3 00
4 - 19

D0392570

THE VANQUISHED

❦ Gods ❧

OTHER BOOKS IN THE PROMETHEUS LECTURE SERIES

Atheistic Humanism
Antony Flew

Naturalism without Foundations
Kai Nielsen

Problems of Life and Death: A Humanist Perspective
Kurt Baier

THE
VANQUISHED

Gods

Science, Religion, and the

Nature of Belief

RICHARD H. SCHLAGEL

PROMETHEUS LECTURE SERIES

Prometheus Books

59 John Glenn Drive
Amherst, New York 14228-2197

Published 2001 by Prometheus Books

The Vanquished Gods: Science, Religion, and the Nature of Belief. Copyright © 2001 by Richard H. Schlagel. All rights reserved. No part of this publication may be reproduced, stored in a retrieval system, or transmitted in any form or by any means, digital, electronic, mechanical, photocopying, recording, or otherwise, or conveyed via the Internet or a Web site without prior written permission of the publisher, except in the case of brief quotations embodied in critical articles and reviews.

Inquiries should be addressed to
Prometheus Books
59 John Glenn Drive
Amherst, New York 14228–2197
VOICE: 716–691–0133, ext. 207
FAX: 716–564–2711
WWW.PROMETHEUSBOOKS.COM

05 04 03 02 01   5 4 3 2 1

Library of Congress Cataloging-in-Publication Data

Schlagel, Richard H., 1925–
    The vanquished gods : science, religion, and the nature of belief / Richard H. Schlagel.
        p. cm. — (Prometheus lecture series)
    Includes bibliographical references and index.
    ISBN 1–57392–898–4 (alk. paper)
    1. Rationalism. 2. Religion and science. I. Title. II. Series.

BL2747.7 .S35 2001
291.1'75 — dc21   2001019034

Printed in Canada on acid-free paper

Dedicated to three very gifted professors
who imparted to me their love of learning

George E. Brooks

Whitaker T. Deininger

Edgar S. Brightman

❦ CONTENTS ❧

❦

6. CRITIQUE OF RELIGIOUS EXPERIENCE 273

BIBLIOGRAPHY 339

❧ PREFACE ❧

Considering the strong polemical stance that I have taken toward religion in this book, I believe I owe the reader a brief description of my religious background. I was baptized a Lutheran, but when I was very young my parents moved to another section of the city which was so overwhelmingly Catholic that there were few Protestant churches, so we joined a nearby Methodist church. Although I had many Catholic friends in my immediate neighborhood, my social life centered mainly in the church where I became president of the youth group called the Epworth League. My mother was active in the Woman's Club but my stepfather, a wonderful person, never attended church or held any religious beliefs, nor tried to influence my beliefs. As most young people, I accepted the teachings of the church without serious reflection. I took communion when it was offered, but I thought of it as just a ritual without much significance. The transubstantiation of the wine and wafer into the blood and flesh of Christ as one consumed it, a dogma of the Catholic church, seemed completely implausible and actually barbaric.

Located in a parish of modest income families, the Liberty Methodist Church in Springfield, Massachusetts, was quite plain, lacking conspicuous religious symbols. The emphasis of the sermons was on living a moral life, rather than on any mysterious, esoteric, or mystical theological doctrines. Being a member of a church community was just something one took for granted. However, in my late teens I did undergo a mildly significant religious period during which I felt a spiritual force in my life guiding my moral choices, an experience in retrospect that I soon out-grew. It was not until I entered college, after serving in the Army Air Force during World War II, that I started questioning the religious beliefs I had acquired in early life.

As a premedical student at Springfield College I was required to take a large number of science courses, particularly in the biological sciences and in chemistry, which conflicted with the creation story in Genesis and with many Christian doctrines. In a course in religion where the professor believed that reading the Bible would be so inspirational that he did not have to explain or justify the text, I left the course feeling it had been a complete waste of time, especially in contrast to my other courses in which I was learning so much. This reaction was not based on any rebel-lion, just a conviction that there was not much in the Bible that was worth knowing (the same belief most Christians have about the Koran). Although I now have a greater appreciation of the literary and inspira-tional impact of the Bible, along with the value and influence of its eth-ical teachings on Western civilization, I have retained the same opinion about its factual content. For me religious beliefs are like shadows that vanish when exposed to the light of reason. I have no greater difficulty in disbelieving in the existence of God and the divinity of Jesus than I do in disbelieving in the existence of Zeus or Satan and the divinity of Buddha or the Dalai Lama.

Although I graduated as a premedical student with a Bachelor of Sci-ence degree, I was so stimulated by the Great Books course I had with Professor George E. Brooks and so incited by the sole philosophy course taken in my final term with Professor Wittaker T. Deininger that I decided to change direction and pursue graduate study in philosophy. Given the one course I had in philosophy, I am grateful to Boston University for accepting me (conditionally on the recommendation of my professors and the Dean at Springfield College) for graduate study. Under the direc-tion of Professor Edgar S. Brightman the department was oriented toward Personalistic Idealism, with Brightman defending (based on a very tragic personal experience) a Platonic view of Christianity: God was unlimited in goodness and love, but constrained in power by an "irra-tional surd." So unexpectedly I found myself in a philosophy department that was religiously oriented, although that did not affect my training in philosophy nor modify my attitude toward religion. Although it was a small department at the time, I received an excellent background in tra-ditional philosophy, especially the history of philosophy and seminars on such philosophers as Kant, Hegel, F. H. Bradley, Samuel Alexander, and A. N. Whitehead. What I learned from these seminars is that speculative metaphysical systems, however brilliantly conceived, such as Whitehead's process philosophy, are no match for the cooperative, exacting, intersubjective investigations of scientists which I had come to admire as an undergraduate. This is even truer of theology, which in my opinion is a gossamer web of concepts with little foundation or significance.

My first teaching position was at The College of Wooster where I was asked to resign early in the academic year for having acknowledged to my students that I was an atheist, but the college generously paid my salary for the entire year. My second teaching position was a one year appointment at Clark University. From there I came to The George Washington University where I have taught for forty-five years. Although I had a heavy course load throughout most of my academic career until recently, the five sabbatical leaves granted me by the university, spent mainly in Paris, not only expanded my cultural background but provided the necessary leisure to do the research for my publications. I have enjoyed my teaching at The George Washington University and should some of my former students read this book, I would like to express my appreciation for their having challenged and stimulated my thinking in so many ways throughout the years. I also want to thank Professor Stiv Fleishman in our department for his comments on chapter 5, even though we disagreed about the nature and tone of my criticisms of Genesis. In addition, I am most grateful to Professor Thelma Lavine, a former colleague and dear friend, for having written (an unrequested but agreed to) supporting letter on my behalf to Dr. Paul Kurtz, the founder and president of Prometheus Books, the publishing house that I especially hoped would print my book. I am very pleased that Dr. Kurtz accepted the book for publication, especially after taking the time to read the manuscript. Also, I wish to thank the editorial staff at Prometheus Books for the fine appearance of the book.

Finally, I want to acknowledge my loving gratitude to my wife Josephine, who teaches French at Saint Johns College High School, for having managed our Paris apartment and arranged our annual travels to Paris and other European countries during the summers and four full year sabbatical leaves. I am especially grateful to her for assuming most of the distracting responsibilities of daily life freeing me to concentrate on my teaching, research, and writing, and for making our life together so enjoyable, exciting, and fulfilling. Furthermore, as with previous manuscripts, she read portions of this book and suggested ways to clarify the arguments and improve the style. That she was willing to do so is especially significant because she does not share the same view of religion that I do. Given my purpose in writing the book, one can imagine how difficult this has been for her and yet she has not let it affect our marriage or prevent our being what we fondly call "soul mates" (despite my disbelief in the soul). Our mutual love of art, music, and the intellectual life, along with the cultural and aesthetic enrichment of travelling, has made up for the one major conflict in our lives. She feels very deeply about religion while, as a philosopher, I believe it is my duty to evaluate it as I see it.

I will conclude with this personal note. Recently, when I was in a reflective state listening to beautiful music, I asked myself what it would be like to believe that there was a God who orchestrates in some mysterious way the musicality of all existence. Momentarily, I realized how reassuring it would be to think that a purposeful agency oversaw to the last note everything that occurs in the vast expanse of the universe, including human existence, a Being that one could turn to for guidance, inspiration, and solace when striving to live well in a world racked by adversity, temptation, and selfishness. I imagined vaguely a kind of Being who would resolve all the uncertainties, injustices, and tragedies pillaging human existence, bringing it to a happy conclusion. In the breadth of a sigh I understood how such a belief could make one feel at home in an otherwise indifferent universe and how comforting this could be. But then reality broke in. All the counter evidence and arguments surfaced upsetting this vain reverie making it seem like a poor indulgence, a bad faith in surrendering to something I knew deep down was untrue. Still, though I could not commit to such a temptation myself, for an instant I felt what an earnest appeal it must have for others.

—Richard H. Schlagel

❧ INTRODUCTION ❧

❧

I n this book I maintain, without serious misgivings or regrets, that the
Age of Religion is coming to an end. There arrives a time when major
institutions of the past become outmoded, whatever their previous glory;
history is a graveyard of discarded religions, philosophies, ideologies,
and political systems (such as pagan religions and kingdoms). This is true
despite the resurgence of conservative religious movements in Muslim
countries, such as the Taliban in Afghanistan, along with the religious
right and Christian creationists in the United States. The unfortunate
influence of the latter was illustrated recently by the decision of the
Kansas Board of Education to remove evolution from the state's science
standards, although this decision will be reversed in the next election
because three creationist candidates for the school board were defeated in
the Republican primaries by moderates pledged to return evolution to
the state's standards. Simlar efforts to restrict the teaching of evolution
are being made by school boards or the legislators in Alabama, Arizona,
Illinois, New Mexico, Nebraska, and Texas, on the grounds that evolution
is not a proven fact, but a theory whose evidence can be challenged.

Yet it is depressing to know that intelligent people can believe that
the myth of Genesis could be used to question all the "consilient" evidence—geological, paleontological, anthropological, embryological,
anatomical, biomolecular, and genetic—supporting the evolutionary
theory (which has been definitely confirmed but like relativity theory still
is called a 'theory' because of its earlier designation). If humankind did

15

not evolve from primates, as the evidence overwhelmingly indicates, why is the genetic makeup of humans about 99 percent identical to that of the pygmy chimpanzees? God would have had to be quite capricious or malicious to have planned such a deception. It is possible, of course, to bury one's head in the Bible but sooner or later the truth will prevail.

My intent in this book is to show, by analyzing the historical background and contents of the Old and New Testaments, along with the origin of the Koran, that the underlying belief system of the Hebraic-Christian and Muslim religions is no longer tenable. Both religions still serve important social, ethical, and psychological functions, but their efficacy decreases as their implausibility increases owing to our greater knowledge of the universe and understanding of human existence. Whereas divine creation, revelation, and God's providential care have been the bedrock of the Hebraic, Christian, and Muslim religions, this has become anachronistic in the modern world. It is true that religions have extolled love, charity, and self-sacrifice that significantly contributed to the civilizing of human beings and led many individuals to lead exemplary lives devoted to the welfare of others, such as the late Mother Teresa, but they also have produced superstition, hypocrisy, bigotry, repression, intolerance, and terrible wars. In any case, the moral consequences or psychological benefits of religious beliefs are no justification of their factual truth, because these same consequences have been derived from beliefs that have long since been discarded as outmoded.

As one Kansan is quoted as saying in justification of creationism: "Evolution is just somebody's nice theory and doesn't impact my life. . . . But if you become a Christian and believe in God's creation that changes everything, everything in your daily life."[1] The flaw in that reasoning is that it could be used to justify any belief, however absurd, as long as it made the person feel better. One can imagine people saying the same thing during the Copernican Revolution in opposition to heliocentrism or a bigot rejecting the fact that there is no genetic evidence of racial inferiority on the grounds that "it is just somebody's nice theory and doesn't impact my life." Another statement by the same person is even more egregious: " 'In the end it comes down to who do you trust. We know who wrote the Bible. Now compare him to whoever wrote this or that scientific paper.' "[2] Although the person has two master's degrees, he obviously does not apply the same standards of rationality to his thinking about religion as I presume he does to his profession, otherwise he would know that we do not have any idea who wrote the books in the Bible while scientific papers are carefully authenticated and peer reviewed before accepted for publication. It is this kind of weak-mindedness that leads others to conclude that many religionists hold the beliefs they do because they stop thinking when it comes to religious convictions. I realize that for many people the truth of evolution is not as important as what they would like to believe about themselves and humankind, but it would be extremely unfortunate if this principle were to guide our educational system because it provides no criterion for distinguishing between truth and falsehood or fact and fiction. Furthermore, as Freud pointed out, every great advance in science—heliocentrism, evolution, and his own theory of psychoanalysis—has been at the cost of man's ego.

In the final chapter I argue that while the early attempts of man to provide answers to questions about human existence and natural phenomena were the *quasi-rational* motive for religious beliefs (as they were of myths), the *experiential* source was dreams, hallucinations, out-of-body projections, and near-death encounters. With no recourse to alternative explanations, these mysterious experiences were accepted as self-authenticating and real. Hearing the commands of the gods, having celestial or apocalyptic visions, experiencing mystical bliss, ascending from the body, and when dying perceiving a divine presence among the living dead were taken as prima facie evidence of a supernatural reality. Many people have similar experiences today, but instead of appearing with a religious motif they tend to conform to the cultural ethos of the present, occurring as astral flights, alien abductions, or near-death encounters with dead relatives and friends. Furthermore, there now is considerable clinical evidence to show that epileptics, schizophrenics, and psychotics have comparable experiences produced by abnormal neuronal discharges in the brain, with some of the great religious leaders of the past (probably St. Paul and Muhammad) displaying analogous symptoms. One investigator, Michael Persinger, has even created a magnetic resonator that, when attached to the head, can induce mystical and out of body experiences by magnetically stimulating the temporal lobes. Consequently, such experiences no longer have to be taken at face value as evidence of a transcendent reality. One cannot be certain that there is not more to these paranormal experiences than the neurophysiological explanations would indicate, but the latter are supported by a growing body of empirical evidence. Unless there is more confirmation, it would be rash to revise the framework of modern science built on such solid empirical foundations to such exacting criteria for the uncertain evidence of subjective experiences that can be (at least partially) explained scientifically, as well as replicated by other means.

I do not expect everyone who perseveres in reading this book will agree with my conclusion. Those who still find in religion an authentic worldview and an inspirational belief system obviously will not be persuaded by these arguments. As all evidence and critiques are grounded on certain presuppositions, the conclusions will be unconvincing if one rejects the underlying assumptions on which the evidence and reasoning are based. For example, those who believe that Genesis contains a cryptic meaning or secret code foretelling later scientific discoveries or that transforming religious experiences are evidence of a numinous reality will not agree with my assessment. But the book is not intended to dissuade people who are dependent upon or convinced of the truth of religion; it is addressed to those who are struggling to decide whether the religious outlook is still viable considering its archaic origins, the recent neurophysiological explanations of religious experiences, along with the impact of secular influences owing to our changing worldview as a result of scientific discoveries. Like many classical philosophical treatises (for example, those of Francis Bacon, Descartes, Locke, Hume, and Kant), this book attempts to facilitate the transition from a previously dominant belief system to another that is more congruent with the current state of knowledge. It is my hope that whoever reads the book will find the critique of Christianity it presents helpful in their attempt to decide if religion has the final answer to the deepest questions of human existence, or whether the search for truth is an ongoing process continuously subject to revision as we learn more about ourselves and the world.

Although focused on the revelatory religions of the Hebrews, Christians, and Muslims, I believe the critical assessment applies also to Eastern mystical religions. In fact, I think there is a simple refutation of Eastern mysticism: considering all the accumulated evidence indicating that consciousness arose very recently in the universe, it could not be the underlying reality as mystics claim. Their view based on mystical experience, like the philosophical system of Hegel claiming that the natural world is merely an objective manifestation of an Absolute Spirit or Cosmic Consciousness, cannot be true if consciousness emerged a short time ago from an antecedent physical universe that, throughout most of the past, did not include it, as biological and astrophysical research attest. Moreover, if consciousness is dependent on the brain, as neurophysiological evidence seems to confirm, and if mystical experiences can be induced by stimulating the temporal lobe, then a Cosmic Consciousness cannot be the fundamental reality: a dependent phenomenon cannot be the cause of that on which it depends. This does not deny mystical experience as such, only the metaphysical or theological claims made on the basis of the experience.

This book abides by Socrates' credo that "the unexamined life is not worth living." The thrust of the argument is that of the two predominant influences that shaped Western civilization, the Hebraic-Christian revelatory religion and the protoscientific speculations of the ancient Greeks, the latter has been vindicated by the remarkable discoveries and theoretical explanations in science that are superseding religious beliefs. Although throughout most of the past two millennia Christianity has been the major ideological and cultural influence in the West, this no longer is true. Unlike revealed religions which rely on a more or less infallible scripture that one must accept on faith because there is little factual support for it, or defer to an authoritarian church claiming to be the representative of God and struggling to preserve the status quo, the ancient Hellenes initiated a *progessive* critical inquiry into the structure of the universe and understanding of man and society. The remarkable advances in science in the twentieth century based on empirical investigations, objective evidence, and rational theorizing are a legacy of and tribute to the ancient Greeks.

Religionists disparagingly call those committed to the scientific worldview "materialists," but our present conception of physical reality is vastly different from the mechanistic-materialistic universe of Newton. Matter no longer is composed of indivisible, irreducible, unchanging material particles whose interactions are determined by mechanistic forces or causes. Instead, based on experimentally probing nature to reveal its infrastructures, atoms have been discovered to be composite, according to the "standard model" consisting of six quarks defined by fractional charges and quantum numbers, along with six leptons such as electrons, muons, and tauons (with their complementary neutrinos) identified by their mass, charge, spin, and modes of decay. The binding forces of the universe are the strong, weak, electromagnetic (the latter two unified into one electroweak force), and gravitational produced by exchange particles: photons, gluons, bosons, and presumably gravitons. No longer conceived in terms of brute matter, physical reality is more accurately defined as force fields or mass/energy, while features like indeterminacy, novelty, and emergence replace mechanistic determinism.

In addition, much to the surprise of contemporary scientists, nature itself creates complex structures with intricate designs that previously would have called for a designer: the novel mutations that drive the evolutionary process; the ingenious coding and deciphering of messenger proteins in genetic replication; the marvelously unfolding convergence in embryological development; the enormous complexity of the neuronal network underlying conscious experiences; and the dynamic internal structure of the atom. As these complex organizations of matter are inherent in nature itself, there is little justification for seeking explanations for them beyond the universe. Although it appears *as if* nature had to be directed or preprogrammed to produce the extraordinary results it does, the more we learn about the causal conditions and actual mechanisms involved the more unnecessary is that assumption. This was the great lesson of Darwin, which has become even more apparent since his day. Today there even are cosmological theories, such as the inflationary and string theories, that attempt to show that the universe is self-existent or self-creative.

Rather than the universe being a dumb machine requiring a mechanic to create and a tinkerer to maintain it, nature itself generates self-directed processes and complicated novel systems: intricate structures realized in self-organization and replication; spontaneous creation of beautiful fractal patterns from chaotic states; and emergence of complex novel forms, properties, and functions. Whereas in the past it was believed that this rational order and marvelous design presupposed an intelligent creator, this inference no longer is necessary, especially as it explains nothing. A legacy of the primitive belief that natural occurrences are manifestations of purposeful psychic forces or agents, we have learned that these intentional explanations contribute nothing to our understanding of the underlying processes or mechanisms producing natural phenomena. Nature itself possesses an intelligible order that in yesteryear would have been attributed to God, but which now can be experimentally discovered and understood. Furthermore, given these inherent resources, it is not as difficult to imagine that intelligent creatures could have evolved from such a rich matrix of creative potentiality in remote corners of the universe. Thus we must revise our conception of nature to include these recently discovered capacities if we want to understand the world intelligently.

Given our greater understanding of nature and increased ability to control and redirect natural processes, we have become nature's cocreators in forming the future within our ecosystem, the earth. In the past humans were limited to anticipating and adapting to a predetermined future, but now we have acquired some capacity for foreseeing and molding the future in our interests. Although this ability was abused in the past half-century, we are learning to appreciate the dire consequences and correct our mistakes. Nowhere does this prospect have more potent challenges (and dangers) than in genetic engineering. We are at the threshold of being able to improve human nature, not as previously by enhancing personal growth externally with greater economic, educational, and cultural opportunities, but from within.

Just as it is possible to diagnose in the embryo certain *physical* genetic defects and eliminate them by restructuring the genome, with genetic engineering it will be possible to modify or eliminate such *psychological* defects as alcohol and drug addiction, attention and learning disorders, child abuse, schizophrenia, psychoses and neuroses, and obesity, which bring so much pain and make it practically impossible for those so afflicted to realize their potential as human beings. Should we shrink from doing so? A common objection is that this would be "playing God," but throughout history humans have attempted to improve the human condition (indicating that it was not perfect to begin with) by domesticating animals, producing agriculture, creating the industrial revolution (and now the information revolution), along with eliminating epidemics and diseases by various biochemical discoveries. What is the difference between that and attempting to improve human nature, whose defects are one of the greatest causes of human suffering today as in the past? It would be irresponsible not to try to prevent these afflictions on the grounds that this would be usurping God's role.

If these remarks have not already alienated the reader, I should forewarn him or her of another possible offense. In my previous books I maintained the kind of impersonal, objective, scholarly approach typical of most research tomes. In this book, however, I adopted a satirical style (usually in the form of parenthetical assertions) when commenting on incredible passages in the Old and New Testaments. In justification I think it is past time that the Bible be treated with reverence, as if it actually were "the word of God," rather than an ancient compilation of writings by unknown authors attempting to reconstruct history from an oral tradition to address the religious needs of specific communities. In my opinion, based on recent biblical scholarship as well as my own research, Genesis is an archaic myth while Jesus is no more than a legendary figure exalted by historical distance and distortion; I have treated them accordingly, hoping this would open the reader's mind to their actual status and significance. I realize that some people will resent this disparaging style, but I believe others will appreciate the frankness and perhaps feel a sense of liberation ("the emperor is naked"). People react in surprisingly different ways, so that what some find agreeable others will find offensive, and vice versa.

I think that attempts by Gerald Schroeder and Maurice Bucaille (discussed in chapter 5) to show that Genesis and the Koran, if properly interpreted, contain hidden meanings that reveal their compatibility with modern science are not only mistaken but offensive because they try to convince those who do not have as strong a scientific background that there is more to these scriptural passages than meets the eye. But the cultural world in which these primitive texts were written is not our world. Not since the seventeenth century has our conception of the world changed as rapidly or radically as during the past one hundred years owing to the remarkable advances in science. This in turn has led to undreamed of technological applications and innovations that have markedly altered our adaptive relations to the world, with many wonderful but also disturbing and destructive consequences. The advantages and dangers for future developments are equally challenging. Yet for these possibilities to be realized to our advantage we must face the world realistically and intelligently, not as dependent children of God. Despite what human beings have believed throughout the past, human destiny depends upon us, not on the gods, who have been vanquished by science if the thesis of this book is correct.

NOTES

1. Hanna Rosin, "Creationism, Coming to Life in Suburbia," *Washington Post*, 5 October 1999, p. A10.

2. Ibid.

OUR CHANGING WORLD

THE RISE OF CHRISTIANITY

Traversing the new millennium stirs up all kinds of reactions, from dire predictions of the apocalypse to prophecies of the second coming of Christ to forecasts of a scientifically created utopia. But who can actually foretell how the next thousand years will alter the destiny of the human condition, anymore than our ancestors a millennium ago could have predicted the face of civilization as it exists today? If the unparalleled developments in the twentieth century are any indication, the transformations will be even more accelerated and astonishing than those during the past hundred years. Already scientists are planning colonies on stations in outer space; anticipating genetically customized babies; prolonging life indefinitely by transplanting cultivated organs, regenerating tissues with stem cells, or arresting the aging process; and envisioning the creation of a robotic subclass of workers.[1]

While these are impressive forecasts of technological innovations, the intellectual and cultural transformations will be just as remarkable if what has occurred during the past century is any indication: globalization of the economy accompanied by a tremendous increase in the standard of living in industrial societies; increased opportunities for educational and artistic fulfillment; remarkable advances and availability of medical services; democratization of many more countries with a significant reduction of class distinctions and privileges; the sexual revolution and approaching equality in the status of women; cultural enrichment owing to international travel; and the computer revolution providing immediate access to unlimited information.

But it is only when we compare life today with how it evolved in the past that we can appreciate fully the enormity of the transformations and their legacy. At the dawn of what is now called the Common Era (C.E.), the marvelous cultural legacy of the ancient Greeks had been assimilated as well as superseded by the expansive military and civic conquests of the Romans, creating one of the greatest empires the world has ever known. Yet despite the grandeur of Rome, it was the occurrence of an incidental event, the crucifixion of an itinerant Jewish teacher named Jesus, that eventually would have the greatest impact on Western civilization for the succeeding two millennia.

In the Occident, the past fifteen hundred years truly can be called the era of Christianity because of its pervasive influence on all aspects of culture: religious, social, intellectual, artistic, ethical, and political. Despite its inauspicious origins among a small group of mostly illiterate Jews attracted to the charismatic preaching of Jesus, his message gradually was spread to the various cities scattered throughout the Eastern Mediterranean basin and Asia Minor. There was something beguiling in a religion that claimed that if we accepted the adversities of this life with equanimity and reverence, we could expect an afterlife filled with glory and beatitude. In none of the competing pagan religions was there as effective a motif as that of a god appearing on earth in human form offering his life as atonement for humanity's sins, along with promising eternal salvation as exemplified in his own resurrection after being crucified. Once Paul eased the way for non-Jews to become converts to Christ, Christianity began to spread beyond the small circle of original Jewish disciples to the larger world of the gentiles.

By the fourth century Christianity had grown to the point where it posed a threat to the Roman authorities. In contrast to the Roman belief that religion was an ancillary support of Imperial Rome, the Christians rejected the Roman gods claiming that religion was superior to the state; a claim perceived as undermining the authority of the Empire and one reason for the success of the barbarian invasions—a punishment for forsaking the traditional Roman gods. Even in the first century the Christians' refusal to acknowledge the Emperor as a god invited persecution. As the prominent New Testament scholar Howard Clark Kee states, toward the end of the first century when Emperor Domitian

> decreed that he should be addressed as *Dominus et Deus* (Lord and God), thereby arrogating to himself the divine honors that the Senate had previously reserved for deceased emperors only, the Christians refused to comply and to take part in religious ceremonies honoring the state gods. The incumbent ruler then subjected them to criminal charges on civil . . . and religious grounds.[2]

By 303 C.E. the four Caesars governing Imperial Rome sought to rid the empire of this "atheistic" scourge. Although some scholars maintain that the persecutions were not widespread, for eight years the Christians were savagely executed with a brutality unusual even for that time. Yet such was the effect of their belief in Christ's promise of ultimate salvation that many of the martyrs displayed a remarkable courage when facing horrible torture or mutilation in the arena: Polycarp, the Bishop of Smyrna, was burned alive because he refused to renounce Christianity; Justin Martyr of Palestine declined to have his friends intercede with the Roman authorities when they decreed his death, declaring that he wished to die like his Savior; Blandina, a slave girl, did not protest when tortured, put in a bag, and then gored to death by a bull; Attalus, a leader of the Christian community, when he would not decry his faith was forced to sit on a chair of red-hot iron and roasted to death. " 'The Christians even when condemned to die, give thanks,' "[3] declared Tertullian.

This heroic fortitude in the face of these atrocities and steadfast adherence to their religion so impressed the Roman populace, as well as the rulers, that an edict of toleration was passed in 311 C.E. conceding the futility of the persecutions. As Will Durant states:

> There is no greater drama in human record than the sight of a few Christians, scorned or oppressed by a succession of emperors, bearing all trials with a fierce tenacity, multiplying quietly, building order while their enemies generated chaos, fighting the sword with the word, brutality with hope, and at last defeating the strongest state that history has known. Caesar and Christ met in the arena, and Christ had won.[4]

It should be remembered, however, that both Jesus and Paul predicted the imminent destruction of the universe at Judgment Day by a catastrophic conflagration (which some believed was indicated by the destruction of Jerusalem along with the sacred Temple by the Roman Legion in 70 C.E.), after which those saved by the grace of God would attain everlasting salvation in the Kingdom of Heaven. So to die a horrible death as a martyr in the expectation that this could gain one an eternal seat in paradise was not such a great sacrifice, although a testament to the strength of the conviction.

Apparently this belief in the impending end of the world was proclaimed so ardently by the early Christians that the burning of Rome at the time of the Emperor Nero was attributed by some Romans to the Christians' desire to hasten the approaching apocalypse. Whether for this reason or some other, Nero's persecution of the Christians in Rome in 64 C.E. was especially cruel. Yet given the choice between the Terrestrial Imperial City and the Heavenly City of God, those yearning for something beyond the material splendor of Rome, with its imposing statues and triumphal arches celebrating the conquests of the Emperors along with numerous temples dedicated to the pagan gods, could turn to a religion that claimed that all of this imperial glory and grandeur was ephemeral compared to the more eternal Kingdom of God. For the less fortunate who lived in the miserable hovels of Rome, the compassionate teachings of the Christians had even greater appeal since it was they "who would inherit the earth."

But it was Emperor Constantine's defeat of Maxentius' legions at the battle of Milvian Bridge in 312 C.E., ordaining his conversion to Christianity, that ended Christian persecution and fostered its expansion. Having had a vision of a "flaming cross in the sky the afternoon before the battle with the Greek words *'en toutoi nika* — in this sign conquer,' " followed in the dawn by a dream in which "a voice commanded him to have his soldiers mark upon their shields the Christian symbol of Christ,"[5] while Maxentius' legions displayed the banner of the Mithraic-Aurelian symbol of the Unconquerable Sun, his victory convinced him of the superiority of the Christian God, a critical turning point in history. As a result, Constantine and Licinius issued the "Edict of Milan" in 313 proclaiming religious toleration throughout the empire and ordered the restoration of the Christian churches and return of Christian property. With Christianity proclaimed the state religion, the vast influence and institutions of the Roman Empire extending from Rome to Constantinople, encompassing Italy, Gaul, Britannia, Greece, Byzantium, and the Near East, along with Alexandria and Carthage in North Africa, facilitated its expansion throughout the Mediterranean world.

But though the number of Christians grew as the apostles carried their message throughout the Levant and Asia Minor, because neither the epistles of Paul nor the canonical Gospels contained sufficient answers to impending doctrinal questions, ritualistic practices, and institutional structures, these had to be determined by the early church fathers such as Bishop Ignatius of Antioch, Clement and Origin of Alexandria, Tertullian of Carthage, Bishop Ambrose of Milan, and Augustine Bishop of Hippo. Among the crucial doctrinal issues were the following: how literally should the virgin birth of Jesus by Mary be interpreted? Did the sacrament of the Eucharist, a legacy of Jesus' last supper with his disciples, involve an actual transubstantiation of the bread and wine into the flesh and blood of Christ or merely a symbolic ritual? Should the raising of Jesus from the dead be interpreted as a bodily resurrection or as a spiritual manifestation to the witnesses, as the Gnostics claimed? Was Jesus the anticipated Messiah of the Hebrews or the redeemer of all mankind? Did his coming expiate original sin or mediate it? Was human salvation or damnation predetermined and thus dependent solely on the grace of God or could the outcome be influenced by good works? Did Jesus consider himself the son of God and thus divine or the son of man and therefore an ideal form of humanity? Was the correct interpretation of the relation of Jesus and the Holy Spirit to God the trinitarian concept of the Godhead as three in one (the Holy Spirit, Christ, and God being cosubstantial and coeternal but with three manifestations) or the unitarian conception of God as supreme with the Holy Spirit and Christ, although divine, part of God's creation?

While derived from the life and teachings of Jesus as depicted in the Gospels, these questions could be given various answers because of the ambiguous assertions attributed to Jesus who spoke mainly in parables, along with the often conflicting accounts presented in the Gospels themselves, the earliest written at least forty years after his death and addressed to different audiences. Thus many Councils had to be convened throughout the centuries to settle doctrinal disputes. It was Emperor Constantine himself who summoned the first synod in Nicaea in May of 325 C.E. to decide between Athanasius's or Arius's conception of the trinity. Though neither doctrine was fully supported by the participants, the Council decided in favor of Athenasius's trinitarian interpretation which became official Christian doctrine as stated in the Creed, although this failed to end the disputes. Constantine's son Constantius reverted to the Arian position and tried to impose it on all Christians, without success.

The Creed also declared creation ex nihilo the orthodox interpretation of Genesis — a conception foreign to all ancient philosophies because of its inherent unintelligibility — despite its disagreement with the original wording in Genesis that it was "the spirit of God moving over the water" that preceded the separation of night and day, implying that creation began with a preexisting water. The belief that the major aspects of the universe originated by "separating out" of a preexisting mass of water was the core of the older Babylonian creation myth, *Enuma Elish*, considered by many scholars to be the basis of the Genesis account.

But though doctrinal decisions were officially announced at the close of these Councils and the advocates of competing interpretations threatened with heresy and excommunication if they persisted in defending the rejected positions, the early history of Christianity was fraught with competing doctrines producing numerous schisms and sects — a forerunner of the Protestant Reformation and contemporary church disputes. Christians who believe that church doctrine is inerrant or infallible because it is based either on divine authority as revealed in scripture or on the Apostolic authority of the Catholic Church ignore the disputatious and somewhat arbitrary nature of the decisions determining these doctrines. The contentious doctrine of the virgin birth of Christ, for instance, now is said to have arisen from a mistranslation of the original Hebrew for "young woman" into the Greek word *parthenos*, meaning "virgin." As two biblical scholars assert:

> In Matthew 1.23 we find Isaiah 7.14 interpreted as a prophecy of the birth of Jesus from a virgin. In fact the original Hebrew does not use the word "virgin" at all. Isaiah was referring to a young married woman, not a virgin. But the Greek parthenos [into which it was translated] does mean "virgin."[6]

Once Christianity was severed from its Jewish roots, a different structural organization had to be substituted for the rabbinate. Borrowing from the Romans, the church was organized into various territorial jurisdictions or dioceses under the supervision of archbishops, bishops, archdeacons, deacons, and priests who eventually were appointed and supervised by a college of cardinals under the Pope as head of the church. Just as the various Roman consuls and proconsuls appointed to rule the dispersed provinces of the Empire usually competed with one another to become the supreme ruler as Caesar or Augustus of Imperial Rome, so the various archbishops or bishops in Antioch, Athens, Alexandria, or Carthage vied with one another for their influence. Still, Christianity now had acquired a structural organization that contributed to its stability and growth.[7]

All that had been the glory of Rome, the indomitable legions, the cohesive administrative and legal code, the extensive economic system and network of roads, the splendid architecture, aqueducts, and monuments, and the excellent educational system finally ended when Odoacer conquered Rome in 475 C.E. What once had seemed an invincible empire collapsed under the weight of its own excesses of conquest, opulence, pomp, self-indulgence, strife, and perversity. What followed has been called "the dark ages" because of the near total eclipse of ancient learning; Justinian closed the "pagan schools" in 529 C.E., including Plato's Academy and Aristotle's Lyceum, while other centers of learning in the West declined or disappeared altogether.

The efficient centralized administrative organization of Rome disintegrated into the decentralized feudal system of independent feuding provinces, bishoprics, principalities, duchies, and so forth. The titles of kings, dukes, barons, knights, lords, serfs, and vassals replaced those of emperor, proconsul, senator, plebeian, and farmer of Rome. A hierarchical structure analogous to that of the Catholic Church replaced the civil institutions of Rome with the Christian religion providing whatever tenuous cohesiveness existed in Europe. Having defeated the Roman legions, for example, when Clovis with a few thousand of his men knelt in the Cathedral of Reims to be baptized at the end of the fifth century, he then ruled Gaul under the "sword of the true faith," which for the French is considered "the baptism of France." Similarly, on Christmas day 800, Charlemagne knelt before the alter of Saint Peter in Rome to pray when Pope Leo III, in gratitude for having been restored to the papacy, perhaps without warning crowned the King, and the congregation thrice cried out "hail to Charles the Augustus, crowned by God, the great peace-bringing Emperor of the Romans!"[8] With that act Charlemagne's realm was transformed into a Holy Roman Empire, setting the precedent that secular rule should be legitimized by the Pope, although this did not always go unchallenged. Aware that there was another "Emperor of the Romans" living in Constantinople, Charlemagne did not use the title.

THE CRUSADES

Extending nearly a thousand years from 500 C.E. to the reawakening of Europe called the Renaissance in the 1400s, the end of the first millennium and beginning of the second marked the apogee of the medieval period. Occurring at the beginning of the new millennium, the Crusades in many ways epitomized the medieval spirit. Motivated by a religious fervor to stem the tide of the advancing Turks who had captured Jerusalem in 1070 and were threatening Constantinople itself, leading Alexius I, the ruler of the Eastern Empire, to appeal to the Latin West for aid, Pope Urban II scoured northern Italy and southern France to amass support. In a magnificent speech in 1095 to the multitude at Clermont in Auvergne, France, Urban described the brutal treatment of the Christians in Jerusalem and the threat to the Eastern Church in gruesome terms, beseeching the Western nobles to renounce their rivalries and join in a Holy War or Religious Crusade to free Jerusalem and defend the Eastern Church. At the end of his speech the ignited crowd thundered the words "'*Dieu li volt*—God wills it.'"[9] No momentary exaltation, Urban persuaded tens of thousands of men—serfs, vassals, knights, barons, counts, dukes, and even monks and clergy—to consecrate themselves, along with their property, to this hazardous effort to serve God. Although no kings were among the nobility of the First Crusade, later ventures included King Louis VII, Emperor Conrad III, Emperor Frederick Barbarosso, King Philip Augustus, Richard I, the Lionhearted, King Andrew, Emperor Frederick II, and King Louis IX.

Of the eight crusades only the first can be considered a true success. Largely a French mission, as were most of the Crusades whose leaders were referred to as "Franks" by the Saracens, it was led by Duke Godfrey, Seigneur of Bouillon, Count Bohemund of Taranto, Tancred of Hautesville, and Raymond, Count of Toulouse. After a treacherous three-year campaign, they finally arrived at the walls of Jerusalem on June 7, 1099, with a force reduced to nearly one-third the original size. The following month they succeeded in breaching the walls and taking the city. Provoked by the ambushes of the Saracens during their devastating march to Jerusalem and by the Muslims fierce resistance during the siege, with unusual religious piety the Christians allegedly slaughtered 70,000 of the Muslim inhabitants and, after herding the Jews into the Temple of Solomon, murdered so many that the pool of blood in the Temple was deep enough to swim in. A gruesome eyewitness account is left by Raymond of Agiles, one of the clergy among the retinue of Count Raymond, who wrote that

> "when our men had mastered the walls of the city and the towers, then wonderful things were to be seen. Numbers of the Saracens were beheaded — which was the easiest for them; others were shot with arrows, or forced to jump from the towers; other were slowly tortured and were burned in flames. In the streets and open places of the town were seen piles of heads and hands and feet. One rode about everywhere amid the corpses of men and horses. But these were small matters! . . . If we speak the truth we exceed belief: let this suffice. In the temple and porch of Solomon one rode in blood up to the knees and even to the horses' bridles by the just and marvelous Judgment of God, in order that the same place which so long had endured their blasphemies against Him should receive their blood."[10]

One might think that this was a cynical satire on the barbarous cruelties of war, but the priest was exultant: " 'This day, I say, glorious in every age to come, turned all our griefs and toils into joys and exultation.' "[11]

Although a Latin Kingdom was established in Jerusalem, its existence was so precarious that St. Bernard left the Abbey of Clairvaux to sound the clarion for a Second Crusade, emulating the success of Urban II. His fervent eloquence was so successful that certain areas of France were depleted of able bodied men who left their properties in the care of their wives. The Franks were led by King Louis VII and the Germans by Emperor Conrad the II; their separate armies were so decimated by the time they reached Jerusalem that, even combined with the force of Baldwin III, the ruler of Jerusalem, when they attempted to recapture Damascus from the Muslims their army was repulsed, forcing the survivors to flee to Antioch and Acre or return to Jerusalem. Shocked by the failure of the Second Crusade, the Latin Christians wondered how a war undertaken on behalf of Jesus Christ could have been forsaken by the

Christian God. Like the Hebrews in the Old Testament who attributed every military success (and failure) to Yahweh, the Christians believed their God would have ensured the success of their efforts to gain control of Jerusalem, the citadel of Christianity, as it is for Judaism.

Though there was considerable internal strife, the Latin Christians ruled Jerusalem from its liberation in 1099 until its recapture in 1187 by the great Muslim leader Saladin; a gifted and though occasionally merciless commander, he was the wisest, most honorable and humane ruler during that turbulent brutal period. Unlike the Christians who slaughtered the Muslims and Jews when they took Jerusalem, Saladin, recognizing that the city contained the holy shrines of the Christians (the Holy Sepulcher), the Jews (the site of the Temple of Solomon), and the Muslims (the Dome of the Rock), after its surrender dealt with the inhabitants very leniently. Nevertheless, a Third Crusade was launched to restore the city to Christian sovereignty.

The first attempt was by the Emperor Frederick Barbarossa who, though acclaimed as a second Moses leading an expedition to the Promised Land, at age sixty-seven was too old for such an undertaking and tragically drowned in 1190 before ever reaching Jerusalem, leaving a desolate army behind.[12] Later in the year a joint effort was made by two young Kings, Richard I, the Lionhearted, who was thirty-one, and the Frank King, Philip Augustus, who was only twenty-three. Joining forces for the siege of Acre that lasted nineteen months, they finally took the city but Philip became so ill that he decided to return to France, leaving the Third Crusade in charge of Richard. Replenishing his army, Richard proceeded to Jaffa to relieve the city from Muslim siege. Excelling in military prowess as Saladin did in civil virtues, when their forces met in battle Saladin admired Richard for his outstanding heroic conduct while Richard admired Saladin for his exceptional honorable character. As examples of their mutual respect, Richard at one point proposed that his sister Joan marry Saladin's brother al-Adil to end the crusades (but the Church did not approve), while Saladin's brother Saphadin, seeing Richard fighting dismounted during a battle, sent two of his own magnificent Arabian horses to him, declaring that " 'it is wrong that a king should fight on foot.' "[13]

Neither achieving a decisive victory in their several combats, they signed a truce in 1192 allowing Richard to keep the cities he had conquered. Palestine would be partitioned but free passage permitted to all Muslims and Christians between their sectors, leaving Jerusalem under Muslim control, though providing for the safety of Christian pilgrims. Having signed the agreement committing each party to a peace for three years, Richard left for England while Saladin died the following year at age fifty-five. As Durant states: "Saladin's moderation, patience, and justice had defeated Richard's brilliance, courage, and military art. . . . The Christian virtues and faults were better exemplified in the Moslem Sultan than in the Christian King."[14]

After the Third Crusade failed in its purpose to free Jerusalem from Muslim control, a Fourth Crusade was organized by Pope Innocent III based on a different strategy. Rather than setting forth for Jerusalem by marching through southeastern Europe to the Hellespont or Bosphorus where they could seek passage to some Christian port in the Levant, or sailing from an Italian port to the Aegean Islands and then to Palestine, it was decided to sail down the Adriatic to Egypt, conquer Cairo, and then march on Palestine. Because Venice was the dominant sea power of the Mediterranean, the Pope finally persuaded the Venetian Republic under Doge Enrico Dandolo, then ninety-four years old and nearly blind, for a suitable price to provide the necessary supplies and war galleys.

Diverted by the plea of the son of the deposed Emperor of Constantinople to restore his father as ruler for an enormous bounty, the great fleet of vessels, despite the opposition and threat of excommunication by the Pope, redirected their expedition to Constantinople. When the usurper of Constantinople refused to abdicate, the Crusaders landed and captured a city more magnificent than imagined in their wildest fantasies. As described in the memoirs of Geoffroi de Villehardouin, Marshall of Champagne, who was among the crusaders:

"You may be assured that those who had never seen Constantinople opened wide eyes now; for they could not believe that so rich a city could be in the whole world, when they saw her lofty walls and her stately towers wherewith she was encompassed, and these stately palaces and lofty churches, so many in number as no man might believe who had not seen them, and the length and breadth of this town which was sovereign over all others. And know that there was no man among us so bold but that his flesh crept at the sight. . . ." [15]

Alexius IV, the son who had bargained for the restoration of the Empire to his father, was crowned co-emperor (having been blinded by the brother who deposed him, his father was unable to rule by himself), but Alexius had ceded so much to the Venetians for their support that a popular revolt erupted during which he was killed. The leader of the revolt, a royal prince, then organized an army to repel the Latin Crusaders but was himself defeated, so Baldwin of Flanders, the ruler of Jerusalem, in 1204 became the governor of what was now the Latin Kingdom of Constantinople, which was divided into smaller feudal domains, each governed by a Latin nobleman.

The city was pillaged with Venice the main vandal and beneficiary.

The ornate architecture of St. Mark's Basilica, along with the delicate arabesque-like columns of the lovely Ducal Palace, were Byzantine inspired, while the jeweled alter of the Basilica, much of its Byzantine art, and the famous four golden copper horses of the Quadriga taken from Constantinople's hippodrome, were spoils. The Venetians also acquired numerous port cities to guard their trade routes and dominance of the Mediterranean, with the aged Enrico Dandolo, who had accompanied the Crusade, given the title "Doge of Venice, Lord of One Fourth and One Eight of the Roman Empire" on his return to Venice. Due to its unscrupulous villainy, Venice had become the "jewel of the Adriatic," a city of enchanting beauty. Surfeited and spoiled by this success, no attempt was made either to conquer Cairo or to liberate Jerusalem.

A Fifth Crusade in 1217 under the Hungarian King Andrew did succeed in returning most of Jerusalem to the Christians. Although Frederick II, the young Emperor of Germany and Italy, had been excommunicated for failing to support the Fifth Crusade, he embarked a year later on the Sixth Crusade. Despite being shunned by the Christians for his excommunication, when he arrived in Palestine he formed an *entente cordiale* with Malik al-Kamil, the new Sultan of Egypt and Syria. This led to their signing in 1229 a treaty by which the Muslims yielded to Frederick the cities of Bethlehem, Nazareth, Acre, Jaffa, and Sidon, plus all of Jerusalem except the Dome of the Rock, sacred to Islam. Although the Christians of Palestine were delighted, Pope Gregory IX rejected this accord with the Muslims and refused to ratify it. Five years later Jerusalem was captured by the Turks and so fell again under non-Christian rule.

A Seventh Crusade was undertaken in 1248 by Louis IX of France, known as the pious King, who was defeated two years later at Mansaurah. Remaining four years at Acre following his defeat with just a remnant of his former army, he returned to France in 1254. After his departure Baibars, the Sultan of Egypt, marched along the coast from Cairo to Antioch capturing each Christian city along the way, killing or enslaving the inhabitants, and leaving Antioch so demolished that it never recovered its previous glory as a city. Once again aroused by the plight of the Christians, King Louis, now in advanced age, embarked on the Eighth Crusade but died en route to Jerusalem in 1270. Prince Edward of England took up the Cross the following year making his way to Acre where he found the task of liberating Jerusalem so futile that he returned to England to be crowned King. Then, in retaliation for a Christian attack on an Arab caravan in Syria, Sultan Kahil marched on Acre and after taking the port city went on to capture the remaining Christian cities of Tyre, Sidon, Haifa, and Beirut. With inglorious defeat the Crusades had come to an end.

While nearly any glimpse of history displays a stupefying dispersion of mad folly and senseless brutality, none surpasses the Crusades. They were a microcosm of the paradoxes of the human condition, combining a noble idealism with the vilest inhumanity. Consisting of eight major campaigns along with lesser forays from Western Europe to the Levant, their proclaimed mission was to rescue Jerusalem from the Saracens and reinstate the sacred relics of the Holy Land. Originally proclaimed in the name of Christ and dedicated to the Christian God, this spiritual motivation more often was overcome by a passion for glory, riches, and titles, along with the quest for kingdoms in the form of fortified castles or cities. Believing they were acting in consonance with God's will, the Christians usually displayed extraordinary courage, accepting martyrdom as a divine blessing secondary only to military success. This is evident in the hortatory remarks by Louis IX (Saint Louis) to the Christian forces before the attack on Damietta, quoted in a letter by a pilgrim named Guy:

> "It is not without the divine permission that we have been brought here to a country so powerfully protected.... Everything is in our favor, whatever many happen to us. *If we are conquered, we shall be martyrs.* If we triumph, the glory of God will be thereby exalted.... Certainly it would be foolish to believe that God, who foresees all things, has incited me in vain. This is His cause, we shall conquer for Christ, He will triumph in us, He will give the glory, the honor and the blessing not unto us, but unto his name...."[16]

This belief that they were emissaries of God destined to reconquer the Holy Land unfortunately led the nobles to make impulsive foolhardy decisions resulting in disastrous consequences, as when the Christian forces led by Guy of Lusignan, King of Jerusalem, needlessly were trapped and utterly destroyed by Saladin at the Horns of Hattin, one of the crucial battles that led to the failure of the Crusades (198–205). A similar disaster occurred when King Louis IX, after his seemingly miraculous conquest of Damietta, was defeated at Mansourah by Baibars al-Brundukdari, the usurper Sultan of Egypt, with a reported loss of 50,000 Christians, virtually ending the Crusades (349). Believing that God would enact some miracle ensuring their success because of the holiness of their cause, they were deceived into taking these tragically fatal decisions. The irony was that the Saracens were making the same religious assumptions, except that they were praying to Allah and usually taking more care to ensure his victory, made easier by the fact that they were fighting in a region well known to them in contrast to the Crusaders. If the outcome depended upon divine guidance or miraculous interference, then the ultimate defeat of the Christians evidently demonstrated the superiority of Allah over the Christian God.

Yet even in defeat it was not the nobles—the Emperors, Kings, Princes, Dukes, Earls, Counts, and Barons, along with the Patriarchs, Archbishops and Viceroys of the Popes—who suffered most from these disastrous campaigns, but the lesser nobles or those of non-noble rank: the knights, squires, priests, archers, crossbowmen, spearmen, and lowest of all, the baggage carriers. Although princes, too, were sometimes wounded or killed, they had the protection of their armor, the advantage of being mounted, and the defense of their guard. If it became apparent that defeat was imminent, it was the duty of the guard to ensure a safe retreat to the nearest sanctuary of a fortified castle or anchored ship. Also, whether in transit, campaign, or siege, the nobles naturally had the best tents, protection, and provisions, while the main body of troops often lived in squalor and misery, dying of "starvation, scurvy, typhus, and the strange disease called *leonardie*, which reduced men to helpless letharge. . . . Scorching heat and rain, winter frosts and mud, made life nearly impossible" (237).

The nobles also were favored by an unwritten but pervasive feudal code protecting them even when they were defeated and captured, so that normally they were treated with respect and accorded hospitality and accommodations according to their rank. Not an iron code, it would be broken if there were hatred between the adversaries or if the taking of a fortified domain was so costly that it aroused the cruel vengeance of the victor. But preserving the lives of captured nobility had a further advantage in that they could be held for enormous ransoms; for example, following his defeat at Mansourah, King Louis, in addition to surrendering Damietta to the Egyptians, was forced to agree to pay a huge ransom "equal to the entire yearly revenue of the King of France." Similarly, when the son and nephew of the Sultan Shawar were captured by King Amaury, Shawar offered "two million pieces of gold for their release" (175).

Yet the treatment of defeated strongholds depended as much on the whim of the conqueror as on any feudal code or moral principles. Occasionally the inhabitants, along with the garrison of a vanquished fortified castle or city, were allowed to leave with their possessions, though usually without them, yet it was just as likely they all would be killed or taken into captivity to be sold later in slave-markets. Sometimes if the garrison had fought bravely it was rewarded by being allowed to go free while the inhabitants were slaughtered; yet at other times everyone was massacred, except the nobility, and the castle or city fortress razed to the ground, as happened to Christian Antioch when it was conquered by Baibars (369). When King Amaury captured the fortified Muslim city Bilbeis all "men, women and children were hacked to pieces in the onslaught . . . [and] Bilbeis became a desert" (174).

Normally the spoils were distributed among the nobles while the
foot soldiers received little reward. In this way the nobility acquired enormous treasures in terms of silver, gold, precious gems, fabrics of silk and
damask, and vast estates of fortified castles or cities. In contrast, the
knights and foot soldiers usually gained very little beyond what they
could steal from the vacated houses or bodies of the slaughtered inhabitants. There was no system of proportional dispensation of the spoils.
Payne describes, for example, the following distribution of the plunder
from Constantinople when it was sacked by the Crusaders and Venetians:

> The great nobles chose the greatest houses for themselves. The marquis
> of Montferrat chose the vast Bucoleon Palace and the Church of Sancta
> Sophia and the nearby houses of the patriarchate. Count Henry of Flan-
> ders chose the Blachernae Palace. The soldiers set up house in the man-
> sions of the rich until they were thrown out by unruly noblemen who
> wanted the mansions for themselves. It was understood that for three
> days all would have license to rape, murder, and pillage. Anarchy
> reigned. The churches were profaned; libraries were sacked; bronze
> statues dating back to classical Greece were overturned and then carried
> away to be melted down. The high altar at Sancta Sophia was covered
> with a sheet of gold and encrusted with jewels. The invaders tore out the
> jewels with their daggers. . . . Three churches were converted into store-
> houses for the gold and silver and costly cloths that were set aside for
> the barons. The rank and file, although promised treasures of their own,
> received very little; and those who took gold and silver valuables were
> summarily executed. The barons regarded the city as their own private
> property. When the massed treasure of all the palaces and churches of
> Constantinople was valued, the barons received 450,000 marks and only
> 100,000 marks was reserved for lesser ranks. Each knight received 20
> marks, each priest and knight's servant received 10 marks, and each foot
> soldier received 5 marks. It was not a very generous distribution of the
> spoils. (pp. 281–82)

Since this was a Christian city that was being plundered, one can imagine
what happened to captured Muslim cities.

The same Prince or Sultan could be kind and merciful on one occasion and barbaric and ruthless on another. Moderation and consistency
seem to have been completely lacking among the leaders, whether Christian or Muslim, probably because of their divine-like status and near
absolute authority. As indicated previously, Saladin is often held up as
the most cultured, humane, and generous of the rulers of his time, yet he
achieved power by the most vicious, deceitful treachery. When Sharwar,
the Sultan of Egypt, was invited by some Emirs to make a pilgrimage to
honor a local saint, he was accompanied by Saladin who rode by his side.

Soon after their departure, "Saladin leaned over, seized Sharwar by the collar, and ordered him placed under arrest and taken to camp. There Sharwar was beheaded" (175). In this ruthless manner Saladin became Sultan of Egypt despite not being Egyptian. These incongruities or contrasts of character were particularly manifest in King Louis IX, eventually sainted because of his deeply religious convictions and practices. His contrasting traits are vividly etched by Payne:

> He was paradoxical: a meditative man who loved action, a reasonable man who believed in the sanctity of improbable relics, a profoundly gentle man who could be mercilessly cruel on occasion. His pride and humility were in harmonious balance.
>
> He collected relics with avidity, including the Crown of Thorns and a portion of the True Cross, both of which he purchased in Constantinople for vast sums. Eventually he built the famous Saint-Chapelle to house them.
>
> In time he acquired the Holy Lance and the Holy Sponge and the Holy Nails, the Purple Robe, a piece of the Holy Shroud, a portion of the Napkin used by Mary Magdalene to wash Christ's feet, a phial of the Virgin's Milk and another of the Precious Blood. Avaricious of relics, he acquired the Virgin's blue mantle and the swaddling clothes of the Christchild. Having exhausted the available treasures of the New Testament, he went in search of the treasures of the Old Testament. He acquired the Rod with which Moses struck the Rock and all manner of strange objects from the ancient past: there is no end to the inventiveness of Venetian and Byzantine merchants. (p. 338)

In a previous book describing the origins and growth of scientific thought from the earlier mythopoetic, theogonic, cultural heritage, I was struck by the converging evidence provided by anthropologists, ethnologists, and comparative psychologists that individuals, along with societies, usually think on several different cognitive levels.[17] Primitive peoples would make careful practical preparations for agriculture, a fishing trip, a hunting expedition, or a war party and then perform magical or religious rites to enlist the favor of the gods, especially concerning the more perilous aspects of the ventures. Although the Presocratic philosophers, credited with originating scientific rationalism, were attempting to understand and explain the world objectively in terms of natural processes, empirical models, and rational laws, their thinking—with the exception of the ancient Atomists—still was deeply affected by animistic, subjectivistic, and anthropomorphic concepts derived from earlier modes of thought.[18]

Even with the development of modern classical science it took four centuries before scientists could accept the emergence of complex self-organizing and replicating structures manifesting design as natural occurrences, rather than divine ordinations. Today one still finds scientists, who in their professional work would never think of not submitting their results to the most rigorous critical tests and intersubjective verification, holding religious beliefs based on no more justification than biblical or church authority and faith, illustrating clearly that two different cognitive levels are at play. The United States is the most advanced scientific and technological society in the world and yet it has more Christian fundamentalists than any European country, also illustrating the coexistence of two vastly different societal cognitive levels.

The description of King Louis IX and what we know of other leaders of the Crusades illustrates the same phenomenon. Here was a ruler of France who had to organize the tremendous preparations for the Crusades, along with planning the strategy and leading the attack on the fortifications of the Saracens, and yet was so naive and gullible that he truly believed he was purchasing actual Christian relics such as phials of the Virgin's milk and Jesus' blood, Mary's mantle and the swaddling clothes of the infant Jesus, a piece of the cloth Mary Magdalene used to wash Jesus's feet, the crown of thorns, the sponge offered to Jesus by the centurions to quench his thirst, the nails used in the crucifixion, and so on. How could any reasonable person believe that these fragile items could have been preserved over a thousand years after Jesus' death? Yet the conviction that when in Jerusalem they were following in the footsteps of Jesus and encountering the Holy of Holies was so deep that it suspended or overruled any critical appraisal. Thus the Crusaders' would accept the advice of deranged prophets despite their better judgment, be passionately motivated in battle by the sight of relics such as a piece of the "True Cross" or the "True Lance," and accept victory or defeat as due to God's condoning or condemning their actions.

What we would accept as natural or chance occurrences, such as the discovery of plentiful sources of water, abundant food from the countryside, hordes of supplies captured by accident from a passing Saracen caravan, or sudden twists of good fortune in battle, were attributed to God's benevolence. On the other hand, the onslaught of draught, plagues, epidemics of cholera, malaria, or diarrhea, and unexpected defeats in battle were seen as rebukes of God. Nothing was viewed as natural or accidental but always as intended by God. When King Louis decided to return to France by sailing from Acre with what remained of his decimated fleet, his ship became stranded on a sand bar just off the coast of Cypress. In panic Louis

> flung himself down on the ship's deck, barefoot and wearing only a tunic, to implore God's aid. The ship floated off the sandbank, but a few hours later they were in the middle of the storm. This gave rise to long

discussions about God's intentions when he let loose storms at sea. Was it punishment for their sins? Was it a warning or a threatening? Was it God's anger or God's love? (p. 359)

Even today when natural disasters or senseless acts of brutality occur, rather than accepting them as tragic but naturally occurring events, one will hear clergymen say "we don't know why that occurred, but God knows." Yet if there were a God who knew and failed to prevent the disaster, then 'he' either would be morally culpable or limited in his capabilities.

Although the intended purpose of the Crusades to return Jerusalem to Christian autonomy failed, the contact with the much richer culture of Byzantium and in many respects the higher civilization of the Muslims had the unintended effect of confronting the Latin West with its cultural, intellectual, and spiritual limitations. Awed by the imperial splendor of Constantinople, the luxuriant lifestyles of the Muslim Caliphs, and the moral superiority of Saladin, the Crusaders were considerably chastened regarding the presumed superiority of their own culture and religious beliefs. Although in itself a disaster because of the destruction of so much architecture, art, and original Greek manuscripts when large areas of Constantinople were burned during its sack by the Crusaders and the Venetians, it did result in many works of the ancient Greeks being reintroduced to the West. For instance, according to Durant it was "William of Moerbeke, Flemish Archbishop of Corinth, [who] furnished Thomas Aquinas with translations of Aristotle made directly from the original," thus replacing Platonism as the new philosophical and cosmological foundation of Christianity.[19] In addition, Christian physicians benefitted considerably from their contacts with their Muslim counterparts who had added greatly to the medical knowledge bequeathed to them by such classical scholars as Hippocrates and Galen.

The trade routes opened up by the Venetians and Genovese brought to the West spices like pepper, ginger, cloves, nutmeg, and cinnamon, cereals and fruits such as maize, rice, sesame, lemons, melons, peaches, apricots, cherries, and dates, along with such luxurious fabrics as silk, damask, muslin, satin, and velvet, plus magnificently woven and dyed carpets. The craftsmanship of blowing and staining glass that became a renown Venetian art on the Island of Murano was largely derived from contact with the Near East, as well as the art of making mirrors by coating the backs of polished glass with a metallic finish like silver. New methods of financing and banking also were imported. As Durant states: "The Crusades had begun with an agricultural feudalism inspired by German barbarism crossed with religious sentiment; they ended with the rise of industry, and the expansion of commerce, in an economic revolution that heralded and financed the Renaissance."[20]

THE RENAISSANCE

But equally significant for the emergence of the Renaissance was the resurgence of the Muslims as a result of their defeat of the crusaders and conquest of the cities of the Levant. When they invaded southern Spain in the thirteenth century the Muslims brought with them a trove of Greek manuscripts that had been preserved in such libraries as Pergamum and Damascus (but which had been gathering dust in the monasteries and abbeys in the West), along with their commentaries and treatises containing their own investigations in mathematics, physics, astronomy, optics, biology, and medicine. When these manuscripts were translated from the Arabic or Seriac into Latin, they reawakened in the West an interest in these dormant scientific subjects. New centers of scholarship arose in the twelfth and thirteenth centuries in cities such as Bologna, Paris, Oxford, Heidelberg, and Prague. It was in institutions like the Sorbonne ("the mother of universities"), Merton College, Oxford, and the Universities of Bologna and Padua that scholastic philosophy thrived before the advent of modern science.[21]

Although the Humanists scoured libraries, abbeys, and monastaries in Europe and Constantinople primarily to recover the literary heritage of ancient Greece and Rome, when they discovered Greek scientific or mathematical manuscripts they seized them as well. Such eminent scholastic scholars of the thirteenth and fourteenth centuries as Robert Grosseteste, Bishop of London, Thomas Bradwardine, William Heytesbury, Richard Swineshead, and John Dumbleton at Merton College, along with Jean Buridan and Nicole Oresme at the Sorbonne in Paris began the critique of Aristotle's geocentric cosmology and dynamic and kinematic mechanics (explanation of celestial and terrestrial motions) that presaged later investigations by renaissance scientists, such as Copernicus, Gilbert, Brahe, Kepler, and Galileo. The invention of printing with movable type in the West by Gutenberg (it had been invented earlier in China) in the middle of the fifteenth century greatly facilitated learning by making available large numbers of inexpensive, small, durable, uniform, and hence more accessible and readable books. Now the texts of scholars, rather than being sequestered in isolated abbeys or monasteries, could be acquired almost immediately by any literate person, thus increasing their circulation and critical examination leading to the expansion of knowledge.

The growth of great trading ports like those of Venice, Pisa, and Genoa attracted people of diverse cultures from every corner of the Mediterranean and beyond, the rich mixture of customs, costumes, languages, and traditions creating a new cosmopolitan outlook markedly different from the provincial world of the Middle Ages. The rediscovery of the continent of America in 1492 not only confirmed the global shape of the earth and greatly extended the world's horizon, it opened up trade routes and established colonies in "the new world." These explorations in turn led to a renewed interest in geography and cartography, creation of elaborate precision instruments for navigation (the beautiful astronomical devices such as astrolabes crafted during the Renaissance seen in museums in Florence, Venice, Paris, and London), and demand for more exact "star charts" needed for guiding these worldwide navigations. The invention of more exact clocks (a number of early clocks in Europe, such as the famous clock in Strasbourg, still display a single hour hand) and demand for calendar reform (one of the motivations for Copernicus's search for a better astronomical system) are indicative of the thirst for more precise knowledge of natural phenomena, in contrast to purely theological pursuits.

As interest in the natural world and secular affairs competed with the nearly exclusive religious orientation of the medieval period, where the Bible had been proclaimed the sole source of truth and font of wisdom, a radical challenge to the hegemony of the Catholic Church was about to take place. In the first half of the sixteenth century a rebellious clergyman in Wittenberg (close to where Copernicus was writing his revolutionary astronomical work, *De Revolutionibus*), decided to challenge the moral authority of the Church. Disillusioned and incensed by its rampant hypocrisy and immorality (Popes like Cesar Borgia, Alexander VI, were selected not for their spiritual qualities but for their political influence, while celibacy among the clergy was honored more in the breach than in the practice, with illegitimate children a not infrequent issue), especially the selling of indulgences to absolve penance, remit sins, and redeem those suffering in purgatory, Luther argued that only God could forgive sins by conferring grace. His conviction that the remission of sins, rather than an ecclesiastical prerogative, depended upon the person's sincere inward repentance threatened to replace the mediating influence of the clergy by personal communion with God. This affront to the Church's power, challenging its exclusive authority in spiritual matters, hardly could be allowed, so Luther was declared a heretic and excommunicated. Thus began the schisms in the Church eventuating in the creation of many protestant denominations and other religious sects.

THE RISE OF MODERN CLASSICAL SCIENCE

At the time that Luther was attacking the excesses of the Catholic church, Copernicus nearby was writing the *De Revolutionibus*, published in 1543.

Some contemporary historians of science are reluctant to categorize the emergence of modern classic science as revolutionary. Still, despite its roots in the critical investigations of the scholastics from the fourteenth to the sixteenth centuries, the *De Revolutionibus* probably did more than any other work to herald the end of the ancient world and the creation of the new. The heliocentric system proposed by Copernicus displaced human-kind from its former privileged position in the center of the universe and eventually liberated the stars from their fixed position in the furthest orbit, dispersing them into a boundless space. Moreover, aspects of Copernicus's heliocentrism had been anticipated in antiquity by the early Pythagoreans and completely foretold by the Hellenistic astronomer Aristarchus in the third century B.C.E. Although essentially a conservative system retaining the main features of Ptolemy's astronomy except for the radical interchange of the positions of the earth and the sun, nevertheless, it was "revolutionary-making" in the words of Thomas Kuhn.[22] In fact, the hypothesis that the orbital revolutions of the planets could more exactly and systematically be calculated from the sun as the center of the universe led Kepler to formulate his three laws of planetary motion that correctly described the orbits of the planets as elliptical, with the sun as the foci. It was Kepler's third law stating that the planetary period squared is proportional to the mean distance from the sun cubed, so that the periods of the revolutions vary with the $\frac{3}{2}$th power of their mean dis-tance from the sun, that enabled Newton to infer that the strength of the gravitational force between two planets diminishes with the square of the distances between them.

Furthermore, after endowing the earth with the two motions previ-ously attributed to the sun, scientists realized that the earth's axial rota-tion from west to east could account more simply for the apparent diurnal revolution of the whole universe from east to west, while its annual orbital revolution westward could explain (as also apparent) such phenomena as the retrograde motion of the planets. With Kepler's laws one could dispense finally with all the geometrical artifices devised in antiquity to "save the phenomena," such as epicycles, eccentrics, and equants (so detested by Copernicus), creating a simpler, more exact, and completely interlocking description of all the planetary motions, the pri-mary aspiration of Copernicus. Finally, the centrality of the sun led Kepler to draw an analogy between the sun's radiation of light through-out the universe and its dispersing a force producing the orbital motion of the planets—one of the first attempts to explain planetary motion by a kind of mechanistic influence radiated from the sun! So he conjectured that the elliptical path of the planets around the sun could be explained by two forces, a propelling force similar to light emanating from the sun and a "gravitational" force between the sun and the planets, the latter due to the kind of magnetic attraction attributed to the poles of the earth by William Gilbert in his *De Magnete*, published in 1600.

In 1609, the same year Kepler published the discovery of his first laws, a Florentine scientist teaching at the Venetian University of Padua saw a Dutch lens grinder demonstrating in Piazza San Marco an elongated optical tube that made distant objects appear larger and closer. Intrigued by the potential of the instrument, Galileo with the aid of an artisan constructed a similar device, initially called an *occhilai* or "spyglass" (in deference to its military signficance), with a greater magnifying power. Realizing its military potential because it allowed its possessor to see distant objects, such as approaching enemy sailing vessels sooner, and thus prepare a suitable reception, Galileo demonstrated to the Doges of Venice from the top of the campanile in Piazza San Marco its capacity of magnifing objects thirty times. In appreciation, the Doges raised his salary as a professor at the University of Padua from 480 to 1,000 florins a year, while also conferring on him a lifetime tenure at the University (which he forsook for the position at the same salary of "Chief Mathematician of the University of Pisa and Philosopher to the Grand Duke," Cosimo de' Medici). But the real significance of the spyglass or telescope (*telescopium*), as it later came to be called, lay not so much in its military potential as in its capacity to enhance telescopic observations.

While Galileo did not invent the telescope, he was the first to use it to supplement naked eye observations of the night sky that had been relied upon since antiquity. As described in his book *Sidereus Nuncius*, published in 1610, these observations included the disclosure of vast numbers of new stars wherever he looked, implying that the universe was immensely larger than previously believed; the discovery of four satellites revolving around Jupiter analogous to the moon revolving around the earth in the Copernican system; vivid images of the mountains and valleys on the moon (precise diagrams of which he drew in his book remarkably similar to photographs distributed by NASA), indicating that the moon's surface was similar to the earth's and not a perfectly smooth crystalline body as maintained by scholastic astronomers; the appearance of revolving white smudge spots near the surface of the sun which he interpreted as clouds, suggesting a further resemblance between the celestial and terrestrial realms; and a clear view of the phases of Venus, which provided significant confirmation of the heliocentric theory that predicted these phases in contrast to the geocentric theory which implied that Venus manifested a continuous crescent or horn shape in its orbital revolution.

Although astonishing even to Galileo, these telescopic discoveries were incredible to other astronomers who accepted Aristotle's ontological distinction between the celestial and the terrestrial worlds, the former composed of an aetherial substance defined as eternal, incorruptible, and weightless, while the latter comprised the four perishable material elements, fire, earth, air, and water. It was not so much his astronomical discoveries, startling as they were, that shocked the scholastic astronomers, but their challenge to the ancient distinction between the celestial and terrestrial worlds, a distinction that had to be rejected if the heliocentric theory were true. For the critical feature of the heliocentric position was the incongruous consequence that a terrestrial body, the earth, would revolve in the heavens, while the sun, a celestial body, would reside in the center of the terrestrial world. How could two entirely different realities located in ontologically distinct realms be interchanged?

Equally anomalous was the fact that as celestial bodies the planets were believed to have an eternal, uniform, circular motion, while a terrestrial body like the earth was either naturally at rest in the center of the universe, or if displaced, would strive to return to its natural place in the center by an accelerated rectilinear motion. These cosmological distinctions in turn were overlaid with theological significance, such as the Kingdom of God existing in the heavens, Christ's bodily ascension into heaven, angels and various heavenly hosts descending from heaven, and the location of hell in the center of the earth, as in Dante's *Divine Comedy*. Even someone as intelligent and learned as Cardinal Bellarmine, the person Galileo appealed to in 1616 not to proscribe the Copernican system, apparently believed that hell was in the center of the earth. As he says:

> "it is indeed reasonable that the place of devils and wicked damned men should be as far as possible from the place where angels and blessed men will be forever. The abode of the blessed (as our adversaries agree) is heaven, and no place is further removed from heaven than the center of the earth."[23]

The naturalization of the celestial realm undermined the credibility of these religious concepts, especially if taken literally. Moreover, passages in scripture which stated or implied that the sun moved and that the earth stood still (Joshua 10:13, Psalm 93:1 and 104:19, and Ecclesiastics 1:5) would have to be rejected, challenging the inerrant truth of the Bible.

While Kepler's laws, as mere calculating devices, did not pose as serious a threat to the ancient geocentric cosmology, despite presuming the truth of heliocentrism (even Pope Urban VIII, the prosecutor of Galileo, was willing to entertain the heliocentric view as a heuristic calculating hypothesis), the dramatic telescopic discoveries of Galileo did. When he presented these discoveries in dialogue form in Italian in his celebrated book, *Dialogue Concerning the Two Chief World Systems* (the English title), published in 1632, they raised a storm of protest among the scholastics and church authorities. Although Urban had granted Galileo permission to publish a book containing a debate between the supporters of the Aristotelian and the Copernican systems, Galileo had not informed the Pope that he previously had been enjoined by Cardinal Bellarmine from "holding, teaching, or defending" the Copernican system.

Moreover, the Pope, who previously had been such an avid admirer of Galileo that he wrote a poem in praise of the *Siderius Nuncius* and proposed to give Galileo's son a pension, had permitted the publication of the *Dialogue* provided Galileo treated both systems impartially, as inconclusive hypotheses, and added an appropriate reference to the Pope's view that in the final analysis astronomers could not fathom God's creation and prove one system over the other. In fact, even though Kepler had shown the mathematical superiority and explanatory potential of the Copernican system, and Galileo had discovered startling new astronomical evidence showing that the celestial realm was not as dissimilar to the terrestrial world as previously believed, no observations themselves at that time could prove that the earth moved, while there was considerable common sense evidence that it was stationary.

If, as postulated in the heliocentric system, the earth had two motions, an annual revolution of approximately twenty miles per second and a diurnal rotation of about a thousand miles per hour, why were these motions not apparent? Why was the earth's motion not felt? Why were objects not thrown from the spinning earth as stones are when released from a rotating sling? Why were the clouds and birds not left behind as the earth rotated or revolved beneath them? If, in contrast to being stationary, the earth traversed a huge orbit, then why were the stars not seen to be displaced when observed from opposite poles of its orbit (the famous argument from parallax)? Why, if the earth rotates eastward a thousand miles an hour, does a projectile thrown straight upward return to the same point, since during its upward and downward trajectory the earth would have revolved some distance eastward (an objection presented by Aristotle)? Known since antiquity, these counter-arguments were the main reasons for rejecting the heliocentric theory and accepting geocentrism, despite the newer astronomical evidence and arguments supporting the former.

Although tentative rebuttals of these objections had been offered by scholastic philosophers, such as Buridan and Oresme in the fourteenth century based largely on the relativity of uniform motions, it was not until Galileo's forceful and systematic presentation of these counter arguments in his *Dialogue* that they became persuasive. While he had included frequent caveats in the *Dialogue* to suggest that Salviati (who spoke for him) was not "absolutely" convinced of Copernicanism, it was apparent to his adversaries, as well as to the Pope, that he had not dealt with the two systems "hypothetically and impartially" as instructed by the Pope. It is obvious throughout his book, the greatest scientific dialogue ever written, that Galileo believed the evidence overwhelmingly favored (if not proved) the Copernican hypothesis, in violation of Pope Urban's instructions.

Furthermore, he often ridicules the arguments of Simplicius (the name taken from a sixth-century scholastic) who defends the traditional geocentric cosmology of the scholastics and of the church authorities, thereby provoking a hostile response. In addition, although in some respects it might have appeared appropriate, having Simplicius, the mocked scholastic, state the position of Pope Urban that regardless of the astronomical evidence God in his omnipotence could have organized the universe in many ways unthinkable to man, was a serious mistake. This perhaps inadvertent misjudgment, when pointed out to Urban by Galileo's adversaries, especially aroused his anger. But it was when the Pope learned that in 1616 Galileo had been "admonished" by Cardinal Bellarmmine, in an unsigned affidavit witnessed by a notary and other church officials, not to "hold, defend, or teach in any way, orally or in writing,"[24] the motion of the earth or stability of the sun, that he reacted in fury. Believing that Galileo had deliberately misled him in their meetings in 1624 when Urban had given him permission to publish a book on the two competing systems by not mentioning the previous affidavit, the Pope henceforth was an implacable foe of Galileo, insisting on his trial by the Inquisition.

While one can understand why the Pope felt deceived, betrayed, and mocked by Galileo still, to use the Inquisition's threat of torture and imprisonment to force Galileo to abjure on his knees his belief in Copernicanism before an ecclesiastic commission, has cast a long pall over the credibility of the Catholic church. It was only in 1992 that a Polish Pope, John Paul II, in tribute probably to his countryman Nickolas Copernicus, finally exonerated Galileo from the false condemnation. But the episode is full of tragic ironies. For though the Church was in error in forcing Galileo to recant his belief in Copernicanism which he avidly held to be true, as it proved to be, the strength of his conviction was based on the false belief that the tides were caused by the agitated motion of the earth produced by its contrasting annual revolution and diurnal rotation. Kepler had informed him of the correct explanation involving the mutual gravitational attraction between the earth and the moon, but Galileo was put off by Kepler's mystical Neoplatonic writings and believed that evoking gravitational forces between the moon and the earth resembled the "occult causes" of the scholastics; Galileo thus rejected this correct explanation. Drawing an analogy between the waves produced in water contained in an agitated pan or in the hold of a tossing ship, he thought the earth's contrasting motions caused the rhythmic flow of the tides in a similar manner.

Nonetheless, though he was humiliated by the Church and initially broken in spirit by a treatment he did not believe he deserved, including his confinement to his villa in Arcetri at the outskirts of Florence for the remainder of his life, he managed to write and furtively publish his second book, *Dialogues Concerning two New Sciences*. It is this work that laid the foundation of subsequent scientific inquiry and earned him the title of "the father of modern science." Along with numerous other inquiries, one main discovery was the correct mathematical formulation and experimental demonstration that a free falling body accelerates proportional to the square of the times—not according to its weight as Aristotle had claimed or as proportional to the space, another popular misconception. His second main discovery was his description of the trajectory of projectile motion as parabolic.

But even more importantly, his triumph over the Church consisted in his liberating scientific inquiry from ecclesiastical control, ensuring its free autonomous development. Furthermore, his conviction that it is experimental inquiry disclosing exact mathematical correlations in nature that is the key to understanding the universe, not scripture or theology, has been vindicated conclusively by later developments in the physical sciences. As he states,

> philosophy [natural science] is written in this grand book—I mean the universe—which . . . cannot be understood unless one first learns to comprehend the language . . . in which it is written. It is written in the language of mathematics . . . without which it is humanly impossible to understand a single word of it . . . wandering about in a dark labyrinth.[25]

Yet while Galileo had completely demolished the ancient Aristotelian cosmology grounded on the ontological distinction between the celestial and terrestrial worlds, and he and Kepler had discovered respectively the correct laws describing gravitational fall and planetary motions, the final unification of these two domains awaited the great Newton.

THE LEGACY OF NEWTON

Succeeding his mentor Isaac Barrow as the second Lucasian professor of mathematics at Trinity College, Cambridge, the realization that the rectilinear descent of terrestrial objects and the elliptical motion of the planets might have the same cause occurred to Newton (according to his own account) as he saw an apple fall in the orchard of his family's estate in Woolsthrope, where he had gone to escape the plague in London in 1666. Although common enough today, the insight that the force causing the moon's revolution around the earth was the same gravitational force that attracted the apple to the earth required the genius of the greatest scientist that has ever lived (because of his formulation of the universal law of gravitation and other eminent contributions to theoretical physics, his exact optical experiments and discoveries along with suggestions for further experimental inquiries, and his outstanding mathematical achievements, especially his discovery, independently of Leibniz, of the calculus). No other scientist has combined these essential scientific abilities, theoretical, experimental, and mathematical, to the degree that Newton did. In his day he was considered preeminent in each of these areas of scholarship.

Having inferred that all physical objects exert a mutually attractive force proportional to the product of their masses, he then had to determine in what way the strength of this force varied with distance to explain how the gravitational force of the sun produced the individual motion of the planets in their successive orbits around the sun. Kepler previously had conjectured that the elliptical motion of the planets described by his three laws depended upon two forces: a propelling force extending from the sun (which he originally called an "anima motrix" but later revised to a physical force analogous to the sun's radiation of light) and a counteracting attractive force drawing the planet into its elliptical path which he interpreted as a magnetic attraction following Gilbert. Drawing further on the analogy with light whose strength diminished with the distance, Kepler initially proposed that the sun's propelling power decreased in direct ratio with the distance (though later he favored the inverse square law).

It takes about eighty-eight days for Mercury to orbit the sun, nine months for Venus, a year for the Earth, two years for Mars, sixteen years for Jupiter, and thirty years for Saturn (with the moon omitted because it revolves around the earth). Aware that the successive orbital periods of planets are not in direct proportion to their distance from the sun, Newton concluded (as did Hooke and Huygens) that the force could not diminish directly with the distance. Instead, he inferred from Kepler's third law (which states that the planets' orbital periods vary with the $3/2$th power of their distance from the sun—not in direct ratio) that the strength of the gravitational force must diminish not directly with the distance, but with the square of the distance. Like Kepler, he assumed that it was the sun that was the main source of the gravitational force causing the planets motion (we now know that given the tremendous thermonuclear energy of the sun, with its equivalence to mass based on Einstein's equation $E=mc^2$, that the sun represents 98 percent of the mass of the universe, allowing the masses of the other planets to be discounted).

Thus Newton introduced his universal law of gravitation that all bodies have a gravitational attraction proportional to the product of their masses and inversely proportional to the square of their distances. Finally eliminating any distinction between the terrestrial and celestial domains, Newton's law unified the cosmos into a single system of laws. Inertial motion had been described in a restricted form by Galileo and generalized by Descartes, and now Newton used inertia to replace Kepler's propelling force as the second force causing the planet's orbital pattern. This use of forces to explain various motions, gravitational, inertial, magnetic attraction, and the newly investigated electrical repulsion and attraction, marked the end of Aristotle's organismic conceptual system and its replacement by Newton's mechanistic framework. Although many scientists in Newton's day were reluctant to admit the reality of forces, thinking of them as "occult powers," he recognized their necessity.

For Aristotle the four terrestrial elements, air, earth, fire, and water (aither was a nonmaterial celestial substance), were analyzable into an underlying substratum characterized by essential and accidental qualities. Growth and change were explained as either due to superficial changes in the qualities of objects (as when leaves change color in the autumn) or to more basic substantial changes (as when leaves are burned). The order in nature was maintained because the essential nature of things, as determined by their species and genus, would allow only the exchange of specific qualities. Living things have an inner striving (or *telos*) to actualize their potential, as when an acorn grows into an oak tree under the proper conditions, nature itself being an efficient cause. It was this inner tendency of all natural phenomena to actualize the potential inherent in their essential natures, as determined by their species and genus, that made Aristotle's system organismic and qualitative.

Scientific knowledge for Aristotle consisted of demonstrating from appropriate, true premises, discovered inductively by "rational intuition," that particular objects or events had the properties they did because they belonged to a higher genus which inherently possessed those properties. A familiar example is the explanation of why humans are mortal from the fact that all animals are mortal, deducing that since the human species falls within the genus animals, it must possess the essential quality of mortality. Similarly, the answer to why the planets (in contrast to the stars) do not twinkle is because they are proximate celestial bodies and no proximate celestial bodies twinkle. In Aristotle's system, while any explanation must specify the material and efficient causes (the underlying substance and productive cause), it also must state the formal and final causes (the generic kind of thing the object is which determines the end it strives to realize).

In the only instance of the *complete* rejection and replacement of an *entire* theoretical framework in the history of science since the adoption of Aristotelianism by the scholastics, the whole of Aristotle's theoretical system had to be discarded. This framework of interpretation, in terms of substance and form, potentiality and actuality, essential and accidental properties, and inherent formal and final causes, was seen as entirely inadequate in contrast to the new mode of explanation in terms of insensible particles (atoms and corpuscles) that have the properties of mass, inertia, acceleration, and momentum, with the scientific explanation of motion based entirely on efficient causes involving mechanical forces. An entirely different theoretical framework was being introduced to explain the various forms of motion.

Because he wrote his extraordinarily influential *The Structure of Scientific Revolutions* after he had written *The Copernican Revolution* (in which he did not propose such a radical irrational interpretation of scientific revolutions), it may have been the *wholesale rejection* of the Aristotelian system, that led Kuhn to his characterization of scientific revolutions (in contrast to "normal science") as "discontinuous, incommensurable gestalt switches," with opposing scientists existing in incommunicable conceptual worlds.[26] But once the mechanistic framework of atomic physics, the methodology of experimental inquiry, and the indispensability of mathematical formalisms were established, the complete rejection of that framework has never recurred.

There were lesser revolutions, such as Lavoisier's refutation of the theory of phlogiston, Darwin's evolutionary theory, Maxwell's theory of electromagnetism, and the geological theory of plate tectonics, but these occurred as modifications in or extensions of the previous conceptual framework, and thus were based on traditional scientific concepts and laws. Nor were the developments of relativity theory and quantum mechanics incommensurable with Newtonian mechanics as sometimes claimed; instead, as Einstein himself said of relativity theory and Bohr asserted of quantum mechanics, they both include Newtonian mechanics as "limiting conditions" of each theory because the classical Galilean transformation laws can be derived from the Lorentz transformation equations of relativity theory when the velocity of a system is insignificant compared to the velocity of light, while Bohr's correspondence principle applies when the magnitude of interactions is large compared to Planck's constant.

In the ancient atomic system of Leucippus and Democritus the physical properties of mass, acceleration, inertial motion, and force of impact had been assigned to the indestructible atoms, with the composition and disintegration of substances explained by the mechanical interactions of these indivisible particles (a mode of explanation explicitly rejected by both Plato and Aristotle as not providing for a purposeful universe). Because of this, it was natural that Newton and the other contributors to the formulation of the mechanistic worldview, such as Bacon, Descartes, Gassendi, Mersenne, Hobbes, Boyle, and Locke, would turn to atomism as the foundation of their new explanatory system. Moreover, while Aristotle conceived of scientific explanation as syllogistic deduction or demonstration from premises stating generic classifications, the new conception of scientific inquiry involved the experimental discovery of correlations in nature that could be expressed as laws in mathematical equations (such as $f = ma$, $E = mc^2$, $\varepsilon = h\nu$, etc.) which applied to theoretically postulated phenomena such as atoms, energy, forces, charges, and so on, subject to experimental tests.

These theoretical developments completely transformed man's conception of the universe and his place in it. The ancient spherical, homocentric universe divided into two qualitatively distinct realms with the Prime Mover (as pure form, pure actuality, and final cause) at the pinnacle of an aspiring cosmos was replaced by an infinite Euclidean universe whose atomic constituents generated such mechanical forces as gravitational attraction, atomic cohesion, gas pressure, electrical repulsion and attraction, heat or energy, and so forth. Theoretical knowledge for Aristotle was divided into three disciplines, mathematics, physics, and what came to be called metaphysics, the latter a "first philosophy" or "theology" that investigated the first principles of things, along with "being qua being" or the ultimate immovable substance (the Prime Mover). Aristotle's description of the Prime Mover shows why Thomas Aquinas believed that Aristotle's cosmological system was more compatible with Christianity than Plato's Demiurge functioning as a divine craftsman imposing order on the resisting world of the Receptacle. As Aristotle states,

> the possession rather than the receptivity is the divine element which thought seems to contain, and the act of contemplation is what is most pleasant and best. If, then, God is always in that grand state in which we

sometimes are, this compels our wonder; and if in a better this compels it yet more. And God *is* in a better state. And life also belongs to God; for the actuality of thought is life, and God is that actuality; and God's self-dependent actuality is life most good and eternal. We say therefore that God is a living being, eternal, most good, so that life and duration continuous and eternal belong to God; for this *is* God.[27]

Thus for Aristotle God or the Prime Mover was an archetypal philosopher whose self-contained existence had its own consciousness as its object of thought.

THE CONFLICT BETWEEN SCIENCE AND RELIGION

The emerging consensus of an atomic-mechanistic universe not only replaced Aristotle's organismic cosmology, it also threatened the biblical account of creation while raising a number of theological problems. In an infinite physical universe with no celestial heaven, where is the Kingdom of God located and where do the angels and heavenly hosts reside? What was the destination of Christ's bodily ascension into heaven? How could a physical body rise? The decline of learning and prevalence of illiteracy during the medieval period meant that the laity accepted uncritically whatever was taught by the Church, especially since the liturgy was in Latin, which few understood. The savants of this period, however, were very much concerned to reconcile religion with the newly emerging scientific worldview. While earlier one could accept the Genesis account of creation as literally true, it's explanatory weaknesses became more evident in the seventeenth century, owing to the renewed confidence in scientific inquiry and man's attempt to understand the universe.

Instead of just taking biblical assertions on faith, one began asking such obvious questions as: How did God "in the beginning create heaven and earth" from nothing? How could the earth exist while being "without form and void"? How could God "bring forth light" as a separate creation in the absence of the sun? How could Cain acquire a wife and beget the human race when his father and mother, Adam and Eve, who were supposed to be the original ancestors of the human race, never had a daughter? While one could accept that a *mythical* account would contain such glaring anomalies, this hardly could be true of a literal, inerrant description of creation as Christians were taught to believe of Genesis. The threat of the new science for some Christians is clearly exemplified in Luther's disparaging comment about his contemporary Copernicus:

People give ear to an upstart astrologer [the term was used for astronomers at the time, but here it may be intentionally derogatory] who strove
to show that the earth revolves not the . . . sun. . . . This fool wishes to
revise the entire science of astronomy; but sacred Scripture tells us that
Joshua [Joshua 10:3] commanded the sun to stand still, and not the
earth.[28]

This does not mean, of course, that the originators of modern science
themselves were not religious. Copernicus was the nephew of a bishop
and a canon of the Catholic church; though a protestant, Kepler was
deeply influenced by the mysticism of Neoplatonism; Galileo's avowed
purpose in writing his proscribed *Dialogue Concerning the Two Chief World
Systems* was to "show the world beyond Italy" that Catholics were as well
informed of the Copernican system as scholars in other countries. Even
Newton, the primary creator of the mechanistic-materialistic worldview,
was deeply religious, although his conscience prevented him from
swearing an oath of allegiance to the Anglican faith to become ordained,
a prerequisite at the time for obtaining a professorship at Trinity College,
Cambridge. He thus had to acquire a royal exemption. After years of
study he could not accept the Athanasian trinitarian concept of Christ,
the Holy Spirit, and God as three-in-one, the accepted Anglican doctrine;
he therefore had to be exempted from taking the oath if he were to accede
to the Lucasian professorship. Although no one seems to know who
interceded on his behalf, he was successful. Nor had the other contributors to the formulation of the atomic-molecular worldview, such as
Bacon, Descartes, Gassendi, Boyle, and Locke, ceased to believe in the
existence of God. They were disavowing the Aristotelian-Scholastic cosmology, not Christianity.

But the adoption of the new scientific framework inevitably brought
about a modification of the conception and role of God, as well as a
reevaluation of the arguments traditionally offered since Aristotle as
rational 'proofs' of God's existence. This was "inevitable" because all religions, as all institutions, exist to satisfy certain human needs, and hence
arise within an historical-cultural context (evident in their different
beliefs and practices) that provides the background conditions for their
emergence. So as the historical-cultural background changes, as just
described in the Christian world, this affects religious beliefs and practices. Furthermore, whether one is Hindu, Buddhist, Taoist, Jewish,
Christian, or Muslim normally is not a matter of choice but an accident of
birth, a fact often forgotten when one considers one's own religion the
only true one or superior to any other. So while belief in the Bible, especially the New Testament, along with personal religious experience and
the pervasiveness of religious institutions within the state still were the

major sources of Christian faith, scientists and philosophers, as a result of the renewed confidence in scientific inquiry and modification in world outlook, were seeking more rational justifications for belief in God. As a consequence, the evidence of God's manifestation in nature was considered as important as revelation, and even superior if the latter conflicted with the former, as Galileo argued.

This alteration of beliefs is evident in the theory of Deism, the doctrine that God created the universe as a self-sufficient, self-governing system that could function on its own without God's intervention. Moreover, because the traditional 'proofs' of the existence of God were based on certain epistemological, theological, or cosmological assumptions, their credibility diminished with the change in conceptual framework and worldview. For example, one of the most famous 'proofs' of the existence of God was formulated by St. Anselm, a Benedictine monk who became Archbishop of Canterbury in the eleventh century. Well known for his assertions that "I do not seek to understand that I may believe, but I believe in order to understand" and that "Truly There Is a God, Although the Fool Hath Said in His Heart, There is No God,"[29] he is especially famous for his "ontological argument," which attempts to demonstrate that one cannot *consistently* deny the existence of God or even think that God does not exist. One can *say* that God does not exist, but then one is not using the word 'God' with its proper meaning or reference, as would be true also if one called water 'fire,' to use his example; that is, the correct conception and description of anything must include its essential or defining attributes.

Beginning with the definition of God as "a being than which nothing greater can be conceived," Anselm argued that if one denies that God exists, then one is denying the essential meaning of God as "a being than which nothing greater can be conceived" because having a conception of God as *existing* includes more — is greater or more comprehensive — than the conception of a nonexisting God. Hence, one either misconstrues the referent of the word 'God' (as a being that could not exist) when one declares God does not exist, or one contradicts the essential meaning of God (which includes existence as essential to God's nature). As Anselm states with scholastic precision:

> . . . it is possible to conceive of a being which cannot be conceived not to exist; and this is greater than one which can be conceived not to exist. Hence, if that, than which nothing greater can be conceived, can be conceived not to exist, it is not that, than which nothing greater can be conceived. But this is an irreconcilable contradiction. There is, then, so truly a being than which nothing greater can be conceived to exist, that it cannot even be conceived not to exist; and this being thou art, O Lord, one God.[30]

Although Descartes repeated this argument in a revised form in his Fifth *Meditation*, it hardly is unassailable for the conclusion is valid only if *in fact* God is that being or referent "than which no greater can be conceived." Does Anselm's claim that only God can be *conceived* in this way establish *the fact* of God's being so? Many things that have been conceived as absolutely necessary or true throughout the past (such as the motionlessness of the earth, that nature abhors a vacuum, or that the soul as a simple substance is indestructible) were later proven false or just discarded. Anselm's conclusion either presupposes the truth of the premise that God's essential nature is to exist or it begs the question in assuming that only God can qualify as the greatest conceivable referent. For someone who does not accept that definition, such as an atheist or even a pantheist, the physical universe or the Absolute would be the greatest possible referent while the theistic conception of God would be as fictitious as the idea of heaven, hell, or the devil. Though Anselm held that his definition of God was the correct one, reinforced by Scripture (in response to Moses' question as to his name, Yahweh 'replied,' "I Am Who I Am" [Exod. 3:13]) and the theological definition of God prevalent in the Middle Ages, it is not as compelling today—another example of the effect of changing cultural and conceptual frameworks on modifying our beliefs.

Two centuries later the dominican monk St. Thomas Aquinas formulated his five 'proofs' of the existence of God based mainly on the recently acquired and translated scientific manuscripts of Aristotle. Advocating a "twofold mode" of religious truths, Aquinas declared that while certain truths like the "triune nature of God" had to be accepted on faith, other truths such as "that God exists . . . have been proved demonstratively by the philosophers, guided by the light of natural reason."[31] Like faith, this illuminating light of reason was endowed by God. But these five arguments (which shall be reduced to three because the underlying logic of two resembles that of two others) show very clearly their rationale depends upon Aristotelian explanatory principles that have lost their plausibility within the new scientific conception of nature.

The first 'proof' is the famous argument for the "Prime Mover," which depended upon Aristotle's nonmechanical definition of motion as "nothing else than the reduction of something from potentiality to actuality." Because "nothing can be reduced from potentiality to actuality, except by something in a state of actuality," the ultimate cause must be pure actuality or the Prime Mover. Furthermore, because any physical motion (as opposed to a self-moving organism) requires a cause, "whatever is moved must be moved by another," but this "also must needs be moved by another," and so forth ad infinitum. But since an infinite series would be nonterminating or incomplete, it would not include a beginning; therefore, "it is necessary to arrive at a first mover, moved by no other; and this everyone understands is God." But it was precisely to replace what had then come to be seen as vacuous definitions and pseudoexplanations that scientists like Boyle and Newton turned to mechanistic concepts like gravitational attraction, inertial motion, and cohesive and repulsive forces to explain motions such as free fall, projectiles, and the revolution of the planets. Once the kinetic theory of atomic motion was introduced, the inference that "whatever is moved must be moved by another" is otiose, although it *was* held that the *original* source of motion, as that of the universe, had to be attributed to God. But the new theoretical framework made Aristotle's argument for a first cause based on his explanation of motion obsolete.

The next argument, called the argument from contingency, maintained that because the existence of material objects is conditional or not inherently necessary, "it is impossible for those always to exist, for that which can not-be at some time is not." Furthermore, "if everything can not-be, then at one time there was nothing in existence," so that "even now there would be nothing to exist. . . ." This therefore requires "the existence of some being having of itself its own necessity" which "all men speak of as God" (analogous to Anselm's ontological argument). But the rationale for this conclusion was avoided even by the ancient atomists who declared that atoms, being indivisible and indestructible, were themselves eternal, along with their motion, thereby obviating a first cause. Like Anselm's argument, Aquinas's begs the question because it assumes that the existence of God does not require an explanation, while the existence of the universe does; that is, God's existence is presumed to be necessary while that of the universe is not. Yet from a contemporary point of view, this assumption is arbitrary since we know the universe exists, whereas whether God exists or not is questionable. But in the seventeenth century the influence of Genesis still was sufficiently strong that even proponents of the atomic-mechanistic worldview felt bound to attribute the origin of the universe to God. As Newton states in a famous passage:

> . . . it seems probable to me, that God in the beginning form'd Matter in solid, massy, hard, impenetrable, movable Particles, of such Sizes and Figures, and with such other Properties . . . as most conduced to the End for which he form'd them; and that these primitive Particles being Solids, are . . . even so very hard as never to wear or break in pieces: no ordinary Power being able to divide what God himself made one in the first Creation.[32]

That the universe be lasting required a creator whose own existence was beyond question, but this is not as evident today for those who are not already committed to a religious view of reality.

The third proof, the argument from design, although rejected by the ancient atomists who claimed that everything occurred of necessity and not for a purpose, eventually became the most influential proof for the existence of God in the eighteenth century. As maintained by Aquinas, the fact that natural bodies, though not endowed with intelligence, normally act uniformly to "achieve their end," presupposes that "some intelligent being exists by whom all natural things are directed to their end; and this being we call God." While this argument led Aristotle to reject either mechanistic necessity or accidental selection as adequate explanations for the recurrence of natural kinds, it also was the basis of Galileo's and Newton's conviction that the original arrangement of the planets could not have occurred merely by natural causes, but required the intentional intervention of God.

It was William Paley, Archdeacon of Carlyle, that in the eighteenth century became famous for his formulation of the argument from design based on the watch analogy. Arguing that if we stumbled on a stone in the forest and were asked how it came to be there, we undoubtedly would answer that in all probability some natural cause were the reason. However, if we found a watch in the path we would be just as convinced that it had been produced intentionally by a human watchmaker because watches display the kind of complex organization of parts, for the purpose of indicating the time, that distinguishes them from stones or other inanimate objects. Drawing an analogy between the mechanisms of the watch and the mechanistic structure of the universe, Paley argued that we can infer that the latter, too, must have been designed by an intelligent being, though vastly superior to the finest craftsman:

> I mean that the contrivances of nature surpass the contrivances of art in the complexity, subtlety, and curiosity of the mechanism; and . . . are not less evidently mechanical . . . than are the most perfect productions of human ingenuity. . . .[33]

As he points out, the most remarkable example is the intricate structure of the eye, which alone would be "sufficient to support the conclusion which we draw from it, as to the necessity of an intelligent Creator."[34]

A century earlier Galileo had argued that if the language of nature is mathematics, then whoever created nature must have been a mathematician. Newton, too, believed that the discovered laws of nature and existence of intricate organic creatures were evidence of divine planning. All the major scientists of the seventeenth century believed that, like all man-made machines, the great cosmic machine required an external intelligence to create its exact laws and to set it in motion, while the existence of mankind and other sentient creatures also attests to God's creative design and purpose which could not arise from purely inanimate matter. As Steven Shapin asserts:

> This "voluntarist" strand was . . . highly developed in English natural philosophy from Boyle to Newton. Nature was to be inspected for the evidence of regularity and patterns that testified to God's designing intelligence. Such evidence spoke to God's "general" or "ordinary prov- idence," and it was to be concluded that natural regularities were con- tinuously and actively maintained by God.[35]

Miracles were accepted as evidence of God's intervention in the world to produce a purpose that required contravening the natural laws of nature.

Yet as appealing as this assumption is, developments in science have shown that it, too, is unnecessary. Prior to Darwin, it was unquestionably reasonable to suppose that organic structures as intricate as the eye, with its marvelous integration of functions, could not have evolved by mere chance. However, when Darwin introduced his theory of the evolution of species based on random genetic mutations whose adaptive advantages were nat- urally selected in a competitive ecological environment, scientists gradually rejected the ancient theory of special creation for this scientific explanation. As will be discussed in chapter 5, the fossil evidence for Darwin's theory of a *gradual* evolution from simpler to more complex organic structures has been challenged by new fossil evidence, yet no prominent paleontologist rejects a naturalistic explanation of evolution for a supernatural one.[36] The discovery of the winding staircase pattern of DNA and RNA by Watson and Crick followed by an understanding of how genetic information is encoded, deciphered, and transmitted, culminating recently in the genome project, has provided a completely naturalistic explanation of the development and function of organisms. Investigations by Ilya Prigogine, Stuart Kauffman, and others of self-organizing dissipative structures,[37] and the disclosure by James Gleick that slight fluctuations can result in catastrophic changes while beautiful patterns can emerge spontaneously from chaotic fractal systems,[38] have shown that nature itself produces unexpected self-generating patterns and amazingly intricate designs. Arising from within matter, these sui generis forms do not seem to require an antecedent intelligent or intentional cause. We are discovering that it is nature that has the inherent capacity to produce these self-organizing, self-replicating intricate patterns.

THE POST-NEWTONIAN PERIOD

To return to the description of the prominent cultural developments in the West during the past two millennia, while Newton's renown is based on his *Principia*, it was his lesser known work, the *Opticks*, that has a tremendous influence on subsequent scientific research throughout the eighteenth century. It presented his major experimental discovery years earlier that when refracted through a prism ordinary 'white' light produces a continuous band of colors or "rays" owing to their different refractive powers, thus demonstrating that rather than being irreducible, ordinary light consists of more basic rays or colors. He also tried to explain the physical properties of these rays in terms of a corpuscular theory. Then, foreshadowing the twentieth-century method of investigating atomic and nuclear structures by bombarding them with smaller particles, he suggested that the penetrating power of light corpuscles due to their heat and velocity might be used to reveal the inner structure of certain substances, such as crystals.[39] Furthermore, his conjectures attributing the pressure of gases to the repelling motion of gas particles, the internal structure of substances and the density and viscosity of fluids to the cohesive force of atoms, along with his speculations regarding the causes of electrical attraction and fermentation instigated and directed research into these diverse natural phenomena during the following two centuries.

One of Newton's first acts as president of the Royal Society, for instance, was to hire Hauksbee to conduct electrical experiments. Soon a succession of discoveries by Stephen Gray, Charles du Fay, and Benjamin Franklin led finally to an understanding of electrical attraction and repulsion in terms of the flow of positive and negative electricity, along with Coulomb's Law that the strength of the electrical attraction varies directly with the product of the charges and inversely with the square of the distances — analogous to Newton's universal law of gravitation, this is a striking example of the uniformities of nature. But the full explanation awaited the later discovery of electrons and their subatomic role. A number of remarkable investigations at the end of the eighteenth century disclosed that three of the four elements considered basic since their classification by Empedocles and adoption by Aristotle, air, water, and earth, were not irreducible but composite: air discovered to contain several elementary gases such as nitrogen, hydrogen, and oxygen; water composed of hydrogen and oxygen; and earth a mixture of diverse components.

Not only were more basic elements being discovered, the investigation of gases such as carbon dioxide and nitric oxide and chemical analyses of substances like hydrochloric acid and water disclosed that these substances were composed of definite proportions of certain elements: CO_2, NO, HCL, and H_2O respectively. Convinced of the truth of Newton's belief in atomism, John Dalton proposed the crucial hypothesis that substances contain a fixed number of atoms (as indicated in the formulas above) combined according to their atomic weights, which could be found by carefully weighing the proportion of elements forming gases or compound substances, as well as by electrolysis.

The nature of combustion involving the fourth element fire was being investigated, Joseph Priestly discovering the new gas later called oxygen. Because at the time combustion was thought to involve an inflammable substance called phlogiston, possessed by the combustible material that was released during the burning process until either all the phlogiston was expended or the surrounding air became saturated, Priestly called the air in which objects burned excessively dephlogistated air. Initially devoid of phlogiston, this air could absorb a large amount, thus enhancing combustion. But it was Antoine-Laurent Lavoisier who determined, by carefully weighing the substances before and after combustion, that despite the reduction in the amount of residue left after a substance was burned, in fact there was an *increase* in weight indicating that something had been absorbed, rather than released, during the combustion, in direct contrast to the phlogiston theory. So although Lavoisier did not discover the flammable substance itself, he correctly described its role in combustion (and respiration), calling it *oxygene*. The beginning of modern chemistry (replacing alchemy which still was prevalent) is generally attributed to the overthrow of the phlogiston theory, along with the correct explanation of combustion in terms of oxygen.

Although Newton's interpretation of light as corpuscular had been opposed at the time by Hooke and Huygens, the enormous prestige of Newton throughout the eighteenth century had led to its being the accepted theory until Young and Fresnel conducted their diffraction experiments at the beginning of the nineteenth century. Concluding that the diffraction patterns (alternating light and dark bands) produced on a screen by light reflected through tiny pin holes, along with its refraction by Island crystal, could be explained more simply on the assumption that the bright bands were produced by reinforced waves and the dark lines by the destruction of the waves that were out of phase, Fresnel went on to measure the wave lengths and amplitudes of specific colors or rays. Furthermore, Newton had predicted that when refracted through a denser medium the light corpuscles would increase in velocity because of the stronger gravitational attraction of the denser medium, while the wave theory predicted that the light waves would be impeded and slowed down. In what is often called an *experimentum crucis*, devising a number of ingenious experiments Faucault showed that the velocity of light was slower in denser mediums like water or glass, thereby disconfirming the particle theory. When Fizeau measured the absolute velocity of light to be 300,000 kilometers per second, the previous fierce opposition to the wave theory gradually subsided to an acceptance.

Later in the century Oerstead demonstrated that a changing electric current produced a magnetic field, while Faraday discovered that a changing magnetic field induced an electric current, the origin of the electric generator. Based on these experimental discoveries, Maxwell devised the equations describing the structure of the electromagnetic field and its changes in time. When it was determined that the speed of light and that of electromagnetic propagation were the same, in one of the greatest theoretical unifications in physics, it was deduced that light, too, was an electromagnetic phenomenon. Einstein referred to Maxwell's discoveries as among the greatest in the history of science.

Concurrent technological innovations during the eighteenth and nineteenth centuries produced the industrial revolution that, like the ancient agricultural revolution, transformed civilization. Machines were invented to mechanize the processes of spinning and weaving wool and cotton, along with manufacturing meedles and nails. The rotary steam engine was developed as a source of power to run the machines in the mills, replacing the less reliable water power. New technologies were introduced to convert coal (which in England was more plentiful than wood) into coke used in the blast furnaces to produce a higher grade of iron, cast iron. These industrial developments in turn initiated radical social and cultural changes.

The demand for factory labor offering higher wages attracted large numbers of farmers to the newly developed manufacturing centers of Birmingham, Manchester, Yorkshire, and Lancashire, introducing two new classes, the working class or proletariate and the increasingly influential entrepreneurial middle class or bourgeoisie, to the previous classes of farmers, landed gentry, and aristocracy. These emerging industrial centers created the need for urban planning, including the building of larger schools, medical facilities, a central sewage system, and greater road access. New financial institutions had to be created to provide the credit or capital to finance the inventions and construction of factories. Additional technological innovations led to the mechanization of farming, the creation of railroads and steamships for faster transportation, the instillation of gas lamps in the cities, the invention of the telegraph, and so forth. A new system of social organization arose radically different from the ancient civilization of the Axial Age.

TWENTIETH-CENTURY SCIENCE

But the experimental discoveries, theoretical developments, and consequent technological applications that would change the world even more dramatically did not occur until the twentieth century. In fact, there have been more significant advances in the sciences of physics, chemistry, astronomy, geology, biology, genetics, medicine, neurophysiology, and electronics in this century than in the whole past history of science, just as there are more scientists living today than in all its previous history. Throughout much of the world, now greatly reduced in size since World War II because of developments in transportation, communication, political integration, and economic interdependence, hardly any aspect of life has remained unaffected by scientific progress.

The catalyst for these changes, following Maxwell's theory of electromagnetism that had eluded Newtonian mechanics, was first the discovery of a particle smaller than the atom, the electron, identified by J. J. Thomson in 1897. This was succeeded by the ground-breaking experimental research of Ernest Rutherford. After having discovered additional evidence of subatomic particles, which he called alpha and beta rays, he used the massive positively charged alpha particle (helium nuclei) to probe the interior of the atom to discover whether the latter had an inner structure. For though atoms had been defined as indivisible and hence irreducible by Leucippus and Democritus in the fifth century B.C.E., and still were considered so by Newton, Dalton, and even Maxwell, there now was evidence suggesting they were composite. For example, the detection of more elementary particles, the determination that each element had a characteristic emission spectrum, the evidence of penetrating X-rays by Röntgen, the discovery of radioactivity by Becquerel, and the isolation of radioactive substances such as radium, thorium, and polonium by Marie and Pierre Curie led physicists to believe that atoms might have an inner structure whose elements and changes could be the cause of the spectral and radiational emissions.

Devising an experiment in which alpha particles were radiated at thin gold foil surrounded by a revolving spectroscope for detecting their angle of deflection, Rutherford's assistant Marsden was astonished to find that while most of the particles penetrated the foil or were deflected at slight angles, a few rebounded directly back to the eyepiece of the observer. Inferring that the rebound must be produced by a massive particle within the gold foil, Rutherford named the particle a "proton," Greek for "first one" to indicate that it was the first atomic particle ever discovered (one did not know yet whether the electron was a constituent of the atom). Unlike the electron which had been detected using a cathode-ray tube, the proton was discovered while probing gold foil and thus was considered a constituent of the atom's interior composition, its positive charge and mass subsequently measured by Rutherford. Realizing the proton would not account for the total mass of the atom, Rutherford's colleague at the Cavendish, James Chadwich, discovered in 1932 a new particle having a mass nearly that of the proton but with a neutral charge, calling it the "neutron."

Because metals are good conductors of electricity, it was inferred that the atoms composing the metals must consist of the nearly massless negatively charged electron along with the massive, positively charged proton and neutral neutron. Although a number of leading physicists were engaged in the attempt to model the interior of the atom, it was the Danish physicist Niels Bohr who succeeded in creating the first successful conception of the interior structure of the atomic. Utilizing Balmer's formula for hydrogen spectra and Planck's constant of action indicating that the absorption and radiation of energy occur in discrete quanta, and using both classical and quantum principles Bohr was able to account for the simple emission spectra of hydrogen, although not for more complex spectra.

Conceiving the atom to be composed of a nuclear proton (the neutron had not yet been discovered) surrounded by swirling electrons in discrete orbits with the innermost designated the ground state, Bohr explained spectral emissions as due to the "jump" of an electron from a higher orbit to the next lower one, the loss of energy equivalent to the emitted quantum of light produced by the quantum jump. Similarly, absorption of energy caused an orbiting electron to leap to a higher orbit whose frequency is proportional to the energy absorbed, according to Planck's equation $\varepsilon = h\nu$. Thus, three of the four basic research areas of twentieth-century physics were established: (1) Planck's theoretical introduction in 1900 of the quantum of action to explain black-body radiation with his equation equating the energy of radiation with its frequency laying the foundation of quantum mechanics; (2) Rutherford's experimental discovery of the proton and Chadwick of the neutron inaugurating particle physics; and (3) Bohr's tentative construction of the atom in 1913 paving the way for later atomic developments that not only accounted for spectral emissions with orbiting electrons, but led to the classification of the elements and explanation of their chemical properties, not by their atomic weights, as Dalton and Mendeleev had, but by their atomic number (the number of protons in the nucleus), with radiation attributed to transformations in the nuclear structure creating isotopes.

Another major contribution to quantum mechanics was Einstein's explanation of the photoelectric effect by light quanta. When homogeneous light (light of the same color or wave length) is reflected on the surface of treated metals, the metallic surface begins to glow due, it was conjectured, to the ejection of electrons from oscillators which were activated by an exchange of the heat or energy of the light. According to the accepted wave theory, the greater intensity of the light source (causing more superimposed waves) should result in the electrons being ejected with greater velocity, but this was found not to be the case. Instead, the energy or velocity of the ejected electrons depended on the color or frequency of the light source, violet light with a short wave length and high frequency ejecting the electrons more vigorously than red light with twice the wave length and half the frequency. Einstein realized that this could be explained by utilizing Planck's quantum of energy and equation equating frequency of radiation with energy, and in one of five famous papers published in 1905, he explained the photoelectric effect on the supposition that light was not composed of waves but of quanta of energy (supporting Newton's previous corpuscular interpretation), the magnitude correlated with the particular color. Thus violet light with higher frequency and greater energy would produce a greater agitation of the oscillators, thereby ejecting the electrons more vigorously than red light, while the total brightness or luminosity would depend on the intensity of the light source, on its containing a greater number of light quanta. These massless quanta of energy later came to be called photons.

Although Einstein's contribution to quantum mechanics was extremely important, both because of the key role photons play in particle physics and also because it was the origin of the paradoxical wave-particle duality of light, his outstanding achievement was the special and general theories of relativity which were uniquely his own contribution. Although he developed his special theory (also published in 1905) from considerations of asymmetries in Maxwell's electrodynamics, the fact that it could accommodate the anomalous results of the Michelson-Morley experiments gave it special significance (although Einstein said he was not directly influenced by the negative results of their experiments). In the *Principia*, Newton had assumed that objects either are at rest in absolute space or move with an absolute velocity relative to an absolute space and time, hence the latter constituted his famous "frames of the universe."

However, because only relative positions and velocities could be measured, as Newton acknowledged, this made his theory of absolute space and time problematic. As no mechanical experiment could settle the issue, near the end of the nineteenth century scientists Albert Michelson and Edward Morley independently attempted to demonstrate optically the motion of light relative to an absolute space. Since absolute space itself is undetectable, they assumed that because it was filled with an immobile ether (to account for the propagation of light waves which it was assumed required a medium as sound does), the revolution of the earth through the ether at about twenty miles per second would create an ether wind or drift, which in turn would affect the velocity of a light beam depending upon whether it was projected parallel or transverse to the ether drift. Using a spectroscope in which a single beam of light was split into two rays by a mirror, so that although both trajectories were of equal distance one ray traveled parallel to the ether and the other transverse to it, when they were reflected back to the spectroscope Michelson and Morley were astonished to find that in contrast to their expectations, the separate rays always returned simultaneously or in phase; that is, there was no interference pattern indicating a time difference in their return.

A striking example of the difficulty of assessing the results of a disconfirmed prediction because all predictions are inferred from a background theory based on various assumptions, along with a network of conceptual implications, it was not at all evident what was the source of the anomalous result: the belief in the earth's orbital revolution; the assumption of the existence of the ether in an underlying absolute space as the source of the ether wind; the conviction that the velocities of the split rays of light would be affected by the ether; the supposition that the classical addition of velocities principle could be applied to light as well as to mechanical velocities; or that some kind of perturbation had offset the expected interference.

However, when Einstein published his special theory of relativity claiming that the velocity of light as measured by different observers moving relative to each other was constant or invariant (the velocity of light *is* affected by the density of the medium in which it is transmitted, for example in air, water, or glass, but the question pertains to the intrinsic velocity of light as measured by observers moving relative to each other), this provided a possible resolution of the problem, despite its paradoxical consequences. According to Einstein's interpretation, accepting the constant velocity of light entailed discarding two of the entrenched presuppositions mentioned above: the assumption of the ether's existence (along with absolute space) and the belief that the classical addition of velocities principle (that velocities varied relative to the velocity of the source and the measurer) that applied to mechanical velocities applied also to electromagnetic propagation. However, the most astonishing consequence was that the velocity of light, as measured by an individual relatively at rest and another moving at nearly the speed of light, would be the same or constant.

Because velocity is a function of the time required to traverse a certain distance, Einstein surmised that for an observer at relative rest and one moving at a relatively high speed to find the velocity of light to be identical, their instruments of measurements must be affected by their respective velocities. Thus if the rods used to measure the distance contracted and the clocks used to measure the time slowed down *in the system moving relative to the one at rest*, just enough so that the measured velocity of light (which should be less in the system moving relative to the system at rest) was identical to that of the system at rest, then this would explain the anomalous result. That is, according to the classical addition of velocities principle, an observer A moving in the same direction as system B should find the measured velocity of B to be relative to its own velocity; instead A finds the *velocity of light* to be invariable. This can be accounted for if the measuring rods and clocks in system A used to measure the velocity of light are contracted and retarded in proportion to A's velocity, thereby explaining why the velocity of light was found to be greater than expected. Because velocity is distance divided by time, shorter rods will give a larger magnitude for the numerator while slower clocks will give a smaller value for the denominator resulting in a greater value for the velocity coefficient, thereby accounting for the degree of contraction and retardation in the system assumed to be moving relative to the other. The different measurements due to the different velocities of the two systems can be calculated with Lorentz's transformation equations.

Thus Einstein's solution is the reverse of classical physics regarding light. While in Newtonian mechanics it was assumed that the length of measuring rods and rhythm of clocks were unaffected by the velocity of the system in which they were used, hence the velocity of light as measured in these systems should be relative to their own velocities, Einstein concluded that because the velocity of light was constant, independent of the velocity of the observer measuring it, the length of measuring rods and the rates of clocks used to determine its velocity must be reduced relative to the system's velocity—the greater the velocity the greater the contraction of the measuring rods and retardation of clocks. If this alteration occurs in all systems proportional to their velocities, this explains why the observers in each system find the velocity of light to be invariant or constant. In the special theory which dealts with *uniform* motions unaffected by accelerating or gravitational forces, this effect was considered to be merely apparent and reciprocal. As the heights of two distant observers appear to be reciprocally reduced by optical perspective (but not actually reduced), in the *special theory* where the motions are uniform, the contraction of measuring rods and slowing of clocks were considered reciprocal and apparent, called the "perspective of velocity,"[40] analogous to the perspective of distances. When Einstein generalized the theory to include accelerating and gravitational forces, these effects no longer were regarded as merely apparent, but considered actual because there were forces generated to cause them.

As Paul Langevin's thought experiment called "the twins paradox" brought out, if one twin were placed on a spaceship that accelerated to within $\frac{1}{20,000}$th the speed of light and then returned to the earth, the space twin's voyage would have lasted two years according to the clock and rate of changes within the space ship, while two centuries would have elapsed according to the earth's time, so that the earth twin would have died long before the other twin returned.[41] This means that intersecting world lines (the contemporaneous trajectories of moving systems) comprise different temporal rates depending on the velocities of the systems creating the world lines. Moreover, because mass also increases with velocity, the speed of light becomes a limiting velocity for any material particle (one possessing mass), while energy and mass become equivalent as stated in Einstein's famous formula $E = mc^2$ (where E equals energy, m equals mass, and c equals the velocity of light squared).

But Einstein's general theory involved more than actual contraction and retardation effects. With his *gedanken experiments* involving elevators in different dynamic conditions, he was able to show that *gravitational effects* could be duplicated in *accelerating systems* outside gravitational fields, while the *inertial conditions* of a system beyond gravity could be replicated in a free falling elevator within a *gravitational field*. From this he deduced the equivalence of gravitational and accelerating forces, along with the equality of inertial mass and gravitational force. The latter equality had been known since Galileo had noted the isochronism of pendular motions and inferred that in a vacuum objects of different masses fall with the same velocity, a fact that had puzzled scientists thereafter. In Einstein's general theory, gravitational attraction and inertia are treated in his field equations as equivalent, thus objects in a vacuum fall with the same velocity because the gravitational force and inertial masses are equal. Like Maxwell's equations which describe the structure of electromagnetic fields instead of forces, Einstein's field equations replace forces by the structure of gravitational fields.

Then, based on the 1919 eclipse observations that confirmed his formula equating mass with energy, from which he had predicted that light quanta as energy would be equivalent to mass and thus be attracted by the gravitational force of the sun, Einstein proposed further that matter was reducible to concentrated energy or to the condensed center of a gravitational field. But since Minkowski had been able to give an objective value to the Lorentz transformation equations used in the special theory by combining space and time into a four-dimensional continuum of events, the concentration of mass or energy in the universe also could be interpreted as a bend or warp in the space-time structure. Moreover, the mathematician Bernard Riemann introduced the non-Euclidean geometry of a curved space that formed a closed sphere, that Einstein adopted as his cosmological model. The whole universe is a closed sphere, finite in volume but unlimited or unbounded in the sense that attempting to go beyond it would result in a continuously curved trajectory. This notion of a finite-infinite universe is the generally accepted cosmological view today.

Three experimental discoveries and theoretical developments occurring mainly in the first two decades of the twentieth century laid the foundations for the greatest progress ever made in science since its inauguration by the ancient Greeks in the sixth century B.C.E.: the introduction in 1900 of a quantum of action by Planck originating quantum mechanics, the discovery by Rutherford of subatomic particles initiating particle physics, and the first tentative conception of the atom by Bohr inaugurating atomic physics. These developments converged in the succeeding decades leading to the creation of quantum electrodynamics (QED), considered by many physicists to be the most successful scientific theory ever constructed. The current unification of physical theory, called "the standard model" consisting of twelve particles (six quarks plus six leptons), three basic forces or exchange particles, electroweak (photons and W^-, W^+, and W^o), strong (gluon), and gravitational (the postulated graviton), has convinced some physicists like Harold Fritsch and Steven Weinberg, along with the astrophysicist Stephen Hawking, that enough is known about the basic laws of matter that "a final theory" may be within reach. Furthermore, some physicists following the lead of Edward Witten believe that a new theory called string theory could bring about the hoped-for final unification of scientific theories.[42]

THE TECHNOLOGICAL RESULTS

These advances reverberating throughout the physical sciences produced remarkable consequences. The discovery of atomic fission made possible the development of the atomic bomb which, despite the tragic deaths it caused in Nagasaki and Hiroshima, brought an abrupt end to World War II and saved thousands or perhaps millions of lives, both Japanese and American, that would have been lost had it been necessary to invade Japan. Also, that the United States possessed the bomb undoubtedly prevented Stalin from imposing communist regimes on the countries of Western Europe as he had on Eastern Europe. Its application for peaceful use has provided an additional source of energy (over 80 percent of the energy in France alone) with nuclear reactors, as well as the usual problems accompanying the application of advanced technology: the risk of radiation and the difficulty of disposing of radioactive wastes.

These atomic-molecular investigations also made possible the sciences of molecular biology and modern pharmacology. The discovery mentioned earlier of the helical structure of DNA-RNA led to the successful sequencing of the human genetic code, disclosing the components and transformations responsible for a person's development and individual characteristics. Using genetic engineering, geneticists already can eliminate some debilitating birth defects, and may be able to prevent such socially undesirable behavior as alcoholism, drug addition, child molestation, abusive behavior, and learning disabilities. Sophisticated electroencephalographic diagnostic procedures are used with MRI (magnetic resonance imaging) along with Pet scanners (positron-emission tomography), creating brain imaging that displays the physiological functions and malfunctions of the brain, enabling physicians to detect tumors and locate the neurological correlates of conscious processes.

Organ transplants and bypass operations are prolonging lives while embryonic stem cells obtained from the inner cell mass of five-day-old human embryos, having the potential to develop into any kind of tissue, will permit physicians to replace degenerating tissue in defective organs by these new cells. Infertility is better understood and more readily correctable, alternative methods of fertilization have been developed, and the discovery of more dependable birth control techniques allows for more effective family planning crucial for stemming the exponential growth rate in world population (despite the opposition of the Catholic Church). A sheep as well as other animals have been cloned. Although providing greater understanding of and control over our lives if used wisely, these discoveries also have dangerous consequences if abused. Yet this has always been true of the application of new technology. If I seem overconfident, I am well aware that we live in a world where a deranged tyrant or a crazed political dissident could annihilate whole populations, if not all of human existence, by unleashing atomic warheads or dispersing lethal doses of bacteria or chemicals into the atmosphere or drinking water. But human existence has always been precarious, as when plagues or epidemics in ancient times destroyed a significant proportion of the population of a region. Nor should we forget that throughout much of the past, human longevity averaged less than half of what it is today, as it still does in certain countries in Africa.

The discovery of chemical pesticides, disease-resisting strains of plants and animals, along with increased yields of harvests and herds due to the green, grain, and gene revolution, have made it possible to support a much larger population at a lesser cost, enabling many more nations to become agriculturally self-sufficient while reducing the tragedies of malnutrition and famine. The tremendous innovations in manufacturing, technology, and mass production have not only raised the standards of living in much of the world by providing greater employment and higher salaries, it has made economically accessible the kinds of material goods people the world over want to enjoy: modern plumbing, electrification, telephones, household appliances, automobiles, television, videos, computers, mass transportation, and so on, which, if used properly, enrich human life. While there is too much emphasis on material possessions as a means of happiness in prosperous societies such as ours, the opportunity for intellectual development, aesthetic enrichment, growth in moral character, and attainment of personal fulfillment requires a degree of prosperity, as impoverished people readily testify. The shock of visiting any country where famine, poverty, disease, and illiteracy, along with the lack of sanitary conditions and modern medical care, are still the norm jolts one into an appreciation of the benefits of science in producing a higher standard of living and quality of life never achieved in the past.

THE DISCOVERY OF OTHER GALAXIES IN AN EXPANDING UNIVERSE

Other discoveries in the twentieth century which have altered radically our conception of our place in the universe are due to astronomy, astrophysics, space exploration, and cosmology. While the notion that cosmic space is filled with innumerable nebular or island universes, some inhabited and others not, had been conjectured by the ancient Greek atomists in the fifth century B.C.E., and the nebulae themselves investigated telescopically in the nineteenth century by William Herschel, the telescope he used was not powerful enough to enable him to decide whether the nebulae were independent island universes beyond the Milky Way or just part of the Milky Way itself. So in the early decades of the twentieth century the extent and duration of the universe still were unknown. It was not until Erwin Hubble built his 100-inch reflecting telescope, greatly extending his knowledge of nebulae, that he could provide by 1924 answers to these ancient questions. First, his telescopic observations penetrated far enough into space to allow him to conclude that our galaxy, the Milky Way, a band of pale light stretching across the stellar realm, was only one of innumerable galaxies in outer space, each consisting of billions of stars, globular star clusters, and interstellar matter. Like stars, the variation in brightness of these nebulae were interpreted as indicating their various distances; the fainter they were the more remote. Though individually they varied in size and dispersion, collectively the large-scale distribution as far as one could see indicated an approximately homogeneous universe. A few years later when the giant 200-inch Palomar telescope was built, permitting astronomers to look back two billion light years into outer space, nearly a million galaxies were observable confirming Hubble's earlier observations.

As important as these discoveries were in revealing the galactic structure of the universe, Hubble's second discovery was even more significant, profoundly changing the astrophysicist's thinking about the cosmos. Using the spectroscope to analyze the light radiated from the distant galaxies, Hubble discovered a shift in the wave lengths toward the red end of the spectrum, an indication of elongated waves. While there were various possible interpretations of this "red-shift," as it came to be called—that dust particles caused the shift to the red or that the aging of the light waves in their journey to the earth was responsible—the phenomenon known as the Doppler effect soon was the accepted explanation. We experience this effect when the whine of a siren from a vehicle becomes shriller as it approaches (because of the shortened waves and greater frequency) and duller when it recedes. Analogously, if the source of light waves advances in the same direction as the waves this will compress them into shorter wave lengths and higher frequencies, while if the source recedes this will cause the waves to be stretched and occur with less frequency. Applied to the light from distant galaxies, this indicated that the galaxies were receding with the shift to the red increasing with the distance (though not violating the constant velocity of light because as the wave length increases its frequency decreases, the product of the two remaining constant). This recession is not just away from the earth but occurs in all directions, so that the galaxies are receding from each other with a speed proportional to their distances, implying an expanding universe.

When Einstein had first formulated his model of a closed spherical universe in accordance with Riemann's curved space, he made what he called "the greatest mistake of his life," the introduction of a cosmological constant or antigravitational force to offset the fact that his equations implied that the universe, rather than being static, was expanding with a positive curvature. When he learned of Hubble's discovery he realized his mistake and accepted the idea of a closed but inflating universe (similar to an inflated balloon). Furthermore, the expansion of the universe attributed to cosmic radiation eliminated a paradoxical consequence of Newton's cosmology which implied that if the dominant force in the universe were gravitational attraction, then the matter of the universe should have been concentrated in the center surrounded by a vast domain of empty space. But an expanding universe due to a radiational force stronger than gravity would explain the existence of galaxies throughout space whose rate of recession was proportional to their distance.

The third major contribution of Hubble was his realization that an expanding universe implied a beginning to the expansion that could be calculated from knowledge of the distance between the galaxies and the rate of expansion. Thus for the first time a reliable answer could be provided for the age of the universe, the time elapsed since the expansion began, to replace the mythical account in Genesis which claimed the universe was created in 4005 B.C.E. An initial calculation gave the age of the universe as 1.8 billion years, about one-eighth the present estimate. Moreover, this smaller figure had the paradoxical consequence that the age of the universe would have been less than that of the earth as calculated by geologists from radioactive disintegration, as well as less than the stars based on the consumption of nuclear fuels in the sun, both of which were computed to be about five billion years old. Now it is believed that the age of our solar system is about five billion years while the age of the universe is roughly fifteen billion years. These discoveries not only refute the biblical age of the universe, they also disprove Eastern mysticism since it seems unlikely that a universe fifteen billion years old consisting of billions of galaxies could depend on a consciousness that emerged on the earth a minute ago (in terms of cosmic time).

With this conception of an expanding universe that implies an initial state at some definite time in the past when the process of inflation began, cosmologists started to theorize as to the nature of this initial state and how the present universe with its various elements and forces might have evolved. Today much more is known about the tremendously condensed, infernal temperature and plasma conditions of the initial state called the "big bang," along with the creation of space and time and the sequential appearance of the various elements, forces, and organizations of matter when the universe gradually cooled as it expanded. The detection of a leftover background radiation (discovered by Arno Penzias and Robert Wilson in 1965) from this initial radioactive state lent considerable support to the theory.

But supposing this general explanation of the origin and age of the known universe is approximately true, a number of unanswered questions remain. What gave rise to the "big bang" that created the universe? Why did the creation occur about fifteen billion years ago? Was there a preexistent state of the universe and, if so, what was it and how did it give rise to the big bang? Are there multiple universes of which ours is merely one balloonlike manifestation? Will the expansion continue forever or as the ratio between the density of the matter of the universe producing the gravitational force and the strength of the radiation change, will the process reverse? Although answers to these bewildering questions seem entirely beyond our reach, a glance at the history of science shows that whenever explanations of previous questions were found, these in turn always generated new mysteries which at the time appeared quite baffling. So it is today, which makes one doubt whether a final theory is attainable. With time, further astrophysical explorations and discoveries aided by cosmological theorizing undoubtedly will provide solutions to these current questions, while also leaving additional quandaries in their wake.

INVOKING GOD IS NO EXPLANATION

What is not feasible is that we turn to religion for the answer. While many religionists[43] have enthusiastically welcomed the big bang theory because it appears to support the Genesis myth that the universe was created at some moment in the past, this is a mistake. Unlike the big bang theory that is based on the experimental evidence of the red-shift and residual radioactivity, along with rigorously established laws and previously confirmed scientific theories, the Genesis account is a myth similar to the older Near Eastern myth, *Enuma Elish*, from which it may have originated. Neither myth was intended as a literal description of the origin of the universe which was beyond the explanatory capabilities of anyone at the time, but merely "a likely story" (as Plato called his cosmological tale in the *Timaeus*) to satisfy human wonder about an occurrence that was beyond comprehension. Narratives were the earliest forms of 'explanation.' In contrast, the big bang and inflationary theories were introduced to explain astronomical data with a conceptual framework that was consistent with past scientific laws and theories, along with being subject to empirical tests and revisions. Breaching this system of scientific explanation by suddenly bringing in God would have no explanatory significance or justification whatsoever!

What would it explain? Could one infer from the usual theistic conception of God how the big bang actually was brought about, why it occurred when it did, or if the expansion will go on forever? If the nature of God is ineffable, as often claimed, how could we derive a meaningful explanation from something that itself is beyond comprehension? One might as well say that Zog or Krog created the universe for any difference it would make! It is sometimes claimed by religionists that the existence of God answers the ultimate question of why there is something rather than nothing. But that, too, is an illusion since it is just as reasonable to ask why God exists, as to ask why the universe exists. Ultimately one has to accept the existence of something, some unexplained explainer. The familiar reply that only God is self-existent is hardly an answer because it rests on a question-begging definition of God. One could as well assume that the universe is self-existent, because at least we know it does exit. In fact, both the inflationary theory[44] and string theory[45] attempt to show how the universe could be created from the initial conditions and grand unified theories. If true, this would make the existence of the universe necessary and self-explanatory.

Based on the history of science, we now realize that no explanation invoking God ever is justified by the evidence, but instead involves a cognitive leap. The belief that events are explainable as acts of a deity has its origin in the primitive supposition, underlying all mythical and early philosophical accounts, that the universe displays a purpose, so it must be the product of intention or will, analogous to the explanation of human actions (illustrated in Genesis and in Plato's conception of the Demiurge as a Divine Craftsman). But while it is appropriate to ask why people act as they do, it now is recognized that asking *in the same sense* why there was a plague, famine, devastating tornado, mud slide, epidemic, or why someone was killed by lightning, born deformed, suffered a paralysing stroke, killed in an automobile accident, or endured a horrible death by cancer, has no meaning. Only a naive person would attribute the sinking of the Titanic or a cholera epidemic to an act of God. As tragic as these occurrences are, they are just natural phenomena brought about by natural causes or human errors of judgment, not the intentional acts of a god. Once people did attribute such disasters to a vengeful deity (the Old Testament is a succession of such acts by Yahweh) to whom they prayed or offered sacrifices, human as well as animal, to gain exemption from God's wrath or to attain his favor. But it is time these primitive beliefs were outgrown and discarded, especially since there is no evidence that the universe has a purpose.

In addition to the unparalleled scientific developments described earlier, the twentieth century will be known for the first explorations of space by satellite and manned spaceships. For as long as there have been hominoid creatures on the earth, they have gazed upward at the pale surface of the moon, this nearest celestial companion, struck by its beauty and periodic phases whose recurrence was the basis for the earliest calendars. When I was young no one even dreamed that we would be able to acquire the technological skill to land on the moon, its remote inaccessibility captured in the well-known expression at the time that "for all we know the other side of the moon might be made of green cheese." Then there was that moment when an astronaut slowly descended the stairs of the landing craft and awkwardly walked on the moon's surface. Even after the fact, when one looks up at the distant moon at night it hardly seems possible that men actually were on its surface. Is there any exploration in mankind's past to compare with it? Surely it will go down as one of the greatest achievements of the twentieth century, even though we take it for granted now as humans usually do.

CONCLUSION

Unlike religions which resist new discoveries and ways of thinking, the influence of science and technology during the past century has introduced more intellectual, technological, and cultural transformations than in all past history. The current revolution in electronics, computers, information access, and communication promises to have as significant an effect on civilization as the previous agricultural and industrial revolutions. In fact, the pace of change has become so rapid that for many people it is unnerving, generating a nostalgia for a more tranquil, calmer, stable time, along with a hostility toward science and technology for bringing us to this unsettling period. However, it is a common human weakness to take for granted improved conditions while exaggerating the disadvantages and adverse consequences. Although often critical of the material benefits of modern industrial society, how many people would be willing to go back to a time when most of the population was illiterate and when famine, pestilence, infant mortality, and poverty were rampant, as they still are in many areas of the "underdeveloped" world, and when the average lifetime was about thirty years, as it was in ancient Rome? It was not religions that improved the living conditions of people throughout the world (even Jesus accepted poverty saying "the poor will always be with us") but science and technology, while religions looked to an afterlife as a recompense for the unredeemable miseries and injustices of this world. In fact, while Marx's characterization of religion as "the opium of the people" because it sedated them into accepting their deplorable status is somewhat severe, it is undeniable that one of the major appeals of religion has been its promise of a better life to come and assurance that "the poor will inherit the earth" to compensate for the deprivations of this life.

Even today there are millions of people in Russia, India, Africa, Central and South America, and Southeast Asia living in the most wretched conditions of poverty, sanitation, and destitution who do not rebel or protest, in some cases because they believe that if they accept their present condition with equanimity they will earn a better status in the next life. Now, however, the prospect of rectifying these economic and social conditions, including the possibility of improving human nature, the major source of evil in the world, by genetic engineering is within our grasp. How we respond to this is the one of the greatest challenges of the new millennium.

Considering the vast transformations during the past two thousand years and the fact that change itself is now institutionalized rather than opposed, except by very conservative religious groups, it is impossible to conceive what human existence will be like a thousand years from now. But one thing can be safely predicted: that the great religions that arose during the axial age, to satisfy basic psychical and societal needs at the time, will be incapable of fulfilling these roles in the future because the intellectual, cultural, and social context will have so changed that their relevance will fade. As Nietzsche claimed, it was a "sorry day for priests and gods when men created science," but not for mankind.

Only by ignoring the contrasting *historical* origins and changing influences of religion and science can one maintain the validity of religion today. The point of describing the rise of modern science was to show how radically different are the two worldviews precluding the kind of reconciliation presently sought by religionists, as well as some scientists. The true nature and value of cultural institutions can be appraised only by taking into account the historical context within which they arose and functioned. If religions were not so firmly institutionalized as they are at present, but had to be freshly grafted onto contemporary society, I believe the incompatibility would be so glaring that the attempt would be abandoned. As we have seen, science has remade the world in which we live, both intellectually and physically. Not only has it provided a clearer perspective on the past, it has radically enhanced our hopes for the future. With this conception of our changing worldviews as background, we shall turn in the succeeding chapters to a critique of the relevance of religions in the modern world.

NOTES

1. End-of-the-Millennium Special Issue,"What Science Will Know In 2050," *Scientific American* (December, 1999).

2. Howard Clark Kee, *Understanding the New Testament*, 5th ed. (Englewood Cliffs, N.J.: Prentice-Hall, 1993), p. 314.

3. Tertullian, *Apologeticus*, Loeb Library, vol. xlv, p. 14. Quoted from Will Durant, *The Story of Civilization*, Part III, *Caesar and Christ* (New York: Simon and Schuster, 1944), p. 649. The description of the martyrs is based on Durant.

4. Durant, *Caesar and Christ*, p. 652.

5. Ibid., p. 654. Durant writes that this account is derived from the great Chris-

tian historian Eusebius who had it on authority from Emperor Constantine himself when he requested that Eusebius write the monumental *Ecclesiastical History*.

6. A. T. and R. P. C. Hanson, *The Bible Without Illusions* (London: SCM Press, 1989), p. 19. Brackets added.

7. Cf. Robin Lane Fox, *Pagans and Christians* (New York: Penguin, 1986).

8. Will Durant, *The Story of Western Civilization*, Part 4, *The Age of Faith* (New York: Simon and Shuster, 1950), p. 469.

9. Ibid., p. 587.

10. Raimundus de Agiles, *Hist. Francorum qui ceperunt Jerusalem*, cap. 38–39. (Migne 155, col. 659). Quoted from H. O. Taylor, *The Medieval Mind*, vol. 1, 4th ed. (Cambridge: Harvard University Press), p. 552.

11. Ibid.

12. Cf. Durant, *The Age of Faith*, pp. 598–99.

13. Robert Payne, *The Dream and the Tomb: A History of the Crusades* (New York: Stein and Day Publishers, 1984), p. 257.

14. Durant, *The Age of Faith*, p. 601.

15. Geoffroi de Villehardouin, *Chronicle of the Fourth Crusade*, Everyman Library, p. 31. Quoted from Durant, *The Age of Faith*, p. 604.

16. Payne, *The Dream and the Tomb*, pp. 341–42, italics added. Until otherwise indicated, the following page references in the text are to this work.

17. Cf. Richard H. Schlagel, *From Myth to Modern Mind: A Study of the Origins and Growth of Scientific Thought*, vol. 1, *Theogony through Ptolemy* (New York: Peter Lang Publishers, 1995), chaps. 2, 3.

18. Cf. ibid., chaps. 4–10.

19. Durant, *The Age of Faith*, p. 611.

20. Ibid., p. 613.

21. The following discussion of the origins and development of modern science is based on my book, *From Myth to Modern Mind: A Study of the Origins and Growth of Scientific Thought*, vol. 2, *Copernicus through Quantum Mechanics* (New York: Peter Lang, 1996).

22. Thomas S. Kuhn, *The Copernican Revolution* (Cambridge: Harvard University Press, 1957), p. 134.

23. Karen Armstrong, *A History of God* (New York: Ballentine Books, 1993), p. 290.

24. Cf. Schlagel, *Copernicus through Quantum Mechanics*, p. 290.

25. Galileo Galilei, "The Assayer," trans. Stillman Drake and C. D. O'Malley, in Drake and O'Malley, eds., *The Controversy On The Comets Of 1618* (Philadelphia: University of Pennsylvania Press, 1960), pp. 183–84.

26. Cf. Thomas S. Kuhn, *The Structure of Scientific Revolutions* (Chicago: University of Chicago Press, 1962), chap. 10.

27. Aristotle, *Metaphysics*, trans. W. D. Ross, Bk. XII, ch. 7, 1072b 23–29.

28. Translated and quoted by Andrew D. White, *A History of the Warfare of Science and Theology in Christendom*, vol. 1 (New York: Appelton, 1896), p. 126.

29. Anselm's *Proslogium*, from *St. Anselm: Basic Writings*, trans. S. N. Deare, 2d ed. (La Salle: Open Court Publishing Co., 1962). Quoted from L. Miller, ed., *Believing in God* (New Jersey: Prentice-Hall, 1996), pp. 24–26.

78　❦　THE VANQUISHED GODS

30. Ibid., p. 25.

31. Thomas Aquinas, *Summa Theologica*, from *Basic Writings of St. Thomas Aquinas*, ed. Anton C. Pegis (New York: Random House, 1945). Quoted from L. Miller, pp. 27–31. The following quotations of Thomas Aquinas are from this work.

32. Isaac Newton, *Opticks*, based on the 4th ed., London, 1730 (New York: Dover Publishing, Inc., 1952), p. 400.

33. William Paley, *Natural Theology*, ed. Frederick Ferré (Indianapolis: Library of Liberal Arts, 1963). Quoted from L. Miller, p. 84.

34. Ibid.

35. Steven Shapin, *The Scientific Revolution* (Chicago: University of Chicago Press, 1996), p. 149.

36. Cf. Richard Dawkins, *The Blind Watchmaker* (New York: W. W. Norton Co., 1986), pp. 6, 21.

37. Cf. Llya Prigogine and Isabelle Stengers, *Order out of Chaos* (New York: Bantam Books, 1984), pp. 142–43 and Stuart Kauffman, *At Home in the Universe* (New York: Oxford University Press, 1995), chap. 1.

38. Cf. J. Gleick, *Chaos* (New York: Pengiun Books, 1987), pp. 114–15, 261, 314.

39. Cf. Newton, *Opticks*, Bk. III, Part I, Quest. 31.

40. Cf. Milič Čapek, *The Philosophical Impact of Contemporary Physics* (New York: Van Nostrand, 1961), p. 202.

41. Ibid., p. 201.

42. Cf. Brian Greene, *The Elegant Universe* (New York: W. W. Norton & Company, 1999).

43. In this context I mean by 'religionist' all those who believe that the rational order in the universe is evidence of a spiritual creator on which it depends, a belief reinforced by scripture and religious experience.

44. Cf. Alan Guth, *The Inflationary Universe* (Reading, Mass.: Addison-Wesley, 1997), pp. 273–76.

45. Cf. Brian Greene, *The Elegant Universe*, pp. 361–70.

THE MYTHIC CALLING
OF ISRAEL

T he review in the previous chapter of the cultural and intellectual
changes during the past two millennia, particularly the résumé of
the growth of modern science since the sixteenth and seventeenth centuries, was intended to show how extensively our conception of the natural world has changed during this period. The world as we know it is
almost entirely different from that of preceding millennia, yet many
people cling to beliefs that are justifiable only within the cultural context
of this earlier period. Unless one is so mesmerized by the biblical tradition
that these fundamental developments have no effect, any understanding
of our Western religious heritage, beginning with the Old Testament, necessarily will be influenced by what we know today in contrast to the primitive naivety of the Axial Age, the period between 800 and 200 B.C.E. when
the great world religions and philosophical cosmologies were created.[1]

GENESIS AS MYTH

This discussion of the Old Testament will focus on the first two books of
the Pentateuch, Genesis and Exodus, because these books particularly
provide the foundational background for our Western religious heritage.
It is only since the nineteenth century, owing to scientific discoveries in
geology and paleontology, along with the higher criticism of the Bible, that
at least among scholars the mythical nature of Genesis and Exodus have
become accepted. Even such outstanding scholars as Newton previously
accepted as true the story of creation presented in Genesis. Christians

traced their ancestry back to Adam and Eve, Muslims traced theirs to Ishmael, the son of Abraham and Hagar, Sarah's Egyptian maid, and the fabulous adventures of Moses were believed to be historical truths. In fact, however, it is not until the memoirs of Nehemiah describing the Persian period in the fifth century B.C.E. that one can be confident that the narrative reflects an eyewitness account of events.[2] The previous books contain a cultic interpretation of prehistory, Yahweh having selected Israel from "all the nations" as his historical protagonist, with other countries used as pawns in the drama. Yet the other nations had their own legends and mythical gods which they, too, believed were controlling their destinies.

Accepting the Old Testament as *the* authentic interpretation of the history of the world is incredible. Knowing what we do today about the age and immensity of the universe, the diversity of peoples on the earth, and the natural evolution of humankind, the Old Testament hardly can be taken as more than a particular mythical account (at least down to the destruction of Jerusalem by Nebuchadresser and the exile) with some strands of fact interwoven with an elaborate theocratic interpretation, and therefore not very different from numerous other cultic accounts. The Pentateuch held no illusions for David Hume:

> Upon reading this book, we find it full of prodigies and miracles. It gives an account of a state of the world and of human nature entirely different from the present; Of our fall from that state; Of the age of man, extended to near a thousand years; Of the destruction of the world by a deluge; Of the arbitrary choice of one people, as the favourites of heaven; and that people the countrymen of the author; Of their deliverance from bondage by prodigies the most astonishing imaginable; I desire any one to lay his hand upon his heart, and after a serious consideration declare, whether he thinks that the falsehood of such a book, supported by such a testimony, would be more extraordinary and miraculous than all the miracles it relates. . . .[3]

In contrast to Hume, scholars like Bernhard W. Anderson maintain that such religious documents, rather than reflecting the primitive state of civilization at the time as interpreted by prophets, priests, and sages, is evidence of a deeper meaning testifying to "the transhistorical realm of religious imagination" (p. 504).

> The stories concerning primeval history, then, are not factual accounts of the sort that the modern historian or scientist demands. These stories are "historical" only in the sense that they plumb the depth of history's meaning and evince those fundamental experiences that have been common to human beings from the very dawn of history. The manner of presentation is poetic or pictorial, for the narrator is dealing with a subject that eludes

the modern historian's investigation—namely, *the ultimate source of the human drama in the initiative and purpose of God*. Above all, the narrative is written in the conviction that Israel's root experiences, Exodus and Sinai, provide the clue to the *meaning of all human history*, right back to the beginning. (p. 160; emphasis added)

It certainly is true that the kind of religious experience that underlies the Old Testament was "common to human beings from the very dawn of history," and though the quotation does not state that Anderson agrees with the "narrator's" interpretation of human history, his book as a whole indicates he does. But why should anyone conclude that the Old Testament, rather than being an archaic account of the prehistory of a people derived from an oral tradition dating from four thousand years ago, hence reflecting the primitive culture of the time, "eludes the modern historian's investigation" because it represents "the ultimate source of the human drama in the initiative and purpose of God"? Are we unable to understand the *Iliad* and the *Odyssey* or other great nationalistic epics or sagas? Other than an ethnic bias, what is there to authenticate that account in contrast to all the other fabulous interpretations of prehistory which now are seen as primitive and outmoded?

In fact, as Anderson correctly states: "From a secular viewpoint . . . Israel's history is a minor sideshow in the larger history of the ancient Near East, and its culture is overshadowed by the more brilliant cultures of antiquity" (p. 8). Still, he draws the chauvinistic conclusion that because "both the Jews and Christians" view the Old Testament as "*sacred* history," it should be regarded as disclosing "the ultimate meaning of human life . . ." (p. 8). But what warrant is there for this conclusion? Why should an epic drawn in the sands of prehistory and washed away by the tides of time be taken as depicting the ultimate meaning of life? Surely the "secular viewpoint" is the valid one. Moreover, it would be extremely ethnocentric to think that "Israel's root experiences . . . provide the clue to the meaning of all human history, right back to the beginning." What significance does this history have for China, Japan, India, or for most non-Hebrews existing today? In Heroditus's *Histories* Israel is not even mentioned; it is insignificant when compared to other nations such as Egypt, Persia, and Babylonia. It was no more significant then, than it is today.

All ancient nations had their particular mythological stories accounting for the creation of the world, the origin of the gods, and their unique destiny as a nation, but we no longer accept these other accounts as true. Is there any reason for conferring this distinction on the Old Testament, except that it is the foundation of *our* religious heritage? Given all the theocratic accounts of the histories of peoples, why should the Israelites' description of Exodus and Sinai be taken as "root experiences" for other peoples? When we compare this narrative with our knowledge of the world today it has no credibility, nor is it even exemplary in its account. The dominant image of God portrayed in the Old Testament, that of a jealous, vindictive, destructive, tyrannical deity often indifferent to human suffering—is appalling! Abraham pleaded in vain to save the cities of Sodom and Gomorrah (Gen. 18:22–33), arguing that it would be unjust to destroy completely these cities if there were any righteous people among them (and surely there must have been some innocent children). In some cases, as was true of Moses when he descended from Mount Sinai or Horeb and found the people worshiping a golden bull, the prophet was so dismayed by the threatening wrath of Yahweh that he pleaded with him to forgive the people and not destroy them (Exod. 32), reminding him of his covenant with them.

As related in the Old Testament, Yahweh punishes Egypt with a series of catastrophes including the death of all first-born sons, followed by the destruction of cities beginning with Sodom and Gomorrah, eventually including nearly all those in Palestine, such as Shechem, Samaria, Hebron, Lachish, and finally Jerusalem, along with the capitals of "the nations," such as Thebes, Nineveh, and Babylon. Seeming to take pleasure in the carnage, Yahweh says of the inhabitants of Jerusalem just before it was demolished by the Babylonians,

> I will give their dead bodies for food to the birds of the air and to the beasts of the earth. And I will make the city a horror, a thing to be hissed at; every one who passes by it will be horrified . . . because of all its disasters. And I will make them eat the flesh of their sons and their daughters, and every one shall eat the flesh of his neighbor in the siege and in the distress, with which their enemies and those who seek their life afflict them.[4]

Yet it is Yahweh himself who used Israel's "enemies" to punish them for their idolatry, disloyalty, and moral transgressions, but the punishment is so devastating that it seems to be administered by a monster.

He treats his loyal prophets so disdainfully that Jeremiah in utter despair declares: "Cursed be the day on which I was born!" (Jer. 20:19). Despite the dedication shown by Ezekiel, the "Lord God" takes from him his beloved wife and then forbids him even to show sorrow or to mourn: " 'Son of man, behold, I am about to take the delight of your eyes away from you at a stroke; yet you shall not mourn or weep nor shall your tears rain down' " (Ezek. 29:15). This he inflicts on a loyal disciple! He is so vain regarding his reputation that when about to destroy Judah, the still remaining southern kingdom of Israel, he says:

"It is not for your sake, house of Israel, that I am about to act, but for the sake of my holy name, which you have profaned among the nations to which you came . . . and the nations will know that I am the Lord . . . when through you [your destruction] I vindicate my holiness before their eyes." (Ezek. 36:22–23)

At the time each nation believed that it was their gods who were in control of events. In 2 Kings 18 it is reported that the Assyrian commander Rabshakeh under King Sennacherib mocked King Hezekiah of Judah, claiming that the Assyrian gods were more powerful than other gods because the Assyrians had conquered the nations. Believing that all events were controlled by Yahweh, Isaiah 41 claims that the conquest of Babylon by Cyrus of Persia was directed by Yahweh, although the famous Cyrus Cylinder "affirms that Marduk, the god of Babylon, selected Cyrus to become 'the ruler of the world' and then went by his side 'like a real friend' " (p. 471). Yahweh does exhibit a better side when he exhorts his people to forgo vain rituals and instead seek justice, appose oppression, and defend the unfortunate.

> Bring no more vain offerings:
> incense is an abomination to me . . .
> When you spread forth your hands,
> I will hide my eyes from you;
> even though you make many prayers,
> I will not listen; your hands are full of blood.
> Wash yourselves; make yourselves clean;
> remove the evil of your doings from before my eyes;
> Cease to do evil, learn to do good;
> seek justice, correct oppression;
> defend the fatherless, plead for the widow.
> (Isa. 1:13–17)

Although occasionally he displays compassion, as when he finally redeems Job from his terrible afflictions, increasing his benefaction "twice as much as he had before" his trial (Job 42: 10), and "repents" of the harm he intended for the Assyrian city of Nineveh sparing it despite the protests of Jonah (Jon. 3:10), he typically is portrayed as an extremely jealous, vengeful god. Other gods were depicted as acting as willfully, capriciously, or destructively, but they no longer are considered more than human constructs projected onto historical events, not actual deities controlling history. While Yahweh usually was portrayed as a monotheistic God, in contrast to the numerous fertility, harvest, nature, and warrior gods worshiped by the other nations, that does not mitigate his extremely primitive, savage, anthropomorphic traits adapted from those of the rulers of the time.

Unlike other ancient nations such as the Egyptians, Assyrians, Babylonians, Persians, and Greeks whose creative energy was displayed in many fields, such as astronomy, mathematics, literature, painting, sculpture, and architecture, the Israelites poured all their creative genius into one work, the Old Testament (although it was the influence of three Jews, Marx, Freud, and Einstein, that was dominant in the twentieth century). Yet despite its faults of stupefying repetitions and genealogies, historical inaccuracies and discrepancies, along with racist claims and primitive anthropomorphisms, the sublime twenty-third Psalm and the didactic wisdom of Proverbs lend it a majestic quality.

Its theophanic interpretation of history created the setting for Christianity which never would have occurred without it, while its dramatic stories became the folklore of Western civilization: Adam and Eve and the Fall, the destructive flood and Noah's Ark, Abraham's test of the sacrifice of Isaac, the Tablet of the Ten Commandments presented to Moses on Mount Sinai, the return of the prodigal son, Jonah's sojourn in the whale, Delilah's betrayal of Sampson, David's slaying of Goliath and later seduction of Bathsheba, King Solomon's wise ruse to determine which of two women was the baby's actual mother, Job's despairing tribulations and final redemption, and so forth. Yet despite its claim by the prophets and priests to be divinely inspired, it is transparently a human creation, an epic morality play in which history is the stage, the prophets and people of Israel the leading actors, other countries supporting players, and the "Lord God" the dramaturgist. So rather than a sanctified document that reveals the hidden meaning of human history in divine epiphanies, the Old Testament will be considered objectively, as one would any other mythical rendering of the origins of a people. If it is claimed that one must have a *prior faith* in the truth of the Old Testament to truly understand it as a theophany, which an objective approach precludes, then in fairness one would have to adopt this same principle when considering other religious writings, such as the Hindu Vedas or Buddhism, so how would one choose among them?

Though for most of Western history the Old Testament was accepted as an inerrant testimony to God's purpose as revealed to the prophets in the books named after them, this patently is not true. The "higher criticism" of the Bible (including the New Testament) beginning in the nineteenth century has contributed greatly to its demystification. While previous readers of the Bible throughout the centuries had found repetitions and discrepancies in the texts, these anomalies were dismissed or ignored because it was considered to be the word of God and thus literally true. Maintaining that it had been revealed by Yahweh to a succession of prophets who were the authors of its various Books, it had to be accepted as infallible. Now, however, it is known that not only did none of the prophets themselves write the books, but the actual authors are unknown (as is true also of the Gospels of the New Testament).

Furthermore, as most Hebraic-Christians learn the biblical stories when innocent of any skeptical attitude and then hear them retold in sermons throughout their lives as if they were factual episodes, there is little incentive to be critical. As noted in the previous chapter, while scientific developments in astronomy, geology, and paleontology raised serious questions regarding the creation story of Genesis, along with biblical statements affirming that the sun revolved around a stationary earth, the actual demystification of the Bible was due to a critical *internal* examination and exegesis by biblical scholars who were members of the clergy. The unfortunate fact is that most religious believers are unaware of this "higher criticism" and quite satisfied to remain in ignorance, because if they were informed it would tend to undermine their beliefs or the certainty of their convictions. Although human beings obviously have a deep need and desire to believe in some kind of spiritual power beyond the physical universe, it is largely because they are so indifferent to scientific developments and uninformed of these critical studies that they still find these scriptural writings compelling. Most Jews and Christians would be shocked to learn, based on biblical scholarship, how little factual evidence there is for the historical narratives presented in either the Old and or the New Testaments.

The span of the Old Testament covers nearly two millennia of the pre-Christian or pre-Common era. This epoch in turn can be divided into seven periods based on the most outstanding events in the life-story of Israel: (1) the ancestral period (c. 1800–1300) covering Yahweh's original covenant with Abraham along with the lives of Isaac, Jacob, and Joseph; (2) the Mosaic period (c. 1300–1250) including the servitude of the Israelites under the Pharaoh in Egypt, their Exodus under the leadership of Moses, and their "forty year" wandering in the desert wilderness; (3) the period (c. 1250–1000) of Joshua's conquest of Canaan and the formation of the confederacy of the twelve regional tribes plus the thirteenth priestly tribes of Levi; (4) the United Kingdom of Israel (c. 1000–922) under the rule first of King Saul, then King David who chose Jerusalem as the capital of Palestine, followed by his son King Solomon who built the Temple in Jerusalem; (5) the period (c. 922–587) of the divided kingdoms with Ephraim (later called Israel) in the north and Judah in the south until the fall of Judah to Nebuchadressar and the exile of the Israelites to Babylon; (6) the period (c. 587–400) of exile in Babylon and the postexilic era comprising the restoration of Palestine and the Temple by the Persian King Cyrus; (7) the later period (c. 400–168) when Palestine came under the control of Alexander the Great and the Hellenistic Seleucid rulers until the revolt by the house of Maccabees, which includes the wisdom literature such as the Book of Daniel and the end of prophesy.[5]

The biblical narrative from Genesis to the recounting of Joshua's conquest of Canaan and establishment of Palestine, presented in the five scrolls of the Torah called the Pentateuch, along with the Books of Joshua and Judges, were based entirely on the oral tradition, and thus are mythical or legendary. As R. P. C. and A. T. Hanson, two Anglican theologians, state, "Everything narrated in the Old Testament about the history of Israel up till the entry into Canaan is either myth or legend. Solid history only begins after the entry, and even then there is a considerable element of legend."[6] Like Homer's *Iliad* and *Odyssey*, there is some tenuous factual basis to this historical recounting, but these scant facts are barely visible owing to their embellishment during a millennium of imaginative retelling. When the diverse strains of this oral heritage were transposed into written form from 600 to 400 B.C.E., it was not to convey an accurate historical account, which in any case was precluded by its misty origins, but to present Yahweh as the creator of the universe and controller of Israel's destiny. Thus the Old Testament is Israel's testimony to its confrontation with God. Despite orthodox Hebrews and fundamentalist Christians who, in their religious zeal ignore the vast body of biblical scholarship, adamantly maintaining that every word in the Bible is literally true, the fact is that it is largely mythical and legendary. Moreover, as Richard Friedman, another biblical scholar who has spent most of his life trying to discover the actual authors of the Bible, states, "It is a strange fact that we have never known with certainty who produced the book that has played such a central role in our civilization."[7]

It is not until the two books of Samuel and Kings that there emerges a more reliable rendering of events, judged by the credibility of the narrative, the historical records of other nations, and recent archeological excavations. Still, it is only when we read the Book of Nehemiah that we find a witness to what actually was being recounted, though these events are overlaid with the thematic context of Israel as Yahweh's chosen people whom he punishes or rewards according to their deserts. But even then it is not as if we were privy to the original scrolls. Until the Dead Sea Scrolls dating from the second century B.C.E. were discovered in the caves at Qumran in 1947, the earliest scripture available was from the ninth century C.E. So we find on the one hand that the first written scripture was based on about a fifteen-hundred-year oral tradition and on the other that the Bible accessible to the West was no earlier than the ninth century, thirteen hundred years later than the original Bible.

PROBLEMS OF AUTHENTICITY, AUTHORSHIP, AND CHRONOLOGY

But the issues of authenticity are even more complex. The Old Testament is the history of Judaism and since the language of the Israelites was Hebrew, most of the Bible originally was written in Hebrew, called the Masoretic text. But because Aramaic had become the lingua franca by the time of the destruction of the Temple, at least "some parts of the latest books in the Old Testament" were "written in Aramaic" (p. 9). Then during the last three centuries B.C.E. the Old Testament was translated into Greek which is called the Septuagint "because of the legendary account of its origin: it was supposed to have been translated by seventy scholars working together in Egypt, who miraculously all separately produced the same translation" (p. 10). This was the work that was known to the early Christians because Greek had become the universal language.

Then at the request of Pope Damascus I who wanted a more authoritative Latin translation, in the late fourth century C.E. St. Jerome produced the official Latin translation of the Old Testament, called the Vulgate, based on the Hebrew Masoretic text (rather than the Greek Septuagint). A revised version containing Greek and Latin translations on opposite pages was brought out by the renown humanist scholar Erasmus in 1516, and became the accepted Catholic Bible used throughout the Medieval Period. Based on Erasmus's translation, Martin Luther produced his own version in the German vernacular in 1534. This was followed in the early 1600s by the famous Authorized King James's version, the beautiful English translation used throughout the English speaking world until recently.

Considering its long history derived from an oral tradition, it is not surprising that the actual authorship of the Old Testament is unknown. But until recently church authorities maintained, and most people acquiesced in believing, that the Pentateuch, comprising the first five books of the Bible (Genesis, Exodus, Leviticus, Numbers, and Deuteronomy), was written by Moses himself and therefore called the "Books of Moses." Yet as Friedman documents, once the Torah (the name used by the Hebrews to refer to the Pentateuch) was completed, rabbis themselves began finding discrepancies and contradictions throughout the Books. As early as the third century C.E. Origin, one of the Church fathers, was pressed to find rejoinders to those who discovered textual anomalies. As Friedman states:

> . . . the tradition that one person, Moses, alone wrote these books presented problems. People observed contradictions in the texts. It would report events in a particular order, and later it would say that those same events happened in a different order. It would say that there were two of

something, and elsewhere it would say that there were fourteen of the same thing. It would say that the Moabites did something, and later it would say that it was the Midianities who did it. It would describe Moses as going to a Tabernacle in a chapter before Moses builds the Tabernacle. (pp. 17–18)

Throughout the following centuries as additional translations, exegeses, and commentaries of the Bible appeared, further textual aberrations were discovered or uncovered. For example, if Moses were the author of the complete Pentateuch how could he have described his own death in Deuteronomy 34? Would he have referred to himself as the "humblest man on earth"? How could he have compiled a list of Edomite Kings (Gen. 36) that included those who lived after he had died? Stylistic variants within the texts also pointed up problems because they "referred to Moses in the third person, used terms that Moses would not have known, described places where Moses had never been, and used language that reflected another time and locale from those of Moses" (p. 9). Among other errant passages, Thomas Hobbes pointed out that the Pentateuch includes references to consequences that had continued "to this day," implying the perspective of a later writer, while Spinoza noted that Deut. 34:9 states that "there has not arisen a prophet since in Israel like Moses," an expression of admiration that would have been used by someone who had known prophets after Moses and could compare them.

Needless to say, those who pointed out these discordant passages were not admired or congratulated but usually repudiated, reviled, and even forced to recant on threat of excommunication with their books burned. Considerable ingenuity was expended to explain these discrepancies while reaffirming Moses' authorship claiming, for example, that later compilers had added lines at various places or had inserted new information or changed names to make the Bible more comprehensible to contemporary readers. Regarding references to events that could not have been known in Moses' day, it was claimed that it was not incongruous for Yahweh to have revealed foreknowledge of events to his chosen prophets. As it became more difficult to ignore, repress, or rationalize the evidence, some clergy argued that even if there had been emendations and additions to what Moses wrote, insofar as these were the work of later prophets guided by the Holy Spirit this would not jeopardize the sanctity of the scriptures.[8]

However, once it was acknowledged that there had been later insertions in the Mosaic texts it was easier for later scholars to detect these additions based on their content and style. While previously the adamant belief in a single authorship had repressed recognition of these differences, the discovery fact there were numerous instances of duplicate renditions of the same episodes became more accepted, acquiring the name of "doublets."

> A doublet is a case of the same story being told twice. Even in translation it is easy to observe that biblical stories often appear with variations of detail in two different places in the Bible. There are two different stories of the creation of the world. There are two stories of the covenant between God and the patriarch Abraham, two stories of the naming of Abraham's son Isaac, two stories of Abraham's claiming to a foreign king that his wife Sarah is his sister, two stories of Isaac's son Jacob making a journey to Mesopotamia, two stories of a revelation to Jacob at Beth-El, two stories of God's changing Jacob's name to Israel, two stories of Moses' getting water from a rock at a place called Meribah, and more. (p. 22)

Like previous cover-ups, at first the doublets were interpreted as merely variations on the same theme, not as substantially different or conflicting accounts, and therefore not evidence of different authors. It was suggested that they even were introduced to bring out other aspects of what was described or to convey an alternative moral lesson. On closer examination, however, it became apparent that there was more involved indicated by the different wording, one version invariably using one key word and the other consistently using another to designate the same referent. It was not simply stylistic variation, but *two consistently independent parallel uses*. Specifically, one version used 'Yahweh' whenever the deity was referred to while the other used 'God' ('Elohim' in the Hebrew). Furthermore, there were other persistent variations in phrasing in the different versions suggesting that these represented *separate* accounts by different authors, apparently patched together to form a single continuous narrative.

Friedman presents a particularly convincing example of a doublet in Gen. 6:5–8:2. If one reads the text through one finds striking discontinuities among various passages; for example, the statements "But Noah found favor in Yahweh's eyes" followed by "These are the generations of Noah," or in the lines "And Noah did according to all that Yahweh had commanded" followed by "And Noah was six hundred years old, and the flood was on the earth." Not only is the continuity interrupted, but in one group of passages the term 'Yahweh' is used throughout while in the other the term 'God' ('Elohim') consistently is used. Presenting the continuous text as it occurs in Genesis, Friedman cleverly distinguishes one from the other by printing one in bold type, allowing the passages in regular type to be read as one text and those in bold type as the other. Read separately (although they are intermixed in the original text), each of them presents coherent independent accounts. The difference is so remarkable that it leaps off the page (cf. pp. 54–59). Despite the compelling evidence, this dual authorship initially was countered by the argument that one of the doublets was the original, which Moses then rewrote into a second version, or that both versions were based on two older accounts, each of which Moses had decided to revise and retain. "But ultimately it was concluded that both of the two sources had to be from writers who lived after Moses. Each step of the process was attributing less and less to Moses himself" (p. 23).

The doublet hypothesis was popular in the eighteenth century, but by the beginning of the nineteenth century biblical scholars found that there was evidence not only of *two* different sources of the five books of the Pentateuch attributed to Moses, but of *four*. In addition to the two versions of a similar story, it was found that the first four books of the Pentateuch also contained lengthy accounts of the kinds of issues, legalistic and ritualistic, that would be of special concern to the priestly class. These included specific moral codes pertaining to marriage, divorce, adultery, and the care of widows and orphans; regulations regarding the treatment of conquered peoples, especially women and children; designations of religious holidays and rituals; specifications of which meat should be purified and offered for sacrifice at the altar and what portion should go to the priests; directions for how the tabernacle or temple should be organized and the sacrifices conducted, and so forth. Unlike the stories of Noah, Abraham, Isaac, Joseph, Moses, and Joshua, these sections of the books of the Pentateuch were written for a different purpose and in a much finer literary style, indicating they had a separate and later authorship. Then a young German scholar, W. M. L. De Wette, showed that the fifth book of the Pentateuch, Deuteronomy, not only was written in an entirely different style but that its content was so strikingly distinct, compared to the other four books, that it, too, called for a separate author. Thus, as Friedman observes, "from the work of a great many persons, and at personal cost for some of them, the mystery of the Bible's origins had come to be addressed openly, and a working hypothesis had been formed. It was a remarkable stage in the Bible's history" (p. 23).

So, rather than the five books of the Pentateuch being a continuous narrative written by Moses, the evidence indicated that different source materials had been used in its compilation. The text that used the name 'Yahweh' to refer to the deity was designated the "J" version because the German scholars leading the research often used the name 'Jehovah' along with Yahweh, hence they took the "J" from the former. The text that was translated as 'God' was labeled the "E" version because 'Elohim' is the Hebrew term for 'God'. Those sections related primarily to priestly concerns dealing with legalistic, ritualistic, and religious matters were designated the "P" segments, while Deuteronomy, considered a separately written document, was referred to as the "D" book. Although this classification took account of what appeared to be different textual sources, it raised additional questions as to the origin of the sources and their chronology. Were the different versions written at different times and if so were they indicative of different stages in the development of Israel's ancient religion?

Regarding the problem of chronology one scholar, Karl Heinrich Graf, came to the following conclusion as described by Friedman:

> . . . the J and E documents were the oldest versions of the biblical stories, for they (and other early biblical writings) were unaware of matters that were treated in other documents. D was later than J and E, for it showed acquaintance with developments in a later period of history. And P, the priestly version of the story, was the latest of all, for it referred to a variety of matters that were unknown in all of the earlier portions of the Bible such as the books of the prophets. (p. 25)

As to whether they indicated different stages of religious development, another scholar, Wilhelm Vatke, concluded that the oldest versions J and E represented the earliest period of Israel's religious development "when it was essentially a nature/fertility religion" (p. 25). Deuteronomy (D), containing the laws presented to Moses and the covenant with the Lord God, constituted a middle stage of Israel's "spiritual/religious" faith. Written last, P designated "the latest stage of Israelite religion" dominated by the priestly class and thus primarily concerned with legalistic and ritualistic matters.

According to Friedman, it was Julius Welhausen (1844–1917) who synthesized these two investigations into what came to be called the "Documentary Hypothesis," a preliminary explanation for the occurrence of the four different sources.

> Welhausen accepted Vatke's picture of the religion of Israel as having developed in these stages, and he accepted Graf's picture of the documents as having been written in three distinct periods. He then simply put the two pictures together. He examined the biblical stories and laws that appear in J and E, and he argued that they reflected the way of life of the nature/fertility stage of religion. He argued that the stories and laws of Deuteronomy (D) reflected the life of the spiritual/ethical stage. And he argued that P derived from the priestly/legal stage. He traced the characteristics of each stage and period meticulously through the text of each document, examining the way in which the document reflected each of several fundamental aspects of religion: the character of the clergy, the types of sacrifices, the places of worship, and the religious holidays. He drew on both the legal and the narrative sections, through

all five books of the Pentateuch, and through other historical and prophetic books of the Bible. His presentation was sensible, articulate, and extremely influential. . . . It tied the source documents to history. It provided a believable framework in which they could have developed. (pp. 25–26)

The real significance of the "Documentary Hypothesis" is that it treats the Pentateuch as one would any other ancient document, submitting it to the usual rational standards of critical historical analysis, rather than considering it sacredly inerrant because it was divinely revealed to Moses. Realizing that this approach could undermine the very foundation of religious belief in treating the Bible like any other secular historical work, religionists[9] often argue that the truth of the Bible must be accepted on faith. But this argument is circular because having faith in the Bible *presupposes* its validity, otherwise why have faith in it, the very point at issue? One can always ask, "Why *should* one have faith in the Bible?" which presupposes some justifying grounds. Furthermore, accepting the Bible on faith precludes any critical appraisal because one already is committed to its truth: any objections will be countered by the argument that if one had sufficient faith one would see through the objections. That is, *once having made the commitment there is no possibility of determining whether it was justified or unjustified.*

It is often argued that similar to establishing personal relations in contrast to testing empirical truths, coming to experience God is an I-Thou relationship which presupposes some positive committment on the part of the individual. This was the point of William James's famous essay "The Will to Believe" and Søren Kierkegaard's definition of "truth as subjectivity." Unlike objective truth which is established on impersonal grounds, according to Kierkegaard *"an objective uncertainty, held fast through appropriation with the most passionate inwardness, is the truth"* defined subjectively.[10] The weakness of this definition of truth, as a passionate inward commitment in the absence of convincing objective evidence, is that it allows for all kinds of fanatical beliefs, either from terrorists, fanatics, or deranged individuals. It could have been the justification for the thirty-nine suicides of Herff Applewhite's Heaven Gate cult, the bombing of the Federal Building in Oklahoma city, or the maiming and deaths caused by Ted Kacynski, the convicted Unabomber. The prevalence of human irrationality and gullibility indicates that it is not difficult to find subjective confirmation of something one wants to believe or to which one is already committed!

Furthermore, on subjective grounds people have believed in many nonexistent entitles, including witches, guardian angels, demons, devils, gods, and so forth. That individuals can form deep personal relations to mental images or constructs that do not have any reality is well confirmed throughout history. Because prior commitment itself is based on a desire or need to believe, how can one determine whether or not one is merely deluding oneself or is a victim of wishful thinking in holding the belief? Subjective conviction by itself has never been a sufficient or reliable criterion of truth. However, as most people *do not want to be freed from certain delusions or self-deceptions*, which serve as psychic crutches, that is no objection. All one has to do is listen to sermons on Sunday morning by tele-vangical ministers to see how easy it is for some people to accept the most absurd beliefs as if they were self-authenticating. It is for this reason scientists have devised rigorous objective criteria for testing the truth of beliefs, realizing how easy it is to be deceived by what one is inclined to believe.

Despite the strong scholarly underpinnings of Welthausen's Documentary Hypothesis which came to be referred to as the "higher criticism," religious opposition to the thesis persisted throughout the first half of the twentieth century. Then to the credit of the Catholic Church, a major change occurred in 1943 when Pope Pius XII issued an encyclical "*Divino Afflante Spiritus*" which "has been called 'a Magna Carta for biblical progress' " (p. 27). Believing that those who wrote the Bible were inspired by the Holy Spirit, the Pope encouraged biblical scholars to be unconstrained in their biblical research. Stimulated by the Pope's encyclical, the Catholic *Jerome Biblical Commentary* appeared in 1968, introduced by the following editorial statement:

> "It is no secret that the last fifteen or twenty years have seen almost a revolution in Catholic biblical studies—a revolution encouraged by authority, for its Magna Carta was the encyclical *Divino Afflante Spiritus* of Pope Pius XII. The principles of literary and historical criticism, so long regarded with suspicion, are now, at last, accepted and applied by Catholic exegetes. The results have been many: a new and vital interest in the Bible throughout the Church; a greater contribution of biblical studies to modern theology; a community of effort and understanding among Catholic and non-Catholic scholars." (p. 28)

A similar freedom was evident among leading Protestant and Jewish biblical scholars, although not among fundamentalists, conservatives, or the orthodox. While some opposition continued during the following decades, Friedman asserts that "at present, however, there is hardly a biblical scholar in the world actively working on the problem who would claim that the Five Books of Moses were written by Moses—or by any one person" (p. 28).

Yet as far as the Documentary Hypothesis is concerned, some scholars are more convinced of the evidence for some of the sources than for the others. Anderson, for example, seems willing to accept the

Deuteronomy and Priestly classifications, but has reservations regarding the distinction between the J and E versions.

> Keep in mind that this is a hypothesis which attempts to account for the observed diversity in the Pentateuch, and like any hypothesis, this one is constantly being subjected to testing in scholarly study and debate. One vulnerable point is found in the Old Epic tradition, specifically the division of this material into two strands, the Yahwist [J] and the Elohist [E], and the dating of each. Some scholars maintain that the hypothesis, stated this way, puts too much emphasis in "documents" or "sources" and fails to do justice to the dynamic of the oral tradition that preceded, and even accompanied, writing. Others question whether the Old Epic tradition has to be divided into separate "Yahweh" and "Elohist" versions; we may be dealing with a single tradition that has been enriched or supplemented in the course of transmission.[11]

Yet the kind of textual evidence pointed out by Friedman in the account of the Flood in Genesis, referred to above, is very convincing. Moreover, Friedman is persuaded not only that there are two sources, but that they can be traced to the two kingdoms of Palestine: "the person who wrote J was particularly concerned with the [southern] kingdom of Judah, and the person who wrote E was particularly interested in the [northern] kingdom of Israel." (p. 67; brackets added) Karen Armstrong says that while the hypothesis "has come in for a good deal of harsh treatment . . . nobody has yet come up with a more satisfactory theory of key biblical events. . . .[12]

My purpose being to indicate that the uncertain historical origins of the Bible preclude its being taken as an infallible or even reliable source of religious beliefs, I will not pursue further the intriguing question as to the more specific origins of the four sources — those who would like to inquire more extensively into the problem should consult Friedman's excellent book. Instead, I want to turn to the first two books of the Pentateuch to present *internal evidence* that they have no factual or historical significance whatsoever. Starting at the beginning with Genesis, it is shocking that there is so much discussion (in books, popular magazines, as well as television) of a mythical story that has little more credibility than the older Babylonian *Enuma Elish* myth by which it was influenced.[13]

CRITICAL EXIGESIS OF GENESIS

In fact, the initial themes of Genesis were common in the myths that existed in the Near East at that time. As Anderson observes: "The motifs of creation, paradise, the flood, and the deliverance of humankind from total destruction were expressed in various forms in the myths and leg-ends of the ancient Near East" (p. 160). It is, I believe, a depressing symptom of our poor secondary educational system and of the appalling ignorance of large segments of our society that in the most technologi-cally advanced country in the world (and one that has produced more Nobel Laureates than all European nations combined) forty percent of the population believe the Genesis account of creation, rather than the 'theory' of evolution or in the Big Bang Theory. Recently in an introduc-tory course in philosophy when I referred to the 'theory' of evolution a student interrupted, emphatically declaring that "there is no factual evi-dence for the theory." The remark was so unexpected and brash that I replied in an uncharacteristically harsh manner, saying that "not only is the evidence for the evolution of species supported by geology, anthro-pology, paleontology, embryology, and genetics, there is not a shred of evidence for any alternative explanation of life on the earth." By now the evidence is so compelling, despite some problems of interpretation and controveries, that evolution no longer should be referred to as a theory, any more than relativity 'theory' should be referred to as a theory. As Steven Weinberg, Nobel Laureate in physics, states: "It seems to me to be a profoundly important discovery that we can get very far in explaining the world without invoking divine intervention, and in biology as well as in the physical sciences."[14]

Yet the pressure of conservative religious groups to have creationism taught in public schools, as an alternative explanation of the origin of humanity, is so strong in many religious communities that the National Academy of Sciences has been compelled to issue a statement that evolu-tion and not creationism must be taught as part of the scientific cur-riculum in public schools to support teachers whose positions are threat-ened if they do not teach creationism. Thus despite a 1987 Supreme Court ruling that creationism *does not* have to be taught, along with evolution, as an alternative explanation of the origin of man because it is merely a religious belief not supported by scientific evidence, there still are those who want to see it taught in our schools as if it were a viable alternative to evolution. The recent attempt by the school board in Kansas to have creationism, rather than evolution taught in the public schools (which, fortunately, was later reversed), is an example of this influence. In justifi-cation of the conservative religious view, Arne W. Owens, a spokesman for the Christian Coalition, stated, "We believe communities have the right to have their values reflected in the curriculum. . . ." [15] Not only does this statement reflect a naive confusion between facts and values, it ignores the fact that truth is also a value.

As indicated previously, there is support for the doublet hypothesis beginning with the creation myth in Genesis which appears in two versions, the oldest (2:4–3:24) immediately following a preceding but later version (1–3:22). The second, oldest account is the most familiar because it is the one that contains the well-known story of Adam and Eve in the Garden of Eden. It is this fable that has inspired so much art, in particular Masaccio's painting in Florence of the "Expulsion from Paradise" (which has just been restored with the appended fig leaves removed) and Michelangelo's magnificent rendering of creation in the Sistine Chapel in St. Peter's.

Whether out of ignorance or lack of concern, in the older version (presented later) the origin of the universe itself is barely mentioned and nothing said of creation in six days. After passing reference to "the day that the Lord God made the earth and the heavens," the story plunges immediately into the creation of man, stating that God "formed man of dust from the ground and breathed into his nostrils the breath of life," thereby making him a living being. Then in Eden, vaguely referred to as "in the east," God planted a garden filled with beautiful and fruitful trees, including the tree of life and the tree retaining knowledge of good and evil. Calling the man Adam, he placed him in the garden saying that he could eat of the fruit of any tree except that containing knowledge of good and evil (and later of life) because if he ate of that fruit he would die.

Concerned that Adam would be lonely, God did not at first give him a mate, but instead created from the ground "every beast of the field and bird of the air" to keep him company, saying that henceforth they would be known by whatever name Adam gave them. But realizing that animals were insufficient companions, God cast a spell over Adam and while he slept extracted a rib from which he formed wo-man to be his lasting companion. Thus it is said that "man leaves his father and his mother and cleaves to his wife, and they become one flesh." The woman he called "Eve" because it is her womb that will beget mankind. Though the man and woman were naked they were not self-conscious of the fact until a serpent led them astray. Approaching the woman who apparently was more susceptible, the serpent informed her that though God had forbad eating of the fruit of the tree of knowledge on pain of death, this was not true because if they ate of the fruit they would not die, but become like God knowing the difference between good and evil. Thus, although the serpent is usually portrayed as the villain, in fact it had revealed God's lie or deception (having been created by God the serpent must have been endowed with this knowledge and like the animals in the comics, it could talk).

Drawn to the luscious fruit and lured to the forbidden tree with the prospect of becoming wise, Eve first ate of the fruit and then tempted Adam to do the same. Immediately they became aware of their nakedness, attempting to cover themselves with an "apron of fig leaves." Hearing the footsteps of the Lord God walking "in the garden in the cool of day" (as gods are apt to do), Adam and Eve in their embarrassment due to their newly acquired knowledge of their nakedness hid themselvles. But God was not to be fooled. "Where are you?" he asked, apparently not as proficient at seeing things in gardens as from his domain on Mount Sinai or from his Heavenly Kingdom. Adam should have let his wife reply because he gave the self-incriminating answer that, being naked, he had hid himself. Again displaying a strange limitation of knowledge for a deity, God replied: " 'Who told you that you were naked? Have you eaten of the tree of which I commanded you not to eat?' " Adam, being the sterling character that he was, immediately incriminated Eve, saying it was she who talked him into eating the fruit of the forbidden tree. Eve in turn blamed the poor serpent who has been reviled by mankind ever since, although we should be grateful to it for encouraging us to free ourselves of our ignorance of good and evil—assuming the validity of John Stuart Mill's argument that it is better to be an Adam enlightened than to be an Adam in blissful ignorance.

Along with having stimulated much art, the fable had immense theological significance because it is the source of the "doctrine of original sin" that harried early church fathers like Augustine and that during the Reformation became such a burning issue for Luther and Calvin. For according to the doctrine, the sin of Adam and Eve was transmitted by coitus to all succeeding generations, requiring God's grace to be expunged. The symbolic significance of the myth is then revealed in God's response to this transgression, indicating why so little is said about the creation of the universe. It is apparent that the real intent of the narrative is to explain the lowly status of the serpent and why it is so despised, why women suffer so much pain in childbirth, why men must labor so hard tilling the soil, and why human beings having been formed from dust are returned to dust. Speaking to the serpent God says:

> " 'Because you have done this . . .
> upon your belly you shall go, and
> dust you shall eat all the days of your life.
> I shall put enmity between you and the woman,
> and between your seed and her seed. . . .' "

To the woman he declared:

> " 'I will greatly multiply your pain in child bearing;
> in pain you shall bring forth children,
> yet your desire shall be for your husband,
> and he shall rule over you.' "

To Adam he decreed:

> " 'Because you have listened to your wife, and
> have eaten of the [forbidden] tree . . .
> cursed is the ground because of you;
> in toil you shall eat of it all the days of your life . . .
> In the sweat of your face you shall eat bread till you return
> to the ground, for out of it your were taken;
> you are dust, and to dust you shall return.' "

Unlike the New Testament, there is no promise of an afterlife. Man shall return to the lifeless dust from which he came. Afraid that Adam and Eve, as in their earlier transgression, would eat of the tree of life and thus become like God, not only in their knowledge of good and evil but in attaining immortality, he banished them from this original state of paradise, placing a cherubim with flaming sword to guard the Garden from reentry. In this episode we have a forecast of God's jealous nature.

Although not as colorful a story, it is the later version of creation that one reads first in Genesis which biblical scholars believe was written several centuries after the older version and contains a much more detailed account of the stages of creation over six days. It begins like the Babylonian *Enuma Elish* myth by assuming the existence of a watery chaos from which God "separated" the most prominent features of the world, light and darkness, day and night, sky and earth. In agreement with all ancient myths, there is no assertion that God created the world from nothing. *Creation ex nihilo*, which is unintelligible if not self-contradictory, later became Christian dogma by a decision of the Council of Nicae in the fourth century C.E. Instead, it is written that "the Spirit of God was moving over the face of the waters."

Accepting the common belief in the Near East at the time that words possess magical causal powers, the creation is described as issuing from what God says: "And God said, 'Let there be light' and there was light. . . ." In the *Enuma Elish* myth, to determine whether the younger god Marduk had sufficient "magic quality" to overcome the powerful god Ti'amat, he was confronted with the following test:

> They placed a garment in their midst
> And said to Marduk their firstborn
> "O Lord, thy lot is truly highest among gods
> Command annihilation and existence,
> and may both come true.
> May thy *spoken word* destroy the garment,
> Then *speak again* and may it be intact."
> He *spoke* — and at his *word*
> the garment was destroyed.
> He *spoke* again, the garment reappeared.
> The gods, his fathers, seeing the power of his *word*,
> Rejoiced, paid homage: "Marduk is king."[16]

Furthermore, St. John's Gospel commences with the statement: "In the beginning was the Word, and the Word was with God, and the Word was God." This statement has stirred considerable theological controversy because the Greek term for 'word' is *logos*, and one interpretation is that creation was based on a pattern of *logoi* in God's mind, the words representing the things to be created. Knowing the name of something at that time meant having a certain power or control over the object named. For example, when God chose Moses to deliver the Israelites from Egypt, Moses asked in whose name he was to act, but God refused to give his name declaring, "*Elyeh-Aster-Elyeh,*" translated as "I Am Who I Am" (Exod. 3:13). Elsewhere God gives his name as JHWH (a form of "to be"), a word so sacred that it was prohibited to pronounce the holy name 'Yahweh' aloud; thus wherever 'Yahweh' occurred in the Bible where it might be spoken it was translated as "The Lord" (in Hebrew of course).[17]

In addition to creation issuing from the power or magic of words, the precise manner often was described by the common process of "separation" or of "separating off." In *Enuma Elish*, the silt forming the earth "separates" where the fresh water meets the salt water. In one of the earliest Greek philosophical accounts of creation, Anaximander described the process by which the primary opposites, Hot and Cold, emerged from the original "*Apeiron*" or "Boundless" as one of "separating off."[18] So also in Genesis "God separated the light from the darkness" (1:4), made the "firmament in the midst of the waters . . . separate the waters which were above the firmament" (1:6–7), calling the latter Heaven. Having separated light (Day) from darkness (Night), while "the earth was without form and void" (1:2) on the first day, 'he' then created the firmament or Heaven above the waters on the second day. On the third day where the waters gathered the dry land appeared (as in the *Enuma Elish* myth), the solidified earth permitting the growth of vegetation, particularly fruit trees.

Although light and darkness and day and night had already been created, anachronistically it is not until the fourth day that the sun, moon, and stars were placed in the firmament; the "greater light [of the sun] to rule the day," and "the lesser light [of the moon] to rule the night" (1:16). They and the stars thus produced the days, seasons, and years. On the fifth day God filled the seas with "swarms" of aquatic organisms, created birds flying above the earth, and had the earth bring forth diverse kinds of land creatures, "cattle, creeping things, and beasts of the earth" (1:24). Finally, unlike the older myth, in this later version man does not appear until the sixth or last day and is created in the image of God (although anthropomorphic, at least in this version God is not said to appear "walking in the garden in the cool of the day," taking on the likeness of man as in Greek epics). He then created wo-man to be man's companion.

Having established man's dominion over these creatures, God provided them all with "every green plant for food" (1:30). As he had at the end of each previous day, God looked upon his work with satisfaction and "saw that it was good." After six days of creation he rested on the seventh day, following the custom in the Near East at the time, and so "blessed the seventh day and hallowed it" (2:2–3).

The reference to the morning and evening of each day of creation definitely implies that each stage took one day, not that the six days were symbolic of large stretches or epochs of time, as biblical apologists have argued to make the narrative more compatible with modern geological and evolutionary theories. Furthermore, declaring that the earth brought "forth living creatures according to their kinds" (1:24) clearly means that all the great variety of cattle, creeping things, beasts, plants, and trees were created at once in their current form. Unlike the conjectures of the ancient Greek philosophers Anaximander and Empedocles, there is not the slightest hint of evolution in either of these biblical versions of creation. In contrast to the philosophical speculations of the Greeks, these creation stories were not meant primarily as explanations but sought to make the world less mysterious and alien by attributing the origins of the universe and living creatures to the intentional acts of a deity. Since the purpose of the Old Testament is to describe the travails of the Israelites as Yahweh's chosen people to fulfill his historic plan, these myths were not offered as factual explanations but as dramatic narratives. Thus there is nothing in the Old Testament of any scientific value or of philosophical significance, although it does contain some beautiful inspirational writing. True also of the New Testament, this is why religious belief has been such an impediment to philosophical speculation and scientific inquiry, in contrast to the inquiries of the ancient Greeks from whom we derive our confidence in the efficacy of empirical investigations and rational explanations.

Until the nineteenth century, the combined effects of the authority of the Bible and the lack of significant counter evidence led most people to accept the Genesis story as the true account of creation. It was believed that the universe (which meant primarily our solar system with perhaps the Milky Way galaxy) was created by God about 6,000 years ago, along with all the known species of existing organisms, during a six day period. Today, however, with so many remarkable scientific discoveries during the interim, it would be nearly impossible to find anyone involved in research in geology, astrophysics, archaeology, paleontology, biology, or genetics who believes the Genesis fable. Even a Pope as conservative as John Paul II declared in November 1996 that the Catholic Church accepted evolution as not just a hypothesis, but as the recognized factual explanation of the origin, transformation, diversity, and proliferation of species, although he retained the (unnecessary) hypothesis that the process was ordained and directed by God.

As reported in the previous chapter, after Erwin Hubble's telescopic discovery in the third decade of the twentieth century of the spectral red-shift implying an expanding universe, the age of the universe from the Big Bang has been calculated to be about fifteen billion years, while the age of the earth from its condensation from a nebular gaseous state to be about five billion years. The first forms of life, primitive algae and bacteria, appeared about a billion years later perhaps due to the injection of some force, such as electricity, into the primal stew of carbon molecules or possibly generated by vast dispersions of microbial matter spewed up from volcanic eruptions on the ocean's floor. The earliest fish, corals, plants, insects, and reptiles arose during the Paleozoic period from 600 million to 300 million years ago. As almost everyone learned from Steven Spielberg's film Jurassic Park, the dinosaurs appeared about 250 million years ago and became extinct 65 million years ago, apparently due to a comet colliding with the earth producing a dense debris that blackened the sky for decades. The consequent darkness and cold killed many plant and animal species, including the dinosaurs. While it was a calamity for the dinosaurs, it has been pointed out that it was a fortunate occurrence for the rise of humans, for as long as the dinosaurs dominated the earth smaller mammals could not evolve, being prey for the larger predators.

The earliest large mammals arose during the Paleocene epoch following the extinction of the dinosaurs, while the earliest hominids, erect bipedal mammals, emerged during the Miocene period about twenty-five million years ago. The fossil evidence shows a remarkably continuous evolution beginning with the branching from our primate ancestors of about six million years ago to the appearance of transitional creatures (omitting some intermediate forms) from Australopithecus afarensis to homo habilis, homo erectus, and homo sapiens, anatomically modern humans that appeared some 200,000 years ago. The latter evolved into Neanderthals that lived from about 150,000 to 40,000 years ago and finally Cro-Magnons that appeared about 40,000 years ago, apparently causing the extinction of the Neanderthals. The discovery by anthropologists in the seventies of the celebrated "Lucy," dating from about three million years ago, has replaced "Eve" as our maternal ancestor. It now appears that sometime between two and three million years ago modern human beings evolved from Lucy's descendants. Needless to say, none of this fossil evidence is compatible with Genesis, nor have any of the attempts to reinterpret Genesis to make it consistent with the paleontological evidence been very convincing.[19]

It was Darwin and Wallace, shortly after the middle of the nineteenth century, who proposed the daring hypothesis of evolution to replace the archaic "special creation" explanation of the origin of mankind and other species. Having taken a five year voyage as official naturalist on the HMS *Beagle* to the archipelagoes around the world, Darwin was amazed at the striking variety of species found on some islands that did not exist either on other islands or on the mainland, suggesting that their diversity must have been produced indigenously. The fondness of Englishmen for breeding horses and dogs plus the fact that his grandfather, Erasmus Darwin, in a book entitled *Zoonomia*, explained organic life according to evolutionary principles, undoubtedly prepared him to interpret the diversity and proliferation of species as due to spontaneous genetic mutations transmitted to younger generations of the same species.

Moreover, it had been observed in London that the population of the peppered moth, which had been predominantly colored grey in 1848, had gradually changed to a darker winged color by 1898 (the period during which Darwin wrote his books on evolution). The change coincided with the proliferation of smokestacks, whose pollution killed the gray lichens that covered the tree trunks on which the moths perched, along with darkening the trunks themselves. Because the darker winged variety of the moth, which originally comprised a much smaller population, was better able to hide from the birds which were their main predators as the darkening effects of the smokestacks took effect, they proliferated. In contrast, the lighter winged moths, being highly exposed, were more depleted by the birds and therefore produced fewer progeny, so their population decreased. When the pollution from the smokestacks was eliminated, the process reversed itself.

Darwin had read Thomas Malthus's *An Essay on the Principle of Population* and had been impressed by his thesis that while the population of humans increases in geometrical proportion, the means of subsistence only increases in arithmetical proportion, hence there is a constant competition for survival. In this situation, as the example of the peppered moth illustrates, those best adapted will tend to survive and propagate while the others will diminish or die out entirely. As an example of how science progresses, one of the serious flaws of Darwin's and Wallace's evolutionary hypothesis was that it was predicated on the occurrence of spontaneous genetic mutations for which there was no independent evidence or explanation at the time. Breeding merely provided evidence for genetic changes as a result of the new combination of male and female chromosomes which would be passed on. It was not until after Francis Crick and James Watson in 1953 discovered the double helix structure of the DNA, combined with the development of molecular biology, that a more complete explanation could be given. No longer restricted to new combinations of chromosomes, as more was learned about the genetic code and how it directed the activity and replication of cells it was discovered that genetic mutations occur frequently due to simple errors in the message transmitted in the gene-replication process or from the effects of cosmic radiation altering the biomolecular structure. These changes can be either minor or major, the latter occurring when a strikingly different genetic template with new instructions is transferred to another gene creating radically new properties. Most mutations are neutral occurring in the noncoding material of the DNA, some are harmful killing the cell or aborting the embryo, but occasionally a rare mutation will confer an advantage. It is the latter that drives evolution, the accumulation of such fostering mutations producing something as intricately structured and precisely functioning as the eye.

More generally, throughout the past it was believed that all life exhibits complicated structures and integrated systems too refined, delicate, and complex to have evolved gradually, in a step by step process. Even Darwin was perplexed by the prospect of gradual random mutations so perfectly adjusted that eventually, without any conscious design or intention, they could produce something as wonderful as the eye. But there are two factors usually overlooked when one attempts to imagine or conceive how this could occur. One is the fact that evolutionary development is not a completely random process, in the sense that any mutational change is equally likely, but that such modifications are restricted by molecular genetic compatibilities, along with embryological constraints.[20] The subatomic alterations in the genes are random in that they are not predetermined, but not in the sense that any kind of transmissible mutation is equally possible. The selective process is due to the natural environment permitting only those mutations that enhance survival to prevail. Thus the guiding influence directing evolution is not antecedent or prospective, but transactional and retrospective. This was the great revolution of Darwin and Wallace. Like all revolutionary scientific developments, initially it was counterintuitive but eventually accepted because it was more consistent with the evidence and more explanatory.

The other factor that makes it difficult to imagine gradual progressive changes having such marvelous cumulative effects is that they occur on a time scale beyond human comprehension.[21] We measure changes on an infinitesimally small scale as compared to paleontological, geological, or astronomical time. To picture the changes we would have to see the process speeded up, as with modern photography we can 'see' a plant grow or an embryo develop. If we could view evolution within those accelerated time frames, perhaps we would find it less incomprehensible because we do accept that an acorn develops into a splendid oak tree or that a fertilized human egg develops into a Marilyn Monroe.

The evidence for evolution is so extensive and interrelated that it is difficult to understand how any intelligent person could reject it. The fossil record is the most prominent evidence. Where there are exposed deposits of layered sedimentary rock, nature displays a genealogical tree having the simplest organisms embedded in the deepest layers of sediment, with the phyla occurring as the trunk and major branches while the more complex arboreal species appear in the rising layers. Since by several means one can fix the date of the various geological strata, this enables paleontologists to assign relatively exact time periods to when different species existed. Then there are the fossil-rich areas near lakes and ancient watering holes, such as Rusinga Island by Lake Victoria, the Olduvai Gorge in Tanzania, or sites in Indonesia, Java, and China, where the skeletal remains of the ancestors of homo sapiens have been partially preserved in the hardened clay, their age determined by radiocarbon dating. The later is an exact calculation based on the content of ^{14}carbon in the organic material, a heavy radioactive isotope of carbon with a mass number of 14 used as a tracer in dating archaeological and geological materials.

Furthermore, there is the evidence from comparative vertebrate anatomy, embryology, and genetics. Regarding the former, despite the amazing variety of life there is a remarkable homology of anatomical structures and functions.[22] Mammalian forelimbs, for example, while serving the diverse actions of grasping in primates, walking and running in four legged animals, and as flippers in seals enabling them to swim, have similar functional components which are adaptive variations from a common ancestor, the amphibians. Also, there is abundant evidence of transitional structures of species, as in the evolution of horses' hooves, the hip sockets of primates as they began to walk upright, and the shapes and brain capacities of primate skulls as they evolved into more human-like creatures.

In embryology there is the dictum that "ontology recapitulates phylogeny," meaning that the sequence of embryological processes replicate to some extent phylogentic changes, as exemplified by the appearance of gill slits in one stage in the development of the human embryo. As for genetics, one would suppose that if 'God had created . . . every living creature . . . according to its kind" (Gen. 1:20), then they would have had their own particular genetic code, yet the genetic code is the same in all species and the cells of all organisms basically function the same. However, the wholly unexpected clinching argument that humans were not "specially created," but evolved from earlier primate forms, comes from genetics. If "God created man in his own image," as Genesis claims, then why is it that the genes of human beings are at least 98 percent identical to that of the pygmy chimpanzee[23]—unless, of course, God is a divine chimpanzee? Furthermore, the recently decoded genome is a kind of bio-graphical text of the history of life on earth.

Returning to our discussion of Genesis, having revealed their naked-ness and thus expelled from the Garden of Eden, in the quaint language of the Old Testament, Adam "knew" Eve and she successively bore two sons, Cain and Abel. Cain grew up to be a farmer while Abel became a shepherd, which brought them into competition when they offered sacri-fices to the Lord. When Yahweh was impressed by the succulent lambs presented by Abel but indifferent to the produce offered by Cain, the latter became jealous and angry at his brother. Having just created human beings, God apparently did not yet know human nature very well, so he was surprised that Cain was upset when he favored the offerings of Abel, asking Cain, "Why are you angry, and why has your countenance fallen?" Not to be assuaged, Cain invited his younger brother to go to the field together where he killed him. Aware that Abel was missing, God asks Cain where he is, whereupon Cain gives the famous answer, "How should I know; am I my brother's keeper?" But the Lord must have seen the blood spilled by Abel for he punishes Cain by compelling him hence-forth to be "a fugitive and a wanderer on the earth" (4:14). When Cain objects that "whoever finds me will slay me," God puts a mark on him with the threat that if anyone slays him he shall be punished sevenfold. But this is perplexing because only four people have existed so far, one of whom is dead, so who are the others that Cain feels threatened by? Has the Lord created other people beyond Eden that he has not told us about? It is to explain such anomalies that theology is called. In any event, expelled from God's presence Cain departs for what sounds like the fairyland "of Nod, east of Eden."

Immediately after stating that Cain had been banished to the land of Nod, the next events are even more perplexing, claiming that he "knew his wife, and she conceived and bore Enoch," after which he "built a city, and called the name of the city after . . . Enoch" (4:17). But this is full of paradoxes. Who was Cain's wife and where did she come from, since there is no mention of Adam and Eve, the first humans, having a daughter? How could Cain have built a city all by himself? It then says, "to Enoch was born Irad," and then lists a chronology of fathers without mentioning wives or daughters, though this is not surprising given the low status of females among these early Hebrews. It is not until Lamesh, the great great grandson of Enoch, that wives are listed (4:19). But even though the status of women was very low (recall Lot offering his two virgin daughters to the crowd to do with them as they will to save the two visitors), at least one would expect that the origin of the wives of Cain and Enoch would be mentioned. It is these kinds of discrepancies that reinforce the conclusion that the Old Testament is a series of disconnected compilations.

The narrative then returns to Eve who bore another son called Seth, which she considered a replacement for Abel (4:25). There is a second later version that claims that Adam fathered Seth when he was 130 years old and, continuing to live an incredible eight hundred years longer, "had other sons and daughters" (5:3–4), in all living to be 930 years old (if one can believe that). Seth became a father for the first time when he was 105 years old, calling his son Enoch after his brother. Like Adam, Seth also had an unbelievably long life during which he had other sons and daughters until he reached 905 years. And so it went with Enoch, who lived to be 365 years old, and his children enjoyed a similar longevity. One of his sons was the legendary Methuselah who outdid them all by living 969 years. Since there was no reliable or standard calendar in the West until the Julian Calendar was introduced in Rome in 46 B.C.E., there is no telling what these figures stand for. It certainly is implausible that any of them lived as long or had children as late as indicated. How could anyone, except an extremely credulous person, accept this as literally true?

Continuing with these longevities, Methuselah at 187 years fathered a son named Lamech who at 182 years had a son called Noah, one of the most famous names in the Old Testament. After stating that Noah waited until he was 500 years old to demonstrate his paternity, producing three sons, Shem, Ham, and Japheth, there then occurs one of those discontinuous, incongruous passages to which I have never seen any previous reference among biblical scholars.

> When men began to multiply on the face of the ground, and daughters were born to them, the *sons of God* saw that the *daughters of men* were fair; and they took to wife such as they chose. . . . The Nephilim were on the earth in those days, and also afterwards, when the *sons of God* came in to the *daughters of men*, and they bore children to them. These were the mighty men that were of old, the men of renown. (Gen 6:1–4; emphasis added)

While some Greek and Roman gods occasionally had intercourse with mortal women, this has never been a part of biblical history. Who were the Nephilim, the "mighty men . . . of old," "the men of renown"? Since Yahweh had no consort, as Osiris had Isis in Egyptian religion, it would be difficult for him to produce sons.

So who were these Nephilim called the "sons of God" who bore children from the "daughters of man"? They are not mentioned by Anderson or in any other book on the Old Testament that I have consulted. Interestingly, however, they are referred to by Gerald L. Schroeder in his book, *The Science of God*, in connection with more primitive species of man, such as Cro-Magnons. According to Schroeder, there is a "Talmudic legend" that holds that in addition to the genealogy of Adam and Eve there existed at the time the Nephilim, a race of people that resembled human beings, but who were inferior because they were not endowed, as were Adam and Eve, with a soul or with the spirit of the Lord (which would conflict with their being "the sons of God"). According to Schroeder, "The word Nephilim comes from the Hebrew root for fallen or inferior. Adam, having a *neshama* [a soul or the spirit of God] would find the Cro-Magnon inferior in spirit if not in body."[24] But as Schroeder's motive is to show that Genesis anticipated later paleontological discoveries, such as the prior existence of a more primitive form of human being, I do not think this interpretation bears textual support.

The statements about the Nephilim occur only in Gen. 6:1–4 and are so perplexing that I do not see how any reliable interpretation can be given, especially as the reference seems to be connected to the longevity of human beings: "My spirit shall not abide in man for ever, for he is flesh, but his days shall be a hundred and twenty years." Yet we have been told previously that the longevity of some was much longer, Methuselah allegedly having lived for 969 years (5:27) and his son Lamech 777 years (5:31). For those who accept that the Pentateuch was based on the oral tradition and represented various unknown sources, some inserted at different times, such perplexing stories do not pose a problem. But how do those who hold that every word in the Bible is an infallible revelation interpret such passages?

Returning to our story of Noah, even though God had created humans and presumably should have known what to expect, he became displeased with his creation. Again there are two versions of this, one in Gen. 6:5–8 and the other in 6:11–22. In the first version God "saw the wickedness of man" and "was sorry he had made man on the earth, and it grieved him to his heart," so he said, "I will blot out man whom I have created from the face of the ground," along with all other creatures except for Noah who had "found favor" in his eyes. There the first version ends and the second begins. According to the second, God not only was disappointed with the humans he created, but for some reason did not foresee the terrible violence that would ensue in the animal kingdom which could not be attributed to the sin of Adam and Eve: "God saw the earth and behold, it was corrupt; for all flesh had corrupted their way upon the earth" (6:12). So God came to a drastic decision, telling Noah that he intended to destroy all living creatures by flooding the earth. Exempting Noah, whom he found "righteous," he instructed him to build an ark according to precise specifications to contain all the paired species of living creatures, along with sufficient food, so that not all would be destroyed.

A charming story, it is full of inconsistencies and of course has no plausibility, it being impossible to contain in an ark, whose dimensions are 300 cubits long (an ancient measurement based on the length of a person's forearm, from the elbow to his or her fingertips), 50 cubits wide and 30 cubits deep, one pair at least of all the species of living things, plus "every sort of food that is eaten." Yet despite the absurdity of the story and the fact that I teach at a secular university in the nation's capital, on several occasions I have had students who claimed that there was archaeological evidence of the remains of an ark on Mount Ararat. One wonders where they get such gross misinformation and how they can be so credulous as to believe it. Also, some time around the fifties, I believe, Immanuel Velikovsky became famous for a brief time for his claim that he had found evidence throughout the world of a flood. The evidence was not sustained, his name soon forgotten, although the story of a flood does appear in the ancient literature of the Near East (which will be discussed in chapter 5).

Regarding the contradictions, there are two different versions of the story, the first stating that Noah should bring into the ark, in addition to his wife, sons, and their wives, two of every sort of living thing, male and female (6:19). A few lines later it says, "take with you seven pairs of all clean animals; the male and his mate, and a pair of the animals that are not clean . . . and seven pairs of the birds of the air . . . to keep their kind alive upon the face of the earth" (7:2). If the Bible were infallible or inerrant, one would have to swallow an awful lot of blatant contradictions. Then after creating a wind that caused the water to subside and the earth to dry, God instructed Noah and his entourage to leave the ark, establishing the first covenant, not only with Noah and his descendants but also with all the other living creatures, promising never again to release a flood destroying nearly all that existed on the face of the earth (9:8–17). From the three sons of Noah "the whole earth was peopled," with another of those stupefying genealogies listing the generations produced by Noah's sons, and Noah dying at 950 years of age.

The fable of Noah is followed by a brief sequel concerning the famous Tower of Babel. The earth having been peopled by the descendants of Noah's sons (as the flood had destroyed everyone else), they all spoke the same language, ancient Hebrew. Those who settled "in the land of Shinar," a plain in Babylonia, decided to build a city with a tower reaching to the heavens. Being of a curious nature, "the Lord came down [one wonders from where] to see the city and the tower which the sons of men had built" (11:5). Again displaying his jealous vindictive nature, Yahweh calls on some unknown cohorts to join him in "confusing their language," lest the people gain too much power, dispersing them throughout the earth—perhaps a crude attempt to explain the diversity of languages and people throughout the continents.

> And the Lord said, "Behold, they are one people, and they have all one language; and this is only the beginning of what they will do; and nothing that they propose to do will now be impossible for them. Come, *let us go down*, and there *confuse their language*, that they may not understand one another's speech." So the Lord scattered them abroad from there over the face of all the earth, and they left off building the city. Therefore its name was called Babel, because there the Lord confused the language of all the earth; and from there the Lord scattered them abroad over the face of all the earth. (11:6–9; emphasis added)

It is unfortunate (except for some beautiful literature and inspirational writing) that the Holy Bible was not named the Wholly Babel, which would have spared us a lot of superstitious nonsense.

THE PATRIARCH ABRAHAM

One of the distant descendants of Noah's sons was Abram (later changed by the Lord to Abraham), whom the Lord chose to be the patriarch of both the Israelites and the nation of Islam. Abram had taken as his wife Sarai (later changed to Sarah) and they first settled in Harar in northern Mesopotamia, but then the Lord directed Abram to go to his kindred's home in the land of Canaan, promising him that " 'I will make of you a great nation,' " and " '[t]o your descendants I will give this land' " (12:2–7). So Abram took Sarai to Shechem (which later would become the capital of the northern kingdom of Israel) to the Oak of Moreh where he built an alter to the Lord.

There was a famine in Canaan, so they left for Egypt where Abram decided to tell the Egyptians that Sarai was his sister (she was indeed his half-sister, both having the same mother) fearing that because of her beauty the Egyptians would kill him to free her for marriage. In fact, when she entered Egypt the sons of the Pharaoh were so taken with her beauty that they praised her to Pharaoh who took her into his house, and for her sake rewarded Abram with plentiful sheep, oxen, asses, camels, and servants, so that he became rich. However, although Pharaoh did not know that Sarai was Abram's wife, the Lord afflicted him with great plagues as punishment for taking her into his home. Somehow concluding that his afflictions were due to having taken Abram's wife, Pharaoh released her and Abram, allowing them to retain the riches he had given to Abram. Leaving Egypt they settled in the land of Canaan where once again the Lord promised Abram that the "length and breadth of the Land" will belong to him and his descendants (with the result that some Jews claim this land as their god-given inheritance to this day). They then dwelt by the Oaks of Mamre in Hebron where Abram again built an altar to the Lord.

After a brief description of a battle in which the forces of Abram defeated the enemies of the Kingdom of Sodom and Salem, the narrative returns to Abram's plaintive plea to the Lord for an heir. Because Sarai had reached the age of menopause and had not conceived, how would it be possible for Abram's descendants to be as numerous as "the grains of dust in the ground or as the stars in the firmament," as the Lord had promised? Believing she would never conceive, Sarai in desperation offered her Egyptian maid Hagar to Abram to take as his second wife. When Hagar realized she was pregnant, she flaunted the fact before Sarai who complained to Abram. Telling her she could deal with Hagar as she pleased, Sarai treated her so harshly that in despair Hagar fled into the wilderness where the "angel of the Lord" found her, ordering her to return to her mistress. But the angel also told her that she would bear a son, "a wild ass of a man," whom she should call Ishmael. Ishmael, who would be half Egyptian, would become the patriarch of the nation of Islam, as Isaac, Abraham's eventual son by Sarah, would become the patriarch of the nation of Israel.

Thirteen years after Hagar bore Ishmael the Lord appeared to Abram saying to him, "I am God Almighty" and will make a covenant with you whereby "you shall be the father of a multitude of nations . . . and kings shall come forth from you" (17:1-6). Changing Abram's name to Abraham and Sarai's name to Sarah, the Lord promised further that his covenant would apply to all of Abraham's descendants who would obtain "all the land of Canaan for an everlasting possession, and I will be their God" (17:9). As a "sign of" the covenant the Lord demanded that Abraham be "circumcised in the flesh of your foreskins," and that "every male throughout the generations" will be circumcised on their eighth day, whether they are born in the household or bought as servants, adding that "any uncircumcised male . . . shall be cut off from his people," having broken God's covenant (17:11-14). God then promised Abraham that Sarah would bear him a son, but Abraham found this so incredible considering their ages that he "fell on his face and laughed, and said to himself: 'Shall a child be born to a man who is a hundred years old' " or to his wife " 'who is ninety years old' "? But God assured him that Sarah would bear a son whom he would call "Isaac."

There then occurs one of those fantastic episodes in the Bible that puts it beyond belief. As Abraham sat in the heat of the day by the door of his tent at the Oaks of Mamre he looked up and saw three men standing in front of him [like Greek gods, the Lord appparently appeared at times as a man], one of whom he somehow recognized as the Lord. After suggesting that they should rest, wash their feet, and partake of the food that Abraham asked Sarah to prepare for them, as they were eating the Lord said to Abraham: " 'I will surely return to you in the spring, and Sarah your wife will have a son' " (18:9–10). Sarah, who had passed menopause ("it had ceased to be with Sarah after the manner of women") laughed to herself, as Abraham had earlier, wondering how this could be possible at her age (the longevities now were quite different than at the time of Noah). Hearing Sarah laugh and understanding her disbelief, the Lord said to Abraham (which has been a justification ever since for accepting all kinds of absurdities narrated in the Bible), " 'Is anything too hard for the Lord?' " But what would have made this credible at the time was the common belief that conception was a gift of the gods of fertility to whom people of all nations offered sacrifice.

With Abraham as their guide, the three men (the Lord and two Angels) left for the infamous Sodom and Gomorrah because, as the Lord said, " 'the outcry against Sodom and Gomorrah is great and their sin is very grave,' " although we are not told what provoked this devastating judgment. When Abraham learns that the Lord intends to destroy entirely both cities, his sense of moral justice is offended:

> " 'Wilt thou indeed destroy the righteous with the wicked? Suppose there are fifty righteous within the city; wilt thou then destroy the place and not spare it for the fifty righteous who are in it? Far be it for thee to do such a thing, to slay the righteous with the wicked. . . . Shall not the judge of all the earth do right?' " (18:23–25)

Acknowledging the validity of Abraham's argument, the Lord agrees that if any righteous people can be found in either city he will spare it.

But later that evening two angels came to Sodom where Abraham's nephew Lot was staying with his wife, two daughters, and two sons-in-law to be. When Lot invited the angels to spend the night at his house, some of the men from the city surrounded the house demanding to know who were his two guests. Refusing their demands, Lot instead incredibly offers to turn over to them his two virgin daughters "to do to them as you please" (19:8). Spurning his offer, the mob so threatened Lot that the angels came to his aid, drawing him inside the house, closing the door, and blinding the men attacking him. Concluding that he was justified in destroying both cities (despite the fact that innocent children and women must have lived there), the next morning the angels told Lot to leave the city with his family, and when his intended sons-in-law refused to go with them, the angels led Lot, his wife, and two daughters out of the city, ordering them " 'not to look back or stop anywhere in the valley . . . lest you be consumed.' " When they had escaped to the neighboring city of Zoar, the Lord "rained on Sodom and Gomorrah brimstone and fire" killing all the inhabitants in the entire valley and destroying everything that "grew on the ground" (19:24–25). Tragically, Lot's wife who followed behind him disobeyed the command not to look back, so she was turned into a "pillar of salt" — if one can believe that.

Not ended, the episode has an incestuous finale which defies credibility. Shortly after reaching Zoar, Lot led his daughters to the surrounding hills where they lived in a cave. Although all the inhabitants of the valley of Sodom and Gomorrah were killed, including the two young men who were to marry Lot's daughters, surely there were people living in Zoar and other neighboring villages. Yet the younger daughter urged that because "there is not a man on earth to come in to us" (that is, to impregnate them), she and her sister should get their father drunk, lie with him and thereby conceive so "that we may preserve offspring through our father" (19:30–35). Apparently these incestuous acts were condoned by the Lord because each daughter bore a son, the older calling her son Moab who became "the father of the Moabites to this day," while the younger called hers Ben-ammi who became the father of the nation of Ammonites. Fables such as these were invented to explain the origin of nations, as Roman historians claimed that Rome was founded by Romulous who was sired by a God and suckled by a wolf.

Of all the stories associated with Abraham, perhaps the most famous is the trial sacrifice of Isaac, the beloved son miraculously conceived by Sarah in her old age. Analyzed for its moral or theological meaning by innumerable theologians and philosophers, such as Kierkegaard, for me its significance merely reflects the barbarous customs of the time, especially the sacrifice of sons and daughters at the altar in periods of great national duress. Recall that in 2 Kings 3:27 the King of Moab, when he was about to lose a battle, "took his eldest son who was to reign in his stead, and offered him for a burnt offering upon the wall"; that in 2 Kings 21:6 Manasseh "burned his son as an offering"; and that one of the Judaic Kings defending Jerusalem sacrificed his eldest son on the ramparts to save the city. In this case, however, it is the Lord who, as a test of Abraham's faith, demands that he take Isaac to the land of Moriah where he was to present him as "a burnt offering." Whoever wrote the narrative introduces a poignant dramatic element when he has Isaac ask his father, " 'Behold, the fire and wood, but where is the lamb for a burnt offering?' " since he had been told that it was a sacrificial journey. Abraham answers, " 'God himself will provide the lamb for a burnt offering, my son' " (22:7–8).

But when father and son reached the sacrificial site, Abraham built an altar, put wood on it, and after binding Isaac placed him on the pyre in preparation for the sacrifice. Because sacrificial animals were killed rather than being burned alive, Abraham took his knife and was just at the point of stabbing Isaac to death when the Angel of the Lord appeared staying his hand, saying to him, " 'now I know that you fear God, seeing you have not withheld your son, your only son, from me.' " Seeing a ram whose horns were caught in a thicket, Abraham sacrificed the ram instead of Isaac. Whatever religious symbolism others may find in this story, to me it is just sheer barbarism. What would one think, for example, of a grandfather who, to test the loyalty of his son, demanded that he kill *his* son, the grandson, even if at the last moment the grandfather withdrew his command? Is the act any less horrible because it is supposed to have been commanded by God?

THE MIRACLES OF MOSES AND THE EXODUS

Since it is not possible to recount all the stories in the Old Testament, and since my purpose is to show that it is a tribal history with no more theological significance than any other tribal narrative, I will turn now to what Anderson calls the "decisive event—the great watershed of Israel's history . . . the Exodus from Egypt."[25] Before he died Abraham instructed a servant to select a wife for Isaac, not among the Canaanites in the region but from Nahor in Mesopotamia, the original home of Abraham. So Rebekah became the wife of Isaac and bore him twin sons, Esau and Jacob. Tricking his older brother out of his birthright (although twins, Esau preceded Jacob from the womb and therefore was the eldest), Jacob became the more important branch of the genealogical tree, his sons becoming the leaders of the twelve tribes of Israel. He married Leah and Rachel in turn, and though Leah had children first because Rachel had difficulty conceiving, Jacob (whose name had been changed to Israel) favored Joseph, the son Rachel finally bore, since "he was the son of his old age" and perhaps because originally he had choosen Rachel to his wife. He had worked for seven years for Rachel's father, Laban, to obtain her, but her father deceived him on the wedding night by substituting Leah, on the grounds that because she was the oldest daughter she should be married first, but Jacob later married Rachel as well. Polygamy was not prohibited in the Old Testament.

The favoritism of Jacob for Rachel's son Joseph aroused hostility among his brothers, which was inflamed when Joseph told them of his dreams prophesying that he would rule over them. This led to the well-known story of Joseph being sold to the Ishmaelites for twenty shekels of silver and taken to Egypt. There his skill in interpreting Pharaoh's dreams led to his being given the later's signet ring, allowed to ride in the second chariot after the Pharaoh, and made governor "over all the land of Egypt" (41:41–44). In those days one who had prophesied successfully or had brought prosperity to the ruler by the administration of his affairs was considered favored by the gods, and was thus richly rewarded. In addition to his important role as governor of Egypt, Joseph was given an Egyptian name and married to the daughter of an Egyptian priest. Having interpreted Pharaoh's dream as revealing that seven years of abundance would be followed by seven years of blight and famine, during the time of prosperity Joseph shrewdly had provisions stored to alleviate the famine years, allowing him to provide for the Egyptians, as well as for his father Jacob and his brothers when they were made known to him during the famine.

Under the leadership of Jacob's sons, the twelve tribes of Israel prospered in Egypt as long as Joseph lived. Their descendants multiplied and were placed in important positions due to Joseph's influence, thus becoming "exceedingly strong so that the land was filled with them" (Exod. 1:7). However, when Joseph and the older Pharaoh died, the new Pharaoh, traditionally identified as Rameses II who reigned from 1279–1213 B.C.E., was alarmed by their growing numbers and power, so he decided to take away their privileges, consigning them to harsh manual labor making mortar and bricks used to construct storage areas for supplies. When the Israelites continued to multiply even under this oppression, Pharaoh decreed to his people that " 'every son that is born to Hebrews you shall cast into the Nile, but you shall let every daughter live' " (1:22).

While the decree was in effect, a family from the house of Levi had a robust son whose mother successfully hid him for three months until the danger of his discovery became so great she decided to put him in a "basket made of bulrushes," covered with "bitumen and pitch," and leave him among the protective reeds by the river's bank. She then instructed her daughter Miriam to observe the baby from a distance to determine whether he was safely found. Shortly after being placed among the reeds, the Pharaoh's daughter came to the river bank to bathe, saw the basket, and asked her maid to retrieve it. Seeing the baby crying the princess took pity on it, recognizing that it was a Hebrew child. When the baby's sister Miriam saw the tender reaction of the daughter of the Pharaoh, she asked if she would like her to find a Hebrew woman to nurse the child. When the princess replied that she would, Miriam cleverly went to get her mother to nurse her baby son. When the child became older, his mother brought him to the Pharaoh's daughter who took him into the household as her son, naming him "Moses" (perhaps derived from an Egyptian suffix meaning "to be born"). Moses grew up in Pharaoh's household where he was raised as a member of the family and given an excellent education. Yet, one day when he went out and observed the treatment of his people, he became so enraged seeing an Egyptian beating a Hebrew man that he attacked and killed him, hoping no one saw him. But the incident became known, so Moses fled to the land of Midian where one day he came to the aid of the daughters of the priest of Midian. In gratitude the priest invited him into his home and later offered his daughter Zipporah to him in marriage. They had a son called Gershom.

Then there occurred one of the most famous episodes in the Old Testament. God, we are told, had not forgotten the plight in Egypt of his chosen people, so one day when Moses was guarding his father-in-law's flock and "came to Horeb, the mountain of God," an "angel of the Lord appeared to him in a flame of fire out of the midst of a bush; and he looked, and lo, the bush was burning, yet it was not consumed" (3:2). Intrigued by a burning bush that was not destroyed (in the Bible fire or burning objects were perceived as the sign of God himself or of one of his angels), Moses turned to observe it, whereupon he heard God calling "Moses, Moses" from the bush. "Here I am," Moses replied, as if God would not have known where he was. Commanding him not to come closer and to take off his shoes because he was standing on holy ground, the Lord identified himself as the God of Abraham, Isaac, and Jacob. Afraid to look upon God, Moses hid his face (3.5–6).

With the usual monotonous historical repetitions typical of the Old Testament, God declares to Moses that he is aware of the suffering Israelites in Egypt and has "come down to deliver them out of the hand of the Egyptians, and to bring them . . . to a good and broad land, a land flowing with milk and honey," the future Palestine. When the Lord says he will send Moses to Pharaoh to lead the people out of Egypt (the previous Pharaoh having died, presumably Moses had nothing to fear by returning), Moses answers, "What am I that I should go to Pharaoh and bring the sons of Israel out of Egypt?" (3:11). But reassuring him, God said he will accompany him, be a "sign" for him, and that when Moses has delivered the people from Egypt he will "serve God upon this mountain," Mount Horeb. There then occurs the famous exchange when Moses asks what name he should give if the captive Israelites ask who sent him to deliver them. In reply God said "I AM WHO I AM," adding, "Say this to the people of Israel, 'I AM has sent me to you' " (3:13–14).

But Moses still hesitated claiming that the Israelites would not believe him, which God interpreted as a request for a "sign," some miraculous act that if performed before the people would convince them that the sender was truly God (recall that as a test of Marduk's powers he was asked to destroy a garment and then make it reappear, which he did). So God commands Moses to take the rod he is holding and throw it to the ground, whereon it turns into a serpent, frightening Moses. Further reassuring him, the Lord tells him to grasp the serpent's tail which turns it back into a rod. As a further "sign" God has Moses' hand turn leprous after withdrawing it from his bosom, then restored when he repeats the act.

That this was intended as a "sign" to convince the people that Moses had God's backing is made evident by the statement:

> "If they will not believe you" God said, "or heed the first sign, they may believe the latter sign. If they will not believe even these two signs or heed your voice, you shall take some water from the Nile and pour it upon the dry ground; and the water which you shall take from the Nile will become blood upon the dry ground." (4:8–9)

At a time when nothing was known about the composition of substances, so that all occurrences seemed mysterious, magical, and subject to God's commands, it was natural to believe in such miracles—as people still believe in the sacrament of communion. But today this is unworthy of intelligent human beings. Rods cannot be turned into snakes or people given and cured of leprosy at will, anymore than bread can be turned into flesh or wine into blood at the altar. It is incredible how easily one's sense of reality can be subverted, even today, within a religious setting. Yet despite the position of the church, most Catholics surely take the sacraments symbolically or ritualistically, otherwise they would gag at having to swallow the actual flesh and blood of Christ if taken literally.

As a last resort to extricate himself from this perilous task, Moses protests that he lacks eloquence: that he is "slow of speech and tongue." But the Lord says that since he made him as he is, he also can teach him what to say. As a final plea Moses says in desperation, " 'Oh, my Lord, send I pray, some other person' " (4:13). But the Lord is adamant, declaring he will send with Moses his brother Aaron who is a more accomplished speaker to dictate the words said by Moses, with even God if necessary telling him what to say. Leaving him no venue of escape, Moses is directed to go back to Egypt to free the Israelites, taking with him his wife, son, and the rod to be used as a "sign" before Pharaoh to perform "all the miracles . . . put in your powers" (4:21). But then there occur several incongruous incidents that presage this incredible story. First, although determined to free the Israelites, for some inexplicable reason the Lord decides to "harden" Pharaoh's heart, "so that he will not let the people go," obstructing his own intention. Then, after Moses and his family set out for Egypt, *without any explanation* "the Lord met him and sought to kill him" (4:24). It is only when his wife Zipporah, using a flint to cut off their son's foreskin, touches Moses' feet with it saying, "Surely you are bridegroom of blood to me," that the Lord decides to spare him (4:24–26). This certainly is a very impulsive, vicious conception of God, to say the least.

Reaching Egypt, Moses and Aaron confront Pharaoh telling him that their God demands that their people be allowed to leave Egypt, but the Pharaoh replies in effect that because their God is unknown to him there is no reason to obey him. When Moses and Aaron predict a curse "of pestilence or the sword" if Pharaoh does not obey, he responds by imposing even harsher conditions on the people of Israel. Telling the Lord that their protests have just made things worse, God directs them to perform the miracle he had shown them to impress the Pharaoh, so Aaron casts his rod to the ground whereupon it changes into a serpent. But the Pharaoh commands "the magicians of Egypt," his "wise men and the sorcerers," to do the same, which they did "by their secret arts" (7:10–12). Even when Aaron's serpent swallowed up those of the Egyptians, the Pharaoh's "heart was hardened" (as God had commanded) and would not grant their request. All this is done to enable the Lord to demonstrate his greater powers:

> ". . . I will harden Pharaoh's heart, and though I multiply my signs and wonders . . . Pharaoh will not listen to you; then I will lay my hand upon Egypt and bring forth my hosts, my people the sons of Egypt, out of the land of Egypt by great acts of judgment. And the Egyptians shall know that I am the Lord. . . ." (7:3–5)

Whoever wrote this was intent on proving that the Lord of Israel was superior to any gods of the Egyptians, even though he is made to appear vain, willful, and cruel.

So the Lord decided to unleash the full fury of his powers if Pharaoh does not release the Israelites, *even though it is the Lord who prevents him from doing so*! First, he tells Moses and Aaron to accompany Pharaoh in the morning when he goes to the Nile to bathe and while he and his servants watch, strike the waters with the magic rod causing all the water in the Nile, rivers, ponds, canals, pools, and vessels to turn into blood, killing all the fish. But again "the magicians of Egypt did the same by their secret arts," so Pharaoh's heart remained hardened, and he would not free the people (7:22). God next instructed Moses to tell Aaron to point the rod over the waters of the rivers, canals, and pools causing a vast horde of frogs to cover all the land and invade all the houses, occupying any empty space. But again Pharaoh's magicians were able to do the same. Yet this time Pharaoh was so upset by the pestilence that he asked Moses and Aaron to entreat the Lord to destroy the frogs, agreeing to let the people leave so that they could sacrifice to the Lord in the wilderness. So the Lord destroyed all the frogs which were so plentiful that when gathered in heaps "the land stank." But once freed of the invasion of frogs, Pharaoh's heart was hardened, reversing his decision to release the Israelites.

Each time the request was renewed and denied it was followed by another disaster caused by the magic rod, leading Pharaoh to agree to free the people, only to have his "heart hardened" again and revoke it. First, the land was inundated throughout with gnats, which even the magicians could not match with their secret arts, followed by swarms of flies, and then a plague that killed all the animals and flocks of the Egyptians, but not those of the Israelites. Following this the Lord instructed Moses and Aaron to throw "handfuls of ashes from the kiln" toward the heaven, the fine dust producing boils and sores on all Egyptians and their beasts. Although this should have changed the mind of Pharaoh, again the Lord hardened his heart with the usual result. Next came hail mingled with fire and thunder, the hail so heavy that it killed any living thing that was not protected by shelter, along with all the flax and barley.

This was succeeded by a plague of locusts so thick that the sky was darkened and all the plants and fruit of the trees devoured. Then the Lord directed Aaron to reach toward the heaven bringing complete darkness over the land, so pitch black that all activity ceased for three days, no one being able to see to move, but again without the desired effect. By now distraught and enraged, Pharaoh commands Moses and Aaron to leave, saying they will die if he sees their faces again. All this wanton destruction was an excuse to humble the Egyptians and impress on the Israelites how superior their magician-God was to the Egyptian. As he says to Moses:

> "Go in to Pharaoh; for I have hardened his heart and the heart of his servants, that I may show these signs of mine among them, and that you may tell in the hearing of your son and of your son's son how I have made sport of the Egyptians and what signs [miracles] I have done among them; that you may know that I am the Lord." (10:1–2)

Deciding finally that he would inflict a catastrophe so cruel that it would bring this terrible impasse to an end, the Lord decides to kill all the first-born of every Egyptian family from the Pharaoh's to "the lowest maidservant . . . and all the first-born of the cattle" (11:4–5). As usual there are several versions of the story, the last two having had a lasting impact because they contain one of the most significant Judaic traditions, the Passover Seder. In order to spare the first-born of the Israelites from the slaughter, each family was told to take a year-old, unblemished, male lamb and on "the evening of the fourteenth day of the month" the whole congregation of Israel should kill the lambs, then take a bunch of hyssop, dip it into the blood, and dab some on "the two doorposts and the lintel of the houses" to mark them (12:5–7). Thus, when the Lord passes though Egypt that night killing "all the first-born . . . both man and beast," the blood on the doorposts and lintel "shall be a sign . . . upon the houses where you are," so that "I will pass over you . . . when I smite the land of Egypt" (12:12–13). After giving detailed instructions as to how the feast of the passover was to be prepared and observed, the Lord said: " 'This day shall be for you a memorial day, and you shall keep it as a feast to the Lord; throughout your generations you shall observe it as an ordinance forever' " (112:14). And so it remains a major Jewish observance to this day despite its doubtful origin.

At midnight, while the people of Israel were confined to their homes as instructed, the Lord massacred all the first-born of the Egyptians and their cattle, causing a great wailing in the land "for there was not a house where one was not killed." The Pharaoh was so bereaved that he immediately summoned Moses and Aaron telling them that they and their people should leave Egypt. He even allowed them to take all their possessions, including their flocks and herds, along with the "jewelry of silver and gold" they had acquired from the Egyptians. This time the Lord did not interfere by hardening the heart of the Pharaoh, so after having "dwelt in Egypt . . . four hundred and thirty years," a multitude of "about six hundred thousand men on foot, besides women and children," left Rameses for Succoth (12:37). What a fantastic story, comparable to those in the *Iliad* and the *Odyssey*.

Instead of taking the shortest route across the land of the Philistines, to avoid a possible war with them the Lord literally led the legions of people south through the wilderness to the Red Sea—or the Reed Sea, as scholars now refer to it—going "before them by day in a pillar of cloud to lead them along the way, and by night in a pillar of fire to give them light. . . ." (13:21). However, once they had left Egypt the capricious Lord again unaccountably "hardened the heart of Pharaoh" causing him and his servants to regret their release and pursue the Israelites by chariot until they overtook them. As the Pharaoh laments:

> "What is this we have done, that we have let Israel go from serving us." So he . . . took six hundred picked chariots and all the other chariots of Egypt with officers . . . and overtook them encamped at the sea. . . ." (14:5–9)

There then ensues what is probably the most famous miraculous event in the Old Testament. Blocked by the sea in front and the advancing

Egyptian army in the rear the Israelites were panicked, but Moses reassured them: " 'Fear not, stand firm, and see the salvation of the Lord, which he will work for you today; for the Egyptians whom you see . . . you shall never see again' " (14:13). To protect them during the night "the pillar of cloud" which, as the Lord, had gone before them as their guide now became "the angel of God" going to their rear to separate them from the Egyptians. As the night passed, Moses, following the instruction of the Lord, stretched out his handheld rod which "drove the sea back by a strong east wind all night, and made the sea dry land, and the waters were divided" (14:21). Advancing on the stretch of dry land miraculously walled in on either side by water, the people of Israel were able to cross the sea that night. But the next morning when the Pharaoh's mounted army and hundreds of chariots followed suit, the Lord directed Moses again to stretch his rod over the sea, causing it to rush back plunging "the chariots and the horsemen and all the host of Pharaoh that had followed them into the sea; not so much as one of them remained" (14:29). Having traversed the dry ground during the night the Israelites were saved. "Seeing the great deed of the Lord, the people feared the Lord; and they believed in the Lord and his servant Moses," which of course was the intended point of the story.

But is it believable today? Not unless one believes that the earth is flat, that storks bring babies, and that leprechauns can reveal hidden treasure. It is a dramatic legend, but nothing more than that. There is no record of this disaster among the Egyptians who would be expected to register the complete destruction of their Pharaoh and his entire army of charioteers. Much wasted time has been spent attempting to devise plausible explanations for the event, such as the fluctuations of the tide, a strong wind momentarily diverting the sea water, or the bed of reeds supporting the hordes of Israelites but not horsemen and chariots. Yet legends are not the sort of things that sustain factual explanations. Just consider how 600,000 men on foot *plus* women and children (even taking into account an exaggerated number) could cross a restricted sea bed in a single night! Retold for centuries before being written down, these fables are the stuff of fabrication and fiction, not fact. Yet they still are believed by many credulous Jews and Christians as if they were historically true. As the two Anglican theologians R. P. C. and A. T. Hanson earlier have admitted in all candor:

> The realization that the Bible is not a scientific textbook first began to dawn on Christians . . . in the last century and has probably been fairly widely accepted by now. Most of us do not regard Adam and Eve as historical characters and do not hold that woman was literally formed out of man's side. But the realization that the story of Israel's origin from Abraham till almost the time of Saul and David is not history but legend

can hardly be described as having affected very many Christians even today. We still hear sermons giving a psychological analysis of Abraham's feelings on Mount Moriah, or a vivid account of how the Red Sea dried up at the waving of Moses' rod. This is not to say that those parts of the Bible which are myth or legend are of no value. Very much the reverse. But we can only appreciate their value if we accept them for what they are and do not pretend that they are something which they are not.[26]

Having miraculously contrived the final exodus from Egypt, the magician-God had to perform additional miracles to insure the survival of the people of Israel. After crossing the Reed Sea, Moses led the Israelites into the wilderness for three days where they were without water. When they reached Marah the water there was too bitter to drink, so the Lord directed Moses to a tree which, when he threw it into the water, made it sweet and drinkable (15:22–25). As they continued wandering in the wilderness they found little food, so again they "murmured against Moses," protesting that he had freed them from the Egyptians only to let them die of hunger. But the Lord heard their complaints and told Moses to tell them that at twilight they will have meat to eat and at dawn they will receive bread. So that evening flocks of quail appeared which provided the people with meat, while the next morning after the dew lifted the ground was covered with a white flaky substance that was as sweet tasting as "wafers made with honey." Calling this nourishing substance "manna," they ate it for "forty years till they came to a habitable land . . . the border of the land of Canaan" (16:31:35). That they could have lived primarily on one substance for forty years, nearly two generations, is of course nutritionally impossible, but literalists ignore that. Still short of water to drink, the people as usual blamed Moses who complained to the Lord: " 'What shall I do with this people? They are almost ready to stone me.' " So the Lord told Moses to strike the rock at Horeb with his magic rod whereupon water poured out of it — if one can believe that a rock can produce water (17:4–6).

There then occurs a lengthy description of the covenants, laws, rituals, and ordinances probably inserted by a priestly writer. The Lord subsequently called to Moses to " '[c]ome up to me on the mountain,' " Mount Sinai, where he gave him "the tables of stone, with the law and the commandments . . ." (24:12). The "Glory of the Lord" settling on Mount Sinai like a cloud for six days, on the seventh day he "called to Moses out of the midst of the cloud" appearing "like a devouring fire on the top of the mountain . . ." (24:12–18). Ascending the mountain Moses remained on it for forty days and forty nights (always a conventional biblical period of time) during which the Lord told him to instruct the people to do the following: present him with very elaborate offerings; construct an ornate ark overlaid "with pure gold inside and out" along with four gold rings attached to the sides so that it could be carried by poles inserted through the rings; make a "mercy seat of pure gold" accompanied by two cherubim formed of hammered gold placed on either end of the seat so their faces looked across at each other and their wings spread over the seat; place the mercy seat on top of the ark and within it the "testimony" the Lord will present to Moses; build a table also overlaid in gold with rings so that it could be carried and on which there should be placed "plates and dishes for incense, and . . . flagons and bowls with which to pour libations," all made of gold; instructions on how to build seven lamps of pure gold decorated with capitals and flowers of hammered gold along with cups on six branches extending from the lamp to hold candles to light the area around the ark; detailed specifications regarding the tabernacle that was to be constructed to hold the altar and the ark along with the congregation; and finally a description of the fine garments, robes, breastplates, girdles, and so forth, which Moses, Aaron, and the latter's sons were to wear as priests "for glory and for beauty" (25–31). Notwithstanding the extravagance of these commands as described, they contain barely a fraction of the riches that were to be assembled to glorify the Lord. Although this horde of people barely had enough to eat and drink to survive, apparently they had carried enough silver and gold from Egypt that they could perform this colossal task requiring the riches of a Croesus.

When the Lord made an end to these demands he presented Moses with "the two tables of the testimony, tables of stone, written with the fingers of God" (31:18). But before Moses descended Mount Sinai with the tables the people, who had grown restive during his absence, asked Aaron to gather their gold jewelry to make a "molten calf." Complying with their request, Aaron fashioned a golden image of a calf which the people proclaimed (forsaking Yahweh) represented the gods who had brought them "out of the land of Egypt." Aaron even built an altar to this god. Knowing that the Israelites had turned away from him to worship a craven image, the Lord informed Moses before his descent that he would "consume" these "stiff-necked people" (32:9). When Moses heard this condemnation he intervened, reminding the Lord of all he had done to save the people of Israel, which would be in vain if he now were to annihilate them, and also of his promise to Abraham, Isaac, and Jacob that their descendants would multiply "as the stars in the heaven." Begging the Lord to "turn from thy fierce wrath, and repent of this evil against thy people," Moses succeeded in his entreaty.

But though Moses prevailed against the wrath of the Lord, when he descended and witnessed the people singing and dancing around the golden calf he, too, became furious. In his anger he threw the Lord's tables to the ground breaking them, cast the golden calf into the fire until it was reduced to powder, and then scattered the powder on the water and made "the people of Israel drink it" (32:19–20). When Moses accused Aaron of complicity in creating an image of false gods, Aaron blamed the people and said that when he threw the gold into the fire the golden calf emerged—attesting to the common recourse to magic to explain events, especially when one did not want to assume responsibility for them. So Moses called those who were on the side of the Lord to come to him, with all of the sons of the tribe of Levi responding to his appeal and gathering around him. Notwithstanding his plea of mercy to the Lord, succumbing to his own fury he commanded them to take their swords and "go from gate to gate throughout the camp and slay every man his brother, and every man his companion, and every man his neighbor," until there fell that day 3,000 men (32:27–28).

Despite this punishment Moses inconsistently returned to the Lord the next morning and while acknowledging that the people had committed "a great sin" in wanting to worship a graven image in disobedience to God's commands, he heroically asked that the Lord "blot out him" and not the people. But the Lord replied that he had chosen Moses to lead the Israelites and that he would punish the latter by inflicting on them a great plague (32:31–34). Directing Moses to lead those who remained to the land "flowing with milk and honey," the land promised to the descendants of Abraham, Isaac, and Jacob, he said he would send an angel before them "to drive out the Canaanites, the Amorites, Hittites, Hivites, Perizzites, and the Jebusites" (33:1–3). Apparently it did not offend the Lord's sense of justice that he was dispossessing these peoples of their ancient lands to favor the Israelites.

But disheartened by the wavering rebellious behavior of the Israelites, Moses asks the Lord for greater assurance if he were to fulfill his mission, specifically requesting that "thy glory" be made known to him. The Lord agrees to show himself with the warning that Moses not observe him directly: " 'you cannot see my face; for man shall not see me and live.' " (33:20). The Lord selected a place "in a cleft of the rock" for Moses to stand to shield him from seeing the Lord's face as he walks by but permit him to see his back after he passes (again this strange appearance of the Lord in human form). In addition, he tells Moses to cut two more tables like the first (which Moses destroyed in his anger at seeing the people worship the golden calf) and carry them the next morning to the top of Mount Sinai. When Moses reached the height of the mountain the next day, he remained there with the Lord forty days and nights, neither eating nor drinking (an impossibly long time to go without water, especially), forging a "covenant" with the Lord which the latter wrote on the tables as the famous ten commandments (34:28).

Marking the culmination of Moses' favored relation with the Lord, he was so transformed when he descended the mountain that "the skin of his face shone" owing to a spiritual radiation (34:29). So pronounced was the glow that when the people saw his face they were afraid to approach him, forcing Moses to cover his face with a veil. By speaking to Moses the Lord confirmed his unique trust in him.

> "If there is a prophet among you, I the Lord make myself known to him
> in a vision, I speak with him in a dream. Not so with my servant Moses.
> . . . With him I speak mouth to mouth, clearly, and not in dark speech;
> and he beholds the form of the Lord." (Num 12:6–8)

Presenting the tablets with the ten commandments to the Israelites, Moses related to them what the Lord told him about delivering them to the promised land.

Notwithstanding the Lord's exceptional regard for Moses, the Pentateuch ends sadly, for despite all that Moses had reluctantly undertaken yet successfully accomplished for the Lord, neither he nor his accompanying people would be allowed to cross the Jordan river and enter the appointed kingdom. The Lord will take him to the top of Pisgah on Mount Nebo where he will be shown the vast fertile plains that will become Palestine, but it will be Joshua's privilege and that of the sons of the followers of Moses to occupy these lands. While one can understand that the Lord might deprive the unfaithful Israelites in this way, why would he deny Moses the privilege? There is a curious episode often cited to explain this, but it just reaffirms the idiosyncratic behavior of Yahweh (or peculiar recounting of whoever was the author) adapted from the rulers of the period.

Once again when the people were without water in the wilderness they criticized Moses, asking why he had led them out of Egypt only to let them die of thirst in this barren country.

> Why have you brought the assembly of the Lord into this wilderness,
> that we should die here. . . . And why have you made us come up out of
> Egypt, to bring us to this evil place. It is no place for grain, or figs, or
> vines, or pomegranates; and there is no water for us to drink. (Num
> 20:4–5)

When Moses and Aaron appeal to the Lord to save them he replies: " 'Take the rod [the magical rod used so effectively in Egypt] . . . assemble the congregation . . . and *tell the rock* before their eyes to yield its water; so you shall bring water out of the rock for them. . . .' " (Num 20:8; emphasis added) Thus Moses and Aaron gathered the people by the rock and Moses said:

> "Here now, you rebels; shall we bring forth water for you out of this rock?" And Moses lifted up his hand and struck the rock with his rod twice; and water came forth abundantly, and the congregation drank. . . . (Num. 20:10–11)

But why should this incident (referred to as the "waters of Meribah") have so offended the Lord that he prevented everyone present from entering the promised land? The reason seems so slight as hardly to be objectionable. While the Lord had instructed Moses to "tell the rock . . . to yield its water," because he was so provoked by the criticisms of the people, instead of *telling* the rock to bring forth water he "struck the rock with his rod twice." So the alleged offense consisted of deriving the water from the rock by *striking* it with the rod, rather than *telling* it to yield the water, a seemingly insignificant difference (unless the Lord was offended because Moses did not give Him direct credit for deriving the water).

> And the Lord said to Moses and Aaron, "Because you did not believe in me, to sanctify me in the eyes of the people of Israel, therefore you shall not bring the assembly into the land which I have given them." (Num. 20:12)

Whatever the reason, despite all their struggles and privations, none of the adult population who participated in the Exodus and wanderings in the wilderness would be allowed the satisfaction of entering the "land of milk and honey." A sad conclusion.

Deuteronomy, referred to as the Fifth Book of Moses, ends with the description of Moses' death. After showing him a mountain view of all the lands that he promised to the sons of Abraham, Isaac, and Jacob, the Lord says to Moses, " 'I have let you see it with your eyes, but you shall not go over there' " (Deut. 34:4). With that Moses dies at age one hundred and twenty years (the longevity specified earlier by the Lord), buried in a valley in the land of Moab where "no man knows the place of his burial to this day." Though his resting place remains unknown, Moses, along with Abraham, Jesus, and Paul, is one of the four most significant figures in the Hebraic-Christian religion. As Deuteronomy concludes: "And there has not arisen a prophet in Israel like Moses, whom the Lord knew face to face, none like him for all the Lord sent him to do . . ." (34:10–11).

NOTES

1. Cf. Karen Armstrong, *A History of God* (New York: Ballantine Books, 1993), p. 27.

2. Cf. Bernhard W. Anderson, *Understanding the Old Testament*, 4th ed. (Englewood Cliffs, N.J.: Prentice-Hall, 1966), p. 513. Until otherwise indicated, the immediately following page references in the text are to this excellent scholarly work.

3. David Hume, *An Inquiry Concerning Human Understanding*, sec. 10, Part II, par. 100.

4. Jer. 19:7–9. The translation is that of the Revised Standard Version (RSV) of the Bible (New York: Thomas Nelson and Sons, 1953), which I shall use throughout the book without further mention. Hereafter, I will indicate the biblical source in the text.

5. These historical divisions are based on Anderson's chart, p. 25. I have revised and extended the divisions somewhat to make them more explicit and inclusive.

6. R. P. C. Hanson and A. T. Hanson, *The Bible without Illusions* (London: SCM Press, 1989), pp. 6–7.

7. Richard E. Friedman, *Who Wrote the Bible?* (New York: Harper & Row Publishers, 1987), p. 15. Until otherwise indicated, the immediately following page references in the text are to this work.

8. For a more detailed account of these developments, including references to the specific contributors, see Friedman, pp. 18–21.

9. As a minimal definition in this context, I mean by 'religionist' those who believe that the Old Testament represents God's revelation to man and thus is infallible.

10. Cf. Søren Kierkegaard, *Concluding Unscientific Postscripts*, Section II, ch 2.

11. Anderson, pp. 21–22. See also the diagram of the dates of these various sources, p. 453.

12. Armstrong, p. 12.

13. For a discussion of the influence see Anderson, pp. 484–85, and Armstrong, pp. 7–9, 63–64.

14. Steven Weinberg, *Dreams of a Final Theory* (New York: Vintage Books, 1992), p. 248.

15. "Science Panel: Schools Must Teach Evolution," *The Washington Post*, 10 April 1998, p. A10.

16 Thorkild Jacobson, "The Cosmos as a State," in H. Frankfort and H. A. Frankfort, *Before Philosophy* (Baltimore: Penguin Books, 1949), p. 193. Emphasis added.

17. The original Hebrew occurs in Anderson, p. 61.

18. Cf. Richard H. Schlagel, *From Myth to Modern Mind: A Study of the Origins and Growth of Scientific Thought*, vol. 1, *Theogony through Ptolemy* (New York: Peter Lang Publishers, Inc., 1995), p. 95.

19. These issues will be discussed in more detail in chapter 5 in connection with Gerald Schroeder's attempt in *The Science of God* to reconcile the account in

Genesis with modern geological and paleontological evidence, equating the six days of creation with our fifteen billion year age of the universe based on Einstein's theory of relativity.

20. Cf. Stephen Jay Gould, *Wonderful Life* (New York: W.W. Norton & Co., 1990), p. 228n.

21. Cf. Richard Dawkins, *The Blind Watchmaker* (New York: W.W. Norton & Co., 1986), p. xi.

22. Cf. Gould, pp. 213, 214, 231.

23. Jared Diamond, *The Third Chimpanzee* (New York: HarperPerennial, 1992), p. 15.

24. Gerald L. Schroeder, *The Science of God* (New York: The Free Press, 1997), p. 142.

25. Anderson, p. 9

26. R. P. C. and A. T. Hanson, pp. 13–14.

THE *CHRISTOS* LEGEND

INTRODUCTION

No other written work in the West has influenced so many people, shaping their moral behavior and beliefs, as the New Testament during the past two millennia. Today Christianity is one of the largest and most influential world religions with people seeking their salvation, literally or figuratively, in the mystique of Christ. Yet, like the Old Testament myth of creation and incredible stories of Jahweh's intervention in human history on behalf of the Israelites, the gospel stories in the New Testament depicting the life of Jesus Christ are largely legendary or fabricated. Although generally accepted by contemporary *critical* biblical scholars,[1] this conclusion will shock many traditional theologians and clerics, along with most Christians.

All one can conclude with any confidence about the historical Jesus is that he was from Nazareth; that Mary and Joseph were his mother and father; that he probably had four brothers and two sisters; that he wandered as an itinerant teacher or preacher in the regions of Galilee, Decapolis, Samaria, and Judea attracting some followers; and that he was crucified in Jerusalem during the administration of the Roman procurator Pontius Pilate about the year 30 C.E. — yet this is not the conception of Jesus held by most Christians. In contrast to what is actually *known* about the historical Jesus, Christians usually *believe* that as the Christ he was sent by God as the sacrificial lamb to redeem humankind; conceived by the Holy Spirit and born of the Virgin Mary in a manger in Bethlehem visited by wise men and shepherds; endowed with the power to perform

128

such miracles as exorcising demons, curing lepers, and restoring sight to the blind; walked on water, calmed a stormy sea; multiplied loaves of bread and fish by the thousands; converted water into fine wine; restored the dead to life; and was crucified but after three days resurrected as a sign of everlasting life. There is slight historical evidence for most of this which depends mainly on the accounts in the gospels written between thirty-five and seventy years after Jesus' death, unsupported by direct eyewitness accounts or written records.

It also is believed that the authority of his teaching derives from God, explaining the wisdom conveyed in his allegories and parables despite his simple family background as a carpenter's son and lack of schooling. Both the Gospels Mark 6:1–3 and John 7:15 describe the astonishment at Jesus' learning and wisdom despite his lack of education. As stated in John: " 'How is it that this man has learning, when he has never studied?' " This implies that Jesus was illiterate, yet his teachings were so provocative they aroused the anger of the Jewish elders, Pharisees and Sadducees, leading to his crucifixion. Challenging their doctrines that righteousness consists in obeying the laws of the Torah and observing the conventional rituals and prohibitions (such as the sabbath, circumcision, Temple sacrifices, not eating bloody meat or meat from strangled animals, and not associating with gentiles or outcasts), he insisted that holiness depends upon fulfilling the two great commandments to love God and to love one's neighbor as oneself. It is further believed he foretold that he was sent by God to fulfill the Old Testament prophesies and redeem humankind of its sins by suffering crucifixion, but that on the third day following his death he would be raised; that on the eve of the day of his passion he had a last supper with his disciples during which he blessed the bread they ate and the wine they drank, declaring that they represented his body and his blood; that he predicted that one of the disciples (Judas) would betray him and that Peter would deny him; that his resurrection would testify to an eternal life in the Kingdom of God for those who were saved; and that after his death the Holy Spirit would descend on the apostles endowing them with the power to carry on his mission by curing the sick, performing miracles, spreading the word of his second coming, and bringing the "good news of the Kingdom of God" to all nations.

In addition, the Catholic Church maintains that Jesus declared that Peter would be the rock (*Petros*) on which the church would be built and that he was martyred in Rome with his remains contained in a shrine discovered under the high altar of the church of St. Peter, thereby establishing the apostolic succession of the Catholic Church. With some variation, these are the tenets Christians are taught to believe about Jesus from the earliest age. The contrast between what actually is *known* about the historical Jesus and what most Christians *believe* about him is devastating, considering that the belief in Christianity depends upon ignoring this contrast. In fact, the Christ that most Christians believe in is a theological construct or a religious artifact that has very little resemblance to what is known about the actual Jesus. Even something as fundamental as the number of disciples being twelve is disputed by some Christian scholars. That twelve is the same number as the sons and tribes of Jacob is itself somewhat suspicious, perhaps another effort to link the New Testament with the Old. As John Dominic Crossan, a scholar of the authenticity of the gospels, says:

> The question . . . is whether such an institution [of twelve disciples] derives from the time of the historical Jesus or whether it was created after his death among certain early Christian groups. I accept the second alternative for two reasons. One is that I find it almost impossible to imagine thirteen men traveling around together among the small villages of Lower Galilee in the first century [because a group of twelve strange men would have aroused the fear of the people in the tiny, rural, hamlets]. . . .
>
> The second and more immediate one is that whole groups in the early church seem never to have heard of this most important and symbolic institution. . . . If the institution of Twelve Apostles, with all its profound symbolic connotations, had been established by Jesus during his lifetime, it would have been more widely known and noted. I conclude, therefore, that the connection between Jesus' missionaries and the Twelve in Mark 6:7 is due to Mark himself and not to the historical Jesus.[2]

If one finds this difficult to accept we have a clear example of a similar mythmaking process occurring today. In 1997 there was a worldwide movement comprising about 4.5 million Catholics on six continents who signed a petition to persuade Pope John Paul II to declare Mary, the mother of Jesus, "co-redemptrix." If it had been approved, the primary role of Jesus Christ in Christian theology of redeeming humanity from its sins would be extended to his mother Mary. Other than the cult of Mary as the mother of the Lord, the primary rationale seems to be that if she had not consented to the immaculate conception (did she have a choice?) by the Holy Spirit, Jesus would not have appeared among mankind as its redeemer. But this petition raises all kind of problems. Although Mary's perpetual virginity was declared by the Council of Constantinople in 681 C.E., there are a number of references in the New Testament to Jesus' brothers and sisters,[3] his brother James becoming the leader of the Christian community in Jerusalem during the time of Paul. How could a virgin in perpetuity give birth to additional children, none of whom were gods? Then there is the credibility of the virgin birth itself, especially as Joseph, learning before their marriage that Mary was pregnant, intended to divorce her quietly (so as not to embarrass her) after their marriage. But before he could leave her he had a dream commanding him to accept the birth as a gift from God (Matt. 1:19–29). Moreover, Mary played a relatively minor role in Jesus' life, illustrated by the fact that when he was told that his mother and brothers were calling for him, he replied that his disciples were his mother and brothers.

> "Your mother and your brothers are outside asking for you." And he replied, 'Who are my mother and my brothers?' And looking around on those who sat around him, he said, 'Here are my mother and my brothers! Whoever does the will of God is my brother and sister, and mother.' " (Mark 3:32–35)

Furthermore, if Mary were declared a co-redemptrix along with Jesus, would that imply that instead of the trinity there should be a 'quadrennity'? Yet despite these doctrinal problems the mythmaking tendency within religions is so strong that even in this secular age there is a groundswell among Catholics to elevate Mary to a position that has no historical justification. This is a revealing example of how Christian theology comes to be formulated; it is not inerrantly revealed by God but decided by church councils composed of human beings who come to their decision based on special influence groups, their own religious beliefs, and their convictions as to what is best for church doctrine.

Returning to our discussion of the source of religious beliefs, like all our fundamental convictions that constitute our background framework for interpreting any experience, religious beliefs are acquired at an early age. In Sunday school or Catechism children are taught dramatized biblical stories illustrating Jesus' life and ethical teachings. They learn that Jesus was born in a manger, that he performed miracles, that he died for man's sins, and that he was raised from the dead, as will those who believe in him. They are taught the example of the "good Samaritan" who, when he passed a man who had been robbed and beaten until nearly dead, unlike others stopped and helped the man, treating his wounds and taking him to an inn where he could rest and eat, promising the innkeeper to pay for whatever further care was necessary. They learn ethical principles such as that one should turn the other cheek rather than return evil for evil; that one should love one's neighbor as oneself even when the neighbor is an enemy; that those who are poor in spirit, mournful, meek, downtrodden but righteous are preferred by God; that rich persons and lawyers (very prescient) will have as much trouble getting into heaven as a camel squeezing through the eye of a needle; and that evil persons will be punished in hell while the good or those saved by grace will be rewarded in heaven.

Children are taught to recite the Lord's prayer with its message that God the Father resides in heaven but his Will will be done on earth; that if we forgive trespasses against us the Heavenly Father will forgive our trespasses, and that we can call on him to save us from temptation and evil. They are assured that they should not be anxious about their lives because everything is in the hands of God and that he who asks in true faith shall be given. Endowing life with a transcendent support and meaning, these doctrines have attracted billions of people. The core of these teachings are summed up in the apostle's creed, repeated in church services:

> I believe in God the Father almighty,
>> Creator of heaven and earth.
> I believe in Jesus Christ, God's only Son, our Lord,
>> who was conceived by the Holy Spirit,
>> born of the Virgin Mary,
>> suffered under Pontius Pilate,
>> was crucified, died, and was buried;
>> he descended to the dead.
>> On the third day he rose again;
>> he ascended into heaven,
>> he is seated at the right hand of the Father,
>> and he will come again to judge the living and the dead.
> I believe in the Holy Spirit,
>> the holy Catholic Church,
>> [or one Catholic and Apostolic Church],
>> the communion of saints,
>> the forgiving of sins,
>> the resurrection of the body,
>> and the life everlasting Amen.[4]

Repeatedly recited and eventually memorized, it becomes internalized and integrated into a person's belief system shaping their conception of reality. As John Shelby Spong, a Bishop of the Episcopal Church, states, "Over and over, year in and year out, the liturgy of the church flowed over the conscious minds of the people until these events became part of the cultural self-identity, thus enabling these concepts to be kept ever fresh in our memories."[5] God as the "creator of heaven and earth" is reinforced by reading the account in Genesis where one learns that God not only created the universe, but also plants, living creatures, animals, and Adam and Eve.

One learns of the doctrine of original sin owing to Eve's and Adam's disobeying God by eating of the forbidden fruit from the tree of knowledge. Awakened to the difference between good and evil, shown in their becoming shamefully aware of their nakedness, they were expelled from the Garden of Eden or Paradise transmitting their sin to all humankind. Learned while one is young, impressionable, and before being taught any science or factual explanations of the origin of the universe and life, these storied accounts become deeply embedded in one's conceptual frame- work—so entrenched or softwired in one's brain that it is psychologically and/or intellectually impossible for billions of people to relinquish these beliefs (such as "creationism") when confronted with overwhelming refuting evidence. Yet had these same children been taught the correct scientific explanation from as early an age, they would have found it no less convincing and Genesis an amusing fantasy, the dependence of our beliefs upon our particular cultural upbringing proof of that. Muslims, Buddhists, and Hindus are not brought up to accept our religous heritage but their own, while most Chinese children now are taught to believe in a naturalistic worldview combining communism with Confucian ethics.

When affirming beliefs that are impossible to defend rationally in rela- tion to what we know about the world today (creation ex nihilo, the virgin birth of Jesus, miracles such as walking on water, exorcising demons, raising the dead to life, transforming water into wine the Christian will evoke faith. Both the Old and New Testaments offer many assurances that faith excels reason. When the woman with the menstrual hemorrhage was cured by touching the fringe of Jesus' garment, Jesus said, "Your faith has made you well" (Matt. 9:22). Similarly, when two men begged Jesus to cure them of their blindness he replied, "According to your faith be it done to you" (Matt. 9:29). In John 7:38 Jesus says, "He who believes in me, as the scripture has said, 'Out of his heart shall flow rivers of living water.' " In Romans 3:28 Paul states that "we hold that a man is justified by faith apart from the works of Law." But the most moving expression of the supremacy of faith occurs in Hebrews 11:1: "faith is the assurance of things hoped for, the conviction of things not seen." How many people have had their desire to believe reinforced by this beautiful assertion!

It is difficult to resist the lure of such an appealing statement. In fact, when their beliefs are challenged many Christians will answer with pride that "it is a matter of faith," as if this were a self-authenticating justifica- tion. Tertullian, a third-century lawyer and leading theologian of Carthage, is famous for having asserted with reference to Jesus' reincar- nation, "I believe because it is absurd," without realizing how self- refuting is such a statement. Among philosophers knowledge often is defined as "justified true belief." Even Tertullian must have held that his belief, however absurd, was in some sense justifiably true, otherwise why hold it? No sane person holds a belief solely on the grounds that it is absurd. Moreover, if absurd beliefs are accepted as true, how can anyone distinguish between what is true and false? All kinds of bizarre beliefs have been held on the basis of faith which in the religous context amounts to saying that "I will persist in believing despite any evidence or arguments to the contrary." Yet if one is at all sensible one cannot avoid asking *why* a particular belief should be held on faith, which leads back to the question of justification and truth.

Do Christians acknowledge the truth of Judaism, the Muslim religion, or Hinduism owing to some people believing in those religions on faith? We have had a recent example (1997) of how blind faith in a charismatic figure (Marshall Herff Applewhite, the leader of Heaven's Gate) can lead to tragic results. A similar example occurred in 1978 at Jonestown at the Peoples' Temple when more than 900 cult members died because the deranged Jim Jones decided it was time. A Christian will rightly reply that there are extremists or irrational individuals in every community, including science, and that one must consider the nature of the beliefs themselves, but this leads to more than faith as a justification — it calls for an evaluation of beliefs and one's faith in them on reasonable, not absurd or purely subjective, grounds.

Returning to the early indoctrination of religious beliefs, those stories learned as children are reinforced later in hymns, liturgies, homilies, and sermons. They are pictured in frescos, paintings, statues, and carvings on church walls, columns, and doors. Especially in Italy one sees marvelous artistic works from Giotto's frescos in the Arena Chapel in Padua depicting the immaculate conception of Saint Anne,[6] the mother of Mary, to those in Assisi representing the life of Saint Francis, to Michelangelo's scenes from the Bible in the Sistine Chapel in St. Peter's, along with his sublime Pietà. Stories, allegories, and moral precepts are taken arbitrarily from the four gospels with no mention of their divergences or inconsistencies, conveying the false impression that they agree in what they relate and thus are historically valid, since any discrepancies would raise doubts about which are true. Repeated in church, Christians are left unaware of the variations and disagreements among them. As John Crossan says regarding the discrepancies in the Gospels:

> If you read the four gospels . . . consecutively, from start to finish and one after another, you get a generally persuasive impression of unity, harmony, and agreement. But if you read them . . . comparatively, focusing on this or that unit and comparing it across two, three, or four versions, it is disagreement rather than agreement that strikes you most forcibly. And those divergences stem not from the random vagaries of memory and recall but from the coherent and consistent theologies of the individual texts. The gospels are, in other words, interpretations. Hence, of course, despite there being only one Jesus, there can be more than one gospel, more than one interpretation.[7]

But being *un*critical of one's beliefs or those of one's tradition is normal. Persons like Anaxagoras, Socrates, Copernicus, Luther, Galileo, Darwin, and Freud are rare. It has taken five centuries to develop the modern scientific attitude that to be worthy of acceptance beliefs must be tested under controlled conditions whenever possible, while those that cannot be tested should be held hypothetically until there is sufficient evidence, and if that is not forthcoming rejected. Thus the commonly heard argument that "one cannot either prove or disprove the existence of God, offered as if that were grounds for believing, is false. There is not an *independent* or separate proof of the nonexistence of something; the *lack* of evidence for its existence constitutes the refutation. Most nonscientific beliefs are not directly falsified but discarded because they have become obsolete: for example, belief in the pagan gods, heaven and hell, dragons and demons, fairies and evil spirits, angels and devils. Even when individuals adopt a critical attitude in their professional work they often are uncritical regarding their personal beliefs. This is especially true of religious convictions which become so embedded in one's network of beliefs, at such an early age, that they largely determine one's conception of reality. What does not fit into this framework of ideas is rejected; furthermore, being so cognitively entrenched they appear self-evident and acquire such an emotional aura, both consciously and unconsciously, that questioning them is quite disturbing, if not immoral. It also explains why forty percent of scientists hold religious beliefs, although only seven percent of the *leading* scientists (rated as members of the American Academy of Sciences) hold such beliefs. This seems to imply that the less talented scientists have more difficulty rejecting their religious beliefs.

It used to be said that scientists were atheists from Monday through Friday and theists on Saturday or Sunday (depending upon whether they were Jewish or Christian), although this no longer is true of the younger generation of eminent scientists. As Steven Weinberg, a Nobel Laureate in physics, states, "On the rare occasions when conversations over lunch or tea touch on matters of religion, the strongest reaction expressed by most of my fellow physicists is a mild surprise and amusement that anyone still takes all that seriously."[8] As for his own belief he says, "It would be wonderful to find in the laws of nature a plan prepared by a concerned creator in which human beings played some special role. I find sadness in doubting that we will."[9] This honesty is uncommon because individuals can be exceedingly critical and objective in certain areas of thought and yet very subjective or traditional in others, as was true of Copernicus, Descartes, and Einstein (who had no difficulty rejecting Newton's absolute frames of the universe, space and time, yet could not bring himself to accept the uncertainties, indeterminisms, and ontological fuzziness of quantum mechanics).

Not only is it *intellectually* unsettling to question fundamental beliefs, it also is *emotionally* disturbing because one *wants* to believe. As the Presocratic philosopher Heraclitus asserted, "It is hard to fight desire; what it wants it buys with the soul," or as Hume declared, "reason is the slave of the passions." Because a primary function of religious beliefs and rituals is to endow human existence with a transcendent meaning or purpose, however mysterious or incongruous, one is loath to give up these beliefs. One *wants* to believe that a divine being is guiding human destiny, although all the empirical evidence indicates that the universe has evolved from an initial state according to entirely natural laws. One *wants* to think that human beings were created in the image of God, rather than being an evolutionary branch from a common primate ancestor whose genetic code is nearly identical to the pygmy chimpanzee. One *wants* to accept an afterlife where one will rejoin one's loved ones in a kind of beatific state (whatever that is) or even be reincarnated in some other form, rather than just cease to exist. One *does not want* to accept all the seemingly senseless tragedies of life — terrible diseases, horrible accidents, horrendous natural disasters, brutal killings — as just the result of fortuitous or evil causes, but instead 'see' them as fulfilling a "higher purpose." Thus there are powerful psychic forces underlying the desire to believe, yet as strong as these emotional disincentives are to a critical analysis of religious beliefs, another factor has played an equally significant role.

RESISTANCE TO BIBLICAL CRITICISM

This other element is the fact that religious leaders themselves have discouraged and resisted critical appraisal of the scriptures for the reasons previously indicated. The early centuries of the history of Christianity were steeped in controversies regarding the correct interpretation of Jesus' mission, especially in relation to Old Testament prophesies and Jewish laws and rituals; which gospels or epistles should be included in the canon of the New Testament; what interpretation of the sacraments and rituals should be approved; whether the Christian community should be open to gentiles as well as Jews and under what conditions; what allegiance Christians should give to the Roman Emperors (who since Augustus demanded that they be treated as gods) along with the other Roman gods and laws; when the apocalypse and second coming would occur; how "the good news" of "the new age" should be spread; which moral principles (such as those concerning marriage and the treatment of widows and orphans) should be followed; and what roles should be assigned to the elders, deacons, and bishops in the newly formed

Christian communities and churches. Despite these controversies, the impression conveyed is that the answers to these questions were revealed from the beginning. Reading the epistles of Paul written in the fifties after the death of Jesus and thus earlier than the four gospels, as well as those named for Timothy, Titus, Philemon, James, Peter, John, and Jude, written in the latter part of the first century and early in the second, one finds all of these questions raised and addressed.

The average Christian, if the issue is raised at all, usually assumes that these questions have been uniformly answered in the gospels of Matthew, Mark, Luke, and John. But this fails to take into account the fact that the gospels were written after Paul's death in 63 C.E. between about 75 to 120, with Mark appearing first and John last. How were the accounts of Jesus' life and the activities of the apostles preserved from the time of his death to when the gospels were written beginning nearly a half century later? Neither Jesus nor the disciples left written records, the latter being simple fishermen while Jesus was illiterate. Acts 4:13 states that the apostles "Peter and John . . . were uneducated, common men." But Jesus' background and profession as a carpenter was just as common. As Crossan says, "He was an illiterate peasant, but with an oral brilliance that few of those trained in literate and scribal disciplines can ever attain."[10] The problem with the latter claim is that we really do not have much solid evidence of what Jesus actually said. Nevertheless, one might object, we have the testimony of the authors of the four gospels who, judging from the way they were written ("Jesus said . . . ," "Jesus went . . . ," "Jesus appeared . . . ," and so forth), must have been eye witnesses to what they recorded. The fact is, however, not only is it *not known* who wrote the gospels, it *is known* that they definitely were not written by the apostles they are attributed to, that they were not based on eye-witness accounts, and that we do not have their original scrolls. As the authors of *The Five Gospels* assert, "The stark truth is that the history of the Greek gospels, from their creation in the first century until the discovery of the first copies of them at the beginning of the third, remains largely unknown. . . ."[11] Rather than functioning as historical records, the gospels are based on an oral transmission during a forty-five-year period along with some indirect evidence that some of the "sayings" of Jesus were preserved. It is sometimes claimed that oral traditions testify to incredible feats of memory, but this is denied by Howard Clark Kee who certainly is not unsympathetic to the New Testament. He reports that in "a detailed study of oral transmission among peoples all over the world, it was determined that there is *not a single verifiable case* of verbatim memory for extensive oral utterance."[12]

Furthermore, with practically no written records at a time when at least seventy-five percent of the people were illiterate and the cultural atmosphere charged with miraculous acts, saturated with supernatural beings, and redolent with prophesies of a coming messiah and predictions of an apocalyptic end to the world, one can well ask how reliable an oral transmission would be within that credulous milieu after nearly half a century. As A. Weigall states in one of the most graphic descriptions of the ethos of those early centuries:

> The constricted Jesus of Christian theology does not belong to modern times. He is dated. He is the product of the early centuries C.E., when men believed in Olympus, and drenched its altars with blood. Magic plays about him like lightning. He walks upon the waters, ascended into the air, is obeyed by the tempests, turns water into wine, blasts the fig tree, multiplies loaves and fishes, raises the dead. All these marvels made him God incarnate to the thinkers of the First Century; all these marvels make him a conventional myth to those of the Twentieth.[13]

The incredible fact, however, is that nearly three-quarters of a century after this was written Jesus still is not regarded as a legendary figure by billions of people, but as a God. One wonders how long it will take before the realization of this will be accepted.

THE COMPOSITION OF THE BIBLE

It was not until the fourth century C.E. that a consensus developed as to which books of Hebrew scripture and which Christian gospels and epistles should be included in the Old and New Testaments comprising the Christian Bible. Like similar compilations, the Bible did not arise sui generis but had to be assembled. Although it is sometimes implied that God delivered to the early Christians the complete Bible as he had handed Moses the tables of laws on Mount Sinai, this of course is not true. The Emperor Constantine, following his conversion to Christianity in 312 C.E. and after declaring it the official religion of the Roman Empire in the Edict of Milan in 313, asked Eusebius to edit an authoritative edition of the Christian Bible as a basis for unifying Christian doctrine. But apparently it was Athenasuis's compilation and Jerome's translation into Latin that standardized the Christian Bible. According to Burton L. Mack:

> The main events along the way include a little assignment that Constantine gave to Eusebius, bishop of Caesarea, sometime around 325–330 C.E.; a festal letter of Athenasius of Alexandria in preparation for Easter in 367 C.E.; and Jerome's translation of the scriptures into Latin in 382 C.E. Constantine asked Eusebius to have fifty copies of "the sacred

scriptures" prepared by professional transcribers for the new churches he planned to build in Constantinople. Eusebius does not say, but scholars assume, that both the Jewish scriptures and early Christian writings were included.[14]

On the advice of his mother who was influential in his conversion to Christianity, the first church Constantine ordered built was the Church of the Holy Sepulchre in Jerusalem, presumably over the tomb of Jesus.

At the time there were considerable differences of opinion as to which of the numerous gospels and epistles then in circulation should be included in the authorized text. It is not known which of these Eusebius included in the Christian Bible or whether he also included the Old Testament in the copies he had made for Constantine. In contrast, the "Festal Letter of Athanasius . . . listed both the writings Christians should consider as the Old Testament, and those to be included in the New Testament."[15] While arranged differently than in the final standardized version, "Athanasius marks the point at which the writings listed for inclusion in the Christian Bible first solidified," [16] although various selections continued to be used and even today there is a difference between what is included in the Catholic and Protestant Bibles. But it was Jerome's translation of the Bible into Latin, both Old and New Testaments, at the request of the Roman Bishop Damasus who wanted a uniform version, that produced the Christian Bible. As Mack states, "the Latin translation he produced became the standard Bible for the Roman church and Western culture until the Protestant reformation in the sixteenth century."[17] Known as the Vulgate, it was translated into English also in the sixteenth century.

Following a history of uncertainty, confusion, and contention regarding the selection of the texts that would be the foundation of Christian doctrine, far more than Peter the Bible became the rock on which the Christian church was built. After Jerome's translation and the gradual emergence of the Catholic Church in the West as the citadel of the Christian faith, the Bible usually was considered the direct revelation of God (although the Catholic Church reserved the right of interpretation if there was a question of meaning). Both the New Testament containing the teachings of Jesus Christ and the Old Testament, including the archaic and mythical Pentateuch, were usually taught as if they were the inerrant word of God. Whenever contradictions or anomalies were found in the text, church authorities tried to find an allegorical interpretation, following the example of the Jewish scholar Philo Judaeus of Alexandria (30 B.C.E.–50 C.E.), a contemporary of Jesus.[18] An allegorical interpretation is introduced when the obvious sense of the text is so paradoxical or obscure that a literal interpretation is precluded, leading scribes to look for a hidden or deeper meaning. As some constraint had to be exercised as to which allegorical interpretations to accept, the Catholic Church appropriated this authority to itself.

Throughout the following fourteen centuries there was some critical exegesis of certain biblical passages and questioning of the authorship of texts, but by and large the Catholic Church repressed any external criticism once an authorized interpretation had been reached. Those who opposed the decisions of the church were faced with severe criticism and possible excommunication, meaning they were not to be among the select who received God's grace and gift of everlasting life. The terror of the Inquisition was established to insure conformity with Catholic doctrine by one means or another. Martin Luther (1485–1546) was excommunicated in large part for advocating that an individual had the right to a direct inspirational interpretation of the Bible and communication with God, who could forgive man's sins without the mediation of Catholic clergy. Giordano Bruno (1548–1600) suffered a harsher fate by being burned at the stake for his heresies. While Galileo in 1633 avoided excommunication and possible martyrdom by abjuring his support for the Copernican heliocentric universe, this was done under *threat* of imprisonment, torture, and excommunication (he was never imprisoned or tortured as is sometimes claimed; in the early period of his stay in Rome before the trial he lived in the apartment of the Medici Ambassador and later was moved, with his manservant, to chambers provided by the Inquisition).[19]

But perhaps what shielded the Bible from criticism more than anything else was the ahistorical outlook that prevailed before the nineteenth century. While anyone today teaching a document written in the past, whether Plato's *Timaeus*, Aristotle's *De Caelo*, Augustine's *Confessions*, Descartes' *Meditations*, Galileo's *Dialogue*, or Marx and Engel's *Communist Manifesto*, will invariably interpret it in relation to the intellectual or cultural background of the time, this historical perspective was largely absent until the nineteenth century. It was not until after the Copernican Revolution, Renaissance, Enlightenment, and Industrial Revolution, when a sense of scientific, artistic, technological, and economic *progress* developed, that one began to interpret cultural traditions and intellectual developments within their historical context when evaluating them.

While we are accustomed to referring to the "Golden Age of Greece," the "Imperial Splendors of Rome," the "Dark Ages of the Medieval Period," the "Intellectual and Cultural Reawakening of the Renaissance," the "Rationality of the Enlightenment," and the "Technological Advances" of the Industrial Revolution as stages of progression (or regression) in human history, this outlook is a recent development. Like the flat perspective in medieval paintings, previous scholars generally had a very foreshortened view of the panorama of history. Often people looked back to an earlier epoch as more glorious than their own, as later ages regarded the achievements of the classical Greco-Roman civilization as overshadowing theirs, and as the Israelites imagined a prehistoric state of paradise. From this perspective works like the Bible were not viewed as reflecting the limitations of the historical setting or cultural context, but as timelessly true. Yet many Christians, along with televangelists who never would accept the miraculous stories in the Bible if reported as occurring today, unconsciously adopt this foreshortened perspective. As Spong asserts, "in such a world as ours, virgin births, cosmic ascensions, physical resuscitations, and people who are capable of walking on water do not occur, and assertions that they do or that they have are less and less believable by anyone."[20] It is a unsettling fact of human nature, however, that events cast in the dim shadows of the past acquire a kind of surrealistic reality which the light of the present would quickly dispatch. In my opinion, this ahistorical view of religion is a major factor in its continued acceptance.

In the nineteenth century this distorted approach to church doctrine changed. Scholars began to examine the causes and underlying conditions that gave rise to the particular social, political, and cultural institutions of an era, asking how they were historically engendered. Rather than history being segmented into successive periods, with earlier ones often believed to overshadow later ones, the historical process took on a progressive dimension. Concepts, beliefs, values, and institutions that served a valid function in an earlier epoch were seen to be irrelevant and outmoded from the perspective of a later one. The notion of history as a mere sequence was replaced by a linear progression.

CRITICAL BIBLICAL SCHOLARSHIP OF THE OLD TESTAMENT

Once the concept of historical development was introduced, like all radical changes of perspective it opened the eyes of biblical scholars to the possibility of regarding the Old Testament as compilations of texts from various sources, the authors and origins of which are largely unknown — this also is true of the New Testament gospels. Traditionally, the Old Testament was inerrant because it was thought to be the direct revelation of Yahweh to the various authors of the books; once the scales fell from their eyes, biblical scholars realized that this could not be true. The first five books of the Old Testament, called the Pentateuch, could not have been authored by Moses, as commonly believed, because it was written over a millennium after Moses lived. The end of the Pentateuch describes Moses' death and the fact that his burial place is unknown, accounts which he himself could not have written. Similarly, historical evidence indicates that the books ascribed to Joshua, David, Solomon, and the prophets could not have been written by them either.

A comparative study of early myths that ascribe the origin of the universe to various gods revealed the influence on Genesis of the older *Enuma Elish* myth, along with the thematic similarity of the Garden of Eden story, the fall, the expulsion from paradise, and Noah's Ark to other ancient fables. The puzzling repetitions of stories and changes in style, the unexpected twists and breaks in the story line, and the paradoxical inconsistencies and factual discrepancies pointed to the arbitrary insertion of incongruent passages in the texts at different times by different authors. As described in chapter 2, based on the divergent but distinctively consistent passages using the terms 'Yahweh' and 'Elohim,' independent discussions of priestly concerns pertaining to the laws and rituals, as well as the uniquely different composition of Deuteronomy, scholars have ascribed the five books of the Pentateuch to four unique sources: Yahweh, designated "J"; Elohim, called "E"; a priestly version called "P"; and Deuteronomy, called "D."

Moreover, the belief that the world was created in six days six thousand years ago, that humankind descended initially from Adam and Eve or later from the descendants of Noah, that people lived to be hundreds of years old, that sticks could be turned into snakes, and that water could be changed into wine or flow from rocks was no longer credible given scientific developments in geology, anthropology, paleontology, biology, chemistry, and physics. As scholars examined the Old Testament more closely and more critically, it began to resemble other ancient myths, while the brutal conduct of Yahweh seemed to be modeled on that of the typical kings of the time. As generally portrayed in the Old Testament, Yahweh is not an admirable god, but instead acts fitfully out of jealousy and anger and behaves like a tyrant when destroying whole nations because of their disobedience. Ironically, he also is responsible for bringing the Israelites to disaster: the loss of their kingdoms, the destruction of Jerusalem and the Temple, and their eventual dispersion.

This critical appraisal is reinforced by the fact that although the Hebrew religion is usually described as monotheistic in contrast to the polytheism of pagan religions, in fact there are various passages in the Old Testament that portray Wisdom as a Consort of God. In Proverbs, for example, Wisdom is depicted as having been the first creation who then assisted God in the formation of the world:

> The Lord created me [Wisdom] at the beginning
> of his work, the first of his acts of old.
> Ages ago I was set up, at the first, before
> the beginning of the earth. . . .
> When he established the heavens, I was there. . . .
> When he marked out the foundations of the
> earth, then I was beside him, like a master workman;
> and I was daily his delight, rejoicing before him always,
> rejoicing in his inhabited world and
> delighting in the sons of men. (8:22–31)

As Howard Clark Kee states, "Wisdom in Proverbs, and especially in Ecclesiastics, is not merely proverbial lore, but is personified as a female consort of God who . . . is God's companion and co-worker in the process of creating the world."[21]

In addition Satan, as the personification of evil (personifications and reifications being characteristic of primitive thought[22]), is Yahweh's adversary in the struggle for humanity's (and Jesus') allegiance. As Kee says:

> By the fourth century [B.C.E.], and perhaps even earlier, Satan was seen
> to be the cosmic opponent of God and his purpose. The seeming mis-
> carriages of justice and the consequent miseries that befall God's people
> are blamed on Satan.[23]

Surprisingly, the Catholic Church still is requiring its members to hold this outmoded belief. For example, the Vatican has recently published an "updated exorcism ritual, the first to be issued by the Vatican since the early 17th century . . . published in Latin . . . in an 84-page leather bound volume."[24] Other than the elimination of some outlandish wording, apparently there is little change in the essential doctrine. Cardinal Jorge Arturo Medina Estevez, head of the Vatican's Congregation for Divine Worship and the Discipline of the Sacraments, spent ten years on the revision. According to him, Catholics are required to believe in the devil; he says that some doubt the existence of the devil as if it were a question of personal choice: " 'But it is not an opinion, something to take or leave as you please. It is part of Catholic faith and doctrine.' "[25] Enforcing these archaic doctrines which today are so unbelievable is producing considerable dissention within the Catholic congregation and causing many to leave the church. Some cloistered clergy may still believe these articles of faith, but not people who live in the real world. It is not that evil does not exist but that it adds nothing, as of old, to personify it.

THE HIGHER CRITICISM OF THE NEW TESTAMENT

Directing this same historical scrutiny to the New Testament produced similar results. When carefully examined, it is apparent that the gospels were *not* written by the authors assigned to them in the New Testament, and that practically nothing is known about who wrote them. Moreover, as indicated earlier, because they were written between about forty and seventy years after Jesus died, with none based on direct eyewitness testimony or on records left by his disciples, there is considerable disparity between what is actually *known* about the historical Jesus and the Jesus portrayed in the gospels. Even before the nineteenth century there had been attempts during the Enlightenment to separate the Jesus of history from the interpretative accounts of the gospels, the latter formulated essentially to portray Jesus as the Christ fulfilling the Old Testament prophesy that God would send a messiah (the Greek word for 'messiah' is '*Christos*') to redeem humanity's sins. This search for the historical Jesus was initiated by a German professor of the Enlightenment, Hermann Samuel Reimarus (1694–1768), who believed that a critical study of the New Testament would distinguish between what Jesus actually said and what the authors of the gospels attributed to him.[26]

But the person whose name is most closely associated with the quest for the genuine Jesus is the nineteenth-century scholar, David Friedrich Strauss, whose classic work, *Life of Jesus Critically Examined*, was first published in 1835. Attempting to distinguish the "mythical" embellishments in the gospels from the actual historical events, this 1,400-page volume of scholarly exegesis, rather than being admired for its scholarship, aroused considerable hostility which "cost him his first teaching post at the seminary at Tübingen" and "hounded him up to the time of his death in 1874."[27] Since then there have been many famous attempts to discover the actual Jesus: Albert Schweitzer's *The Quest for the Historical Jesus* (1906); the recent study by Burton L. Mack, *Who Wrote the New Testament?*, with the provocative subtitle, *The Making of the Christian Myth*; John Shelby's *Liberating the Gospels*; and John Dominic Crossan's *The Historical Jesus: The Life of a Mediterranean Jewish Peasant*.

But the work that probably has aroused the most interest and criticism recently is the study by the "Jesus Seminar" published under the title: *The Five Gospels: The Search for the Authentic Words of Jesus* (1993). The translation of the New Testament that it represents, called the "Scholars Version," was produced by an initial collaboration of thirty scholars in 1985 which eventually included more than two hundred fellows, who were free from any ecclesiastical or religious constraints. As stated in the preface:

It is the collective report of gospel scholars working closely together for six years on a common question: What did Jesus really say? The Fellows of the Jesus Seminar represent a wide array of Western religious traditions and academic institutions. They have been trained in the best universities in North America and Europe. Together and singly, they first of all inventoried all the surviving ancient texts for words attributed to Jesus. They then examined those words in the several ancient languages in which they have been preserved. They produced a translation of all the gospels, known as the Scholars Version. And, finally, they studied, debated, and voted on each of the more than 1,500 sayings of Jesus in the inventory. *The Five Gospels* is a color-coded report of the results of these deliberations. It answers the question "What did Jesus really say?" within a narrow range of historical probabilities.[28]

Their "answer" includes the unsettling conclusion: "Eighty-two percent of the words ascribed to Jesus in the gospels were not actually spoken by him."[29] While there can be sincere disagreements about the stylistic criteria the Fellows used in their selection of authentic Jesus sayings and the weight assigned to them, one would have expected that this dedicated scholarly achievement would have been applauded and well received, but that was not the case.

Critical scholarship is regularly under attack by conservative Christian groups. At least one Fellow of the Jesus Seminar lost his academic position as a result of his membership in the group. Others have been forced to withdraw as a consequence of institutional pressure. . . . Public attack on members of the Seminar is commonplace, coming especially from those who lack academic credentials.[30]

Yet as the historic example of Galileo illustrates, the truth of doctrines cannot be legislated by ecclesiastical authorities within the Christian churches. If less than twenty percent of the sayings of Jesus recorded in the gospels are actually by him, then no devotional sincerity, dogmatic adherence to traditional beliefs, or threatening criticisms will make it otherwise. Sooner or later the truth will prevail.

HOW RELIABLE ARE THE GOSPELS?

It should be evident from the previous discussion that those Christians who have internalized the worldview of the Bible normally have done so at an early age and without knowing the historical contingency of the biblical texts. Even those "born-again-Christians" who have converted in later life (some while completing prison terms), have done so believing that the Jesus Christ portrayed in the gospels is the authentic historical Jesus. Because it is not in the self-interest of church authorities to raise questions or doubts regarding "sacred scripture" or the teachings and liturgy of the churches based on it, there is a kind of unspoken conspiracy implying the absolute truth of the Bible. Nor is this altogether unfortunate considering the inspirational nature and moral teachings of much of the Bible that have proven so comforting, inspiring, and morally uplifting and reinforcing throughout the ages, as exemplified in the recently deceased Mother Teresa.

But when questions *are* raised how are they answered? Given the fact that the gospels, along with the epistles, are the nearly exclusive sources of information about Jesus and that they were not based on written testimonials or composed by individuals who actually had known Jesus, what were *their* sources and how reliable are they? We know from the epistles, especially those that Paul addressed to specific Christian brethren ("Corinthians," "Galatians," "Philippians," "Thessalonians," "Romans," and others) that Christian communities had been established in the Near East (the Levant), Asia Minor, Greece, Macedonia, and even Rome before the gospels appeared. Moreover, as the epistles were written within the first decades after the death of Jesus (who died at the early age of about thirty), there must have been individuals (Peter, James, John, and Barnabas, for example) visiting these communities who had associated with Jesus or talked with those who had. Thus a body of information accumulated, known as the "oral tradition," containing reports of the crucial events in Jesus' life and ministry. Unlike the disciples of Jesus who as simple fisherman were illiterate, but like Paul who was well educated in the Hellenistic tradition, there must have been Christian converts anxious to make a record of Jesus' history and sayings to be used in church services on the sabbath. As authors of the gospels presumably were from these communities, New Testament scholars infer that they were influenced by this oral tradition, along with whatever written accounts of Jesus' life and sayings might have existed when they wrote the gospels.

This must have been true especially of the author of Mark, the first gospel to appear and therefore the oldest. Although Matthew was placed before Mark when the New Testament was complied and was thought by scholars as late as the early decades of the twentieth century to have been the first gospel written, a later line by line comparison of the texts of the four gospels revealed extensive repetitions by Matthew and Luke of Mark, indicating its priority, while the portrait of Jesus and stylistic differences in John showed that it was written independently of the other three. Because of the "common view" of Jesus presented in Mark, Matthew, and Luke, they are called "synoptic gospels" in contrast to John. The evidence for the dependence of Matthew and Luke on Mark, along with their commonality, is summarized by the Jesus Seminar as follows:

1. Agreement between Matthew and Luke begins where Mark begins and ends where Mark ends.
2. Matthew reproduces about 90 percent of Mark, Luke about 50 percent. They often reproduce Mark in the same order. When they disagree either Matthew or Luke supports the sequence in Mark.
3. In segments the three have in common, verbal agreement averages about 50 percent.
4. In the triple tradition, Matthew and Mark often agree against Luke, and Luke and Mark often agree against Matthew, but Matthew and Luke only rarely agree against Mark.[31]

But what, then, are the sources of Mark and John and of those sections of Matthew and Luke that are not found in Mark? As indicated previously, by the time the gospels were written a consensus had emerged that Jesus was the *Christos* (messiah) predicted by the Old Testament prophets who was sent by God to perform miracles and destined to be the sacrificial lamb bringing "the good news" of the Kingdom of God. The textual variations in Matthew and Luke from Mark, along with the uniqueness of much of John, represent *different expressions* of this essential theme by their authors. Moreover, as Kee points out, their appropriation of the oral tradition did not produce *a verbatim repetition based on exact recall because any public oration of important historical events was expected to be a dramatically enhanced retelling of the episode.*[32] This was true as well when the accounts were being written, since this provided even greater opportunity for exaggeration, embellishment, and adaptation to the particular communal audience.

Yet the question of source influences is very complex. Among those passages in Matthew and Luke which show *no dependence* on Mark there are some of Jesus' sayings, consisting mainly of allegories and parables, that are so strikingly similar they suggest a common independent source. To account for this "a German scholar hypothesized that there once existed a source document, that he referred to as *Quelle*, which in German means 'source.' "[33] This common source is now referred to as the "Sayings Gospel Q." At first just a hypothetical reference source, the "Sayings Gospel Q" has now acquired the status of an actual document, although there are some scholars, such as Michael Goulder and Spong, who disagree. Because there is no existing manuscript of Q, scholars have had to infer its contents by comparing the parallel passages in Matthew and Luke. Burton L. Mack has written a book entitled *The Lost Gospel: The Book of Q and Christian Origins* (1993) and in a later book he describes the significance of Q as if it were known to exist.

Q will put us in touch with the first followers of Jesus. It is the earliest written record we have from the Jesus movement, and it is a precious text indeed. . . . It has enabled us to reconsider and revise the traditional picture of early Christian history by filling in the time from Jesus until just after the destruction of Jerusalem when the first narrative gospel, the Gospel of Mark was written.[34]

This assurance that the textual content of the four gospels can be supplemented and elucidated by the recovery of very early manuscripts has been abetted by the unexpected discovery during the nineteenth and twentieth centuries of a treasure trove of ancient papyri scrolls and an important codex (a precursor of books, a codex consists of the same sized sheets of manuscript tied together on one side). In 1844 the Codex Sinaiticus (named for the location where it was found), comprising New Testament scripts from early in the fourth century C.E., was found in St. Catherine's monastery in the Sinai peninsula. This was followed by the recovery later in the nineteenth century of a fourth-century copy of the Greek Bible that had been lost in the vaults of the Vatican library. Then in the twentieth century ancient papyri scrolls began to be uncovered in earthen jars buried in the sands of Egypt in places such as Oxyrhynchus.[35]

In the early 1930s another significant papyri discovery occurred dating from the first half of the third century C.E. named the Chester Beatty papyri for its purchaser. Then the extraordinary Nag Hammadi collection was unearthed in Egypt in 1945, consisting of a "fourth-century C.E. repository of Coptic Gospels," "Christian Gnostic texts," and "a complete copy of the Gospel of Thomas, lost to view for centuries, along with the text of the Sacred Book of James, and the Dialogue of the Savoir."[36] Then the extraordinary Dead Sea Scrolls, dating *from* the third century B.C.E., were found by a shepherd in the late 1940s, many from a large *scriptorium* or writing room in a remote cave in the rugged stone hills on the northwest shore of the Dead Sea. Here the Essenes, a Jewish sect which had rebelled against the Hashmonean control of the Temple after the latter's successful Maccabean revolt in 167 B.C.E., had taken refuge. When they were relentlessly pursued and killed, as part of the Roman campaign to destroy Jerusalem after 67 C.E., they left behind this treasure of scrolls in their caves.[37]

These remarkable ancient texts, some predating, some contemporaneous with, and others following the appearance of the four canonical Gospels, have enabled scholars to obtain a much clearer picture of the difference between the historical Jesus and the Christ of faith portrayed in the gospels. It is now generally agreed that the variations among the gospels — some so radical as to preclude their all being true — can be attributed to the fact that though the authors were using similar sources on Jesus' life and sayings, they were presenting their own creative interpretation according to their particular religious situation, unique inspirational talents and, according to Spong, the need to replace the liturgy of the synagogue with Christian liturgy for the new church services. As previously pointed out, although the average Christian assumes that the various stories they learn about Jesus from his birth to his death and resurrection are consistently presented in each of the gospels, a comparative reading soon dispels this illusion.

According to Bishop Spong the primary intent of the authors of the gospels was not to write an historically accurate account of the life and teachings of Jesus, but to relate Jesus' mission to the prominent events described in the Old Testament, so familiar to the Jews who composed the congregations of the early church, enabling them to be used as liturgy on the Christian sabbath the way the Pentateuch was used by the Jews on their sabbath. As Spong says, "sacred God experiences of the Jewish past were wrapped liturgically and homiletically around the God experiences found in Jesus of Nazareth."[38] This further illustrates the importance for an adequate understanding of the gospels of connecting them to the historical background in which they were written. Christians usually overlook that the apostles, evangelists, and authors of the gospels, along with the original converts, were Jewish and naturally interpreted what they learned about Jesus from their own scriptural background and liturgical heritage.

This would help to explain why there is so little historical authenticity to the gospels and why the major occurrences in the life of Jesus were interpreted so differently by the authors. Yet for Spong this does not revoke Christian belief.

> I do not today regard the details of the gospel tradition as possessing literal truth in any primary way. I do not believe that the Gospels offer us either reliable eyewitness memory or realistic objective history. I do believe that the Gospels are Jewish attempts to interpret in a Jewish way the life of a Jewish man in whom the transcendence of God was believed to have been experienced in a fresh and powerful encounter. I do believe that the God met in Jesus is real, and that by approaching the scriptures through a Jewish lens, saving reality can be illuminated and — even more important — can still be entered.[39]

So although Spong has frankly conceded that the gospels are not historically or literally true, he nonetheless maintains that they, along with the Old Testament, convey a "God encountering experience." But what is the justification for this conclusion? Can one uphold the validity of the god experience while denying the historical truth of the documents in which the experience is recounted? It would be analogous to asserting that while the play *Hamlet* is a fictional literary work, the character Hamlet is real. Although the *experience of encountering* Hamlet when reading or seeing the play is real, this does not negate the fact that Hamlet is a fictional character within the play. Similarly, God and Christ (not Jesus) are fictional characters within the Old and New Testaments, along with Adam and Eve, the talking serpent, Noah, Gabriel, and the Holy Spirit. Other than ethnocentrism, on what basis could Spong distinguish as authentic the "God encountering experience" in the Bible from that of other religions? Why is it so difficult for critical biblical scholars like Spong to take the next obvious step and acknowledge that this "saving reality" is an artifact of history? It is no harder than giving up belief in Santa Claus.

THE GOSPEL DISCREPANCIES

One would expect that the gospel first written, Mark, the one on which Matthew and Luke primarily relied for their own accounts, would present the least distorted portrayal of Jesus. But if this is so, then many of the cherished beliefs about Jesus presented in the other gospels will have to be discarded, their absence in Mark indicating they had been added by later authors with considerable variation. Regarding the birth of Jesus, in Mark we find no mention of the virgin birth nor of the delightful Christmas story charmingly narrated in Matthew and Luke whose celebration has so enriched the Christian world (if one overlooks the commercialization). After stating that "Jesus Christ, the Son of God," will appear to fulfill the prophesy of Isaiah, Mark begins with a description of John baptizing people in the river Jordan for the forgiveness of sins, preaching that " 'after me comes he who is mightier than I, the thong of whose sandals I am not worthy to stoop down and untie' " (Mark 1:7). Jesus is simply presented as coming from Nazareth to be baptized by John, after which "the heavens opened and the Spirit descended upon him like a dove, and a voice from heaven declared, 'Thou art my beloved Son; with thee I am well pleased' " (Mark 1:10–11). (It is amazing how the heavens could open and spirits descend in these ancient times.)

In contrast, Matthew (following custom I shall use the names given the gospels as if they were the actual authors, although the reader should remember that they are not) begins with a lengthy genealogy tracing Jesus' lineage back to the fathers of Judaism, Abraham and David, before describing his birth. The Gospel then goes on to say that when Joseph learned after they were betrothed that Mary was pregnant, he decided to divorce her quietly (so as not to embarrass her) after they were married, but that "an angel of the Lord" appeared to him in a dream, saying:

"Joseph . . . do not fear to take Mary [for] your wife, for that which is conceived in her is of the Holy Spirit; she will bear a son, and you shall call his name Jesus, for he will save his people from their sins." (Matt. 1:20–22)

Following the instructions of the dream Joseph married Mary and to preserve her purity did not have sexual relations with her until after Jesus was born (although it is curious as to how this could be known). Then the familiar story is told of Jesus being born in Bethlehem where the Wise Men, guided by a star in the East, went to worship him and present him with gifts. When they had departed an angel of the Lord again appeared to Joseph directing him to take his family to Egypt to escape the wrath of Herod who, having been told of the birth of "the king of the Jews," wanted him killed (the similarity of this story of Herod and Jesus to that of Pharaoh and the infant Moses has led some scholars to conclude it was borrowed from the earlier one). All of this was to fulfill the prophesies of Isaiah 7:14, Micah 5:2, and Jeremiah 31:15. Only then is John the Baptist introduced with a somewhat different account of his mission.

Turning to Luke we find still another version. Unlike Mark and Matthew, Luke begins with a statement addressed to an unknown Theophilus justifying his narrative, saying that he intended to write an "orderly account" for him about those recent occurrences "just as they were delivered to us by those who from the beginning were eyewitnesses [an indication that the author himself was not an eyewitness] and ministers of the word . . ." (Luke 1:2; brackets added). In contrast to Mark and Matthew, Luke describes how John the Baptist came to be born, again echoing the story of Abraham and Sarah giving birth to Isaac in their old age (for Spong these repetitions illustrate the influence of the Old Testament on the authors of the gospels). This story, too, begins with an aged couple, Zechariah and Elizabeth, who had no prospects of having children because "Elizabeth was barren, and both were advanced in years" (Luke 1:7). But similar to Abraham, when Zechariah (who was a priest) was in the temple burning incense an "angel of the Lord" spoke to him saying that his prayer had been answered, that "your wife Elizabeth will bear you a son, and you shall call his name John" (Luke 1:11–13). As Abraham, Zechariah protested that he and Elizabeth were too old to have children, but the angel replied that he was Gabriel sent by the Lord to bring him this good news.

During the sixth month of Elizabeth's pregnancy Gabriel again was sent on a mission by the Lord, this time to Mary in Nazareth, a virgin betrothed to Joseph. Gabriel declared, " 'Hail, O favored one, the Lord is with you!' " (Luke 1:28). Mary was confused by what this meant, so Gabriel explained that because "you have found favor with God . . . you will conceive in your womb and bear a son, and you shall call his name Jesus" (Luke 1:31). When Mary asks, " 'how can this be, since I have no husband?' " Gabriel answers, " 'The Holy Spirit will come upon you . . . therefore the child to be born will be called holy, the Son of God' " (Luke 1:35). Mary then decides to go "with haste" to Judah where she encounters Elizabeth who, on being greeted by Mary, felt the baby in her womb "leap with joy," which Elizabeth considered a sign that she had been greeted by "the mother of my Lord" (Luke 1:43–44). (How this could have been known later is a mystery.) Mary stayed with Elizabeth for three months and returned to her home after Elizabeth gave birth to John, later known as the baptizer. All of this makes for a charming story, but does it have any authenticity, especially since it does not occur in the other gospels?

When Caesar Augustus decreed that a census of the Roman empire be taken, Joseph took Mary, who was now in her last stage of pregnancy, to Bethlehem because they were of the lineage of the house of David connected with Bethlehem (this has been challenged by Crossan on the grounds that not only was there no worldwide census taken under Octavius Augustus, but also that the custom was to register in one's own residence, not at a distant one[40]). There then occurs those poignant lines that have became so endearing, lending to the Christmas season its special aura:

> And while they were there, the time came for her to be delivered. And she gave birth to her first-born son [implying that she would have other sons] and wrapped him in swaddling cloths, and laid him in a manger, because there was no place for them in the inn. (Luke 2:6–7)

(It is these swaddling clothes and vial of the Virgin's milk that Saint Louis, during his crusade, allegedly purchased and placed in Saint Chapel in Paris.) Unlike Matthew, in Luke it is shepherds rather than Wise Men who are told by the angel of God where to find the babe in the manger. The story ends with the familiar lines: " 'Glory to God in the highest, and on earth, peace among men with whom he is pleased' " (Luke 2:14).

As is generally true, John is very different from the other three Gospels. John does not mention Jesus' birth at all, but instead presents a Hellenistic interpretation of Jesus Christ as the Word or Light that was with God at the beginning of creation; this interpretation is completely absent from the other gospels. The Greek for 'word' is 'logos,' a concept that played a central role in the philosophies of Heraclitus and the Stoics. Thus the author of John gives this philosophical interpretation of Jesus:

> In the beginning was the Word, and the Word was with God, and the Word was God . . . [and] all things were made through him. . . . In him was life, and the life was the light of men. . . . The true light that enlightens

every man was coming into the world. He was in the world, and the world was made through him, yet the world knew him not. . . . And the Word became flesh and dwelt among us, full of grace and truth; we have beheld his glory, glory as of the only Son from the Father. (John 1:1–14)

What an astonishing difference among the gospel stories purporting to convey an actual account of the life of Jesus. There is no mention of the virgin birth of Jesus in either Mark or John, which is especially significant of Mark because it is considered the prior and most reliable account. Although both Matthew and Luke include the story of the virgin birth, they do so in different ways, just as they do different versions of Jesus' birth in Bethlehem. Only Luke contains the story of Jesus' birth in the manger and John the Baptist's birth by Zechariah and Elizabeth, while only the Gospel of John equates Jesus with the Word and the Light. Which version should one accept as true? Even fundamentalists or evangelists should realize that two radically different descriptions of an event, along with the complete omission of it in other versions, cannot all be true, if true at all.

Since both Matthew and Luke included large sections from Mark, why did they add their own versions and what was their source? These are not pointed out when the clergy quote the gospels, encouraging people to believe whatever stories they want regardless of their inconsistencies, reasonableness, or truth. Is it really believable that having learned that his betrothed "was found to be with child" Joseph had a dream in which "the angel of the Lord" revealed to him that the Holy Spirit was the cause of the conception? How reliable would such an account be after having been transmitted orally and transcribed nearly a century after it occurred? How did the Holy Spirit impregnate Mary and where did the other twenty-three chromosomes come from to constitute the complete genetic component of Jesus? It is disconcerting that, as obvious as they are, these questions normally are not raised. That people continue to believe such a fantastic story is not evidence of a divine gift of faith, but simply of a naive credulity.

What do we find when we examine other crucial events in Jesus' life? In those cases that do not involve supernatural interventions there often is considerable agreement, supporting the thesis that the other authors of the gospels borrowed from Mark or had access to another common source. Regarding Jesus' cleansing the temple, for instance, the accounts in Mark 11:15, Matthew 21:12, and Luke 19:45 are nearly identical, each reporting that he drove out those who were buying and selling and overturned the tables of the money changers, repeating his admonition: "Is it not written, 'My house shall be called a house of prayer for all the nations?' But you have made it a den of robbers" (Mark 11:17).

The greatest variation occurs as usual in John, which adds that it was oxen and sheep that were being sold in addition to pigeons, and that Jesus wove a whip of cords to drive everyone from the temple. The admonition of Jesus also is changed, addressing only those selling pigeons: " 'Take these things away; you shall not make my Father's house a house of trade' " (John 2:16). Moreover, it is in John alone that Jesus says, in reply to the Jews who ask for a sign, " 'destroy this temple, and in three days I will raise it up,' " which his disciples later interpreted (implausibly) as referring to Jesus' body and his resurrection after three days (John 2:19–22).

There usually is agreement, at least among the three synoptic gospels, regarding Jesus' miraculous cures: healing the leper, paralytic, hemorrhaging woman (the daughter of Jairus, one of the rulers of the synagogue), deaf mute, blind man, and demonics. As to the miracles, there is general consensus that Jesus calmed the stormy sea, walked on the sea water, and multiplied the loaves of bread and numbers of fish on two occasions (one to feed the multitude of five thousand and another to feed four thousand), but only John reports his turning water into fine wine at the marriage at Cana when Jesus' mother informed him that there was no more wine (2:1–11). Although there are several instances of Jesus raising someone from the dead, as when he brings to life a widow's only son (Luke 7:12–15), the most well-known instance, that of Lazarus, occurs only in John.

It is a peculiar story in many respects, initially because Jesus knew that Lazarus who was the brother of Mary and Martha whom he "loved," was very ill. Yet when the sisters asked his help in saving their brother, Jesus delayed two days in responding. By that time Lazarus had died and Jesus implies that he knew this would happen, but allowed it to occur so that his cure would be more dramatic and persuasive: "Jesus told them plainly, 'Lazarus is dead; and for your sake I am glad that I was not there, so that you may believe' " (John 11:14). By the time Jesus did arrive in Bethany, Lazarus, who had been dead for several days, had already been placed in a tomb within a cave. When Jesus asked to see him, even Martha demurred, saying, " 'Lord, by this time there will be an odor, for he has been dead four days' " (John 11:39). But lifting his eyes heavenward to call on the Lord, Jesus "cried with a loud voice, 'Lazarus, come out,' " whereupon the "dead man came out, his hands and feet bound with bandages, and his face wrapped with a cloth" (11:43). In terms of what we know today about the metabolism and physiology of the body as well as brain death, it would be impossible to restore a person to life after four days, which is probably why the occurrence is not mentioned in the synoptic gospels. But it is one of the most famous of Jesus' miracles. This is an excellent example (unless Lazarus was in a coma and his body preserved in the cold cave, which would obviate its being a miracle) of how a completely implausible occurrence has gained currency among Christians because it is told in the Bible.

Many of the most familiar sayings and actions of Jesus are reported only in one or two of the gospels. The famous Beatitudes occur in Matthew 5:3–12 and in an abbreviated form in Luke 6:20–22, while the Lord's Prayer is presented in both Matthew 6:9–13 and Luke 11:2–4. The crucial statement on which the Catholic Church bases its apostolic succession, "you are Peter, and on this rock [*Petros*] I will build my church," occurs only in Matthew 16:18. So does the story of Jesus paying the half-shekel tax for himself and Peter by directing Peter to "go to the sea and cast a hook, and take the first fish that comes up, and when you open its mouth you will find a shekel; take that and give it to them for me and for yourself" (Matt. 17:27). Although it is a marvelous tale, it is hardly credible. If one replies, "not for Jesus Christ the son of God," this again begs the question because the reason for believing that Jesus is divine is scripture, which hardly can be authenticated by claiming that Jesus is divine. No non-Christian would find the incredible stories in the Bible believable, any more than Christians normally believe in the divinity of Krishna or the Dalai Lama.

Luke also contains stories that do not appear in the other gospels, such as the well-known accounts of the good Samaritan (10:33–35) and the prodigal son (15:11–32). Furthermore, only Luke presents information about the early life of Jesus, such as the story of Jesus' parents, who went to Jerusalem for the Feast of the Passover and as they were returning home noticed that he was missing. Thinking that he must have accompanied relatives or friends they continued on their journey, but failing to find him they returned to Jerusalem, where they searched for him for three days. Jesus, who was only twelve years old at the time, finally was discovered in the temple "sitting among the teachers, listening to them and asking them questions," so "that all who heard him were amazed at his understanding and his answers" (2:46–47). When his parents scolded him saying that he had made them anxious, Jesus replied that he was in his proper house, the temple of God. One would think that such an important anecdote, testifying to Jesus' prodigality, would be repeated in the other synoptic gospels, but it is not.

Luke also contains the ambiguous reference to Jesus' paternity, stating that he began his ministry when he "was about thirty years of age, being the son (as was supposed) of Joseph . . ." (3:23). Mark describes those who knew his background as being amazed at his abilities, but dubious of his claim to be the son of God.

He . . . came to his own country, and . . . on the sabbath he began to teach
in the synagogue; and many who heard him were astonished, saying,
"Where did this man get all this? What is the wisdom given to him?
What mighty works are wrought by his hands! Is not this the carpenter,
the son of Mary and brother of James and Joses and Judas and Simon,
and are not his sisters here with us?" And they took offense at him
(Mark 6:1–3).

Aware of their misgivings, Jesus makes the oft quoted reply, " 'A prophet
is not without honor except in his own country, and among his own kin,
and in his own house' " (Mark 6:4). Because of this skepticism it is said
"he could do no mighty work there" (Mark 6:5).

In John, too, there is an expression of wonder at Jesus' wisdom, the
Jews asking, " 'How is it that this man has learning, when he has never
studied?' " (7:15). (This is a confirmation of the fact that Jesus was illiterate.) To this Jesus replies that he was not teaching on his own authority
but that of God. From this one can infer that Jesus must have been an
extremely gifted teacher, a charismatic, but one canalso appreciate why
his family (although his brother James became one of the important disciples in Jerusalem after his death) and others were dubious about his
claims to be the son of God, when they knew the actual circumstances of
his birth, family background, and education. Who among us would
accept his brother—or any other living person for that matter—as a god?
Strangely, it is the historical distance that somehow endows these events
with an aura of credibility they would never have if reported today!

There usually is general agreement regarding other major events in
Jesus' life, at least among the synoptic gospels, except for the description
of the tomb scene and Jesus' appearance during the resurrection, which
varies considerably. Mark and Matthew present the same account of the
Last Supper, including Jesus' blessing the bread and the wine and
offering it to the disciples, saying, " 'this is my body' " and " 'this is my
blood of the covenant, which is poured out for many' " (Mark 14: 22–24).
Luke presents an abbreviated account, referring to the bread as Jesus'
body but omitting the wine as his blood. Surprisingly, given the significance of this event in the synoptic gospels, it is not even mentioned in
John! The accounts of Peter's denial and Judas' betrayal are in general
agreement in the synoptic gospels, except that only Matthew reports that
Judas, having repented of his betrayal, returned the thirty pieces of silver
and then hanged himself (Matt. 27:3–5). The account in John as usual is
quite different, not mentioning either the thirty pieces of silver or that
Judas identified Jesus for the soldiers by kissing him.

As for Jesus being brought before the high priest, questioned by
Pilate, mocked by the soldiers, and finally crucified, there is considerable

agreement among the synoptic gospels, except that Luke has Jesus cry with a confident voice just before he died: " 'Father, into thy hands I commit my spirit!' " (Luke 25:40) In contrast, in both Mark (15:34) and Matthew (27:46), Jesus cries in despair, " 'My God my God, why has thou forsaken me?' " —a verbatim repetition of a statement that occurs in the Psalms.[41] The account in John is still different, with Jesus carrying his own cross to the place of the skull (called Golgotha in Hebrew), whereas in the synoptic gospels the soldiers ask Simon of Cyrene to carry the cross, and at the end Jesus simply says before dying, " 'It is finished.' " Given these discrepancies it is tempting to believe that where there is the most agreement, that account is more likely to be true, but to what extent *any* of these stories, if at all, portray what actually occurred is largely conjecture.

When we turn to Jesus' entombment and resurrection, we find so little agreement among the gospels that our suspicions seem confirmed that these incredible stories were added by the authors in their own manner to support Jesus' prediction that after three days he would rise. The account in Mark, presumably the most reliable, is the briefest. Mark says that after the sabbath Mary Magdalene, Mary the mother of Jesus, and Salome carried spices very early in the morning to the tomb to anoint Jesus' body. As they arrived they wondered who would roll away the heavy stone blocking the entrance to the tomb (which had been provided by Joseph of Arimathea). They were amazed to find the stone removed, and after entering the tomb they saw "a young man sitting on the right side dressed in a white robe" (Mark 16:5). Noticing that the women were startled, the young man said they should not be alarmed, that Jesus had risen, pointing to the empty place on which he had been laid, and that they should leave and tell "his disciples and Peter that he is going before you to Galilee; there you will see him, as he told you" (Mark 16:7).

But when they left, the three women were so astonished and frightened that they "said nothing to anyone." The account in Mark in my Revised Standard Version ends there, but is followed by several footnotes indicating that there are other versions. According to one footnote, after Jesus arose he first appeared to Mary Magdalene who went and told the others, but they did not believe her when she said she had seen him and that he was alive. A second footnote says "he appeared in another form" to two disciples (this also occurs in Luke), but they, too, were not believed when they told the others. A third footnote states that he appeared among the eleven disciples and when they were at table he rebuked them for their "unbelief and hardness of heart" in refusing to accept the testimony of Mary Magdalene and the two disciples. According to this last version, he then said to the eleven at table, " 'Go into all the world and preach the gospel to the whole creation. He who believes and is baptized will be saved; but he who does not believe will be condemned . . .' " (Mark 16: f.n. 15–16). This is one place where Jesus is quoted as having directed the apostles to spread the word to everyone, not just to the Jews, indicating that being saved depended only on being baptized and believing, not on fulfilling certain rituals such as circumcision.

The version in Matthew is quite different. Only two of the three women mentioned by Mark, Mary Magdalene and Mary the mother of Jesus, went to the tomb the day after the sabbath. When they arrived there was a great earthquake accompanied by "the angel of the Lord" descending from heaven and rolling back the stone at the entrance to the sepulchre, on which he then sat. As usually the case, anyone who has been in the presence of the Lord is described as radiant with "garments white as snow," an appearance so striking that the soldiers guarding the tomb "trembled and became like dead men" (Matt. 28:4). As in Mark, the women were told not to be afraid, that Jesus had risen, the angel pointing to the empty place where he had lain and directed them to "go quickly and tell his disciples that he has risen from the dead and . . . is going before you to Galilee; there you will see him" (Matt. 28:7).

So the two women left quickly, this time with "great joy" as well as fear, running to tell Jesus' disciples. But as they went they met Jesus himself, clasping his feet in reverence. Reassuring them, he said they should tell his disciples to go to Galilee where they would see him. When the women left to do as Jesus had directed, some of the guards from the tomb went into the city and informed the chief priests of what had happened. Alarmed that people would believe that Jesus had actually risen as had been predicted, the priests gave money to the guards to say, " 'His disciples came by night and stole him away while we were sleeping' " (Matt. 28:13). Accepting the bribe, the guards apparently convinced most of the Jews involved that this is what happened, but the eleven disciples (Judas the absent one) went to Galilee where "they saw him and worshipped him," although some among them were incredulous. To convince them, Jesus utters the words found only at the end of Matthew:

> "All authority in heaven and on earth has been given to me. Go there-
> fore and make disciples of all nations, baptizing them in the name of the
> Father and of the Son and of the Holy Spirit, teaching them to observe
> all that I have commanded you; and lo, I am with you always, to the
> close of the age." (Matt. 28:18–20)

Containing an explicit reference to the trinity, this quotation is especially important, although it occurs only in Matthew. As in Mark and Matthew, Luke relates that after Jesus had died a man named Joseph from Arimathia went to Pilate and asked for permission to take the body and bury it. The request was granted and he removed the body from the cross, "wrapped it in a linen shroud" and placed it in a rock-hewn tomb.[42] The women who had followed Jesus to Galilee, having seen the tomb and how the body was placed, prepared spices to anoint the body. Here the account in Luke begins to diverge from that of Mark and Matthew. When the women took the spices to the tomb at the dawn of the day following the sabbath, they found the stone rolled away and the body missing when they went inside. Perturbed by its absence, they noticed two men "in dazzling apparel" standing near them, before which they bowed. The men then said to them:

> "Why do you seek the living among the dead? Remember how he told you, while he was still in Galilee, that the Son of man must be delivered into the hands of sinful men, and be crucified, and on the third day arise." (Luke 24:5–7)

Leaving the tomb the group of women, including Mary Magdalene, Joanna, and Mary the mother of Jesus, went to the apostles to tell them what they had seen but were not believed. Then a curious episode occurs. Two of the disciples were walking to Emmaus, a village outside of Jerusalem, recounting what the women had told them, when Jesus joined them but for some reason was unrecognized. When Jesus inquired of the two men what they were discussing, they asked him, " '[Are you] the only visitor to Jerusalem who does not know the things that have happened there in these days?' " (Luke 24:18). Apparently feigning ignorance, he asks, " 'What things?' " So the two disciples recount the recent events concerning the prophet Jesus, including the women's discovery of the two angels in the tomb and the missing body, confirmed later by several apostles. Even though he rebuked them as "foolish men" reluctant to believe the prophets, recounting to them the scripture since the time of Moses, including the fact that Christ would suffer before entering into his glory, still they did not recognize him! It was only after he accepted their invitation to stay and share dinner with them, while he was blessing the bread as they ate, that "their eyes were opened and they recognized him," but then "he vanished out of their sight" (Luke 24: 31).

The following day the two disciples returned to Jerusalem joining the others who reported: "The Lord has risen indeed, and has appeared to Simon" (Luke 24: 34). Simon is the other name of Peter; therefore, the fact that Jesus appeared to Peter before any other disciple contributed to the tradition which recognized Peter as "the first of the apostles" from whom the apostolic succession of the Catholic Church is derived. As Elaine Pagels says, for nearly 2,000 years, orthodox Christians have accepted the view that the apostles alone held definitive religious authority, and that their only legitimate heirs are priests and bishops, who trace their ordination back to the same apostolic succession. Even today the pope traces his—and the primacy he claims over the rest—to Peter himself, "first of the apostles," since he was "first witness of the resurrection" [according to the Gospel Luke].[43]

The two disciples then described what had happened to them the previous day and how Jesus had become known to them at the breaking and blessing of the bread. At that very moment Jesus reappeared among them, causing them to become startled and frightened because they "supposed they saw a spirit." Aware of their consternation, to reassure them he pointed to the wounds on his hands and feet (due to his having been nailed on the cross), and asked for something to eat as a sign of his bodily presence. This ambivalence as to whether Jesus appeared in his resurrection as a spirit (or as one version in Mark states, in "another form") or as having an actual physical body has stirred much theological discussion. The Gnostics defended Jesus' spiritual presence but the official Christian position affirms his actual bodily resurrection and ascension into heaven. Again according to Pagels:

> Gnostic Christians interpret resurrection in various ways. Some say the person who experiences the resurrection does not meet Jesus raised physically back to life; rather, he encounters Christ on a spiritual level. This may occur in dreams, in ecstatic trance, in visions, or in moments of spiritual illumination. But the orthodox condemn all such interpretations; Tertullian [c.150–c.230] declares that anyone who denies the resurrection *of the flesh* is a heretic, not a Christian.[44]

Tertullian's view represents the doctrinal position of Christianity today, although it is difficult to imagine where all those resurrected bodies are now located and what they are doing.

But the fact that one version of Mark claims that Jesus arose in "another form," while Luke reports that when he joined the two disciples on their walk to Emmaus they did not recognize him even though they were walking and talking together, and that he later disappeared and then reappeared in a somewhat ghostly fashion, raises serious questions regarding the orthodox interpretation. Considering the crucial role that Jesus' resurrection has played in Christianity, promising an everlasting life for all those who believe in him and its uniqueness among most religions, the authenticity of these accounts is extremely important. The significant point, of course, is that none of the authors of the gospels, whoever they were, was witness to the events following Jesus' alleged resurrection and that the accounts they give are quite discrepant at crucial points: the opening of the tomb, who was seen at the tomb, where and to whom Jesus appeared, and how long he appeared.

Luke concludes with Jesus declaring to the eleven apostles " 'that everything written aboaut me in the law of Moses and the prophets and the psalms must be fulfillled' " (Luke 45), affirming his messianic role. Stating that "Christ should suffer and on the third day rise from the dead" and that "repentance and forgiveness of sins should be preached in his name to all nations" (Luke 24:47), Luke confirms that Jesus' mission would not be restricted to an enclave of Jews, but would be spread abroad among the gentiles. Jesus then led them to Bethany, blessed them and departed from them, presumably rising into heaven.

As expected, the account in John varies considerably from the synoptic gospels. According to John, Joseph of Arimathea was not the only one who took the body of Jesus and placed it in the tomb since he was aided by Nicodemus who brought with him "a mixture of myrrh and aloes, about a hundred pounds' weight" (John 19:39). After Jesus had been anointed with the spices, his body was wrapped in "linen cloths" and placed in a new tomb in a garden near the crucifixion. Then on the day after the sabbath only Mary Magdalene is said to have gone to the tomb while it was still dark, found the stone removed, and without entering ran to Peter "and the other disciple, the one whom Jesus loved" (John 20:2), telling them that the Lord had been removed from the tomb but that she did not know where he had been taken.

Before continuing the tomb account, some mention should be made of the strange reference to the disciple "whom Jesus loved." What does it signify? Although the phrase only occurs in John, it does so in four places. The first reference takes place at the last supper when Jesus says:

> "Truly, truly, I say to you, one of you will betray me." The disciples looked at one another, uncertain of whom he spoke. One of his disciples, *whom Jesus loved*, was lying close to the breast of Jesus; so Simon Peter beckoned to him and said, "Tell us who it is of whom he speaks." So lying thus, close to the breast of Jesus, he said to him, "Lord, who is it?" (John 13:21–25; emphasis added)

It is obvious from the context that this disciple, whose name is not mentioned, is considered to have a special relation with Jesus. Peter acknowledges as much when he asks the disciple "who will betray Jesus?" implying that he believed the beloved disciple had Jesus' confidence more than the rest of them. Yet he, too, did not know who the betrayer would be, so Jesus answers by saying it is " 'he to whom I shall give this morsel when I have dipped it' " (John 13:26), passing the morsel to Judas, the son of Simon Iscariot. But while Jesus knew that "Satan entered into him," the other disciples did not know what Judas's betrayal portended. As indicated above, the second reference occurs when Mary Magdalene leaves the empty tomb running to Peter who is said to be with "the beloved disciple."

The third instance takes place about ten days later when Jesus revealed who he was by the Sea of Tiberias, the morning after a number of the disciples had accompanied Peter on a nightly fishing trip. Having caught nothing by daybreak, they returned to an area of the beach where Jesus was standing, but they did not recognize him (again a curious lapse of recognition considering how long they had been together). When he learned they had returned empty-handed, he instructed them as their boat was still a ways from the shore, to cast their net on the right side of the boat whereupon they filled the net to overflowing. It was then that the disciple whom Jesus loved, apparently being the only one to recognize Jesus, said to Peter, " 'It is the Lord!' " (John 21:7).

The last reference, even more perplexing, occurs near the end of the gospel when Peter, walking with Jesus, turns to find following them "the disciple whom Jesus loved, who had lain close to his breast at the supper . . .' " (John 21:20). Peter then asked Jesus, " 'Lord, what about this man?' " to which Jesus gives the enigmatic response: " 'If it is my will that he remain until I come, what is that to you?' " (John 21:22). The word then spread that this disciple was not to die, yet this is not what Jesus had said. Finally it is added, " 'This is the disciple who is bearing witness to these things, and who has written these things; and we know that his testimony is true' " (John 21:24).

What is one to make of this? Why is this unnamed disciple referred to as "the one whom Jesus loved," whose special relation to Jesus allowed him to lie close to his breast at the last supper? This is a very sensitive issue, but in candor must be addressed. What kind of affection was involved? (It would be really ironic considering the Catholic Church's position and that of the religious right on homosexuality, if Jesus had been homosexual.) But why should one of the disciples be singled out as being especially loved by Jesus? Is the fact that it is not mentioned in the other gospels due to its embarrassing implications, or is it just another example of a fabricated insertion? But there would be no reason for the author of John to include these assertions if he did not think there was some basis, since they do not serve any religious purpose or add to our understanding of Jesus' last days. As is usually the case, there is no answer to this kind of question because the evidence is lacking for any justifiable conclusion.

However, if Jesus were a homosexual this could explain his alienation from his family because homosexuality was not condoned by the Jewish community. In the Gospel of Thomas (55) Jesus' hostility to his family is especially evident: " 'Whoever does not hate father and mother cannot be a follower of me, and whoever does not hate brothers and sisters . . . will not be worthy of me.' "[45] If he had been estranged from his family because of his homosexuality, then this would explain his evident hostility. The explanation usually given is that as the son of God Jesus identified with his heavenly Father whose angelic hosts would have been his natural siblings, but the previous conjecture is simpler and more plausible.

Returning to the account of Jesus' resurrection in John, after Mary Magdalene had informed Peter and the beloved disciple that Jesus had been removed from the tomb, the men ran to the tomb where they discovered the linen cloth and napkin that had been placed on his head (allegedly purchased by Saint Louis), but no body. They then left while Mary Magdalene, who had also returned to the tomb weeping, "stooped to look into the tomb" and saw two angels in white, sitting where the body of Jesus had lain, one at the head and one at the feet. They asked her, " 'Woman, why are you weeping?' " (John 20: 12–13). She answered that it was because her Lord had been taken away and she did not know where. Having said this, she turned around and suddenly faced Jesus but did not recognize him (again that she and the disciples did not recognize Jesus is puzzling considering the time they had spent with him). Jesus, too, demanded why she was weeping and she, "supposing him to be the gardener," asked that, if he had taken Jesus away, to tell her so that she could care for his body. Addressing her as "Mary," she then recognized him but when she attempted to embrace him he said, " 'Do not hold me, for I have not yet ascended to the Father; but go to my brethren and say to them, I am ascending to my Father and your Father, to my God and your God' " (John 20:17). Mary left to tell the disciples what she had seen and been told.

That evening Jesus appeared among the disciples saying, " 'peace be with you' " and showed them his wounds. But Thomas, one of the disciples who was not present when the others told him they had seen Jesus, refused to believe them saying, " 'Unless I see in his hands the print of the nails, and place my finger in the mark of the nails, and place my hand in his side, I will not believe' " (John 20:25). However, eight days later when Jesus again appeared to the disciples, Thomas was among them and when invited by Jesus to examine his wounds, he no longer doubted, declaring, " 'My Lord and my God!' " (John 20:28). But Jesus was not pleased by the fact that Thomas required empirical evidence to believe, saying, " 'Have you believed because you have seen me? Blessed are those that have not seen and yet believe' " (John 20:29). This is a dramatic instance of Christians being exhorted to place faith above objective evidence, however bizarre the belief—an example cited by evangelical preachers to belittle and dismiss reasonable objections to incredible Christian doctrines.

Jesus then appeared to the disciples a third time (as described above in connection with the beloved disciple) when they returned empty-handed from their all-night fishing trip. Having enabled them to fill their net, Jesus invited them to have breakfast of bread and fish with him. Although they now had recognized him, none dared ask, " 'who are you?' " (John 21:12) meaning, I suppose, his status as the risen Christ. He then asked Peter three times if he loved him and when Peter replied each time that he did, Jesus in effect asked him to care for his flock when he was gone. The gospel ends with Peter asking what should be done with the disciple following them who had been Jesus' beloved.

It should be apparent that the purpose of comparing some of the crucial episodes in the life of Jesus, as presented in the various gospels, is to show how often they diverge in terms of narrations, additions, and omissions. While there is also agreement due to their using to some extent common sources (the main one being Mark and the Q Gospel if it exists), there are glaring discrepancies. Because each of the gospels is written in such a way as to convey the impression that the narrated episodes in the life of Jesus were directly observed by the author, and thus must be historically accurate, Christians are usually left unaware of these differences, especially as they are used indiscriminately in liturgical and homiletic worship. Crucial doctrines, such as the annunciation and Joseph's reaction, the manger story, the tomb scene, and the resurrection, are so divergently portrayed as to have little authenticity when examined critically. As Spong says regarding the various stories in the gospels:

> So vivid are these details, so clear are the pictures they paint, that there remains a general consensus in both church and society that these stories surely were literally created from vivid eyewitness recollections. The assumption is made, without much internal debate, that what we read here are literal and historic facts. Indeed, to think otherwise for most church people is almost inconceivable. *Yet that easy leap from familiar data to historic accuracy has been challenged increasingly in the last century, not by critics of the christian faith who have abandoned organized religion in droves, but rather by the world of New Testament scholarship.*[46]

This certainly undermines the fundamentalists' claim that the New Testament scripture is inerrant or infallible because it is the revealed word of God. How is one to decide which of the divergent accounts is true, or if any are? If one replies that we can appeal directly to God, how do we know that it is God who is answering and not some wish fulfilling fantasy? For most people it really does not matter, but for those who are seeking the truth, it does.

NOTES

1. As the authors of a recent critical translation of the New Testament Gospels state: "To be a *critical* scholar means to make empirical, factual evidence—evidence open to confirmation by independent, neutral, observers—the controlling factor in historical judgments. Noncritical scholars are those who put dogmatic considerations first and insist that the factual evidence confirm theological premises." Robert W. Funk, Roy W. Hoover, and the Jesus Seminar, *The Five Gospels: The Search for the Authentic Words of Jesus* (New York: Macmillan Publishing Co., 1993), p. 34. In other words, *critical* scholars adopt the same canons of inquiry used in historical research and in science generally. Traditional Christian scholars will argue that this objective critical approach is unsuitable for understanding the Bible because it consists of sacred scripture which must be considered infallible because it was revealed by God. However, the transparent circularity of this argument often has been pointed out; the evidence for the existence of the Hebraic-Christian God is derived from the Bible, whose truth in turn is guaranteed by the existence of God.

2. John Dominic Crossan, *Jesus: A Revolutionary Biography* (New York: HarperCollins, 1994), pp. 108–109.

3. Referring to Jesus, Mark 6:3 states: "Is not this the carpenter, the son of Mary and brother of James and Joses and Judas and Simon, and are not his sisters here with us?"

4. There are many versions of the apostle's creed. I have selected a brief one. The statement in brackets has been added because it is said in Protestant churches in place of the previous statement.

5. John Shelby Spong, *Liberating the Gospels* (New York: HarperCollins Publishers, 1996), p. 4.

6. The Immaculate Conception of Mary by Saint Anne, her mother, to exempt Mary's soul from original sin sometimes is confused with the virgin birth of Jesus by Mary due to the intercession of the angel Gabriel. But the latter is not designated an "immaculate conception," but a "virgin birth."

7. Crossan, p. x.

8. Steven Weinberg, *Dreams of a Final Theory* (New York: Vintage Books, 1992), p. 256.

9. Ibid.

10. Crossan, p. 58. This, however, must be qualified because the authors of *The Five Gospels* have concluded, based on meticulous analysis, that only eighteen percent of the statements attributed to Jesus in the Gospels are authentic.

11. Robert W. Funk, Roy W. Hoover, and the Jesus Seminar, p. 9.

12. Howard Clark Kee, *Understanding the New Testament*, 5th ed. (Englewood Cliffs N.J.: Prentice Hall, 1993), p. 83. Emphasis added. Kee cites the study by

H. M. and N. K. Chadwick, *The Growth of Literature*, 3 vols. (Cambridge: Cambridge University Press, 1932–1940).

13. A. Weigall, *The Paganism in our Christianity* (New York, 1928), pp. 18–19. Quoted from Frederick B. Arts, *The Mind of the Middle Ages: A.D. 200–1500* (New York: Alfred A. Knopf, 1962), p. 459n. 9.

14. Burton L. Mack, *Who Wrote the New Testament?* (New York: HarperSanFrancisco, 1995), pp. 287–88. In addition to being the bishop of Caesarea and councilor to Constantine, Eusebius was a church historian having written the outstanding *Ecclesiastical History*. This book is one of the most reliable (which is not to say that it is completely accurate) sources of information about the first four centuries of the history of Christianity, including the activities and fates of the evangelists, the sources of and compostion of the gospels, and the siege and destruction of Jerusalem and the Temple from 67 to 70 C.E. The information about Eusebuis and Athenasius is contained in Kee, the index.

15. Ibid., p. 287.

16. Ibid.

17. Ibid., p. 290.

18. Kee gives this account of Philo. "Perhaps the most prolific of the eclectic philosophers of the first century C.E. was a Jew named Philo. Born into a prominant family among the nearly third of a million Jews of Alexandria, Philo distinguished himself in public affairs as leader of an embassy in the court of the Emperor Gaius Caligula (37–41 C.E.) to protest absuses suffered by the Jewish community in Egypt. He stood out as well in intellectual circles as the first thinker to join together in thoroughging fashion rational philosophy and the revealed religion of the Jews." Kee, p. 27.

19. Cf. Richard H. Schlagel, *From Myth to Modern Mind: A Study of the Origins and Growth of Scientific Thought*, vol. 2, *Copernicus through Quantum Mechanics* (New York: Peter Lang, 1996), pp. 162–69.

20. Spong, p. 325.

21. Kee, p. 48.

22. Cf. Richard H. Schlagel, *From Myth to Modern Mind: A Study of the Origins and Growth of Scientific Thought*, vol. 1, *Theogony through Ptolemy* (New York: Peter Lang, 1995), p. 97.

23. Kee, p. 46.

24. Sarah Delaney, "Vatican's Updated Exorcism Rules Differ Little from those of 1614," *The Washington Post*, 27 January 1999, p. A22.

25. Ibid.

26. Cf. Funk, Hoover, and The Jesus Seminar, p. 2. This research by Profesor Reimarus is being pursued today by the Jesus Seminar.

27. Ibid., p. 3.

28. Ibid., p. ix.

29. Ibid., p. 5.

30. Ibid., p. 35.

31. Ibid., pp. 10–11.

32. Cf. Kee, pp. 83–84.

33. Funk, Hoover, and The Jesus Seminar, p. 12.

34. Burton L. Mack, p. 47.

35. This information is contained in Funk, Hoover, and The Jesus Seminar, pp. 8–9.

36. Ibid., p. 9.

37. Kee, pp. 62–65.

38. Spong, p. 326. In developing this thesis Spong was influenced by the writings of Michael D. Goulder, such as *The Evangelist's Calendar – A Lectionary Explanation of the Development of Scripture* (London: SPCK, 1978). According to Spong, p. 92, Goulder's thesis is that "at least the synoptic Gospels were developed against the background of a Jewish liturgical year rather than as biography, history, or any other kind of literary writing process."

39. Ibid., p. 20.

40. Cf. Crossan, p. 20.

41. This statement, "My God, My God why has thou forsaken me?" occurs in Psalm 22:1. It is an especially significant example, emphasized by Spong, of how much the authors of the gospels borrowed from the Old Testament. Mark took this verbatim from the Psalms and Matthew took it from Mark. Neither Luke nor John repeat it, perhaps because it indicates that Jesus died in a state of despair, believing that he had been abandoned by God.

42. The story of the "lost shroud of Turin" is a fascinating one. Claiming that the linen shroud found in Turin carried the imprint of a dead body that could have been that of Jesus, it was believed by many christians that it was the orignal shroud. But carbon dating of the linen proved that it was of much later origin, from the thirteenth or fourteenth centuries, although this is contested by those who would like to believe it is authentic.

43. Elaine Pagels, *The Gnostic Gospels* (New York: Vintage Books, [1979[1989), p. 11.

44. Ibid., p. 5.

45. Quoted from Crossan, p. 59.

46. Sprong, p. 235. Emphasis added.

THE GOSPEL OF PAUL AND SPREAD OF CHRISTIANITY

The four gospels discussed in the previous chapter purported to relate, according to their particular versions, the life and mission of Jesus ending either with his crucifixion or his resurrection. For an understanding of how the gospel ("good news") after Jesus' death was spread by the apostles ("sent men"), we have to rely mainly on the Acts of the Apostles and on the Epistles, particularly those letters written by Paul which are considered the most authentic. But it is the Book of Acts, especially, believed to have been written by the same author as the Gospel of Luke which, according to Kee, "has given us nearly all the information we have about the historical beginnings of the church . . . [and] some additional tradition about Paul which we could not infer from Paul's letters. . . ."[1]

In fact, Luke's detailed recounting in Acts of Paul's final journey by ship from Caesaria to Rome, particularly the gripping description of the shipwreck on the island of Malta (Acts 27:1–26), and the fact that Luke's narrative changes from the third person plural "they" to the first-person plural "we," convinced some scholars that such a dramatically vivid and detailed account could be written only by someone who actually had accompanied Paul. However, because Paul does not describe this journey in his letters, and given the obvious discrepancies between the accounts of Paul presented in the Acts and those in the Epistles, Kee denies that whoever wrote the Acts was present during the events, attributing the strong sense of vividness to the author's literary skill.

Although it is possible that Luke had access to traditions or even to sources deriving from Paul, the sense of immediacy arises from Luke's literary achievement. And whatever his sources may have been, he has shaped and adapted them with great skill to serve his particular aims.[2]

If true, the author of Luke certainly was an extraordinarily gifted narrator, although this was not unusual for the time.

THE ACTS OF THE APOSTLES

While the Acts is important as the source of information about the activities of the evangelists following Jesus' death, such as Peter, Stephen, Barnabas, Timothy, Philip, John, James (the brother of Jesus), and Silas, the focus is mainly on Paul, his conversion and his extended travels to bring the "good news" of the redemption to "all the nations." The Acts begins with a reference to the "first book" of the author, presumably the Gospel of Luke, but while that Gospel ended with Jesus appearing after his resurrection only for a day or two, in the Acts he appeared "to them during forty days" at the end of which, "as they were looking on, he was lifted up, and a cloud took him out of their sight . . . into heaven. . . ." (Acts 1:3–10)[3] A dramatic image, it has been the subject of many Renaissance paintings but is suitable more for artistic imagination than historical fact.

At the suggestion of Peter, the first act of the apostles was to select a replacement for Judas the betrayer, choosing Matthias (1:26). Then on the day of the Pentecost, the seventh Sunday after Jesus had risen, the Holy Spirit descended on the apostles, endowing them with the capacity to speak in as many tongues as there were native languages among the community of Jews who had come to Jerusalem from many nations. When the other Jews heard the disciples speaking in this manner, some were astounded and some were incredulous, the latter concluding that the apostles must have been intoxicated because many of the languages they spoke sounded like gibberish. In protest Peter said, "these men are not drunk, as you suppose," for they fulfill the prophesy of Joel that God, when his Spirit descends upon us "will show wonders in the heavens above and signs on the earth beneath . . ." (2:15–19). So as Jesus had foretold, "many wonders and signs were done through the apostles" (2:43) when the Holy Spirit entered them, for they were able to perform miracles and cure people in his name.

For example, when Peter and John later were going to the temple they met a forty-year-old man who had been lame from birth asking for alms. Replying that they had no silver or gold, Peter directed the man to look upon them, whereupon his "feet and ankles were made strong" so that he was able to walk (3:6–7). This miraculous act indicates that at this time Peter was the most prominent of the apostles. As a further example of their spiritual powers, when a husband and wife named Anani and Sapphira sold a piece of their property to give to the brethren, but with-held a portion of it without informing Peter, he divined their deception, telling them they had "lied to God," following which they each dropped dead at different times. When word of these wonders and signs spread, the people brought their sick to be healed with the number of converts growing from 120 when Jesus died (1:15) to "multitudes both of men and women" (5:14).

Unfortunately, this success aroused jealousy and resentment in the high priest of the Sadducees who had Peter and John arrested, only to be surreptitiously released from the prison at night by "an angel of the Lord." However, things did not fare so well with Stephen initially given the task of serving food to the widows, but who was so "full of grace and power [that he] did great wonders and signs among the people" pro-ducing additional antagonism (6:8). When some Jews from the syna-gogue engaged him in disputation, his "wisdom and spirit" were found to be superior to theirs arousing even more hostility. Confronting those Jews, Stephen accused their fathers of having persecuted the prophets and murdered Jesus, concluding with the devastating reprimand: " 'You stiff-necked people, uncircumcised in heart and ears [an expression of severe criticism used by Jahweh in the Old Testament], you always resist the Holy Spirit" (7:51). Enraged by this reprimand the Jews were about to apprehend him when he was seized by the Holy Spirit and, looking up to heaven, saw " 'the heavens opened and the Son of man standing at the right hand of God' " (7:55–56). (It is amazing how so many things could be seen in a non-existent heaven.) But this vision only incensed them fur-ther, so they seized Stephen carrying him out of the city where they stoned him to death. His last words were: " 'Lord, do not hold this sin against them' " (7:60).

Saul, or as he was later called, Paul, is now mentioned for the first time as being present when Stephen was stoned to death and not inter-fering because, as a Pharisee, he was a fierce opponent of the disciples of Christ. When, for example, "a great persecution arose against the church in Jerusalem" causing the brethren to be dispersed, Saul is described as having "laid waste the church, and entering house after house . . . dragged off men and women and committed them to prison" (8:3). Then, recounting how the scattered disciples Philip, Peter, and John succeeded in attracting "multitudes" in Samaria, converting a government minister (referred to as a eunuch) in the service of Candace, the Ethiopian Queen, to the way of Jesus, the account returns to Saul's persecution of the evan-gelists and his conversion. "Breathing threats and murder against the dis-ciples of the Lord," who were seen by Saul as threatening the stability of the region, he was on his way to Damascus to obtain incriminating evidence of the activities of the evangelists when he had his epiphany.

> Now as he . . . approached Damascus . . . suddenly a light from heaven flashed about him. And he fell to the ground and heard a voice saying to him, "Saul, Saul, why do you persecute me?" And he said, "Who are you, Lord?" And he [the Lord] . . . said, "I am Jesus, whom you are persecuting; but rise and enter the city, and you will be told what you are to do." (9:3–6)

This vision of Jesus was the basis of Paul's repeated claim that though he had not been one of the original disciples, he was equal to them in authority because he, too, had seen the Lord Jesus.

Although the men traveling with Saul did not share his vision, they heard the voice and were astonished. After falling from his horse, Saul stood up but was unable to see, so he had to be led to Damascus by hand where for three days he remained blind, neither eating nor drinking. Then a disciple in Damascus named Ananias was told by the Lord to go to Saul and, by laying hands on him, restore his sight. Ananias was reluctant to do so, knowing of Saul's persecution of the evangelists, but the Lord insisted saying, " 'Go, for he is a chosen instrument of mine to carry my name before the Gentiles and kings and the sons of Israel; for I will show him how much he must suffer for the sake of my name' " (9:15–16). Going to Saul as he was bidden, Ananias restored his sight whereupon Saul was filled with the Holy Spirit. Joining the disciples when visiting the synagogues, he proclaimed that "Jesus . . . is the Son of God," confounding those who had known of his previous cruelty to the followers of Christ. It is because the Lord revealed that he had chosen Paul (as he was now called) "to carry my name before the Gentiles and kings" that he believed that his special mission was to bring the word of Jesus Christ to the greater world of the gentiles.

Yet the Jewish elders, angered by Paul's conversion and the arguments he used to show that Jesus was the Christ sought to kill him, but he was saved when the disciples lowered him down the city wall at night in a basket. Fleeing Damascus, Paul went to Jerusalem where the disciples initially were apprehensive because of his previous persecutions, but then were persuaded by Barnabas of his sincerity. At first he was safe in Jerusalem preaching with the disciples and, because of his superior education, disputing with the Hellenists. After a while, his life was endangered again, forcing him to flee to Caesarea and then to Tarsus, his birthplace. For a time the churches in Samaria, Galilee, and Judea were allowed to grow peacefully, attracting many converts.

The narrative returns to Peter, who cures the paralyzed man named

Aeneas and then restores to life the devout woman Tabitha, who had fallen sick and died. But it is his encounter with the Roman centurion Cornelius, a man known for his piety and charity, that is of special interest because it depicts God's revelation to Peter, as he had revealed to Paul, that the gentiles were to be included among those who were to receive the Holy Spirit in the name of Jesus Christ. One evening Cornelius had a terrifying vision in which he was instructed by the Lord to bring Peter to his residence. The following day Peter also had a vision, after falling into a trance, of a great sheet filled with all kinds of animals, reptiles, and birds descending from heaven. Apparently because the trance had occurred while Peter, being hungry, was preparing food, "there came a voice to him: 'Rise, Peter, and kill and eat' " (10:12). Replying that he could not eat anything that was "common and unclean" the voice answered, " 'What God has cleansed, you must not call common' " (10:15) — a dramamtic instance of the role of trances in the New Testament.

As Peter was trying to decide what this meant Cornelius' men arrived taking him to Caesarea. When he saw Peter, Cornelius fell to his feet, but Peter raised him saying that he, Peter, was just another man. Noticing that there were Jews as well as non-Jews in the company of Cornelius, despite the Hebraic law prohibiting Jews from associating with people of other nations, Peter suddenly realized the meaning of his vision: "God has shown me that I should not call any man common or unclean" (10:28). He then declared to Cornelius, " 'Truly I perceive that God shows no partiality, but in every nation any one who fears him and does what is right is acceptable to him' " (10:34). While he was saying this the Holy Spirit descended on the gentiles, as well as on the circumcised, and they began praising the Lord so Peter "commanded them to be baptized in the name of Jesus Christ" (10:48). When the brethren in Jerusalem learned of this they criticized Peter for accepting the gentiles into the community; however, after he described his vision and its meaning as he had interpreted it they were silenced saying: " 'Then to the Gentiles also God has granted repentance into life' " (11:18). So now both Peter and Paul endeavored to spread the word of Jesus among the gentiles, a crucial change that lead to Christianity's emergence as a world religion, rather than just becoming another vanishing sect.

The death of Stephen described previously was accompanied by a renewed persecution of the church in Jerusalem forcing many of the apostles to scatter to such places as Phoenicea, Cyprus, and Antioch where they then had considerable success in spreading the word among the Jews. When the disciples in Jerusalem learned of this, they sent Barnabas to Antioch to preach and because he was so well received, he decided to go to Tarsus to bring Paul back to Antioch. There they taught together for a year. It was "in Antioch the disciples were for the first time called Christians" (11:26).

Meanwhile in Jerusalem King Herod added to the persecution by killing James, the brother of John, and imprisoning Peter. But when Peter was bound in chains sleeping between two soldiers with sentries guarding the doors of the prison, an angel of the Lord appeared as a light shone in his cell, causing the chains to fall from his hands and allowing him to walk from the prison unnoticed. The escape was so remarkable that even Peter "did not know if what was done by the angel was real, but thought he was seeing a vision" (12:9). Once released from the prison he passed through the gate to the city "which opened . . . of its own accord," coming to himself as the angel left him (12:10–11). When he went to the house of Mary everyone was astonished to see him, especially when he told them of his miraculous escape (a delightful story too good to be true).

But Herod would pay dearly for his sins. The peoples of Tyre and Sidon had requested an audience with the King to plead for peace. Then, on the appointed day, Herod appeared dressed in his royal robes,

> took his seat upon the throne, and made an oration to them. And the people shouted, "The voice of god, and not of a man!" Immediately an angel of the Lord smote him, because he did not give God the glory; and he was eaten by worms and died. (12:21–23)

It is unfortunate that "an angel of the Lord" was not active in the days of Stalin, Hitler, the rape of Nanking, Pol Pot, Idi Amin, or Milosovic.

The Acts then describes how "the Holy Spirit" selected Paul and Barnabas to carry the word to Seleucia, Cyprus, and various cities in Asia Minor. Invited by the rulers of the synagogue to preach, Paul stood up and, drawing on his extensive knowledge, recalled the history of the Jews to the time of King David, affirming Jesus' continuity with David by claiming that "God has brought to Israel a Savior, Jesus, as he promised" (13:23). He concluded by recounting the life and message of Jesus.

Paul was so successful in his oration that on the "next sabbath almost the whole city gathered together to hear the word of God," arousing the jealousy and wrath of the unconverted Jews (13:44–45). Responding to the latter's hostility, both Paul and Barnabas boldly replied that because many Jews refused to accept the promise of an eternal life brought by Jesus Christ they were taking their message to the Gentiles: "For so the Lord has commanded us saying, 'I have set you to be the light for the Gentiles, that you may bring salvation to the utmost parts of the earth' " (13:47). So once again the primary theme of the Acts, that the mission of the apostles was to carry Jesus' word to all the nations, is proclaimed.

This swing between successful preaching and fierce opposition continued until in Iconium the people "stoned Paul and dragged him out of the city, supposing that he was dead" (14:19). He recovered but such persecution supports his claims in his letters that he had suffered much during his missionary travels. Continuing to visit and preach the gospel in various cities in Asia Minor, Paul and Barnabas finally sailed back to Antioch where they had begun their dual mission, only to confront a dispute as to whether gentiles could be saved without being circumcised, the ritual initiated by Abraham which had become a law of Moses. Because the issue had been raised by disciples from Judea, Paul and Barnabas were selected to go to Jerusalem to help settle the controversy. Arriving in Jerusalem they told of the multitudes they had attracted during their travels, especially among the uncircumcised gentiles, but the Pharisees who were present objected, declaring, " 'It is necessary to circumcise them, and to charge them to keep the law of Moses' " (15:5).

Coming to the support of Paul and Barnabas, Peter asked why the Pharisees made "trial of God by putting a yoke upon the neck of the disciples," arguing that salvation does not depend upon obeying rules but is granted by "the grace of the Lord Jesus . . ." (15:10-11). James similarly replied that in his judgment "we should not trouble those of the Gentiles who turn to God, but should write to them to abstain from the pollution of idols and from unchastity and from what is strangled and from blood" (15:19-20). Having reached a consensus, it was decided to send apostles to the various cities to spread the word of the decision and to quell any disputes. But when Paul and Barnabas were about to leave, a disagreement arose between them regarding who they should take as companions. They decided to separate, Barnabas taking John (called Mark) with him to Cyprus and Paul choosing Silas to go with him to Derbe and Lystra. In his subsequent preaching Paul announced the decision he had reached in Jerusalem to excuse the gentiles from circumcision, with the result that "the churches were strengthened in the faith, and . . . increased in numbers daily" (16:5). Accompanied by Timothy (the son of a devout Jewish woman and Greek father; although a convert he never had been circumcised, so to please the Jews Paul had him circumcised), Paul and Silas brought the ministry to many regions as directed by "the Holy Spirit" and "the Spirit of Jesus." Then one night Paul had a vision of a man from Macedonia calling him to come there to preach the gospel, again attesting to the significant role of visons in guiding the actions of the evangelists (16:9–10).

Embarking from Troyas, near the Bosphorus, the three men sailed directly to Samothrace, Neapolis, and finally to Philippi, a Roman colony and the leading city of Macedonia. There they stayed preaching until Paul, annoyed by a slave girl who performed divination, had her power exorcised. But having "brought her owners much gain by soothsaying," they were furious when they realized that Paul had destroyed her powers, dragging him and Silas before the magistrates and charged them with disrupting the city. When the crowds joined in attacking Paul and Silas "the magistrates tore the garments off them and gave orders to beat them with rods" (16:22). Following a severe beating, the two were thrown into the inner prison with their feet fastened in the stocks to prevent escape.

Then, as usual, a miraculous occurrence intervened. Around midnight when "Paul and Silas were praying and singing hymns to God . . . suddenly there was a great earthquake, so that the foundations of the prison were shaken; and immediately all the doors were opened and everyone's fetters were unfastened" (16:25–26). Yet rather than escape, they remained in their cell until morning when the magistrates decided to release them. However, when informed of this Paul objected, declaring that because he and Silas were Roman citizens the magistrates had violated Roman law by having them beaten publicly and thrown into prison without any trial. Learning of this the magistrates became alarmed, apologizing to Peter and Silas and helping them to leave the city safely.

And so the story repeats itself with Paul and Silas going to various cities, initially having success in preaching the gospel, but eventually arousing the jealousy and hostility of the Jews who accused them of civil disturbance by preaching that there was a higher law than Moses and a greater King than Caesar. From these accounts we realize how apprehensive the leaders of Judaism and the Roman authorities were of any civil disturbance. Despite the stabilizing influence of the Roman Empire, the vast diversity of peoples and religions under its rule made the leaders frightened of any new ideologies or political movements. It is for this reason that in his letters Paul emphatically urges the apostles in the various communities to obey the local laws and not challenge the authorities. As Jesus had said, "Render to Caesar the things that are Caesar's, and to God the things that are God's" (Mark 12:17). As for the Mosaic laws, the apostles argued that their preaching was not intended "to demolish them but to fulfill them," the coming of Jesus Christ interpreted as a confirmation of the Old Testament prophesies, as well as bringing new commandments.

Eventually Paul arrived in Athens, the origin of Hellenistic culture and still the center of the major philosophical schools, where he was joined by Silas and Timothy. Although Alexandria and Rome had for several centuries replaced Athens as the dominant cultural influence of that region of the world, Athens still retained something of its past luster as the citadel of learning. But because it also was host to many religious sects, when Paul arrived "his spirit was provoked . . . as he saw that the city was full of idols" (17:16). So he began arguing in the synagogue with the Jews and in the marketplace with the Greeks, illustrating how the gospel was spread. He even engaged the Epicurean and Stoic philosophers in debate, something the illiterate apostles were unable to do. Some called him a "babbler" while others, curious to hear his views, invited him to speak on the Areopagus,[4] saying, "May we know what this new teaching is which you present? For you bring some strange things to our ears; we wish to know therefore what these things mean" (17:19).

Paul used this occasion to compliment the Athenians for their religious ardor while also criticizing them for their idolatrous beliefs. Referring to an altar with an inscription "To an unknown god," Paul declared that the "God who made the world and everything in it, being Lord of heaven and earth, does not live in shrines made by men" (17:23–29), nor can he be depicted by the imagination of man in gold, silver, or stone. He argued that before God had sent his only son to instruct man these idolatrous beliefs were understandable, but now that a higher truth had been revealed by someone whose authority was confirmed by "raising him from the dead," there was no excuse for continuing them (17:30). This reference to the resurrection of Jesus Christ was "mocked" by some Athenians but aroused curiosity in others, among them Dionysus the Areopagate. (Dionysus was converted by Paul and according to tradition became the first Bishop of Athens who was later martyred).

Departing from Athens, Paul continued his travels to many cities in Greece and Asia Minor. Going first to Corinth, he met Aquila and his wife Priscilla who had left Italy because of Emperor Claudius's decree that all Jews had to leave Rome. Paul decided to stay with them so he and Aquila could practice their trade as tentmakers, confirming Paul's claim in his letters that he preferred to support himself rather than depend upon the aid of the church. He also continued to preach, proclaiming to the Jews that Jesus was the Christ. When "they opposed and reviled him" he said to them, " 'Your blood be upon your heads! I am innocent. From now on I will go to the gentiles' " (18:6). Although many of the Corinthians were persuaded by Paul's preaching and asked to be baptized, when some Jews rose up against him he left Corinth with Aquila and Priscilla for Ephesus. From there he went to Caesarea, down to Antioch, then to Galatia and Phrygea, returning again to Ephesus, all the while preaching the gospel.

During his return to Ephesus it is said that "God did extraordinary miracles by the hands of Paul, so that handkerchiefs or aprons were carried away from his body to the sick, and diseases left them and the evil spirits came out of them" (19:11–12). When some of the itinerant Jewish exorcists, including seven sons of the Jewish high priest Sceva, attempted to emulate Paul, an evil spirit in one of the possessed men protested: " 'Jesus I know, and Paul I know; but who are you?' " The demonic man sprang on the exorcists with such ferocity that he overpowered them, causing them to flee "naked and wounded" (19:15–16). (It is this kind of story that makes the Bible such interesting reading but so implausible.) When word of this spread through Ephesus among the Greeks as well as the Jews, many began extolling the name of Jesus Christ while "a number of those who practiced magic arts brought their books" worth "fifty thousand pieces of silver" to be burned in sight of everyone (19:19).

But the patron goddess of Ephesus being Artemis, the goddess of fertility, the silversmiths who made their living by making silver shrines and statues of Artemis became alarmed at Paul's attack on idolatry. As their leader Demetrius exclaimed:

> "Men, you know that from this business we have our wealth. And you see and hear that not only at Ephesus but almost throughout all Asia this Paul has persuaded and turned away a considerable company of people, saying that gods made with hands are not gods. And there is danger not only that this trade of ours may come into disrepute but also that the temple of the great goddess Artemis may count for nothing, and that she may even be deposed from her magnificence, she whom all Asia and the world worship." (19:25–27)

When the people heard this they shouted: "Great is Artemis of the Ephesians!" An illustration of the fact that one people's god is another people's idol, one is remined of all the statues and trinkets of Jesus and of the Virgin Mary. Yet this episode is significant for a number of reasons, attesting not only to Paul's great success in preaching, but also showing how the promulgation of a new religion could be viewed as not only provoking civil disturbance, but also as posing an economic threat.

So as usual Paul was forced to leave departing again for Macedonia. But after three months the Jews plotted against him, so accompanied by a number of disciples he sailed for Troas where they were joined by another group which, according to the narrative, included the author of Acts, who writes that "we sailed away from Philippi . . . and in five days we came to them at Troas, where we stayed for seven days" (20:6).[5] There then follows an itinerary of their travels by ship to Assos, Mitylene, Chios, Samos, and Miletus where Paul called the elders of the church in Ephesus to join him. It was there that he gave a deeply moving oration depicting with great modesty his mission:

> "You yourself know how I lived among you . . . serving the Lord with all humility and with tears and with trials which befell me through the

> plots of the Jews; how I did not shrink from . . . testifying both to Jews
> and to Greeks of repentance to God and of faith in our Lord Jesus Christ.
> . . . But I do not account my life of any value nor as precious to myself,
> if only I may accomplish my course and the ministry which I receive
> from the Lord Jesus, to testify to the gospel of the grace of God."
> (20:18–24)

Then, following a sorrowful farewell when he tells them that they "will
see my face no more" because he was going to Jerusalem, Rome, and then
to Spain, which he considered his final destination, he beseeches them to
care for the weak and the poor. His final words recall those of Jesus, perhaps the most quoted in the New Testament, "how he said, 'it is more
blessed to give than to receive' " (20:35).

Sailing from Miletus Paul and his group went to Cos, Rhodes, Patara,
Phoenicia, Cyprus, Tyre, Ptolemais, and then Caesaria. There he stayed
with Philip the evangelist, telling his followers that he planned to go to
Jerusalem. Then a prophet from Judea named Agabus took Paul's girdle,
"bound his own feet and hands," and predicted that this would happen
to Paul if he went to Jerusalem. But Paul was adamant, saying, " 'What
are you doing, weeping and breaking my heart? For I am ready not only
to be imprisoned but even to die at Jerusalem for the name of the Lord
Jesus' " (21:13). So Paul, along with some of the disciples from Caesarea,
went to Jerusalem where "the brethren received us gladly" (21:17).

But though the "brethren" were delighted to greet him the other
Jews, when they saw him in the temple, roused the crowd to apprehend
him saying:

> "Men of Israel, help! This is the man who is teaching men everywhere
> against the people and the law and this place [the temple]; moreover he
> also brought Greeks into the temple, and he has defiled this holy place."
> (21:28)

Inciting most of the city against him, the crowd "seized Paul and dragged
him out of the temple" where they were about to kill him when, learning
of the tumult, the tribune (accompanied by soldiers and centurions) intervened. Arresting Paul and binding him with chains, the tribune asked
Paul what he had done to cause this turmoil. Unable to learn anything
because of the clamor, he ordered that Paul be carried by the soldiers to
the barracks because of the menacing crowd.

When the centurion arrived Paul asked if he could speak to him,
explaining that he was a Jew from Tarsus and that he would like to
address the Jewish people. Paul was granted permission and spoke to the
crowd in Hebrew, which initially calmed them. He recounted how earlier

he had attacked the followers of the Way until, on his journey to Damascus he had seen a vision of the Lord Jesus who instructed him to cease his persecution and instead help spread the word to the gentiles. They had been quiet up to that point, but the throng erupted at the mention of the gentiles, again calling for Paul's death. Returning him to the barracks the tribune "ordered him to be examined by scourging," whereupon Paul replied, " 'Is it lawful for you to scourge a man who is a Roman citizen and uncondemned?' " (22:25). Taken aback by the question, the tribune replied skeptically that he had acquired his own citizenship "for a large sum," to which Paul countered that he "was born a citizen" (22:28). There was a strong penalty against binding and threatening a Roman citizen without the latter having been allowed to confront his accusers, so the tribune immediately unchained Paul.

The following day, wanting to learn why the Jews accused him, the tribune brought Paul before the high priests and the council which he had summoned to question him. But when Paul declared that he had lived in good conscience before God, the high priest Ananias was so offended by this declaration that he ordered those close to Paul to hit him on the mouth, leading Paul to cry out, " 'God shall strike you, you whitewashed wall! Are you sitting to judge me according to the law, and yet contrary to the law you order me to be struck?' " (23:3). When the crowd exclaimed that Paul was reviling the high priest, he responded in defense that he did not know he was the high priest for he was aware that it was written, " 'You shall not speak evil of a ruler of your people' " (23:5). This is a salient example of how the two religions, Judaism and Christianity, despite their differences were so intertwined that Paul felt obligated to respect the Jewish law even though he was being assaulted at the command of the high priest.

Discovering that the crowd was composed of both Pharisees and Sadducees, Paul cleverly realized that he could cause dissension by declaring that as a son of a Pharisee he believed in the resurrection of the dead, a doctrine the Sadducees rejected along with the existence of angels and spirits. Hearing this the Pharisees declared, " 'We find nothing wrong in this man. What if a spirit or an angel spoke to him?' " (23:9). Such a commotion arose that the tribune, worried for the safety of Paul, ordered him to be returned to the barracks. Yet the following night the Lord reassured Paul saying, " 'Take courage, for as you have testified about me at Jerusalem, so you must bear witness also at Rome' " (23:11).

Still seeking vengeance, a group of about forty Asian Jews hatched a plot, with the compliance of the chief priest and elders, to convince the tribune to release Paul to them with the understanding that they "would determine his case more exactly," but in fact they intended to kill him.

Fortunately, the son of Paul's sister learned of this plot and informed the tribune. To bring an end to the confrontation the tribune commanded that two hundred soldiers and spearmen, along with seventy horsemen, spirit Paul away by night to Felix, the governor in Caesarea, with a letter explaining the situation (23:12–25). Arriving safely in Caesarea Paul presented his letter to the governor. When Felix learned that Paul was from the province of Cilicia under his jurisdiction, he said that he would hear the case when Paul's accusers arrived, placing him in Herod's praetorium (the guardhouse within the palace grounds) in the interim.

Five days later the high priest Ananias arrived with some elders and presented the case against Paul. Praising Felix for his reforms and expressing their gratitude to him for preserving peace, in effect they painted Paul as a rabble rouser, describing him as " 'a pestilent fellow, an agitator among all the Jews throughout the world, and a ringleader of the sect of the Nazarenes' " (24:5). Denying these accusations Paul challenged his accusers to prove them, but admitted that

> "according to the Way, which they call a sect, I worship the God of our fathers, believing everything laid down by the law or written by the prophets, having a hope in God which these themselves accept, that there will be a resurrection of both the just and the unjust." (24:14–15)

Thus Paul argued that he had not broken any of the Jewish laws and that he was on trial solely because of his belief in the resurrection of the dead (24:21), a doctrine denied by the Sadducees, although they are not mentioned.

The case then dragged on for two years. Paul was kept in custody but allowed some liberty and the right to receive friends, when for some unexplained reason Felix was replaced by Porcius Festus. After three days Festus decided to go to Jerusalem from Caesarea where he met with the chief priests and elders of the Jews who, pressing their accusations against Paul, asked that he be "sent to Jerusalem, planning an ambush to kill him on the way" (25:3). Festus refused, saying that if they had a case against him he would consider it at Caesarea, since Paul was being kept there. So when he returned to Caesarea Festus heard the charges and Paul's continued defense that the accusations were unfounded because he had not done anything against the laws of the Jews, the temple, or Caesar. However, wishing to placate the Jews, Festus asked Paul if he wanted to be tried by him in Jerusalem, to which Paul replied decisively:

> "I am standing before Caesar's tribunal, where I ought to be tried; to the Jews I have done no wrong, as you know very well. If then I am a wrongdoer, and I have committed anything for which I deserve to die, I do not seek to escape death; but if there is nothing in their charges

against me, no one can give me up to them. I appeal to Caesar."
(25:10–11)

Knowing full well that the Jews intended to kill him despite their base-
less accusations, Paul wisely appealed to the legal authority of Rome.
After conferring with his council Festus answered, " 'You have appealed
to Caesar; to Caesar you shall go' " (25:12).

As it happened, King Agrippa and his wife Bernice arrived in Caesarea in honor of Festus's succession, so Festus decided to use the occasion to try Paul's case. Apparently intrigued by it, Agrippa asked to have
an audience with Paul himself. So the next day amidst great pomp,
Agrippa and Bernice were welcomed in the audience hall by the "military tribunes and the prominent men of the city." Reviewing the case
before this eminent audience, Festus concluded by saying that because he
had found that Paul "had done nothing deserving death" and yet had
"appealed to the emperor, I decided to send him [except that] I have
found nothing definite to write to my lord about him" (25:25–26). Thus,
he decided to bring Paul before this tribune and before King Agrippa
"that, after we have examined him, I may have something to write"
because "it seems to me unreasonable, in sending a prisoner, not to indicate the charges against him" (25:25–26).

Then for the umpteenth time Paul recalled his earlier conversion and
later mission; he concluded by declaring that Christ had to suffer to fulfill " 'what the prophets and Moses said would come to pass . . . and that,
by being the first to rise from the dead, he would proclaim the light both
to the people and to the Gentiles' " (26:22–23). Hearing this Festus, with
his secular Roman background, exclaimed: "Paul, you are mad; your
great learning is turning you mad" (26:24). Denying that he is mad, Paul
says that King Agrippa himself knows about these things, even believing
in the prophets which evoked from the King the abrupt response: " 'In a
short time you think to make me a Christian!' " (26:28). To this Paul
replied, " 'Whether short or long, I would to God that not only you but
also all who hear me this day might become such as I am — except for
these chains' " (26:29). Hearing this and withdrawing to consult among
themselves, the distinguished council concluded, " 'This man is doing
nothing to deserve death or imprisonment,' " with Agrippa telling Festus
that Paul " 'could have been set free if he had not appealed to Caesar' "
(26:31–32).

Thus to comply with Paul's request to be tried before Caesar, it was
decided that he should sail for Italy along with some other prisoners
under "a centurion of the Augustan Cohort, named Julius" (27:1). The
Acts then concludes with such a detailed, graphic description of the perilous voyage to numerous ports, including a disastrous shipwreck on the

Island of Malta recounted in the first person plural 'we', that it is difficult for the reader to believe that the author of the Acts was not a member of the entourage keeping an exact log of the journey that he used when writing the Acts. Yet, as previously stated, the consensus of scholars is that this was not the case. In the opinion of Kee:

> All that can be said is that the author of Acts may have utilized as one of his sources a travel account concerning Paul, although one must acknowledge that this document was more reliable in some of its topographical and regional detail than in its historical account of the career of Paul as a whole.[6]

Apparently writing such gripping travel stories was not uncommon at the time, as illustrated by Xenophon of Ephesus who wrote a "vivid story of the perilous travels of two devotees of Isis, whose wanderings take them to Athens and Ephesus, culminating in a storm at sea from which they are miraculously delivered. The similarities to the Acts are obvious."[7]

Arriving finally at Syracuse on the island of what is now Sicily, Paul's group continued to Rhegium on the toe of Italy, then to Puteoli near Pompeii, and thence to Rome. Learning of their arrival the brethren "came as far as the Forum of Appius and Three Taverns to meet us. On seeing them Paul thanked God and took courage" (28:15). While in Rome he was permitted to stay in his own lodgings but remained bound by a chain and had a soldier guarding him. With this limited freedom he was able to receive the Jewish community, telling them he had come to Rome to teach that Jesus had been sent to fulfill the law of Moses and the prophesies of the Old Testament: "some were convinced by what he said, while others disbelieved" (28: 24). Aware of this dissention, Paul rebukes them, telling them that the Holy Spirit had been right in prophesying through Isaiah that the Jews would "indeed hear but never understand," leaving them with the final judgment: " 'Let it be known to you then that this salvation of God has been sent to the Gentiles; they will listen' " (28:28). Free to preach "openly and unhindered," for two years Paul spread the word of the Kingdom of God and that Jesus was the Lord. With that the Acts ends without revealing what would be the final fate of Paul in Rome, although tradition has it that he was executed by Emperor Nero.

With this summary of Acts before us, the central question (as with the gospels) pertains to its historical validity, especially as it is our main source of information about the early history of the successes and failures of the evangelists, particularly Peter and Paul, in spreading the gospel to distant communities. Keeping in mind that the author of Acts, like the authors of the gospels, did not intend to present an historically accurate account (in the modern sense) of the mission of the apostles, does "this mean," as Kee asks, "that Acts is worthless as a historical source?"[8] Although the author displayed tremendous literary skill in writing the Acts as if he were witness to the events narrated (especially when he used 'we' in relating the treacherous journey of Paul's entourage from Caesarea to Rome), scholars for the most part have decided that the Acts was written about thirty years after Paul's death. However, this stylistic skill in presenting events as if the author were present should not be considered a deception, being an accepted literary practice at the time.

Despite the fact that Acts was not intended primarily as an historical document, but as a dramatic portrayal (similar to modern historical biographies) of the struggle to establish Christian communities in the major cities of the Near East, Asia Minor, Islands of Cyprus, Crete, and Rhodes, the Peloponnesus to Macedonia, and Rome, it does portray the accomplishments of Peter along with the itinerary and mission of Paul, whose travels are believed to have comprised about 10,000 miles. More importantly, it conveys a reliable account of the intended church doctrines as they were being formulated and preached at this time: (1) to establish a continuity between the lineage of David and Jesus; (2) to show that the coming of Jesus, along with his death and resurrection, were a fulfillment of the Old Testament prophesy that "a young woman [not a virgin] shall conceive and bear a son, and shall call his name Immanuel" (Isaiah 7:14); (3) that despite Jesus' humiliation and suffering, after three days he was raised from the dead and is now seated at the right hand of God; (4) that his preaching was not intended to destroy the laws of Moses but to fulfill them; (5) that the Jews who were responsible for Jesus' death were wrong to turn away from him and deny that he was the Messiah or Christ; (6) that God himself in numerous revelations to Paul and other evangelists directed that the word be spread among the gentiles who were more receptive than the Jews; (7) that not committing adultery and not eating unclean foods were the essential conditions for male gentiles becoming Christians, not their having to be circumcised; (8) that the Christian communities should obey the local laws as well as the laws of Moses (except for circumcision) to avoid persecution; and (9) that because neither the apocalypse nor the second coming of Jesus (as Paul had taught in his letters) appeared to be imminent, the mission of the apostles was to spread the word and establish churches wherever possible. Little did they realize how successful this effort would prove to be with Christianity becoming, within four centuries, the state religion of the Roman Empire and eventually growing into one of the largest and most dominant religious institutions in the world.

THE PAULINE EPISTLES

Although the Acts of the Apostles was written well after Paul is believed to have been martyred in Rome about 62 C.E., it was discussed first because it presents a much more detailed account of Paul's life, from his conversion trance in 34 C.E. to his arrival in Rome in 59–60, than contained in his letters.[9] Except for a few references to his conversion, revelations, and persecutions with harrowing escapes, his letters mainly address the various doctrinal, ethical, and administrative problems posed by his newly established churches, along with admonishing the brethren to love one another and live exemplary lives. Unlike most letters that relate the writer's personal experiences at the time, Paul's epistles are predominantly didactic, intending to resolve religious disputes relating to rituals and faith or to prescribe the correct moral conduct of the brethren among themselves and to the external community.

While he alludes to some kind of disfigurement and lack of oratorical eloquence that apparently detracted from his speaking effectiveness, his letters in contrast display an astute knowledge of Hellenistic philosophy, especially Stoicism. Convinced that his gospel was guided by divine revelations, he asserts that he was speaking in the name of God, not man. As he states in 2 Corinthians, "they say, 'His letters are weighty and strong, but his bodily presence is weak, and his speech of no account," (10:10), but adds that even "if I am unskilled in speaking, I am not in knowledge . . ." (11:6). Declaring that it was God who "was pleased to reveal his son to me in order that I might preach among the Gentiles" (Gal. 1:15), he maintained that these revelatory encounters with Christ gave him an authority equal to those apostles who had actually known Jesus, as he had not.

Because not all of the letters attributed to Paul were actually written by him, it is important to distinguish the authentic from the inauthentic, even when the latter convey a message that is in doctrinal agreement. According to Kee:

> Careful analysis of the language and content of these writings shows . . . that the so-called Pauline writings fall into the two following categories: (1) those unquestionably by Paul: Romans, 1 and 2 Corinthians, Galatians, Philippians, 1 Thessalonians, and Philemon; (2) a letter about which questions have been seriously raised, where the evidence is ambiguous: 2 Thessalonians; (3) letters that are not by Paul, but which have been developed out of his thought: Colossians and Ephesians; (4) letters that bear his name, but which clearly come from another time and set of circumstances in the church: 1 and 2 Timothy and Titus (the so-called Pastoral Letters); (5) a letter that does not bear Paul's name and which evinces a wholly different thought and religious vocabulary from that of Paul: the letter to the Hebrews.[10]

While Peter and the other apostles, including James the brother of Jesus, confined their preaching mainly to Palestine, it was Paul's spreading of the gospel in cities in Jerusalem, Syria, and Cilicia along the eastern Mediterranean coast, villages in Cappadocia, Lycia, Galatia, Asia, and Bithynia in Asia Minor, city-states in Achaia, Thracia, and Macedonia to as far northwest as Illyricum, as well as the islands of Crete, Cyprus, and Rhodes in the eastern Mediterranean, that attracted the first converts of the early Christian churches. Thus his follow-up letters to these communities contain the most authentic picture we have of the problems confronting these early churches. Addressed to the relatively small groups of converts in these scattered cities (although he boasts of attracting large numbers), they show their struggles to establish themselves as a viable religious sect with a unique gospel in a hostile world of Jews, Greeks, Romans, and other nations.

THE LETTER OF PAUL TO THE GALATIANS

What may have been the first of Paul's surviving letters, addressed to "the churches of Galatia" (1:2), was written not long after his second journey to Jerusalem in 51 C.E., fourteen years after his first visit which took place three years after his conversion in 34, and thus seventeen years later. Written in an angry tone, the letter rebukes the Galatians for "turning to a different gospel" which would "pervert the Gospel of Christ" (1:6–7). Indicative of the doctrinal conflicts among these first Christian churches, composed mainly of Jews who had been brought up to obey the Torah and laws of Moses, the two crucial issues were whether male converts should be circumcised and whether obeying the traditional Hebrew laws and rituals was necessary for salvation according to the new covenant. Paul is opposed to both conditions. As for the first, he says, "in Christ Jesus neither circumcision nor uncircumcision is of any avail, but faith working through love" (5:6), adding that the whole law is fulfilled in one word: "You shall love your neighbor as yourself" (5:14). Perhaps the most well-known and beautiful commandment attributed to Jesus by the gospels, the origin may have been due to Paul since his letters preceded the gospels. Again he says, "neither circumcision counts for anything, nor uncircumcision, but a new creation" (6:15). It is not a ritual act of mutilation that will allow one to enter the Kingdom of God, but being reborn symbolically in the body of Christ.

As for the second condition, obeying the Mosaic laws and other rituals, he is just as adamant: "we have believed in Jesus Christ in order to be justified by faith in Christ, and not by works of the law, because by works of the law shall no one be justified" (2:16). Because God sent his son to redeem human beings from their sins, it is not by *works* but by *grace* that they are saved. Claiming to have been "crucified with Christ," it is not Paul who lives "but Christ who lives in me . . ." (2:20). He does not deny that the law of Moses is useful or valid, especially as it has helped to keep people under "restraint," but now that the Lord has come the law has been superseded and all are one in the new covenant of Christ's love.

> Now before faith came, we were confined under the law, kept under restraint until faith should be revealed. So that the law was our custodian until Christ came, that we might be justified by faith. But now that faith has come, we are no longer under a custodian; for in Christ Jesus you are all sons of God, through faith. For as many of you were baptized into Christ have put on Christ. There is neither Jew nor Greek, there is neither slave nor free, there is neither male nor female; for you are all one in Christ Jesus. And if you are Christ's, then you are Abraham's offspring, heirs according to promise. (3:23-29)

This is a powerful message that opened Christianity to the world. Like the revelation to Peter recounted in Acts, Paul had an epiphany which he interpreted as meaning that there should be no distinction between Jews, gentiles, and Christians once they are baptized into the new covenant or body of Christ. He now removes the distinction between male and female, freeman and slave, in the covenant of freedom. This assertion of equality, so different from the ethos of the Greco-Roman culture, played a crucial role, as we shall find later, in attracting converts to the faith. Furthermore, he proclaims this equality and unity not in his own name, but in that of Christ the Lord: "For I would have you know, brethren, that the gospel which was preached by me is not man's gospel. For I did not receive it from man, nor was I taught it, but it came through a revelation of Jesus Christ" (1:11-12). In addition, as the last statement in the lengthy quotation above asserts, Paul does not consider his gospel a repudiation of Jewish history but as fulfilling it. Despite the belief of the Jews that they were "God's chosen people," Paul maintains that "the scripture, foreseeing that God would justify the Gentiles by faith, preached the gospel beforehand to Abraham, saying 'In thee shall all nations be blessed.' Consequently, those who are men of faith are blessed with Abraham who had faith" (3:8-9). Accordingly, through faith in Christ Jesus "the blessings of Abraham" descended upon "the Gentiles," so that they too could "receive the promise of the Spirit through faith" (3:14).

THE LETTER OF PAUL TO THE ROMANS

While the letter to the Galatians was directed to the Jewish brethren in the Christian communities Paul had helped establish in Galatia, the letter to the Romans, written approximately three years later in 56–57, was addressed to the gentiles. Although the church in Rome had been founded by Jews, apparently a conflict among the Israelites and the apostles had led Emperor Claudius to pass a decree about 49 C.E. expelling all Jews from Rome, leaving the gentiles in control of the church.[11] Thus the letter to the Romans was not written to Jews nor to converts Paul had previously known, but to a congregation mainly of gentiles that he expected to visit in the near future after going to Jerusalem on his way to Spain. In contrast to his harsh criticism of the Galatians for listening to those who "pervert the Gospel of Christ," his letter to the Romans is addressed to "all God's beloved in Rome, who are called to be saints" (Rom. 1:7), adding "I long to see you . . . that we may be mutually encouraged by each other's faith, both yours and mine" (1:11–12).

There then follows the most comprehensive exposition of Paul's gospel contained in any of the epistles. He begins by chastising the wickedness of humans who, believing they are wise actually are fools, refusing to see God manifested in his creation. Even Greeks and barbarians are without excuse because ever "since the creation of the world his invisible nature, namely, his eternal power and deity, has been clearly perceived in the things that have been made" (1:20). Instead of the true God they worshiped idols and images "resembling mortal man or birds or animals or reptiles" (1:23). When they refused to acknowledge him, God turned away giving "them up to a base mind and to improper conduct" involving "all manner of wickedness, evil, covetousness, malice" (1:28–29). As Kee states, "Human beings are not out of right relationship with God because they commit sins; rather, their sinful acts and attitudes are the consequence of their alienation from the creator."[12]

Although Paul places the Jews before the Greeks, he says that in punishment and rewards "God shows no partiality" (2:11). In contrast to the Israelites who claimed that to please Yahweh everyone must obey the laws and rituals, Paul declares that since the gentiles have not been taught the Mosaic commands it is not obeying the law that is crucial for them, but "righteousness before God."

> When Gentiles who have not the law do by nature what the law requires, they are a law unto themselves. . . . They show that what the law requires is written on their hearts, while their conscience also bears witness and their conflicting thoughts accuse or perhaps excuse them on that day when, according to my gospel, God judges the secrets of men by Jesus Christ. (2:14–16)

Since according to Kee there "is no linguistic equivalent in Hebrew or Aramaic of the word 'conscience', this quotation is further evidence of the influence of the Stoics on Paul because of their belief that the *logos* or law of nature is manifested in humanity's conscience.[13] In addition, this statement conforms to Paul's deepest conviction that all human beings are equal before God.

Although the letter is written mainly for the gentiles in Rome, Paul again confronts the issue of whether it is necessary to be circumcised in obedience to the law, maintaining as usual that circumcision is of value for the Jews only if they are in the right relation to God: "He is a Jew who is one inwardly, and real circumcision is a matter of the heart, spiritual not literal" (2:29). But if that is true, he asks, does circumcision have any value even for Jews? His answer is that it does because it identifies one as a Jew and the Jews have been "entrusted with the oracles of God" (3:2). It does not matter that some were unfaithful because their unfaithfulness does not "nullify the faithfulness of God" (3:3).

He then raises the subtle theological question of whether the Jew's "wickedness," since it "serves to show the justice of God," means that "God is unjust to inflict [his] wrath on us?" (3:5). Alternately, if through humanity's falsehood "God's truthfulness abounds to his glory," why should anyone be "condemned as a sinner?" (3:7). That is, if doing wicked deeds and asserting falsehoods enhance God's glory, "why not do evil that good may come [of it]?" (3:8). His answer to these questions will be forthcoming after he discusses the origin of sin. At this point he mainly claims that Jews are no better or worse than others because "all men . . . are under the power of sin . . ." (3:9).

Because all human beings are sinners, no one can be justified simply by obeying the law or following the rituals. Justification depends upon God's grace as a gift "through the redemption which is in Christ Jesus, whom God put forward as an expiation by his blood, to be received by faith" (3:24–25). Asserting that "we hold that a man is justified by faith apart from works of the law," he asks whether "we then overthrow the law by this faith?" (3:28–31) Rather inconsistently he replies "by no means! On the contrary, we uphold the law" (3:31). No justification for this conclusion being given, instead he turns to the example of Abraham, declaring that it was not by his works nor because he was circumcised that he was justified, but by his faith: "The promise to Abraham and his descendants, that they should inherit the world, did not come through the law but through the righteousness of faith" (4:13). One wonders whether it was reading passages such as these that led Luther and Calvin to attribute redemption and salvation to God's grace, since these theological issues were not raised in the gospels. Neither Jesus nor the original twelve disciples would have had, as Paul did, the education in Hellenistic philosophy to raise these kinds of subtle questions.

One may ask, why are we all sinners? Paul's explanation relies on the myth of Genesis. He attributes the pervasiveness of sin to Adam's disobedience rather than to Eve's, probably because of the greater significance attributed to the male in procreation. Thus sin entered the human race by inheritance from Adam bringing with it death, but thanks to the grace of God, who sacrificed Jesus Christ to redeem humanity's transgressions, human beings will be saved through righteousness. So while Adam was the origin of sin and death, Christ is the source of salvation and everlasting life: "Then as one man's [Adam's] trespass led to condemnation for all men, so one man's [Christ's] act of righteousness leads to acquittal and life for all men" (5:18). Thus Paul is able to answer his previous question as to whether we should remain sinners to enhance grace. Because Christ died to redeem humanity's sins but then was resurrected, when human beings are baptized their former sinful selves die to be reborn in a new creation. "We were buried therefore with him by baptism unto death, so that as Christ was raised from the dead by the glory of the Father, we too might walk in newness of life" (6:4). Due to Christ's sacrifice on the cross, human beings have "been set free from sin" becoming "slaves of righteousness," thereby attaining eternal life (6:18). "For the wages of sin is death, but the free gift of God is eternal life in Christ Jesus our Lord" (6:23).

Paul then advances the curious notion that the law itself induces sin by enticing one to do what is forbidden:

> . . . if it had not been for the law, I should not have known sin. I should not have known what it is to covet if the law had not said, "You shall not covet." But sin, finding opportunity in the commandment, wrought in me all kinds of covetousness. Apart from the law sin lies dead. (7:7–8)

Paul identifies sin with his flesh or with the "members" of his body that overpower his will or moral precepts. Thus there is an element of Manichaeanism or Socratic dualism in Paul's gospel, a conflict between the evils or sins of the flesh and the sense of right or origin of moral principles in the mind.

> So I find it to be a law that when I want to do right, evil lies close at hand. For I delight in the law of God, in my inmost self, but I see in my members another law at war with the law of my mind and making me captive to the law of sin which dwells in my members. Wretched man that I am! Who will deliver me from this body of death? (7:21–24)

Thus God by Christ's atonement and indwelling Spirit has attained what the law never has achieved, freedom from sin and death. Moreover, whatever torment, persecution, or physical suffering befalls one at the present is inconsequential compared to the glory that is to come (8:18). How must these reassuring words have ministered to those who were to become martyrs to Christ!

There also is Calvin's doctrine of predestination submerged in Paul's gospel when he states, "those whom he predestined he also called; and those whom he called he also justified; and those whom he justified he also glorified" (8:30). He asks, "Who shall bring any charge against God's elect?" (8:33), since no power can stem God's love nor thwart the intercession of Christ.

> No, in all these things we are more than conquerors through him who loved us. For I am sure that neither death, nor life, nor angels, nor principalities, nor things present, nor things to come, nor powers, nor height, nor depth, nor anything else in all creation, will be able to separate us from the love of God in Christ Jesus our Lord. (8:37-39)

Yet despite this abridgement of the Jewish law, along with the baptismal transformation or rebirth into the body of Christ, Paul cannot renounce his Jewish heritage. It was Jesus, a Jew after all, whom he believes fulfilled the Old Testament prophesy as the true descendent of Abraham and David. Declaring that he has "great sorrow" and "unceasing anguish" in his heart, he wishes that he

> were accursed and cut off from Christ for the sake of my brethren, my kinsmen, by race. They are Israelites, and to them belong the sonship, the glory, the covenants, the giving of the law, the worship, and the promises; to them belong the patriarchs, and of their race, according to the flesh, is the Christ. (9:1-5)

But that is impossible because he now is a believer in Christ and it was his "kinsmen by race" who demanded Jesus' crucifixion, refusing to accept him as the Messiah because he was not a deliverer in the conquering image of David and Solomon.

Yet who ultimately is to blame since everything is in accordance with God's will? Even if one accepts the incredible mythical story that humanity inherited sin through Adam's disobedience, was God's foreknowledge so restricted that he was unaware that Adam would be tempted by Eve to eat of the forbidden fruit, thus coming to know sin and death? Or did God know but was unable to prevent it, implying a limitation on God's part? After all, according to Genesis God did "create man in his image," so God ultimately is responsible for his creation. When faced with this ultimate question Paul falls back on the lame reply: who are we to question God or to demand an explanation for his creation?

> But, who are you, a man, to answer back to God? Will what is molded say to the molder, "Why have you made me thus?" Has the potter no right over the clay, to make out of the same lump one vessel for beauty and another for mined use? What if God, desiring to show his wrath and to make known his power, has endured with much patience the vessels of wrath made for destruction [the damned], in order to make known the riches of his glory for the vessels of mercy [the saved], which he has prepared beforehand for glory. (9:20–23)

While I have great respect and admiration for Paul's superior learning, acute intelligence, superb literary style, lofty moral principles, and deeply compassionate empathy for humankind, I find this answer very disappointing. Would any just God create one group of people so loathsome that he has to destroy them to "make known his power . . . [and] the riches of his glory" for another group that he has preordained to be saved? This notion of mankind as a "vessel" for God's willful creation, in my opinion, is more demeaning than being descended from primates. It not only reduces human beings to artifacts of God, it precludes even questioning the wisdom of God's creation. No thinking person can accept this and assume responsibility for his or her life. If one maintains that we have to accept the paradox on faith, we can reply that there is the alternative choice that there is no God —'that only the foolish can say in their hearts that there is a god'.

Driven by the question of the destiny of his own people who have turned Christ away, some of whom have never even heard of Christ, Paul asks, "how are men to call upon him in whom they have not believed? And how are they to believe in him of whom they have never heard?" (10:14). Has God forsaken the Israelites? Is their fall beyond redemption? Paul's answer is that "through their trespass salvation has come to the Gentiles, so as to make Israel jealous" (11:11). The fact that most Jews have rejected the new covenant has led to its being offered to and accepted by the gentiles, with Paul apparently believing that once the Jews see the benefits of this faith, they, too, will seek righteousness in Christ Jesus.

> In as much then as I am an apostle to the Gentiles, I magnify my ministry in order to make my fellow Jews jealous, and thus save some of them. For if their rejection means the reconciliation of the world [of the Gentiles], what will their acceptance mean but life from the dead. (11:13–15)

He goes on to say that "I want you to understand this mystery," that it is not "until the full number of Gentiles come in" that "all Israel will be saved" (11:25–26). So as "regards the gospel they [the Israelites] are enemies of God . . . but as regards election they are beloved for the sake of their forefathers" who had faith in God's promise (11:28). This is Paul's answer to the perplexing question as to why the gospel is spreading among the gentiles and not the Israelites, and what this portends for the future of the Jews.

He then entreats the brethren in Rome, by "the grace given to me," to live according to the values and moral teachings of Christ so radically different from those accepted at that time.

> Bless those who persecute you; bless and do not curse them. Rejoice with those who rejoice, weep with those who weep. Live in harmony with one another; do not be haughty, but associate with the lowly; never be conceited. Repay no one evil for evil, but take thought for what is noble in the sight of all. If possible, so far as it depends upon you, live peaceably with all. . . . Do not be overcome by evil, but overcome evil with good. (12:14–21)

It was this inversion of noble and slave values or power and weakness, so contrary to Greek morlity, that Nietzsche later will ridicule and condemn.

Like Jesus, he urges the acceptance of the governing authorities, asserting that because they "have been instituted by God . . . he who resists the authorities resists what God has appointed, and those who resist will incur judgment" (13:1–2). Thus he holds the naive view that one must accede to political authorities because they were "instituted by God," a justification of the divine right of kings. One should pay one's taxes and be a debtor to no one. Above all, one should follow the fundamental commandment to "love your neighbor as yourself" because "love is the fulfilling of the law" (13:9–10). In another beautiful passage, he affirms his belief in the imminent passing of human history as the dawn of another era approaches.

> Besides this you know what hour it is, how it is full time now for you to wake from sleep. For salvation is nearer to us now then when we first believed; the night is far gone, the day is at hand. Let us then cast off the works of darkness and put on the armor of light; let us conduct ourselves becomingly as in the day, not in reveling and drunkenness, not in debauchery and licentiousness, not in quarreling and jealousy. But put on the Lord Jesus Christ, and make no provision for the flesh, to gratify its desires. (13:11–14)

He declares his intention to visit the saints in Jerusalem, bringing them aid from Macedonia and Achaia (Greece), and thence to Rome on his way to

Spain. Alas, it is believed he was martyred in Rome about 64 C.E. under the reign of Nero. Like Moses "his burial place remains unknown to this day."

PAUL'S FIRST LETTER TO THE CORINTHIANS

Except for the letters to the Galatians and the Romans, Kee does not indicate the chronology of the other letters, perhaps because there is insufficient evidence. What he does say is that the

> four letters we know as 1 and 2 Thessalonians and 1 and 2 Corinthians were apparently all written in a space of a few years after Paul returned from the visit to Jerusalem he described in Galatians. His missionary activities had taken him across the Aegean Sea to the mainland of Greece, first to the region Attica, where he visited Athens and settled down for an extended period of work in Corinth. The exact chronology cannot be determined. . . .[14]

Because in the concluding remarks to his first letter to the Corinthians (16:1–2), Paul requests that they set aside a gift to Jerusalem as he *previously* had requested of the Galatians, it would seem natural to discuss this letter after the previous one.

Although not famous for its philosophical schools nor as a center of research as were Athens and Alexandria, located on a narrow isthmus separating the Peloponnisus from mainland Greece, Corinth was known for its architecture, *dioclos* (a wooden ramp permitting ships to be drawn on rollers across a strip of land four miles long connecting the Saronic and the Corinthian Gulfs), and wealth, its riches referred to by Paul. While the letters to the Galatians addressed only one central issue, whether the Jewish laws and rituals had been superseded by faith in Jesus Christ and affirmed the equality of everyone baptized into the covenant, the letters to the Corinthians address a wide spectrum of problems that one would expect to arise in a newly established church.

While not in the same angry tone as the previous letter, Paul reiterates that his purpose in writing is to reduce "dissension," "quarreling," and "division." Having learned that there are factions in the church who divide their loyalties among Paul and two other evangelists, Apollos and Cephas, as well as Christ, he exhorts them to forgo their differences and become united in Christ. Declaring that no man is wise, only God, he rebukes the Jews for seeking signs and the Greeks for desiring proof of the existence of God, declaring that faith in the crucified Christ is all that matters.

> For Jews demand signs and Greeks seek wisdom, but we preach Christ
> crucified, a stumbling-block to Jews and folly to Gentiles, but to those
> who are called, both Jews and Greeks, Christ [is] the power of God and
> the wisdom of God. For the foolishness of God is wiser than men, and
> the weakness of God is stronger than men. (1:22–25)

Saying that on his earlier visit to Corinth he did not proclaim the gospel
"in lofty words or wisdom" but "in much fear and trembling" (1:1–2),
relying on the spirit and power of God, he advises that each of the evangelists mentioned earlier, Apollos, Cephas, and himself, should be lis-
tened to for what each has to offer rather than be compared for their
superiority. "This is how one should regard us, as servants of Christ and
stewards of the mysteries of God" (4:1). As he will say later: "Knowledge
puffs up, but love builds up" (8:1).

He then addresses what he considers a scandalous situation, a son
living with his stepmother. Although not incest in the strict biological
sense because the woman was not actually his mother and could have
been of similar age, nonetheless Jewish law prohibited any sexual relations between children and their legal parents. Incensed by what Paul saw
as the indifference of the Corinthians to this immoral situation, he admonished them to expel the son from the community (blaming the son rather
than the stepmother): "you are to deliver this man to Satan for the destruction of the flesh, that his spirit may be saved in the day of the Lord Jesus"
(5:5). This position later was a justification for torture and death during
the Inquisition. He exhorts the Corinthians "not to associate with any one
who bears the name of brother if he is guilty of immorality or greed, or is
an idolater, reviler, drunkard, or robber—not even to eat with such a one"
(5:11). All those should be cast out lest they contaminate the rest of the
community. He is opposed to the brethren settling their grievances in a
court of law outside the church and in fact condemns all lawsuits (a suggestion appropriate for the United States today) (6–7). Homosexuals are
considered in the same category as adulterers and thieves (6:9–10).

Replying to letters asking for advice about sexual and marital relations, Paul evinces considerable tolerance, understanding, and wisdom.
Although his own preference is for celibacy, he acknowledges the sexual
demands of others and encourages betrothals and marriages according to
one's needs. He prefers celibacy because marriage brings on "worldly
troubles," making it more difficult to be devoted to the Lord: "The
unmarried man is anxious about the affairs of the Lord, how to please the
Lord, but the married man is anxious about worldly affairs, how to please
his wife . . ." (7:32–34). But if one is tempted sexually then one should get
married and remain faithful: the "husband should give to his wife her
conjugal rights, and likewise the wife to her husband" (7:3). They should

not "refuse one another" except by agreement or for some religious reason, then "come together again, lest Satan tempt them through lack of self-control" (7:5). (It is interesting how evil is personified as Satan who then gets blamed for these moral transgressions.) Paul avows that he wishes "that all were as I myself am, celibate," but recognizes that "each has his own special gift from God" (7:7).

He believes that the unmarried and the widowed should remain "single," but if that is beyond their "self-control" they should marry. Speaking initially in the name of the Lord, he says that a husband should not divorce his wife and that a wife should not separate from her husband, but if she does she should remain single or try to be reconciled" (7:10–11). Then on his own authority he declares that if the brethren are married to husbands or wives who are unbelievers, as long as the latter consent they should not divorce, for the unbeliever is "consecrated" by the believer, which also ensures that the children from such a marriage are not unclean but holy (7:12–14). However, "if the unbelieving partner desires to separate" they should be allowed to do so for no one knows whether an unbelieving husband or wife can be saved (7:15–16). Again stating that it is only his own opinion (not a dictate from God), he is in favor of maintaining the status quo regarding the current social situation, asserting "that in view of the impending distress [the imminent apocalypse] it is well for a person to remain as he is" (7:26). Although everyone "should remain in the state in which he is called" (7:20), a slave can gain his or her freedom by legal means if possible, but not by rebellion. Yet it really does not matter for "he who was called to the Lord as a slave is a freeman," while "he who was free when called is a slave of Christ" (7:22).

Paul then addresses a question which particularly illustrates the kinds of problems that arose for those making the transition from non-Christian beliefs and rituals to those of the new covenant. As often pungently described, the Jewish temples and pagan shrines resounded with the cries and reeked with the odors from the animals that were being slaughtered and cooked for offerings to the gods. Some portion of what was left of these sacrificed animals was retained by the priests for their consumption, while the rest was sold in the marketplace. It still was believed by some converts that a religious benefit could be derived from eating the leftovers of these offerings, so the question posed to Paul was whether the brethren should participate in this ritual. Declaring that outsiders believe in idols and false deities while Christians who worship one supreme being realize that these other images and gods have "no real existence" (8:4–5), Paul argues analogously that for the brethren who know that "food will not commend us to God" (8:8), eating or not eating sacrificed food has no significance. The problem is that some recent converts "through being hitherto accustomed to idols, eat food as really offered to an idol; and their conscience, being weak, is defiled" (8:7). So because some brethren are tempted by this ritual to expect religious benefits, Paul recommends that even those who know better should not be seen eating such food lest they encourage the weak to do likewise (8:9–10). He constantly reminds the brethren that they should set a good example to others, both within and without the church.

How should men and women appear and behave in church? The answer is based on their natural status: "that the head of every man is Christ, the head of a woman is her husband, and the head of Christ is God" (11:3). This reference to "heads" leads him to declare that any man "who prays or prophesies with his head uncovered dishonors his head," while any woman who prays or prophesies with her head unveiled dishonors her head . . ." (11:4–5). He asserts that it is a woman's "pride" to have long hair, which serves as a covering or veil, while wearing long hair is "degrading" to men. He is disturbed that when the brethren dine together in church having brought their own food and drink, the more wealthy begin to eat before the poorer arrive, the former getting drunk while the latter go hungry (11:21). Rather than forming such factions, he urges the church members to consider themselves one body, just as the body of each person is a functional unity (12:12). But like our own bodies, the church does have a hierarchical organization.

> Now you are the body of Christ and individually members of it. And God has appointed in the church first apostles, second prophets, third teachers, then workers of miracles, then healers, helpers, administrators, speakers in various kinds of tongues. (12:27–28)

It is interesting that workers of miracles and healers are ranked lower on the scale than aspostles, prophets, and teachers.

We come now to those beautiful passages about love that reveal Paul in his most inspired spiritual and literary form. What he says at these times is as sublime as anything attributed to Jesus or to the prophets of the Old Testament, in my opinion, although Paul would have disclaimed any personal credit for them, attributing their origin to the Spirit of God within him.

> If I speak in the tongues of men and of angels, but have not love, I am a noisy gong or clanging cymbal. And if I have prophetic powers, and understand all mysteries and all knowledge, and if I have all faith, so as to remove mountains, but have not love, I am nothing. If I give away all I have, and if I deliver my body to be burned, but have not love, I gain nothing. (13:1–3)

How, then, is love manifested? His answer is one of the finest statements in all literature and more compelling than any found in philosophy.

> Love is patient and kind; love is not jealous or boastful; it is not arrogant or rude. Love does not insist on its own way; it is not irritable or resentful; it does not rejoice at wrong, but rejoices in the right. Love bears all things, believes all things, hopes all things, endures all things. (13:4–7)

If only we could abide by this while facing reality as it is without illusory beliefs or vain hopes!

> Love never ends; as for prophecy, it will pass away; as for tongues, they will cease; as for knowledge, it will pass away. For our knowledge is imperfect and our prophecy is imperfect; but when the perfect comes, the imperfect will pass away. When I was a child, I spoke like a child, I thought like a child, I reasoned like a child; when I became a man, I gave up childish ways. For now we see in a mirror dimly but then face to face. Now I know in part; then I shall understand fully, even as I have been fully understood. So faith, hope, love abide, these three, but the greatest of these is love. (13:8–13)

After these splendid passages which, along with those of Shakespeare, are among the most well known and cherished in the Western world, Paul turns to the relative merits of speaking in tongues and prophesying within the church which, judging from his criticism, must have been very boisterous. Speaking in tongues occurs when a person is so overcome with religious fervor that he or she begins babbling unintelligibly, "speaking into the air," as Paul graphically puts it, while those who prophecy convey some revelation or teaching that is instructive. Paul is not against speaking in tongues for those so possessed, but he prefers prophecy for its edification, while the former is senseless. Not to be outdone, however, he says, "I thank God that I speak in tongues more than you all; nevertheless, in church I would rather speak five words with my mind, in order to instruct others, than ten thousand words in tongue" (14:18–19). Thus he admonishes the brethren to be moderate in what they say when they come together in church, whether it be speaking in tongues, prophesying, or singing hymns. Although women often were given positions of responsibility in the churches and accorded an equality considerably greater than in the Greco-Roman culture, Paul maintains that "in all the churches of the saints, the women should keep silent in the churches" (14:33). If there is something they wish to know, they should "ask their husbands at home."

He next addresses one of the central questions of Christianity — the belief in the resurrection of Jesus exemplifying triumph over death. Declaring that according to scripture Jesus was crucified to redeem our sins, Paul then relates how he was entombed and raised on the third day, appeared to Peter first, then to the other disciples along with James his brother, and finally to them all. Somewhat on the defensive as to the authority of his preaching because he had not been one of the disciples who had been with Jesus in person, Paul humbly claims that because Jesus had appeared to him in the trance on the road to Damascus, he, too, had experienced his presence.

> Last of all, as to one untimely born, he appeared also to me. For I am the least of the apostles, unfit to be called an apostle, because I persecuted the church of God. But by the grace of God I am what I am, and his grace toward me was not in vain. On the contrary, I worked harder than any of them, though it was not I, but the grace of God which is with me. (15:8–10)

Because some converts apparently were questioning the reasonableness of the resurrection, Paul declared that if one denied that Jesus had been raised, not only had Paul's preaching been in vain, but he had also failed to convey truly God's intention to sacrifice Jesus to redeem man's sin. Thus Christianity would lose its essential message.

> If Christ has not been raised, your faith is futile and you are still in your sins. Then those also who have fallen asleep [died] in Christ have perished. If in this life we who are in Christ have only hope, we are of all men most to be pitied. (15:17–19)

So if it is not true that Jesus was resurrected, then the dead will perish and those who believe in Christ are to pitied for their credulity.

Naturally, Paul rejects this apostasy: "For as in Adam all die, so also in Christ shall all be made alive" (15:22). What would be the meaning of baptism into a new creation if, as Shakespeare claimed, "We are such stuff As Dreams are made on; and our little life is rounded with a sleep"? (*Tempest*, Act 4, Scene 1) Paul has a very dim view of human nature if there is not the promise of an afterlife: "If the dead are not raised, 'Let us eat and drink, for tomorrow we die' " (15:32). But this is a very depressing conception of human beings (consistent with the doctrine of original sin) implying that without the prospect of a reward of an afterlife human beings would prefer the lowest forms of pleasure. In contrast, John Stuart Mill defended a different view of humankind: "Human beings have faculties more elevated than the animal appetites, and when once made conscious of them, do not regard anything as happiness which does not include their gratification."[15] Thus higher pleasures have their own inherent attraction for Mill, regardless of any reward in the afterlife. Perhaps Mill's view of human nature was too optimistic, but many would agree with his famous comparison.

> It is better to be a human being dissatisfied than a pig satisfied; better to be Socrates dissatisfied than a fool satisfied. And if the fool, or the pig, are of a different opinion, it is because they only know their own side of the question. The other party to the comparison knows both sides.[16]

Apparently some brethren persisted in asking, if the dead are raised, how is it done? If their earthly body perishes do they acquire a new one and, if so, of what kind? Paul attempts to dispel the doubt with an affirmation, but not an explanation.

> Lo! I tell you a mystery. We shall not all sleep, but we shall all be changed, in a moment, in the twinkling of an eye, at the last trumpet. For the trumpet will sound, and the dead will be raised imperishable, and we shall be changed. For this perishable nature must put on the imperishable, and this mortal nature must put on immortality. (15:51–53)

In a famous statement Paul declares, "Death is swallowed up in victory" (15:54). However, his expectation that this transformation was imminent was not confirmed, as the many cartoons about "the world is coming to an end" attest. How different, but truer to life, is the answer of Shakespeare:

> . . . all our yesterdays have lighted fools
> The way to dusty death. Out, out brief candle!
> Life's but a walking shadow, a poor player
> That struts and frets his hour upon the stage
> And then is heard no more. It is a tale
> Told by an idiot, full of sound and fury
> Signifying nothing. (*Macbeth*, Act 5, Scene 5)

Paul concludes this first letter to the Corinthians with the request that they, as the Galatians, set aside something "on the first day of each week" for a gift to Jerusalem, which he will arrange to have sent when he arrives in Corinth after passing through Macedonia and Asia. He concludes with the admirable exhortation: "Be watchful, stand firm in your faith, be courageous, be strong. Let all that you do be done in love" (16:13–14).

PAUL'S SECOND LETTER TO THE CORINTHIANS

Unlike the previous letter to the Corinthians in which he counsels them on many practical problems confronting the nascent church, along with conveying some theological doctrines, Paul's second letter contains very little that is new or original, except for a description of a former mystical experience. Apparently a follow-up letter to his first one as well as an earlier visit, it contains an expression of his and God's concern for their welfare, a vivid summary of his persecutions and sufferings (11:23–29), an apology for the severity of his first letter, and the usual admonition to remain true to the faith. Having praised the Corinthians to Titus, when the latter after a visit to Corinth joined him in Macedonia Paul lauds their reception of him, declaring "I was not put to shame . . . our boasting . . . has proven true" (7:14).

Praising the Corinthians as those who "excel in everything—in faith, in utterance, in knowledge, in all earnestness, and in your love for us" (8:7), he asks for a generous offering for "the saints," presumably those in Jerusalem. Cleverly playing one off the other, he writes that despite the "extreme poverty" of the churches of Macedonia, their generosity "overflowed in a wealth of liberality on their part" (8:2). So in light of the abundant riches of Corinth he has boasted to the Macedonians that he is confident the Corinthians will excel in their offering when Titus and another of the brethren return to Corinth to receive their gift, "lest if some Macedonians . . . find you are not ready, we will be humiliated—to say nothing of you—for being so confident" (9:3–4). Asking that they not only give generously but willingly, he provides the inducement that has become so familiar in church offerings that "God loves a cheerful giver." (9:7)

Then in a series of passages he brags of his authority, declaring "that I am not in the least inferior to these superlative apostles" for "even if I am unskilled in speaking, I am not in knowledge" (11:5–6). Claiming to have "robbed other churches . . . in order to serve you" (11:8), he boasts of "visions and revelations of the Lord" (12:1). Resorting to subterfuge in refering to "know[ing] a man in Christ" to represent himself, he describes a mystical experience he had years earlier.

> I know a man in Christ who fourteen years ago was caught up to the third heaven—whether in the body or out of the body I do not know, only God knows. And I know that this man was caught up into Paradise—whether in the body or out of the body I do not know, God knows—and he heard things that cannot be told, which man may not utter. On behalf of this man I will boast, but on my own behalf I will not boast, except of my weakness. Though if I wish to boast, I shall not be a fool, for I shall be speaking the truth. (12:2–6)

Though puzzling in its indirect style and indefinite description, it would appear that Paul had an out-of-the-body experience similar to those that are reported today. In a religious trance he had a vision of himself ascending into heaven as if removed from his body. It is these kinds of out-of-the-body experiences, along with dreams, trances, and visions, that have been the hallmark of many religions in the past.

Perplexed by his physical weakness and indifferent speaking ability despite his other gifts, he offers this explanation:

> And to keep me from being too elated by the abundance of revelations, a thorn was given me in the flesh, a messenger of Satan, to harass me, to keep me from being too elated. Three times I besought the Lord about this, that it should leave me; but he said to me, "My grace is sufficient for you, for my power is made perfect in weakness." (12:7–9)

So as usual Satan is blamed, with God's acquiescence, to keep Paul humble. The letter ends with the familiar entreaty: "Mend your ways, heed my appeal, agree with one another, live in peace, and the God of love and peace will be with you. Greet one another with a holy kiss" (13:11–12).

THE LETTER OF PAUL TO THE PHILIPPIANS

Written while in prison because he says he is pleased at being able "to advance the gospel . . . throughout the whole praetorian guard," Paul does not indicate when or from where the letter was written. Unlike some of his other letters that are critical of the behavior of the brethren, he writes with deep admiration for the Philippians who are so well organized that the letter is addressed not only to the "saints in Christ Jesus who are at Philippi," but also to the "bishops and deacons." While he believes that their "prayers and the help of the Spirit of Jesus Christ" will permit his deliverance from prison, he is uncertain whether he should continue to live to serve Christ or die to be with him, although he feels duty bound to continue his mission.

> For to me to live is Christ, and to die is gain. If it is to be life in the flesh, that means fruitful labor for me. Yet which I shall choose I cannot tell. I am hard pressed between the two. My desire is to depart and be with Christ, for that is far better. But to remain in the flesh is more necessary on your account. (1:21–24)

Asking that their "manner of life be worthy of the gospel of Christ" so that he can be proud of them, he adds that "each of you look not only to his own interest, but also to the interests of others."

Paul then turns to a crucial theological inquiry into the status of Jesus: was he the son of man or the son of God? According to Paul, Christ Jesus originally existed "in the form of God" and then gave up this divine status to take on "human form" and be sacrificed, thereby earning even greater exaltation (although it is curious how Paul could know this). Thus the Philippians should be mindful of others as they are of Christ Jesus,

> who, though he was in the form of God, did not count equality with God a thing to be grasped, but emptied himself, taking the form of a servant, being born in the likeness of men. And being found in human form he humbled himself and became obedient unto death, even death on the cross. Therefore God has highly exalted him and bestowed on him the name which is above every name, that at the name of Jesus every knee should bow, in heaven and on earth and under the earth, and every tongue confess that Jesus Christ is Lord, to the glory of God the Father. (2:6–11)

Along with this important theological interpretaion of Jesus, the letter is instructive in that it shows the devotion among the apostles. Paul refers to Timothy, apparently imprisoned with him, serving the gospel at his side "as a son with a father" (2:22). After their release from prison he hopes to send Timothy, along with Epaphroditus, his "brother and fellow worker and fellow soldier" who just had recovered from a serious illness, to serve as messengers and to minister to their needs (cf. 2:25–26). He also mentions two women, Euodia and Syntyche, who should be helped because "they have labored side by side with me in the gospel together with Clement and the rest of my fellow workers, whose names are in the book of life" (4:2–4). Thus the spiritual solidarity and moral integrity of these early Christian churches are not only encouraged and reaffirmed by Paul's letters, there is a constant exchange of apostles to strengthen these religious ties. The letter closes with a curious reference, left unexplained by Paul, to greetings from all the brethren or saints who are with him, "especially those of Caesar's household" (4:21).

THE FIRST LETTER TO THE THESSALONIANS

The first letter begins by praising the Thessalonians who had "become an example to all the believers in Macedonia and Achaia" (1:7). They, in fact, have "turned to God from idols, to serve a living and true God, and to wait for his son from heaven . . . who delivers us from the wrath to come" (1:9–10). Apparently written after a visit to Philippi where he says he "had already suffered and been shamefully treated," he indicates that he had more success among the brethren in Thessalonia who themselves had suffered and been much afflicted by their countrymen. Remaining in Athens Paul sent Timothy "to establish you in your faith and to exhort you, that no one be moved by these afflictions" (3:2–3). This is an indication of how some of these early churches suffered from persecution, yet Paul was comforted to learn, upon Timothy's return, that they had remained steadfast in their faith.

Instructing them as to how they should live, he asks that they "abstain from immorality; that each one of you . . . take a wife for himself in holiness and in honor, not in the passion of lust like heathen who do not know God. . . ." (4:3–4) He turns then to the question whether only those who are living will be saved when Jesus returns or also those who have "fallen asleep." Declaring that just as he had died and then was resurrected, so with great authority and fanfare when Jesus comes he will first raise those who are asleep and then those who are alive.

> For the Lord himself will descend from heaven with a cry of command, with the archangel's call, and with the sound of the trumpet of God. And the dead in Christ will rise first; then we who are alive, who are left, shall be caught up together with them in the clouds to meet the Lord in the air; and so we shall always be with the Lord. (4:16–17)

A glorious vision, it hardly is credible that the dead somehow will appear in the clouds and in the air, though this has been a source of consolation to those who dread death. But is it really possible to believe that God will sound a trumpet and that the billions of dead throughout history (including Neanderthals and Cro-Magnons?) will rise and commingle in the clouds? Some argue that such declarations should be taken metaphorically or symbolically, but apart from the fact that Paul undoubtedly intended them to be taken literally, they do not have much credibility even if taken symbolically. Christianity, it seems to me, is based on the two pillars of credulity and wishful thinking. As to "the times and the seasons," though the coming of the Lord often has been announced Paul avoids any precise prediction, saying "that the day of the Lord will come like a thief in the night" (5:2)—not an especially reassuring simile. Perhaps for that reason Paul adds that those reborn in Christ Jesus are not living in darkness but in the light of day and therefore have nothing to fear: "For God has not destined us for wrath, but to obtain salvation through our Lord Jesus Christ, who died for us so that whether we wake or sleep we might live with him" (5:9–10). The letter ends with the usual stylized request that they live according to the teachings of Christ and the will of God.

THE SECOND LETTER TO THE THESSALONIANS

Although the second letter to the Thessalonians concludes with the statement: "I, Paul, write this greeting with my own hand . . . the mark in every letter of mine," questions have been raised about its authenticity.[17] At least written in the manner of Paul, after commending the Thessalonians for their growing faith and increasing love for one another, the letter addresses two issues: the first perhaps related to what had been said in the previous letter about the coming of the Lord, and the second pertaining to charges of idleness among them. As to the first problem, the letter states that they are "not to be quickly shaken in mind or excited, either by spirit or by word, or by letter purporting to be from us, to the effect that the day of the Lord has come" (2:2). The letter adds that they should not be deceived by anyone, for

> that day will not come, unless the rebellion comes first, and the man of
> lawlessness is revealed, the son of perdition, who opposes and exalts
> himself against every so-called god or object of worship, so that he takes
> his seat in the temple of God, proclaiming to be God. (2:2–4)

The terms "man of lawlessness" and "son of perdition" never having been used by Paul previously, this is one reason, along with the peculiarity of the message, for questioning the authenticity of the letter.

While difficult to interpret, the passage suggests that there is some kind of lawless agency already at work in the world, an emissary of Satan, who is for the present restrained by the Lord Jesus. But when this mysterious power reveals himself by "pretended signs and wonders," as well as by "wicked deception for those who are to perish, because they refused to love the truth and be saved," he then will be destroyed by the coming of Christ (2:6–10). This conflict seems to be a kind of test to distinguish between the faithful and the faithless: "God sends upon them a strong delusion, to make them believe what is false, so that all may be condemned who did not believe the truth but had pleasure in unrighteousness" (2:11–12). Paul then expresses his confidence that the Thessalonians will not be among the deluded and the condemned because God, through Paul's gospel, chose them "from the beginning to be saved, through sanctification by the Spirit and belief in the truth" (2:13).

The second problem arose because some among the Thessalonians, taking advantage of the generosity of the others (or perhaps due to a kind of listlessness in expectation of the anticipated apocalypse), were living in idleness. Recalling the fact that when he was with them he paid for his food and "worked night and day that we might not burden any of you," he "commands" that they "keep away from any brother who is living in idleness and not in accord with the tradition that you received from us" (3:6). Paul assumes that by avoiding such people and not treating them as an enemy, as he says, their shame will be enough to change their ways (3:14–15).

Except for the brief letter to Philemon which adds nothing to our understanding of Paul's mission, this concludes the review of his authentic letters. I have decided not to discuss the other letters in the New Testament; they are there to be read and a number of New Testament scholars, such as Kee, have studied them extensively. What I wanted to learn from Paul's letters was his main contributions to the rise of Christianity. What has emerged is that he believed that God revealed Jesus Christ directly to him, initially commanding him to cease his persecution of the disciples of Jesus and to suffer as an apostle in spreading the word of the new covenant. Insisting always that his gospel came not from himself but from God, he preached the virtues of righteousness and brotherly love. Despite his own background as a Pharisee, he was visionary in claiming that adherence to such Mosaic laws as circumcision, along with dietary and temple rituals, were inconsequential compared to having faith in and being reborn in Christ Jesus, thus opening the church to the gentiles. It was this avowal of tolerance and openness that were mainly responsible for the survival and growth of Christianity.

Expecting the return of the Lord during his lifetime, Paul interpreted the sacrifice and death of Jesus, followed by his resurrection, as the atonement for humanity's inherited sin owing to its disobedience and the redemptive promise of immortality for the true believers. Very much aware of the moral weakness of humankind, he attributed its salvation not to good works or righteousness itself (which he nonetheless extolled), but to God's grace. Undergoing considerable persecution and suffering, he spread these doctrines by example in preaching and in writing during his extensive travels throughout the Near East, Asia Minor, Greece, and Macedonia. While Jesus is the acclaimed divine inspiration of Christianity, it actually was Paul who ensured its survival and whose teachings provided much of the doctrinal background for the church. As Rodney Stark says, "when historians speak of the *early* church, they do not mean the church in Jerusalem [headed by the apostles Peter and James, the latter the brother of Jesus] but the Pauline church—for this is the church that triumphed and changed history."[18]

THE RISE OF CHRISTIANITY

Although Paul was not the only apostle or evangelist spreading the word of the gospel, his estimated 10,000 miles of travel to the various cities mentioned in his letters was by far the most extensive and effective. For that reason the description of his perilous voyages described in the Acts of the Apostles, along with the nature of his preaching, counseling, and organizational instructions conveyed in his letters, provide the most immediate and direct information about the establishment of the first Christian churches. Considering that Jesus' own mission was restricted to the region of Galilee, how did this tiny breakaway Israeli sect, initially comprising the eleven apostles and several members of Jesus' family, grow large enough within four centuries to challenge Greco-Roman paganism and become the state religion of Imperial Rome under Constantine, eventually becoming the prevailing religion in Western civilization? Since miracles played such an important role in authenticating these early religions, it has been argued that the tremendous success of Christianity against overwhelming odds itself attests to a divine provenance, another self-authenticating miracle.

Yet when the rise of Christianity is examined from a more sober or realistic viewpoint, utilizing the methods of the social sciences, the need for a supernatural explanation is obviated. These methods, employed in current sociological investigations of the growth of more recent 'religions' such as Mormonism, Christian Science, and Scientology, along with cults like the Unification Church (more familiarly known as the Moonies), have enabled sociologists to extrapolate how the early Christian communities developed into larger churches in the major cities located around the Mediterranean basin. I shall summarize the results of these studies to complement what was portrayed in the Acts and the Epistles of Paul regarding the rise of Christianity.[19]

Jesus died about 30 C.E., with Paul's conversion occurring a few years later in 34. Believing that the revelation from Jesus Christ commanded him to spread the gospel, he must have begun his apostolic mission shortly thereafter. Then in the year 50 the Apostolic Council in Jerusalem decided that the other apostles should attempt to spread the word of the new covenant beyond Jerusalem by going to the outlying urban centers. How was this accomplished? Because the evangelists were Israelites with an entrée to the synagogues established by the Hellenistic Jews of the diaspora in the major Mediterranean cities, it seems likely that they would go to these places, perhaps carrying letters of introduction from family members or friends. This supposition is reinforced by Paul's frequent references to his preaching in the synagogues where initially he was welcome. It was not until he began to attract a large following, arousing jealousy and resentment among the Pharisees and the Sadducees, as he often writes, that he then was forced to flee to avoid persecution and imprisonment, sometimes without success.

But though apostles such as Paul and Peter were compelled to leave as they attracted more converts, the fact that Christian communities were established, despite their departure, meant that they had been successful in attracting a core of believers. While the original converts probably were drawn by the preaching of the apostles in the synagogues, as well as from personal contacts among the families or friends they stayed with, for these groups to grow into churches they had to increase by drawing additional members. Here is where recent sociological studies of the expansion of religious groups, such as the Mormons and the Unified Church, are helpful. The studies show that proselytizers are least effective when they approach strangers or those already attached to a religion, whereas they are most successful attracting relatives and friends who do not belong to any church and are somewhat indifferent to religion.

Thus it was found that people with no religious affiliation, rather than being more resistant to persuasion, are more likely to be attracted to a novel religious movement than those who already have strong ties to a particular religion. As Stark says, "*New religious movements mainly draw their converts from the ranks of the religiously inactive and discontented. . . .*"[20] However, the new religion should not be too unfamiliar or bizarre, people being "*more willing to adopt a new religion to the extent that it retains cultural continuity with conventional religion(s) with which they already are familiar*" (p. 55). The latter would seem to be confirmed by the fact that the early converts to Christianity were from the synagogues. That the apostles themselves were Jewish, preaching to Israelites within the synagogues and frequently quoting the Old Testament while describing Jesus as a descendant of Abraham, Moses, and David, certainly maintained cultural continuity with Judaism. Furthermore, the new religion had the added appeal of identifying Jesus as the Messiah prophesied in the Old Testament (Isaiah 7:14; 9:6), a deliverer who brought redemption of sins and everlasting life to the converts. This surely was a strong incentive despite the fact that the religious solidarity among the Jews offered considerable resistance to conversion.

But even more important than continuity with an older tradition in attracting new adherents is personal ties. The realization that to be accepted in a preferred group is greatly facilitated by adopting its beliefs and practices *is the strongest motivation* for converting to a particular religion. The evidence for this is compelling. That husbands and wives would like to convert their spouses is well known, while children normally adopt the religion of their parents. Striking examples of this is the influence the mothers of Constantine and Augustine had on their sons' conversions. Young people of marriageable age are encouraged, if not pressured, to marry within their religion, race, or nationality. In ancient times, if the head of a prominent or prosperous household adopted a new religion it was common for all the members of the household to do likewise, including not only the immediate family but also the servants and slaves. Though not always successful, caesars, kings, and lords generally expected their fellow countrymen to worship similar gods. Military leaders felt more secure and confident of their commands when their soldiers were of the same faith; conversely, countrymen, subordinates, servants, and slaves often were eager to adopt the religion of their superiors for anticipated preferences and benefits.

Although for a long time it was believed that Christianity had its greatest appeal among the poorer exploited classes, such as the servants and slaves, who found in the Christian values of brotherly love, equality, humility, and God's preference for the poor and the downtrodden some compensation for their own lowly status and treatment, this view has been challenged in recent years. Despite the fact that Joseph, Jesus' father, was an illiterate carpenter by trade and thus from the lower class, as Jesus was, and his original disciples poor illiterate fishermen, it is now believed that the early converts to Christianity were not from the lower classes, but from the middle or lower upper classes. Although Paul was a tentmaker by trade, the Acts state that he had a fine Hellenistic education, could speak Hebrew as well as Greek, was able to hold his own against the philosophers of Athens, and certainly was anything but illiterate considering the inspired literary quality and lofty expressions of his epistles.

As his letters indicate, Paul seemed to have attracted fairly well-to-do converts in cities like Antioch, Corinth, Athens, Philippi, and Ephesus. Some of his letters refer to the meetings and suppers in the homes of the members of the church, implying that they must have been quite large to accommodate such gatherings. Also the fact that in some letters he cautions the women against putting too much emphasis on fine clothes, expensive jewelry, and fancy hairdos attests to the wealth of some of the families. In addition, his criticism of some people at communal suppers who had plentiful food and wine without sharing with the less fortunate, indicates class divisions.

However, it was not until the conversion of Constantine in 312 C.E. that the incentive to convert from the Greco-Roman pagan gods to Christianity was transmitted from the heads of households to those of lesser status. Prior to that the evidence suggests that it was the children's nurses and tutors, along with the servants and slaves (who were not always poor or deprived, some being well rewarded by their masters) in the prosperous homes who, after their own conversions, were able to attract the children and mothers of the household to Christianity. This occurred in the urban centers where the more prosperous and prominent families lived, not among the poorer farmers living in the countryside. In confirmation, recall the conclusion of Paul's letter to the Philippians in which he writes, "All the saints greet you, especially those of Caesar's household" (4:22). This indicates that even that early there were members of Caesar's retinue (referring to appointed kings or rulers locally) who were Christians. At the beginning of that letter he says that during his imprisonment he was able "to advance the gospel, so that it has become known throughout the whole praetorian guard" (1:12), the elite imperial bodyguards. This, too, attests to the spread of the gospel among the higher classes.

Since most of the children's nurses and many of the servants in these households were women, they were especially placed to attract outsiders to the church. But the situation is much more involved and interesting. Demographic studies, based on ancient manuscripts and burial cites with markers, indicate that "among Christians there soon were far more women than men, while among pagans men far outnumbered women" (p. 96). Unlike the Greeks and Romans who, greatly preferring sons (as in China tody), practiced female infanticide on a large scale, advocated abortions to eliminate unwanted births (for example, conceptions before marriage or by adultery), and favored birth control (utilizing drugs, intrauterine devices, and alternative methods of sexual gratification from vaginal intercourse) in order to reduce the size of families, the Christians following Jewish laws that prohibited these practices, rejected them. Thus three main causes of female mortality were eliminated. In addition, the higher social and legal status afforded women in Christian, as compared to pagan, communities explains why more women were converted to Christianity than men.

Stark provides a graphic description of the low status of women in Athens, perhaps partially explaining the prevalence of homosexuality among Athenian males, since young men would have been better educated, more cultivated, and thus more interesting companions than women.

> The status of Athenian women was very low. Girls received little or no education. Typically, Athenian females were married at puberty and often before. Under Athenian law a woman was classified as a child, regardless of age, and therefore was the legal property of some man at all stages in her life. Males could divorce by simply ordering a wife out of the household. Moreover, if a woman was seduced or raped, her husband was legally compelled to divorce her. If a woman wanted a divorce, she had to have her father or some other man bring her case before a judge. Finally, Athenian women could own property, but control of the property was always vested in the male to whom she "belonged. . . ." (p. 102)

Although Roman women were better educated, more respected, and exercised greater influence in society than Athenian women, their position still was not enviable. As in Athens, they often were married by puberty or younger, twelve years considered the marriageable age: "Octavia and Agrippina married at 11 and 12, Quintilian's wife bore him a son when she was 13, Tacitus wed a girl of 13, and so on" (p. 105). Girls compelled to marry when even younger were considered to be engaged until their twelfth year, at which age they were recognized as "legitimate wives." Even supposing girls in that society matured earlier, this custom must have been regarded as cruel, for Plutarch notes, " 'the hatred and fear of girls forced contrary to nature' " (p. 107). Furthermore, their husbands were normally much older, making it difficult to establish an equitable relationship.

There is considerable evidence of hostility among Roman husbands and wives, husbands often complaining of how difficult it was to get along with their wives, leading to a large proportion of bachelors in Roman society. This, along with the much higher female mortality described earlier and the marked preference for small families, contributed to a notable depopulation of Roman citizens in the centuries coinciding with the growth of Christianity. To encourage families to have at least three children, Julius Caesar, along with Emperors like Augustus and Trajan, passed various decrees from child subsidies (as in contemporary France) to land grants to promote larger families. They even imposed "political and financial sanctions upon childless couples, upon unmarried women over the age of twenty, and upon unmarried men over the age of twenty-five" (p. 115). Yet nothing prevented the decrease in the population which now is believed to have been a significant factor in the decline of Rome.

In contrast, females in Christian communities enjoyed a more agreeable situation. Female babies were not killed or exposed to the elements, abortion (the methods of which were so primitive that if they did not kill the mother they often left her infertile) was outlawed, birth control (which also endangered the life and fertility of the mother) was not practiced, and Christian girls married at a later age (cf. p. 107). Adultery, a common practice among both sexes in the empire, was considered immoral and divorce not encouraged among the Christians. Although Paul always placed men above women in status, he advocated equality and mutuality in their personal relations. Moreover, as numerous references to women (Phaebe, Prisca, Mary, Apphia, Euodea, and Syntyche) in his letters indicate, he acknowledged their importance as "fellow workers," Phaebe even becoming a deaconess (Rom. 16:1–2). In this respect the Christians diverged not only from the pagans, but also from the Jews who did not allow women to officiate at the religious ceremonies in the Temples.

For these reasons, an increasing number of women in pagan households found the moral code of their Christian attendants more appealing than that of their own religion. They in turn were in a position to influence not only their children, but also their husbands who, if they converted, tended to bring the entire household with them. Furthermore, the predominance of female Christians along with the greater number of males in the surrounding pagan societies increased the probability that some Christian women would choose their husbands from among the Greeks and Romans. Unlike the Jews who discouraged exogamous marriages, both Paul and Peter sanctioned marriages between Christians and gentiles, confident that when the pagans saw the chaste, respectful, and modest behavior of their Christian wives, they, too, would be attracted to the new covenant. In this way the community of Christians gradually expanded to include more gentiles. Paul's relaxation of the Jewish laws pertaining to circumcision and dietary restrictions facilitated this inclusion and consequent growth in numbers. This increase was abetted also by the Christian regulation that the children of 'mixed' marriages should be brought up Christian.

But another crucial factor contributed to the greater proportional increase of Christians during these first four centuries, the occurrence of two deadly epidemics. During the fifteen-year duration of the earlier epidemic which began in 165 C.E., probably due to colera, "from a quarter to a third of the empire's population died from it, including Marchus Aurelius himself in 180 in Vienna" (p. 73). This was followed in 251 by another epidemic, this time perhaps due to an outbreak of measles which again decimated the population. At its peak, it is estimated that "five thousand people a day were reported to have died in the city of Rome alone" (p. 77). Although not usually mentioned as contributing to the decline of Rome, Stark believes that the decrease in the birthrate mentioned previously, along with the drastic reduction in the population caused by these devastating epidemics, were in fact an important cause. He quotes Hans Zinnser's dramatic statement that " 'again and again, the forward march of Roman power and world organization was interrupted by the only force against which political genius and military power were utterly helpless—epidemic disease. . . .' "[21]

However, considering that Christians were no more immune from these virulent epidemics than the pagans (which would have been an excellent occasion for the Christian God to display 'his' superior power over the pagan gods by protecting the Christians, but apparently did not seize the opportunity), how did this affect their disproportionate growth rates at the time? The answer, as in the case of lower female mortality among Christian women, lies in their higher moral principles. To be considered righteous, according to Christian ethics, one not only had to "love God" but also "love one's neighbor as oneself," a notion very foreign to the gentiles who were much more selfish and competitive. Thus Christian morality translated into a highly motivated sense of communal solidarity and social concern. Even though salvation ultimately depended upon God's grace, longing to be in God's grace meant that one lived for others, including the pagans or gentiles. Thus when the epidemics struck, in contrast to the pagans who tended to abandon those who fell ill and flee from the catastrophe, as the great Roman physician Galen is said to have done, the Christians generally remained steadfast in caring for the sick, even at the risk of contracting the disease and dying.

Without any understanding of bacterial or viral infections or how diseases are caused and transmitted, epidemics were entirely mysterious and terrifying, intensifying the sense of futility, panic, and chaos. Not having the slightest inkling of their actual causes, it was natural to attribute them to the anger, punishment, or caprice of the gods. Yet without knowing what were the transgressions, how could one redress these offenses or appease the gods? For the pagans there seemed to be no explanation or effective recourse, while the Christians looked upon the devastation as testing their faith and belief. In addition, they were less afraid to expose themselves to the disease or to die, not believing, as most of the pagans, that this would be their end, expecting that their sacrifice would be rewarded in the afterlife. Thus the faith and beliefs of the Christians enhanced their self-sacrificing care of others, including the gentiles.

Dionysus, Bishop of Alexandria, has left a vivid description of the behavior of the Christians at the peak of the second epidemic around the year 260.

> Most of our brother Christians showed unbounded love and loyalty, never sparing themselves and thinking only of one another. Heedless of danger, they took charge of the sick, attending to their every need and ministering to them in Christ, and with them departed this life serenely happy; for they were infected by others with the disease, drawing on themselves the sickness of their neighbors and cheerfully accepting their pains. Many, in nursing and curing others, transferred their death to themselves and died in their stead. . . . The best of our brothers lost their lives in this manner, a number of presbyters, deacons, and laymen winning high commendation so that death in this form, the result of great piety and strong faith, seems in every way the equal of martyrdom.[22]

One might question the accuracy of this account considering that it was written by a Christian Bishop, but even the Emperor Julian who was no friend of the Christians, about a century later in 362 reluctantly had to admit that the " 'recent Christian growth was caused by their 'moral character, even if pretended,' and by their 'benevolence toward strangers and care for the graves of the dead' " (pp. 83–84). Julian was not referring to the behavior of Christians during the epidemics but in general, attributing the "growth" of Christianity to their "moral character," even though he was reluctant to acknowledge that it was sincere.

This, then, brings us back to the question of how the contrasting responses of the Christians and the pagans to the terrible epidemics led to a disproportionate growth in the number of Christians, since they were as susceptible to infection and death as the pagans. The answer turns out to be rather simple, if the explanation by William McNeill is correct.

> "When all normal services break down, quite elementary nursing will greatly reduce mortality. Simple provisions of food and water, for instance, will allow persons who are temporarily too weak to cope for themselves to recover instead of perishing miserably."[23]

According to Stark, "Modern medical experts believe that conscientious nursing *without any medications* could cut the mortality rate by two-thirds or even more" (p. 89). Attempting to calculate more exactly how the difference in caring for the sick between the pagans and the Christians affected their survival rates, Stark concluded that in "a city having 10,000 inhabitants" the ratio of Christians to pagans of 1 to 249 in 160 C.E. changed to 1 to 134 in 170, a significant shift in just one decade (cf. p. 89).

So if what has been said is true (the fact that the Christians were devoted to caring for the gentiles along with one another, while the gentiles did not have a framework of beliefs or devout faith to support such self-sacrificing activities, abandoning the sick to die in miserable isolation), then this could account for the greater percentage of survivors among the Christians. If one combines this with the lower mortality rate among the female Christians and the increase in growth rate in general, owing to their rejection of dangerous abortion and birth control practices, then this would obviate the need for a miraculous explanation for the rise of Christianity.

Yet even apart from these factors Stark has calculated, based on an estimated population of the empire of 60 million and projected growth rate among the Christians of nearly 40 percent per decade (3.42 percent per year), that starting with 1,000 Christians in 40 C.E., by the year 350 the population would have grown to 33,882,008, a figure that appears miraculous, but in fact is just a normal exponential growth rate (cf. pp. 6–7). Furthermore, because the Christian population was growing and the Roman declining, the percentage of the Christian to Roman population would have increased from 0.0017 percent in 40 C.E. to 56.5 percent by 350.

Thus an immense Christian gain would have occurred without their having made a single convert during this period. But, as noted, these same trends ought to have resulted in many converts. For one thing, if, during the crises, Christians fulfilled their ideal of ministering to *everyone*, there would be many pagan survivors who owed their lives to their Christian neighbors. For another, no one could help but notice that Christians not only found the capacity to risk death but were much less likely to die. (p. 90; brackets added)

So if during the first four centuries one combines these additional population increases with the normal exponential growth rate estimated by Stark, then what seems to be the astonishing rise of Christianity no longer appears so extraordinary. Rather than explaining this success as due to divine intervention, it can be attributed to the superior moral values of the Christian religion, which was influenced by the more humane ethical practices of the Israelites. I believe these sociological studies round out or fill in the accounts given in the Acts and the Pauline Epistles of the manner in which these early Christian communities originated and expanded, becoming the official religion of the Roman Empire in the fourth century. Based on the network of apostolic exchanges among these early churches, along with the reasons for the successful growth of the initial Christian communities, what this sociological approach grounded on statistical evidence does not explain, with the exception of the greater appeal of the moral behavior of the Christians, are the kinds of inner religious experiences that led to the initial conversions. These will be discussed in the final chapter, chapter 6.

NOTES

1. Howard Clark Kee, *Understanding the New Testament*, 5th ed. (Englewood Cliffs, N.J.: Prentice Hall, 1993), p. 214.
2. Ibid.
3. Unless otherwise indicated, the following references in the text are to the Acts.
4. 'Areopagus' literally means the 'Hill of Mars', a place on a hill overlooking the Agora or Greek marketplace where the Athenian Court of Morals and Manners met to discuss philosophical or religious issues. Cf. Kee, p. 208.
5. As indicated previously, that the author of Acts actually traveled with Paul and thus was a witness to his later journeys is generally discredited. Paul died in 63 C.E. before the destruction of the temple, while the Acts is considered to have been written after its destruction in 70 C.E.
6. Kee, p. 185.
7. Ibid.

8. Ibid., p. 212.

9. These dates are based on Kee, p. 224. His dates follow that of Robert Jewett, *A Chronology of Paul's Life* (Philadelphia: Fortress Press, 1979), pp. 96–104.

10. Kee, pp. 223–24.

11. Cf. ibid., pp. 187, 242.

12. Ibid., p. 244.

13. Ibid.

14. Ibid., pp. 282–83.

15. John Stuart Mill, *Utilitarianism*, chap. 2, par. 6

16. Ibid.

17. Kee, p. 224.

18. Rodney Stark, *The Rise of Christianity* (San Francisco: Harper Collins, 1997), p. 45; brackets added.

19. My discussion is based mainly on the research presented in Rodney Stark's excellent book just quoted. I also found two other fine studies especially useful: Wayne A. Meeks, *The First Urban Christians* (New Haven: Yale University Press, 1983) and Ramsey MacMullen, *Christianizing the Roman Empire: A.D. 100–400* (New Haven: Yale University Press, 1986). Also Robin Lane Fox's *Pagans and Christians* (New York: Alfred A. Knopf, Inc. 1987) is an excellent study, although I came upon it too late to incorporate in this work.

20. Stark, p. 54. Until otherwise indicated, the following references in the text are to this work.

21. Hans Zinsser, *Rats, Lice and History* (New York: Bantam Books, [1934]1960), p. 99. Quoted by Stark, p. 74.

22. Dionysus, "Festival Letters," quoted by Eusebius, *Ecclesiastical History*, trans. G.A. Williamson (Harmondsworth, Middlesex: Penguin Books, 1965), 7.22. Quoted by Stark, p. 82.

23. W. H. McNeill, *Plagues and Peoples* (New York: Doubleday, 1976), p. 108. Quoted from Stark, p. 88.

5

THE INCONGRUITY OF
RELIGION AND SCIENCE

"**W**hat can we know or justifiably believe?" has been one of the most tantalizing questions asked by human beings since the dawn of civilization. Is tradition comprising folklore, common sense beliefs, and some kind of religious heritage a reliable source of knowledge? Is the evidence of our senses extolled by empiricists and at least crucial for survival, the most secure basis of knowing? Or is science with its inherent self-correcting safeguards utilizing experimental tests under replicable conditions the only trustworthy form of knowledge, especially considering the remarkable discoveries and advances attained by the various sciences in the twentieth century? "Why not a combined selection from of all of these?" one might answer, but this reply is too facile because religious beliefs derived from an archaic past cannot be reconciled with what we have since learned about the universe, while the Copernican Revolution taught us that our ordinary experiences based on sensory observations can be fundamentally deceptive. Yet even scientific knowledge, with its constant revisions and unresolved paradoxes, such as the wave-particle duality and the indeterminate superposition of non-commutative properties in quantum mechanics, along with the mind-brain impasse in neuroscience, raises serious questions about its ultimate veracity. That some epistemic claims within these different sources of beliefs have proven false does not mean, of course, that they all are, but it does raise misgivings about their overall truthfulness.

216

CONCEPTUAL-LINGUISTIC FRAMEWORKS OR BELIEF SYSTEMS

Regardless of the answers to these questions one thing can be asserted with relative assurance: that all knowledge claims and beliefs are framework dependent. Without a background conceptual-linguistic framework no experience would be interpretable, intelligible, or communicable. Even mystical experiences, if claimed to be a source of knowledge or justification of certain beliefs must be interpreted in some conceptual system, otherwise they are just ineffable. Like melodies that haunt a composer's consciousness or poetic themes that lurk in the minds of poets, until the rhythms are set in musical notation and the rhymes fixed in verse they are merely ephemeral states of mind. Only when the reputed revelations, sensory stimuli, or experimental results are interpreted within a religious, common sense, or scientific framework do they become possible knowledge.

What makes these basic frameworks intelligible is that the physical signs (spoken or printed words, mathematical notation, or scientific symbols) possess a meaning in the sense of being understood and having a discernible reference. The terms in the system must be meaningful (or they will be as unintelligible as the proverbial Greek) and their referents identifiable (for example, 'hippopotamus', 'magenta', 'neutrinos', and 'prokaryotic cells'). Both of these semantic modes of meaning, intensional or connotative and extensional or denotative, underlie the intelligibility of a linguistic system, along with the syntax or grammatical structure. Initially, we learn the meaning of nouns, pronouns, adjectives, verbs, and adverbs, the essential referentials in language, by causal proximity and ostensive definition: by associating the word with the object, action, or quality as it is pointed to. In contrast, the meaning of articles, prepositions, conjunctions, declaratives, and so forth, along with the grammar or syntax, are learned through using the language in interaction with people.

These conceptual-linguistic frameworks with their two modes of meaning and syntactic structure not only make interpretation and communication possible, they comprise a network of implicative or entailment relations that is the basis of our inferences, reasoning, and arguments. For example, the biblical name 'Moses' connotes the exodus from Egypt, the parting of the dead sea, the burning bush, and the ten commandments, while the term 'quark' designates subnuclear particles with fractional charges introduced to explain the properties and interactions of nucleons. Whether we can follow a person's discussion and reasoning depends upon understanding these webs of meanings, while fundamental disagreements (if they are not due to misunderstanding) usually are a sign of basic differences in the background conceptual-linguistic frameworks. When we query the truth of an assertion, whether religious, common sense, or scientific, we could be questioning the validity of the statement on the occasion in which it is expressed, but if there is a basic disagreement it is more likely that we are challenging the background system of beliefs in which the statement is embedded and which gives it its meaning. Any justification of a religion based on its sacred origin or infallibility begs the question because it presupposes the truth of the religious system, the very point at issue. Having evolved within a particular historical epoch with its underlying cultural and intellectual presuppositions, all conceptual frameworks are subject to reinterpretation in light of later discoveries and intellectual developments.

THE TWO MAJOR CULTURAL INFLUENCES ON WESTERN CIVILIZATION

In the West there have been two major cultural influences that have formed our basic framework of beliefs: the Hebraic-Christian revelatory, fath-based religion and the proto-scientific interpretation of the universe initiated by the ancient Greeks. Throughout much of past history these two belief systems were integrated by modifying the older religious framework to accommodate the newer discoveries of science, but since the nineteenth century the disparity between them has grown, evincing what has been called a "warfare."[1] Despite this fact, today there is a strong movement in the United States to reconcile these conflicting conceptual systems based on the conviction that current scientific developments, such as revisions in Darwin's theory of evolution and the big bang theory, support ancient religious texts or imply a convergence of science and religion.[2] However, a close examination of the underlying presuppositions of these different cultural traditions reveals how implausible is such a reconciliation.

The earliest attempts to account for the origin of the world occur as myths, theogonies, and theophanies. Surprisingly, the world's major religions and philosophical ideologies appeared roughly within the same time frame from 800–200 B.C.E., a period called the "Axial Age."[3] Apparently, the economic, social, and cultural conditions around the globe at that time led to the replacement of the tenuous earlier oral traditions with a more stable written record of the origin of the universe and life, along with the derivation and justification of the particular mores, festivities, liturgies, and political institutions of the various ethnic regions. Thus Osirianism arose in Egypt, Zoroastrianism and Mithraism in Persia,

Orphiasm in Greece, Taoism and Confucianism in China, Hinduism and Buddhism in India, and Judaism in Canaan or Palestine. It was Judaism, of course, that contributed the fundamental religious background to Western civilization, giving rise to Christianity along with the dominant religion of the Near East, the Muslim religion.

Founded on the belief that a divine being (Yahweh, God, or Allah) had been revealed to a succession of prophets (or in the case of Jesus Christ, to an incarnate God), these epiphanies when recorded became sacred scripture. Comprising revelations to Abraham, Moses, Nathan, Isaiah, and so on in the Old Testament, Jesus Christ, Peter, and Paul in the New Testament, and Muhammad in the Koran, these sacred writings have been considered by billions of people to be the infallible word of God. Not only inerrant, the Old and New Testaments are believed to contain the only knowledge worth knowing, as declared by Augustine: "Nothing is to be accepted except on the authority of Sacred Scripture, since greater is that authority than all powers of the human mind."[4] This exclusion of any beliefs not sanctioned by scripture, along with the eclipse of classical learning, were the main reasons scientific investigations were not pursued in the West during the Middle or Dark Ages. Instead, divine inspiration, religious experience, and faith were extolled as the only acceptable sources of knowledge for all ages.

While one can understand why individuals like Augustine (354–430 C.E.), given the intellectual and cultural ethos of the time held such a belief, that vast numbers of educated people still hold this conviction, despite the tremendous change in our worldview due to scientific discoveries and theoretical advances since the Renaissance, is extremely perplexing. As a philosophy professor at a secular university in the nation's capital I am dismayed to find how many entering students know more about the Genesis story of creation, the life and teachings of Jesus, or the tenets of the Koran than they do about the scientific contributions of Copernicus and Kepler, Galileo and Newton, Dalton and Lavoisier, Darwin and Leakey, and Einstein and Hawking.[5] It is as if they still were living in the distant past rather than in the contemporary world.

However, a growing number of Old Testament scholars acknowledge that the account of creation in Genesis that originated four thousand years ago, at a time when people knew practically nothing about the universe, is mythical or legendary. As R. P. C and A. T. Hanson, two Anglican theologians state, "Everything narrated in the Old Testament about the history of Israel up till the entry into Canaan is either myth or legend."[6] Yet there are millions of people throughout the world who believe that the entire Old Testament is literally infallible. In certain regions of the United States there is strong opposition to accepting scientific evidence for the theory of evolution plus the deceptive belief that the big bang theory of the origin of the universe confirms Genesis. But a glance at Genesis itself reveals how implausible are these convictions.

RÉSUMÉ OF THE TWO CREATION STORIES IN GENESIS

Most biblical scholars now agree that the two creation stories in Genesis, despite their long history of divine inerrancy, are mythical. So the issue is not whether Genesis is a myth, but the fact that millions of intelligent people still persist in thinking it is a true account of creation, as the recent but aborted decision by the Kansas Board of Education to have creationism taught with evolution illustrates. However, not only is the diverse but converging evidence for the evolution of species overwhelming, there are two creation stories in Genesis which are strikingly divergent with no factual basis or explanatory value. Quite simply, they are merely mythical narratives introduced because the level of intellectual development at the time could not sustain a better explanation.

As pointed out in chapter 2, the older of the two Genesis stories presented secondly barely touches on the origins of the world, dwelling instead on the creation of Adam and Eve, their original sin arising from their disobedience, their expulsion from paradise, and the absurdity of their having fathered humankind without ever producing a daughter. There is brief mention of the creation of birds, cattle, and beasts of the fields, though nothing said of creatures of the sea, indicating the incidental importance of those aspects. In contrast, the more recent of the two versions presented at the beginning of Genesis offers a much fuller account of the creation of the world, including the earth as well as the "lights in the heaven," fish, plants, animals, and man and woman. Though more detailed, the description is redolent with incongruities, anachronisms, gaps, and falsehoods: "light was separated from darkness," called day and night, prior to the two luminaries, the sun and the moon, being created; the earth originally "a void without form" emerged as dry land before there was a sun to heat it; birds appeared at the same time as fish; the variety of fish, "sea monsters," cattle, reptiles ("creeping things"), and beasts arose fully formed according to their kinds; man was created in "God's image" to have "dominion" over all living creatures; and finally, all of these creations or generations took just six days. The way of creation was by verbal fiat—God "calling forth" the various items. Although he was satisfied with his creation calling it "good," he later became so disgusted with the living animals he had brought forth that he destroyed them all, except for those admitted into Noah's ark. As literature this is admirable; as science it is ludicrous.

So why should I take the trouble to recount and frankly belittle it? The answer is because millions of people are led to believe that it is literally true, the revealed word of God. In the United States the religious fundamentalists promote creationism over evolution based on two assertions just quoted in Genesis: (1) that God created plants, fish, and living creatures each "according to its own kind," as if every species of flora and fauna arose in the beginning as it exists today; and (2) that God "made man in our image, after our likeness," so that human beings could not have descended from an ancestral primate, as paleontological evidence compellingly indicates. Yet it is not only the fundamentalists that support Genesis based mainly on faith, but even scientists trained in the critical evaluation of evidence. For example, Gerald L. Schroeder, who earned B.S., M.S., and Ph.D. degrees in physics from MIT, where he taught for several years before moving to the distinguished Weizmann Institute in Israel, has recently written a book with the curious title, *The Science of God: The Convergence of Scientific and Biblical Wisdom.*

ATTEMPTS AT MELDING SCIENCE AND RELIGION

While I believe that most scholars, whether their research is in biblical studies or in one of the sciences, would consider the title of Schroeder's book an oxymoron because the revelatory evidence for belief in God (typically subjective, private, infallible, and God-authenticating) is so fundamentally different from scientific evidence (typically objective, intersubjectively confirmable, contingent, and subject to experimental tests), Schroeder believes that they both are true if seen "from very different perspectives."

> What appear to be diametrically opposed biblical and scientific descriptions of the creation of the universe, of the start of life on Earth, and our human origins are actually identical realities but viewed from very different perspectives. Once these perspectives are identified, they coexist comfortably with all the rigorous science and traditional belief anyone could demand.[7]

Schroeder believes that science and religion must be compatible because "current surveys consistently report that in Western countries most people (in excess of 70 percent), believe in some form of evolution and in a Divine Creator" (p. 2). But is the fact that millions of people hold what are considered by the leading scientists in that domain of science to be incompatible beliefs justification for thinking that the beliefs actually are harmonious, just different perspectives on the same evidence, or for recognizing that people are capable of simultaneously holding beliefs that are "diametrically opposed" but compartmentalized to different levels of consciousness? Having cited specific illustrations of this previously, I will add nothing further now except to say that Schroeder himself appears to be a striking example of this, in that he believes in much of Genesis while also being committed to science, intending to show that the two are harmonious.

Schroeder claims that one of the basic sources of the conflict between science and religion is due to a literal interpretation of the Bible, especially Genesis, his focus of attention: "Literalism is simply not an effective way to extract meaning from the Bible" (p. 10). One should be aware that "two millennia ago . . . the Talmud stated explicitly that the opening chapter of Genesis . . . is presented in a manner that conceals information" and that the "kabalistic tradition has come to elucidate that which is held within those verses," not with mysticism, but with a "logic so deep that it might seem mystical to the uninitiated" (p. 10). But those scholars who have studied Genesis impartially have admitted its mythical content, not that it conceals some deep esoteric meaning. In contrast to the Talmud and Cabala which had to rely on the extremely limited knowledge at the time for their elucidation of a hidden meaning in Genesis (with bizarre consequences as we shall see), Schroeder believes that contemporary science provides the key for unlocking this secret meaning.

Although he decries a literal reading of the Bible, it is obvious that Schroeder believes most of the Genesis story, which is why he is impelled to provide a deeper interpretation or explanation of its meaning to bring it in harmony with modern science. For example, he refers to Adam and Eve not as mythical personages, but as the couple from whom the human race began. Without qualification or reservation he states that after Adam and Eve ate from the tree of knowledge, "God expelled them from Eden. The rest is History" (p. 14). He says that after Cain killed Abel and God exiled Cain, "Adam and Eve restarted the process with their third son, Seth" (p. 14). Genesis states that "to Seth also a son was born, and he called his name Enosh" (4:26), but how could Seth have had a son if Adam and Eve were the first created man and woman and they did not have a daughter? Schroeder's reference to the Talmudic legend regarding the possible existence of pre-Adam subhuman women (to be discussed later), with whom Adam might have had sexual relations and produced a daughter, rather than resolving the enigma, magnifies it. Equating the biblical calendar year of 5757 with the year 1996, based on calculating "the ages of the generations of humankind as they are listed in the Bible and the rulers thereafter . . . since Adam" (p. 45), is further evidence of his literal belief in Genesis.

In addition, regarding the Noah saga of the flood, he claims that the different life spans of people recorded in Genesis before, and ten generations after the flood indicate that the author of Genesis was aware of evolutionary developments.

> The Bible documents one evolutionary change in a physical trait, the trait of longevity (Genesis 5 and 11). The biblical data record a transition that might as well have come from a modern text on animal husbandry and breeding.
>
> Prior to the flood at the time of Noah, the life spans of the persons being discussed ranged from 365 years to 969 years, with the average being 840 years. Sexual maturity (the age at which a woman first gives birth) was reached at 65 to 187 years (average 115 years). Both averages are approximately ten times the current values ... far from today's reality. (p. 15)

Accepting these preposterous ages of the pre-flood descendants of Adam and Eve, Schroeder then relates the biblical account of Sarah laughing when she overheard the Lord telling Abraham that she would conceive at age 89, long past her time of child bearing (Gen 17:17). Using her age and Abraham's age of 99, Schroeder argues that "just ten generations after Noah, life spans had so decreased that ... an explicit miracle" was required for Sarah to conceive (p. 15). Comparing the "trend of shortening life span and more rapid sexual maturity ... observed in domesticated animals" with the shortened life span of the post-Noah Israelites, Schroeder states, "Both Maimonides in the twelfth century and Nahmanides in the thirteenth suggest that changes in the environment following the flood favored ('selected for' in modern terms) shorter life spans" (pp. 15–16). By using the term "selected for" Schroeder wants to connect this with evolution.

Schroeder's point in discussing this is to show that the "the biblical concept is that change takes place over time and through generations, just as did the development of the world in the first chapter of Genesis" (p. 15). But for the attempt to have any validity *one would have to accept* the improbable ages of the pre-flood Israelites. Why would one introduce this explanation *unless one believed* the Genesis narrative and the implausible longevities of pre-Noah individuals? The myth of Genesis originated about four thousand years ago in the oral tradition which began to be recorded about twelve hundred years later, around 800 B.C.E. In that distant past how reliable were the numbers for the given life spans of the Israelites? Is there any independent evidence that contemporary people in other countries lived that long (although there were not supposed to be any other people other than the Israelites at that time)? What number system was in use and how was it recalculated when transliterated from the oral to the written tradition? Did the Israelites in that remote time even have a number system that ranged as high as nearly 1,000 years? Furthermore, the explanation assumes the reality of Yahweh's destructive flood to vent his dissatisfaction with his own creation and Noah's preservation of the mates *of all forms of animal life* in his Ark (a spatial impossibility), for which there is no independent historical evidence.[8] What kinds of changes in the post-Noah environment, suggested by Maimonides and Nahmanides in the late Middles Ages, would have brought about in "ten generations" a one-tenth reduction in the life spans? Finally, there is nothing in the actual Noah narration itself to indicate that the author(s) intended to "document one evolutionary change as a physical trait, the trait of longevity," as Schroeder suggests (p. 15).

I think such attempted explanations do not indicate that Schroeder actually rejected a literal interpretation of Genesis as he says, claiming to have discovered a deeper meaning to harmonize Genesis and science, but that he is a 'closet literalist' who imposes modern interpretations on the ancient text to make it appear more credible than it is. We shall find further evidence of this later in his attempt to "demonstrate a harmony" between scientific theories of evolution and the narrative accounts in Genesis. Not actually uncovering any deeper meaning in Genesis, he has to reinterpret or emend certain passages to make it appear that what they state is consistent with modern scientific theories. This endeavor to show that important discoveries and advances in science were implicit in ancient scripture, waiting to be deciphered, is attempted not only by Schroeder but also by interpreters of the Koran.

Rather than accept the fact that these early religious documents, based on the presumption of divine revelation supported by the belief system of the time, have become outmoded as we have attained more knowledge about the world, these authors persist in believing that they are timelessly true. For example, just as Schroeder learned Hebrew to reinterpret passages in Genesis to eliminate discrepancies with science, Maurice Bucaille, a surgeon by profession, learned Arabic to read the Koran in its original language to refute the notion "that science and religion are incompatible."[9] Although he readily accepts the fact that the Bible contains many passages that are incompatible with science which biblical scholars have ignored, he does not think this is true of the Koran because Muhammad insisted that Allah is revealed in the works of nature, as well as in prophesy. As Bucaille says,

> we know that, for Islam, religion and science have always been considered twin sisters. From the very beginning, Islam directed people to cultivate science; the application of this precept brought with it the prodi-

gious strides in science taken during the great era of Islamic civilization, from which, before the Renaissance, the West itself benefitted. In the confrontation between the Scriptures and science a high point of understanding has been reached owing to the light thrown on Qur'anic passages by modern scientific knowledge. Previously these passages were obscure owing to the non-availability of knowledge which could help interpret them. (p. ix)

While it is true, in contrast to the biblical tradition, that Muhammad encouraged scientific inquiry which partially accounts for the impressive scientific achievements by the Muslims in the later Middle Ages, is it credible to believe that revelations to an illiterate prophet recorded in the Koran in the seventh century contain passages that have been enigmatic because they describe astronomical structures and natural processes in ways that could not be understood until the era of modern science? When one examines the application of this method in Bucaille's text, one sees how misleading is the claim. Citing certain passages from the Koran which have an ambiguous or puzzling meaning, Bucaille produces a retranslation to make them conform to later scientific theories, asserting that this is what they originally meant, even though this requires reinterpreting or distorting the original texts as they appear in authorized translations.

For example, in the fourth century B.C.E. the Greek astronomer Heraclides had hypothesized that rather than the whole universe rotating around the earth diurnally, as the observation of the rising of the sun in the east and setting in the west imply, it would be simpler if the much smaller earth rotated on its axis from west to east, this opposite rotation producing the *apparent* rising and setting of the sun. But because of terrestrial objections to attributing an axial rotation to the earth which is not experienced, Heraclides' hypothesis was rejected by the two leading astronomers of antiquity, Hipparchus and Ptolemy. It was not until the sixteenth and seventeenth centuries that the founders of modern science, Copernicus, Kepler, and Galileo, accepted this simpler explanation despite terrestrial objections.

Yet Bucaille argues that a passage in the Koran should be *translated* and interpreted as stating that the alternation of night and day is caused by the axial rotation of the earth. The passage he translates is sura 39, verse 5: " 'He coils the night upon the day and He coils the day upon the night' " (p. 163). Bucaille says (and he cooperated in translating his book from French into English), " 'To coil' or 'to wind' seems . . . to be the best way of translating the Arabic verb *kawwara*," whose original meaning "is to 'coil' a turban around the head . . ." (p. 163). Then referring to the American astronauts' view of the earth from their spaceships, especially the illuminated side of the earth due to the sun's light, he draws the following conclusion:

The earth turns on its own axis and the lighting remains the same, so that an area in the form of a half-sphere makes one revolution around the Earth in twenty-four hours while the other half-sphere, that has remained in darkness, makes the same revolution in the same time. This perpetual rotation of night and day is quite clearly described in the Qur'an. (p. 164)

Consulting an English translation of sutra 39, verse 5 in a scholarly edition of the Koran that contains both the original Arabic and the English translation, I was surprised to read the following: "He makes the Night Overlap the Day, and the Day Overlap the Night: He has subjected the sun and the moon (To His Law): Each one follows a course For a time appointed. . . ."[10] Not only is the word 'coil' not used, but even Bucaille's own illustration of its meaning "to coil a turban around the head" does not support the idea that it is the earth's rotation *under the heavens* (rather than the coiling of the heavens around the earth or the overlapping of night and day) that produces the *apparent* turning of the heavens *above* the earth.

But even more damaging is the reference in the sura to the sun and the moon (omitted by Bucaille in his quotation) following "a course For the time appointed" which, though admittedly vague, still suggests that their "appointed course" is related to the transition of day and night as stated in the Bible (Gen. 1:4), otherwise why mention it in the same context? That Bucaille omitted this reference to the movement of the sun and the moon in connection with the alteration of day and night, while *there is no reference at all in the sura to the earth's rotation*, shows to what lengths he went to try to reconcile the Koran with science — to eliminate any conflict between the geocentric view held at the time the Koran was written and the later heliocentric theory adopted by modern science. The whole book is based on this kind of revisionist translation of ambiguous Arabic passages into French or English to make them agree with later scientific discoveries or theories.[11] It also contains errors as when Bucaille says that the "process of perpetual coiling . . . is expressed in the Qur'an just as if the concept of the Earth's roundness had already been conceived at the time — which obviously was not the case" (p. 164). Apparently Bucaille does not know that the sphericity of the earth had been accepted by the ancient Greeks at least since the time of Plato.

To cite another example of an even more far-fetched interpretation, in the seventh century when the Koran was written, the accepted view of the universe was the geocentric conception of Aristotle and Ptolemy: an earth-centered spherical universe within which the seven planets (Moon, Mercury, Venus, Sun, Mars, Jupiter, and Saturn) in successively distant and larger orbits circle the earth, with the sphere of the fixed stars forming the outer periphery of the universe. Although the heliocentric model of the universe had been introduced by the ancient Greek astronomer Aristarchus in the third century B.C.E., it had been rejected by Hipparchus and Ptolemy, so the geocentric conception prevailed. In passage after passage the Koran refers to the "seven heavens" which include the moon and the sun, but I will quote sura 78, verse 12, as stated in Bucaille: "Did you see how God created seven heavens one above the other and made the moon a light therein and made the sun a lamp?" (p. 146). Despite these numerous references to "seven heavens one above the other," incorporating the moon and the sun coinciding with the geocentric system of the universe held at the time, Bucaille professes to find a more advanced cosmological conception implied in a single ambiguous sura.

Based on the fact that sura 65, verse 12 states (without any elaboration) that "God is the One Who created seven heavens and *of the earth . . . a similar number*," and because the number 7 in Arabic can mean in addition to seven units "an indefinite plurality," Bucaille concludes that to "understand these verses, reference must be made to . . . the existence of cosmic extra-galactic material . . ." (pp, 141, 143; emphasis added). He finds this conclusion reinforced by sura 32, verse 4: "God is the One Who created the heavens, the earth and what is between them in six periods [the latter a reference to the biblical six days of creation]" (p. 143). As this is similar to the Genesis account, as is much of the description of creation in the Koran, the most obvious meaning of 'between' is what extends from the earth to the heavens, the latter containing the moon and the sun. However, Bucaille interprets 'between' to mean "outside the Heavens and outside the Earth," again referring to extra-galactic universes (p. 143). But both of these interpretations are idiosyncratic, to say the least! In every other instance where the term 'earth' is used it is used in the singular, not the plural, and in every context in which 'between' is used it clearly refers to the domain between the earth and the heavens, as in sura XXI, verse 16: "Not for (idle) sport did We Create the heavens and the earth And all that is between!"[12]

It is a long stretch to claim that the 'between' as used in these suras does not designate what exists between the earth and the heavens, but refers to a plurality of worlds *outside* our earth and heaven: that is, outside our solar system which comprised the ancient universe. It was not until the sixteenth and seventeenth centuries, owing to Copernicus, Kepler, Galileo, and Newton, that the heliocentric system was accepted and the conception of a finite spherical universe replaced by that of an infinite universe. Furthermore, it was not until Hubble built the 100-inch telescope in the 1920s that there was sufficient evidence to conclude that there were extra-galactic universes beyond our Milky Way. So is it credible that these suras refer to these later astronomical developments that occurred ten to thirteen centuries later? Based on my own studies, these views were not even held by the Arabic astronomers during the great period of Muslim scientific inquiry in the later Middle Ages. Moreover, if the Koran was so prescient as to mention the existence of other galaxies, then why does it only refer to seven heavens (or planets) rather than ten, omitting the existence of Uranus, Neptune, and Pluto which were later discovered? Surely if galaxies were known to exist, then these additional planets would have been known to exist also. Furthermore, if the Koran contains such advanced concealed information, why is the description so similar to the Old Testament which Bucaille admits contains doctrines incompatible with modern science?

But while one can forgive this specious reasoning in a physician who was not trained to critically evaluate theoretical frameworks, it is much more difficult to excuse in someone like Professor Schroeder who was trained in physics at MIT. In discussing the theory of evolution in relation to the account in Genesis, he makes much of the fact that the fossil evidence does not support the *gradualist* interpretation of evolution held by Darwin and most evolutionists until recently. Referring to the creation story in Genesis, rather than to Koranic verses, Schroeder, like Bucaille, claims that recent developments in science enable one to recognize deeper meanings hidden in Genesis. In Schroeder's case the disclosure is due to recent paleontological developments regarding Darwin's theory of evolution which he claims agree with the Genesis story of creation. Schroeder has an extensive and accurate knowledge of these developments, as well as the current difficulties in attempting to explain the biomolecular genetic mutations that drive evolution. I do not disagree with his understanding of the material, but with the conclusions he draws from it.

Although there is considerable controversy over the *specifics* of Darwin's explanation of evolution, especially his gradualist interpretation (as compared to the more recent theory of "punctuated equilibrium" introduced by Niles Eldridge and Stephen Jay Gould to account for the fossil record of the Burgess Shale), almost none of the participating scientists believes that this is a justification for the kind of religious explanation supported by Schroeder and other religionists. As Richard Dawkins, a defender of a gradualist interpretation that nonetheless acknowledges variable rates of transition in the evolutionary process, states:

> Both schools of thought despise so-called scientific creationists equally, and both agree that the *major* gaps are real, that they are true imperfections in the fossil record. Both schools . . . agree that the only alternative explanation of the sudden appearance of so many complex animal types in the Cambrian era is divine creation, *and both would reject this alternative*.[13]

Moreover, as Boyce Rensberger states in a news article, the "evidence for evolution is so overwhelming that scientists say the probability of its being true approaches 100 percent."[14] The reason scientists doing research in the field are so persuaded by the truth of evolution, despite certain problems of interpretation, is the "consilience" of the evidence, as Gould states: "We know that evolution must underlie the order of life because no other explanation can coordinate the disparate data of embryology, biogeography, the fossil record, vestigial organs, taxonomic relationships, and so on."[15] In contrast to Schroeder who believes that the fossil evidence and the biogenetic mechanisms driving evolution require a purposeful creator, all the major investigators believe it is a natural process ultimately explainable scientifically. In fact, Gould states that "contingency is both the watchword and lesson of the Burgess Shale [containing the record of the Cambrian explosion]" (p. 288).

To evaluate Schroeder's argument, a brief discussion of recent criticisms of Darwin's theory of evolution is necessary. Darwin claimed that later (more recently) advanced lifeforms evolved their more complex structures due to the interplay of two factors: (1) accidental changes (although usually designated as "random" to exclude a purposeful cause, this does not mean that *any possible* mutation is equally likely) in the biomolecular structure of the genetic material produced by internal or external causes (although Darwin did not know this, the internal cause could be some modification in the genetic message while the external could be a cosmic ray), and (2) natural selection. The slight changes in the organism's morphology produced by the mutations (if not initially fatal) would either favor or impede the organism's struggle for survival in a competitive ecosystem of limited resources or habitats, especially if the ecology was changing, as often happens. Thus nature "selects" posteriorly those organisms best fitted for survival by handicapping their competitors, allowing the more successful ones to reproduce and proliferate the advantageous mutations. Given sufficient time, an accumulation of these slight mutations within the expanding population would account for the evolutionary development from simple to more complex organisms recorded (if imperfectly) by the fossils embedded in successive layers of geological strata.

Based on the newly discovered geological and fossil record, what then was known about the breeding of animals, and especially Darwin's observation of the proliferation of species on archipelagos and atolls during his five-year global voyage on HMS *Beagle*, this was an exceedingly reasonable explanation of the evidence. However, it provoked considerable controversy and antagonism because it challenged the millennia-old biblical story of the abrupt creation of all living creatures, including humans, by

God about six thousand years ago, claiming that like other organisms human beings, too, had evolved or descended from more primitive species, the primates. Darwinism especially infuriated those who believed the scriptural doctrine that man had been created in the image of God. But despite the strong opposition based on religious beliefs, the century following the publication of the *Origin of Species* in 1859 witnessed a gradual, if reluctant, acquiescence in his theory as supporting evidence accumulated, at least among leading paleontologists and biologists.

However, the celebration of the centennial of Darwin's great publication hardly had passed when the reexamination of a remarkable fossil record, called the Burgess Shale, challenged Darwin's thesis that evolution consisted essentially of a *continually gradual* transition from simpler to more complex organisms. Actually, the new fossil evidence had been discovered in the second decade of the twentieth century by the renowned paleontologist Charles Doolittle Walcott, secretary of the Smithsonian Institution. Accumulating an enormous collection of fossil specimens dating from the Middle Cambrian Period (about 550 million years ago) embedded in the Burgess Shale of British Columbia, Walcott brought the collection back to Washington where it was carefully stored in drawers in the Smithsonian Institution. Although Walcott was aware of the great significance of the discovery affirming the abrupt appearance during the Cambrian period of between fifteen and twenty new phyla (finding some too unfamiliar and strange to classify, he tried to "shoehorn" them into traditional phyla, according to Gould), his administrative duties at the Smithsonian prevented him from publishing the full results of his remarkable discovery.

Then, beginning in the seventies, Harry Whittington and two of his graduate students at Cambridge University, Simon Conway Morris and Derik Briggs, after carefully examining Walcott's collection, began publishing articles on the Burgess Shale that revolutionized paleontology, superbly described in Gould's book, *Wonderful Life*. According to the Burgess Record of the Middle Cambrian period, the history of life on earth had not been a *prolonged gradual process* of evolution from very early single celled organism to the rich diversity of fauna found on the earth today. Instead, all the major body plans or phyla of living creatures found on the earth arose suddenly in the Cambrian period with no evidence of evolutionary precursors. Furthermore, not only did the sudden appearance of these distinctly new phyla show no sign of an evolutionary heritage or of phylogenetic transitions, they also did not display the expected subsequent branching into the familiar tree of life. On the contrary, most of the phyla died out shortly thereafter, leaving fewer existing phyla to proliferate into the arboreal transition of species.

Briefly, the chronology appears as follows: the earliest evidence of life, judging by the amount of ^{12}Carbon produced by photosynthesis in rock sediments, occurred 3.5 billion years ago or roughly 1.5 billion years after the formation of the earth. For the next 2.4 billion years "or nearly two-thirds of the entire history of life on earth, all organisms were single-celled creatures of the simplest, or prokaryotic design" (p. 58). These prokaryotic cells, consisting of bacteria and algae, were so primitive that they lacked "a nucleus, paired chromosomes, mitochondria, and chloroplasts" (p. 58). Then larger cellular organisms with added nuclear structure, called eukaryotic cells, that include the familiar amoeba and paramecium, appeared in the fossil record some 1.4 billion years ago. Though more complex than their predecessors and therefore evidence of an important evolutionary advance, they still were not multicellular. Prior to the Precambrian explosion, one phylum of multicellular organisms appeared in what is known as the Ediacara fauna 700 million years ago, but it is questionable whether these multicellular fauna were ancestors of the Cambrian explosion or of a failed attempt at multicellular life, according to Gould.

Thus the Precambrian record does not appear to contain any organisms that would provide an evolutionary origin of the Cambrian proliferation of new phyla. The approximately 100 million years of Ediacara fauna may have produced two new soft-bodied fauna and another with hard body parts called the Tommotian, but the latter had such simple skeletons that they, too, may have been a failed experiment, rather than precursors of the fauna found in the Burgress Shale (cf. p. 59). As Gould summarizes this early saga:

> Nearly 2.5 billion years of prokaryotic cells and nothing else — two-thirds of life's history in stasis at the lowest level of recorded complexity. Another 700 million years of the larger and much more intricate eukaryotic cells, but no aggregation to multicellular ... life. Then, in the 100-million-year wink of a geological eye, three outstanding different faunas—from Ediacara to Tommotian, to Burgess. Since then, 500 million years of wonderful stories, triumphs and tragedies, but not a single new phylum, or basic anatomical design, added to the Burgess complement. (p. 60)

This record, evidently, does not support the gradualist interpretation of evolution proposed by Darwin, but displays a pattern of long eons of evolutionary stagnation followed by the sudden appearance of an extraordinary eruption of phylogenetic novelty. The designation "punctuated equilibrium" is intended to capture the sense of extended epochs of quietism punctured by bursts of novelty. But nearly as unexpected and puzzling is the fact that this Cambrian explosion was followed by a period of drastic phyla extinction—or "decimation" as Gould prefers to call it—with the relatively few survivors producing a plethora of new species. It now appears that these mass extinctions occur much more frequently and with greater devastating effect than previously realized. One such episode, called the "Permian Debacle," that occurred about 225 million years ago, close to 160 million years before the Cretaceous period that witnessed the destruction of the dinosaurs, "may have wiped out 95 percent or more of all marine species" (p. 229). Yet despite the striking ecological opportunity and the subsequent diversification of species following this debacle, it did not produce another Cambrian explosion of new phyla. Again Gould presents a clear picture of this pattern of events:

> The Burgess Shale includes a range of disparity in anatomical design [body plans or phyla] never again equaled, and not matched today by all the creatures in all the world's oceans. The history of multicellular life has been dominated by decimation of a large initial stock, quickly generated in the Cambrian explosion. The story of the past 500 million years has featured restriction followed by proliferation within a few stereotypical designs, not general expansion of range and increase in complexity as our favored iconography, the cone of increasing diversity, implies. Moreover, the new iconography of rapid establishment and later decimation dominates all scales, and seems to have the generality of a fractal pattern [repetition in decreasing scale of similar design]. (p. 208)

It is important to realize that this totally unexpected fossil record does not *in any way* invalidate evolution, but does seem to confute the two Darwinian themes of gradualism with accrued complexity. As a result it raises its own particular questions: (1) what produced the sudden diversity of phyla not foreshadowed in the Precambrian period? and (2) what specifically determined which phyla would win in the decimated struggle for survival? While there is as yet no definite scientific answer to these questions, as so often was true at certain stages in the advance of science, they are the kinds of questions that scientists typically resolve. Yet Schroeder offers a number of arguments and statistical analyses to show that science is incapable of answering these questions because they presuppose a purposeful creator whose existence is affirmed in Genesis. Moreover, while the fossil display of the Burgess Shale seems to be incompatible with traditional Darwinism, Schroeder argues that the sudden occurrence of diverse phyla in the Cambrian period is what one would expect from the Genesis claim that God on the fifth day suddenly created all living creatures, each "according to its kind."

But whatever agreement there is between the Genesis story and the fossil record of the Burgess Shale lies in the eye of Schroeder, not in their actually coinciding. First of all, none of these issues is even addressed in the Adam and Eve "J" version, so Schroeder has to rely on the "P" version for his evidence. According to that narrative, it is not until the fifth day that God says, "Let the waters bring forth swarms of living creatures, and let birds fly above the earth . . ." (Gen. 1:21). The aquatic creatures included "great sea monsters and every living creature . . . with which the waters swarm . . . and every winged bird according to its kind." Thus all the kinds of aquatic life and birds were created *fully formed* in one act. There is not the slightest hint of evolution in this. The fourth day of creation is followed by a fifth day with God declaring, "Let the earth bring forth living creatures . . . cattle and creeping things and beasts of the earth according to their kinds" (Gen. 1:24).

Keeping in mind the paleontological chronology of the history of life recounted previously how, literally in God's name, can anyone maintain that the "biblical parallel to this account is striking"?[16] According to Genesis, water existed *without life* two-thirds of the duration of creation. There was *no evolution* of aquatic organisms or of birds, just the immediate creation of "every living creature . . . with which the waters swarm . . . and every winged bird according to its kind" (Gen. 1:21). So *every extant* aquatic form of life as well as birds were immediately created in all their various kinds. Earthly creatures *did not evolve from aquatic life*, but were brought forth independently: "cattle and creeping things and beasts of the earth according to their kinds" (Gen 1:24). Presumably the "beasts of the earth" would include saber-toothed tigers, wooly mammoths, dinosaurs, and flying reptiles with twelve-foot wingspans called pterosaurs (all of which, of course, would easily fit into Noah's Ark). Finally God said, "Let us make man in our image" (in the "P" version, 1:26), but "formed man of dust from the ground, and breathed into his nostrils the breath of life" (in the "J" version 2:7). Contrast that story of the creation of living creatures with Boyce Rensberger's description of what paleontologists conclude:

> . . . Paleontologists have found many transitional fossils representing intermediate forms in the evolution of one major form of life into another.
>
> There are, for example, excellent skeletons of extinct animals showing the transitions from primitive fish to bony fish, from fish to amphibian (the first four-legged creatures walked on the ocean bottom, not on land), from amphibian to reptile, from reptile to mammal (it happened about the time the first dinosaurs were arising), from reptile to bird (the bird-sized *Archaeopteryx* specimen from southern Germany, for example, has feathers and dinosaurlike teeth) and even from land animal to whale (there are fossil whales with four legs, and modern whales still have remnants of hind legs buried in their flesh; their front legs have changed into flippers).

There is abundant fossil evidence showing transitional diversifica-tions among mammals into rodents, bats, rabbits, carnivores, horses, ele-phants, manatee, deer, cows and many others. One of the most finely divided sequences of transitions documents the evolution of apelike crea-tures through half a dozen intermediate forms into modern humans.[17]

Given these striking differences between the story presented in Gen-esis and the evidence we now have for evolutionary theory, how can they be harmonized? How can the extensive fossil record of the transition of species, along with "intermediate forms," be reconciled with the asser-tion that God created "living creatures, each according to their kind"? How can those images of human's precursors from six million years ago, Australopithicus africanus, Homo habilis, Homo erectus, Homo sapiens, Neanderthals, and Cro-Magnons, be resolved into God's immediate cre-ation of man in his own image (implying that God resembles humans, a preposterous notion)? If human beings did not evolve from lower pri-mates but were created as a separate beings, why is our genetic code 98–99 percent identical to that of the pygmy chimpanzee and why do all living organisms have similar genetic coding?

Furthermore, despite the sudden occurrence of the original body forms or phyla during the Cambrian explosion, the transitional species that evolved later could not have existed in the initial burst of creation. Since the dinosaurs evolved during the Cretaceous period some 400 mil-lion years after the Cambrian explosion, they hardly could have been alive during the earlier era; nor, obviously, could human beings have existed then. Yet Schroeder states (my critical comments are within the braces {} in the text):

> For the 3,300 years of its existence, Genesis has presented to us its account of the origin of life. Liquid water appeared on Earth and life appeared immediately thereafter {but there is no mention of life arising on earth when water appeared on it in the "P" version, which states that the *dry land* appeared then vegetation. Therefore, Schroeder must be conflating the "P" with the "J" version, which says that life did not arise on earth until "a mist went up from the earth and watered the whole face of the ground" (2:6)}. The Bible tells us (correctly) not only the timing of the origin of life (at the appearance of liquid water), but also proposes the mechanism for its origins: "The earth brought forth [life]" (Gen. 1:11) {"bringing forth life" is supposed to be a mechanism of origin?}. No men-tion of a special creation is associated with the start of life {so creationists are mistaken in believing such statements as "God created . . . every living creature . . . according to their kinds" (Gen 1:21) implies "special creation"?}. The earth itself had the special properties to orchestrate {'orchestration' is a mechanism of explanation?} the beginning of life. In

modern terms, those properties are described as self-organization of life and/or catalysts {"bringing forth life" is supposed to mean "self-organization" and/or "catalysts"?}. (p. 29)

If this is an example of what Schroeder means by uncovering a deeper meaning in Genesis to demonstrate that it agrees with modern science, then I believe we have to declare the effort fraudulent. At least in this instance, Schroeder has not provided evidence of uncovering a hidden meaning but merely of *imposing* a modern interpretation on very simplistic, vague, imprecise biblical terms or statements. This is precisely what Muslim apologists, such as Bucaille, do to support their claim that there is no disagreement between the Koran and modern science.

These examples occur frequently, as illustrated again in the following quotation from Schroeder:

> The Burgess fossils do not question the development of classes [species] of life. It is no secret that each individual phylum first appeared as simple aquatic forms and became more complex with the passage of time. The Book of Genesis proclaimed this fact 3,300 years ago: first came aquatic animals, then winged creatures and land animals, then mammals. That's Genesis 1! The Bible knows about development. (pp. 39–40)

But this statement conflates two different meanings of 'development': (1) development as a succeeding series of events, and (2) development as a process of structural change or evolutionary transition. Genesis clearly supports the first meaning, but not the second! On the fifth day "God said, 'Let the waters bring forth swarms of living creatures and let birds fly above the earth . . . according to their kind.' " On the sixth day "God said, 'Let the earth bring forth living creatures . . . cattle and creeping things and beasts of the earth according to their kinds.' " Then on the same day "God said, 'Let us make man in our image.' " Obviously this consists of a *sequence* of events, but where is there a whiff of *development* in the sense of a *transitional change* or *evolution*? The first passage does not even state that the birds were created after the aquatic creatures but with them. Had the author intended a temporal sequence he would have stated "and then let birds fly." These kinds of misrepresentations, in my opinion, suggest a person too eager to justify something for which there is no basis. When functioning as a scientist, I do not think Schroeder would condone this. Yet as he honestly admits regarding his religious point of view: "Subjectivity is difficult, perhaps impossible, to avoid. I have an agenda, to demonstrate a harmony between science and the Bible" (p. 51). He has a right to his agenda, of course, but not to distort passages in Genesis to make it appear that they state something entirely different from what they do.

There are many reasons why Genesis is considered a myth by most biblical scholars, beginning with the fact that it is derived from a four-millennia-old oral tradition. But another reason is the discrepancy between the 6,000-year biblical age of the universe in contrast to the contemporary estimate of about fifteen billion years. Schroeder states that in 1996 the duration of human life based on the biblical calendar was 5757 years, derived from the generations listed in the Bible following the creation of Adam and Eve (cf. p. 45). This, of course, is absurdly short since the fossil record indicates that Homo sapiens have been around nearly 500,000 years and Cro-Magnon man (our most immediate ancestor) about 40,000 years. Yet even more incredible, from the scientific point of view, is the claim that the universe and all living creatures were created in just six days, although that is what is to be expected of a mythical account. Given the undisputed geological and cosmological evidence for the approximate age of the universe, there have been numerous attempts to stretch those six days to fit the modern estimate. The attempt by Schroeder to do this, using Einstein's theory of relativity, is one of the most ingenious.

To understand Schroeder's discussion it is necessary to take a brief excursion into relativity theory. In classical Newtonian mechanics it was believed that the temporal rate of physical processes was unaffected by their velocities or by the strength of the gravitational field in which they occurred. This meant that however great the velocity of the system or intensity of the gravitational field, clocks (as well as physical, biological, and radiational processes) would still maintain the same rhythm or rate of change. Relativity theory altered all of that. In systems approaching the velocity of light or in dense gravitational fields, all physical processes slow down, retard, or dilate (along with contracting in space and gaining mass). The classic illustration of this is the *Gedanken experiment*, called the "twins paradox," introduced by Paul Langevin in 1911 to illustrate the consequences of relativity theory.[18] Suppose one of a pair of twins is placed in a spaceship which, during one year as timed by the clocks within the ship, accelerates to just $1/20,000$ less than the speed of light, reverses, and then returns to the earth the following year. Everything in the spaceship, including the aging of the twin, indicates a passage of time of two years. As velocity increases the rate of physical processes underlying the passage of time decreases so that time slows down, while the rate of physical processes and the passage of time increase when the velocity decreases.

According to classical physics, the second twin who remained on the earth would have lived through the same duration of time as her twin, thus having aged two years when the spaceship returned to the earth. However, according to relativity theory, such a tremendous acceleration of the spaceship close to the velocity of light would have caused an enormous slowing down or retardation of all the processes within the spaceship, while the rate of changes on the earth would have remained the same because the conditions were unaltered. The two world lines (as they are called), intersecting at the initial launching from and return to the earth of the spaceship, would comprise *two years* of events on the spaceship and *two centuries* on the earth, owing to the different velocities of the two systems. The twin on earth, along with several generations, would have died by the time the first twin returned. From the perspective of the spaceship, it is as if all the processes on the earth were speeded up as in an old black and white movie, compressing two centuries into two years, while from the perspective of the earth it would appear that all the events in the spaceship occurred in slow motion, so that only two years of events took place in their two centuries of time.

So in contrast to Newton who believed that the flow of time was an absolute unaffected by velocities ("all motions may be accelerated and retarded, but the flow of absolute time is not liable to any change"[19]), Einstein proposed that because the velocity of light is constant, the rate of the flow of time varies with the particular velocity or gravitational force of the system in which it occurs. When confirmed in 1919 this revision of Newton's "absolute frames of the universe" (since it applies to space as well as time) is what brought Einstein immediate worldwide fame. Because time is a dependent rather than an independent variable, the measurement of the time of distant events, along with the duration of events, also varies with the physical conditions of the observer who relies on the information conveyed in light signals to calculate the time of remote cosmic events. As Schroeder states, "The clock of the universe is the light of the universe. Each wave of light is a tick of the cosmic clock. The frequencies of light waves are the timepiece of the universe" (p. 50). But as the frequency of light waves also depends on the physical conditions, these measurements will vary with the different conditions. It is this latter discovery by Einstein that enables Schroeder to equate the biblical creation time of six days with our computation for the age of the universe from the big bang as fifteen billion years.

Measuring the age of the universe means looking back in time, inferring from the frequency of the current radiational wavelength to what it was when emitted by the big bang. Because the length of light waves are elongated or stretched (the Doppler effect) as their source recedes, shifting to the longer wavelengths at the red end of the spectrum, the age of the universe can be calculated from the ratio of stretched wavelength, as currently measured, to the unstretched wavelength when first emitted (cf. 54). Thus Hubble in the twenties inferred, from the telescopically observed shift to the red in the wavelengths coming from distant stars, that the universe must be expanding or inflating. Because expanding space produces longer wavelengths and slower frequencies (their product maintaining the constant velocity of light), this has the same effect of dilating temporal units or slowing the flow of time that increased velocities or stronger gravitational fields do, described previously. As Schroeder states:

> Three aspects of the universe produce identical effects on radiation frequency. Positive differences in velocity, gravity, and the stretching of space as the universe expands all increase (stretch) the wavelength of radiation. Since the frequency of radiation (and hence the beat of the cosmic clock) is lowered in direct proportion to the increase in wavelength, this increase in wavelength slows the perceived passage of time. The first two of these three phenomena relate to differences in the flow of conventional time—biological time [as in the twins paradox]— between specific locations. The third, the universal stretching of space, equally alters the perception of time's flow as reckoned by the universal time clock. (p. 53)

It is this different between the beat of the cosmic clock at creation, compared to the beat of the current background radiation due to the expansion of the universe, that allows Schroeder to equate the six days of creation with our estimated age of the universe as fifteen billion years.

> If we can understand how the expansion of the universe since the big bang has altered the frequency of cosmic background radiation, we may be able to understand how the six days of Genesis "contain all the secrets and all the ages of the universe" [a quotation cited by Nahmanides in Exod. 21:2 and Lev. 25:2 which I have not been able to find in my version of the Bible]. In essence we seek to map cosmic/Genesis time onto time as we perceive it in our corner of the universe. (p. 54)

To simpily a long story, Schroeder says we can do this by comparing the current wave frequency of the cosmic background radiation leftover from the big bang (discovered by Arno Penzias and Robert Wilson at Bell Laboratories in 1965) with the wave frequency of the initial radiation generated by the primal explosion called the big bang. This initial wave frequency is calculated from current experiments indicating the "ambient temperature" at which radiant energy changes into matter. At this transitional temperature protons and neutrons are produced by quark confinement.

We know the temperature and hence the frequency of radiation energy in the universe at quark confinement. . . . It is measured right here on Earth in the most advanced physics laboratories and corresponds to a temperature approximately a million million times hotter than the current 3°K black of space. That radiant energy had a frequency a million million [a trillion 10^{12}] times greater than the radiation of today's background radiation. (p. 57)

By comparing the difference between the lesser wave frequency of the *present* background radiation, owing to the intervening spatial expansion of the universe, with the tremendously greater frequency of the *initial* radiant waves, Schroeder is able to equate the six biblical days of creation with our calculation of fifteen billion years. Because cosmic time is determined by the wave frequency, the trillion times greater frequency of the original cosmic radiation, compared to the current background radiation, means that the flow of time initially was a trillion times faster than our current rate of time. The ticking of earth clocks will be a trillion times slower than the primordial wave frequency clock: one day of this initial cosmic time will be equivalent to a trillion earth days. As Schroeder states, "The cosmic timepiece . . . *today*, ticks a million million times more slowly than at its *inception*" (p. 58; emphasis added). Because of this slower present time flow any temporal measurement today of the times or durations of past events will be a trillion times greater than if measured then.

So now we can see how our present fifteen billion year calculation of the age of the universe, based on our slower clocks, can be contemporaneous with the biblical six days of creation representing the vastly greater flow of time then. According to Schroeder, this is what the Psalms (90:4) meant when it stated, "A thousand years in Your time are as a day that passes, as a watch in the night" (p. 42). More precisely, dividing our age for the universe of fifteen billion years by a trillion (10^{12}) produces a figure of .015 years. Then multiplying this by 365 to convert from years to days yields a result of 5.475, or roughly six days. Conversely, dividing the biblical six days by 365 to convert from days to years and then multiply this figure of .016 years by a trillion produces 16 billion years, essentially the present calculation of the age of the universe. Thus, "in terms of days and years and millennia, this stretching of the cosmic perception of time by a factor of a million million, the division of fifteen billion years by a million million reduces those fifteen billion years to six day!" (p. 58).

This certainly is an ingenious argument reflecting Schroeder's excellent physics background, much more persuasive than other vague assertions that the six days of creation were not intended literally, but that 'days' should be interpreted as 'eons' or 'epochs,' even though this is not a true translation. Should we agree, then, that the author of the "P" version (the six days are not mentioned in the older "J" version) intended by the "generations" of "six days" what we mean by a span of fifteen billion years? I am sure it comes as no surprise that I find this interpretation is based on too many implausible presuppositions to be acceptable, even though the calculations work out.

The initial objection is that this calculated correlation or equivalence is based on the belief that Genesis is not an ancient myth, but a profound document containing hidden truths, despite Schroeder's disavowal of a literal interpretation. It is apparent that for him Adam is not a mythical figure but the first human being created, since Schroeder accepts the biblical calendar of 5761 years (in our year 2000) "calculated by adding the ages of the generations of humankind as they are listed in the Bible and the rulers thereafter" (p. 45). But this genealogy does not conform to the paleontological evidence that our lineage descends from someone like Lucy in the African continent, not from Adam in "Eden in the east" (according to the older "J" creation myth). Furthermore, Schroeder claims that comparing the description of the six days of creation with the flow of events in the rest of the Old Testament following the creation of Adam, pointed out by ancient commentators, indicates an explicit division between the six days of creation and the rest of human history following Adam: "The description of time in the Bible is divided into two categories: the first six days and all the time thereafter" (p. 45).

In addition, he says that "the starting date of the biblical calendar was set at the creation of the souls of humankind (Gen. 1:27), and not at the creation of the universe . . ." (p. 45). Not only are souls not mentioned in the creation stories, but how confident could one be, based on a calculation of the generations since Adam, that six days had been omitted from the Hebrew calendar? It seems that these ancient commentators went to extraordinary efforts to try to make the Genesis accounts credible. For example, the third line of Genesis states that at that stage of creation "the earth was without form and void." The term 'void' was used at the time as indicated in Hesiod's *Theogony* (II, 116): "First of all, the Void came into being. . . ." The ancient Greek word for 'void' was 'chaos', which did not mean our conception of a calamitous disorganized state, but more like a 'yawning gap,' an indeterminate state 'without form and void'. But according to Schroeder we should accept the thirteenth century interpretation of Nahmanides that the Hebrew word *'bohu'* (void) "means filled with the building blocks of matter" (57). But how likely is it that the meaning of 'void' in Genesis, derived from an archaic oral tradition, meant anything as sophisticated as the contemporary conception of the "building blocks of matter," especially since God created the world by verbal fiat ("Let there be. . . .")? In a similar vein Schroeder claims that the word 'generations' used in the statement, "these are the generations of the heavens and the earth when they were created" (Gen 2:4), is not restricted to the six days of creation but conveys the "realization that somehow the days of Genesis contained the generations of the cosmos . . ." (p. 46). But coming as a concluding statement directly after the description of the six days of creation, the context does not support Schroeder's interpretation. I can understand that it was tempting for later commentators, such as Nahmanides as well as Schroeder, to read into these ancient verses a more contemporary significance, but this is not sound scholarship.

Furthermore, it seems to me that Schroeder's conclusion "that the events of Genesis map onto the corresponding discoveries [events] of science" (p. 59) is flawed because it equivocates between claiming that the difference between the two flows of time, the one at the creation of the universe and the other encoded in the current background radiation, is just a matter of perception or is actual. When discussing the twins paradox, I pointed out that from the earth's perspective it "appeared" that the rate of physical processes in the spaceship slowed down to a time flow of two years, while from the point of view of the spaceship it "appeared" that all the physical processes on the earth had been speeded up so that a time flow of two centuries had passed. Although this description is justified, it is misleading if interpreted to mean that the difference is merely apparent and not actual. In the general theory of relativity the rates of physical processes vary in different regions of the universe because the physical conditions (velocity and gravity) vary. These different temporal rates are not merely *apparent* but *actual*; they are referred to as the "proper times" of the particular system, with each proper time being equally real. Unlike classical mechanics these "proper times" are not synchronized by an absolute flow of time, even though they are contemporaneous in the sense that they can have a common beginning and ending. When the one twin left the earth and returned on the spaceship, the "proper time" of the space flight was two years while the "proper time" on the earth was two centuries.

This crucial relativistic concept is so counterintuitive that it is difficult to grasp. There is one passage in Schroeder's book where this equivocation between considering the flow of time as merely perspectival (analogous to objects appearing smaller from a distance) and as an actual change is apparent. At the time of the transition of radiant energy into matter (when protons and neutrons were formed from quarks) .00001 (10^{-5}) seconds after the primal explosion, the frequency of radiation was a trillion times greater than today's background radiation. The following passage equivocates between stating that this is a "perceived" difference or a real change in the "the proper rates of events."

The radiation from the moment of quark confinement has been stretched a million millionfold. . . . That stretching of the light waves has slowed the frequency of the cosmic clock—expanded the *perceived* time between the ticks of the clock—by a million million. "This also applies to *proper rates* of events as one sees by the application of a sequence of Lorentz time dilation factors."[20] (p. 57; emphasis added)

The first two sentences refer to the effect of the stretched light waves on "perceived time," while the last quoted sentence refers to the actual changes in the "proper times" correlated by the Lorentz transformation equations, as Schroeder correctly states.

Despite the ambiguity in this quotation, it is clear from his discussion that Schroeder intends that the temporal changes are not merely perceptual, but refer to actual changes in the "proper rates of events." "Each planet, each star . . . has its own unique gravitational potential, its own relative velocity and, therefore, its own unique rate at which the local proper time passes, its own age" (p. 49). This is true also of different stages in the evolution of the universe. The proper rate at the initial radiation was a trillion times faster than a present: one interval of time would contain a trillion more events than today. Schroeder claims that the author of the "P" version of creation meant by six days of creation the time as it would have been calculated at this intense radiation, not as the fifteen billion years calculated from today's clocks. So the difference is more than perceptual because the world line of six days represents a different proper time than our world line of fifteen billion years, even though they can be made contemporaneous by dividing our calculation by a trillion and changing years to days. However, as we saw in the twins paradox, the fact that two world lines are contemporaneous does not mean that they can be synchronized: that the events in one can be correlated with the events in the other, as if *the two series of events* were merely compressed or stretched into the same interval of time, rather than including different extents of events because of the difference in their proper times.

It is this ambiguity that makes it difficult for me to evaluate Schroeder's argument. Based on the difference in frequencies of the primordial radiant waves with the current background radiation waves, I can understand how "this stretching of the cosmic *perception of time* . . . reduces those fifteen billion years to six days!" (p. 58; emphasis added) But does this mean that the two spans of time include the same progression of events, so that the six days of creation contain "all the secrets and ages of the universe" (p. 46)? Schroeder seems to argue for both interpretations: that of "local proper times" and also of an "undifferentiated frame of reference," as the following quotation indicates:

. . . as the universe expanded and cooled, vastly different local gravities and velocities evolved, having different rates at which local proper times flowed. For our understanding of Genesis time, we must maintain the undifferentiated frame of reference that pervaded the universe at its beginning. (p. 53)

But the six days of Genesis also include the periods of the creation of plants, fish, animals, and Adam after the initial explosion when the universe had expanded. How do these fit into an undifferentiated frame of reference?

It is this difference that I do not understand. In an article in a recent *Scientific American*, a time frame for the evolution of the universe from the big bang to the present is illustrated in units of seconds, minutes, years, and millennia.[21] I found it difficult to match this diagram with Schroeder's attempt to map the six days of biblical creation onto earth time (cf. p. 60), although I did find his correlation between certain days in Genesis and the geological time periods on the earth somewhat more compatible (cf. p. 67). In any case, Schroeder's attempt to harmonize the creation story in Genesis with modern cosmology assumes that astrophysicists agree that the primordial explosion of the big bang represents an absolute beginning or "singularity" of the entire universe, in the sense that the biblical statement "in the beginning God created the heavens and the earth" has been interpreted as an absolute beginning of the physical world (despite the fact that "the Spirit of God was moving over the face of the waters" at the time of creation) (Gen 1:2).

Based on the claim that the laws of physics do not apply to the singularity (the apex of the big bang) because of the extraordinary prevailing conditions, a new argument for the existence of God has been introduced, claiming that either one must look beyond the singularity for an explanation—presumably to God—or that no explanation is possible. As Paul Davies asserts, "If the laws of physics break down at the singularity, there can be no explanation in terms of those laws. Therefore, if one insists on a reason for the big bang, then this reason must lie beyond physics [implying a religious explanation]."[22] However, leading cosmologists such as Stephen Hawking and James Hartle argue that recent evidence from quantum mechanics indicates that there may be no singularity:

. . . the quantum theory of gravity has opened up a new possibility, in which there would be no boundary to space-time and so there would be no need to specify the behavior at the boundary. There would be no singularity at which the laws of science broke down and no edge of space-time at which one would have to appeal to God or some new law to set the boundary conditions for space-time. One could say: "The boundary condition of the universe is that it has no boundary." The universe

would be completely self-contained and not affected by anything outside itself. It would neither be created nor destroyed. It would just BE [as
religionists have claimed of God].[23]

Thus Hawking comes to a conclusion similar to Laplace when he
replied, 'I have no need of that hypothesis' to Napoleon's query 'where is
the place for God in your system?' As Hawking states:

> So long as the universe had a beginning, we could suppose it had a cre-
> ator. But if the universe is really completely self-contained, having no
> boundary or edge, it would have neither beginning nor end: it would
> simply be. What place, then, for a creator?[24]

If this were true, then it would negate Schroeder's argument altogether.

Similarly, Alan Guth, one of the creators of the inflationary model of
the universe, has proposed that the universe might have originated from
an initial vacuum state which he refers to as "nothing," but which actually is a seething caldron of energy referred to as a "false vacuum." This
is a fascinating attempt to find the universe self-explanatory in terms of
its own laws.

> While the attempts to describe the materialization of the universe from
> nothing remain highly speculative, they represent an exciting enlarge-
> ment of the boundaries of science. If someday this program can be com-
> pleted, it would mean that the existence and history of the universe could
> be explained by the underlying laws of nature. That is, the laws of
> physics would imply the existence of the universe. We would have
> accomplished the spectacular goal of understanding why there is some-
> thing rather than nothing—because, if this approach is right, perpetual
> "nothing" is impossible. If the creation of the universe can be described
> as a quantum process, we would be left with one deep mystery of exis-
> tence: What is it that determined the laws of physics.[25]

What this speculation suggests is that the conception of "necessary
existence" can be transferred from a theological issue regarding God to a
scientific question pertaining to the universe, which is a sounder location,
it seems to me. The essential point is that while scientists are committed to
enlarging and improving our understanding of the universe with remarkable results, Schroeder is defending as finally true a twenty-eight hundred
year old cosmogony based on the supposition that one version of Genesis
contains hidden truths that can be decoded and confirmed by recent
developments in science. But what is the basis for believing that only the
first of the two versions, both presented in the beginning three chapters of
Genesis, should be reinterpreted to conform with modern scientific theo-

ries and the other ignored? What justifies one, except ethnocentrism, in believing that of all the ancient myths, this is the only one that is true? One cannot evoke God because the evidence for the existence of God is in the document we are questioning. If the author of that version of Genesis were that wise and knowledgeable, then why did he not present a more reasonable explanation of the creation of the universe and living creatures in the first place?

Throughout, past centuries claims have been made that the Bible contains a hidden code allowing those who can decipher it to predict future events. Recently a book making that claim was on the *New York Times* "Best Seller's List." This is what the author of the book proclaimed:

> Events that happened thousands of years after the Bible was written — World War II, the Moon landing, Watergate, both Kennedy assassinations, the election of Bill Clinton, the Oklahoma City bombing — all were foretold in the code. . . . The date the Gulf War would begin was found before the war started. The Rabin assassination was found a year before the murder.[26]

There are many questions that this claim raises. If these events were foreseen, then why not all events including the 1958 and 1967 Arab-Israeli wars? It does not seem possible that just a select number of events were foretold in the Bible and not all future events, considering how interdependent events are. Moreover, considering all the intervening events since the Bible was written that would have to occur in a precise sequence for these predictions to be realized, it would have to be concluded that all of history is predetermined. This would eliminate any free will or the possibility of influencing events since they already would have been preordained, as John Calvin maintained. Again, this is so implausible that it is more likely that the predictions are retrodictively 'found' or 'read into' the biblical text based on some strange statistical correlation. This is precisely what turned out to be true.

Several months after I wrote the above, I was elated to read the following rebuttal of Michael Drosnin's book in the *Washington Post*. Taunted by statisticians who refused to believe such predictions, and attributed them to some statistical fluke, Drosnin proposed a challenge: using his methods, search *Moby Dick* to see if one could find similarly remarkable lists of predictions. In fact this has been done with fascinating results.

> Australian computer scientist Brendan McKay did just that [search *Moby Dick* for similar predictions]. The chilling but entirely coincidental list included such names as "M. L. King" which appeared near the phrase "to be killed by them" and "Kennedy" near "shoot" and "Lincoln" near "killed" and even "Princess Di" near "mortal in these jaws of death."[27]

Thus McKay found that certain word correlations in *Moby Dick* predicted killings or assassinations similar to those predicted from the Bible, meeting the challenge of Drosnin.

SCHROEDER'S CRITICISMS OF EXPLANATIONS OF EVOLUTION

Returning to a discussion of Schroeder's critique of evolution, the largest portion is devoted to calculating the improbabilities of even Neo-Darwinian theories being able to explain *convergent* evolutionary developments (such as the evolution of the eye in two such different phyla as the octopus and humans), the *divergent* origin of chimpanzees and humanoid creatures from a common ancestor, and the *emergence* of life from a primordial inorganic ecology in terms of what we know of biomolecular processes, random mutations, and natural selection. For Schroeder, the statistical improbability (or even impossibility) of these processes having occurred from what we currently know of the structures and mechanisms involved justifies belief in a divine "programmer" to explain the outcomes. In his view, without a divine consciousness preselecting the goals and preprogramming the necessary and sufficient means for attaining them, they could not have occurred. Unlike Gould, Schroeder does not view evolution as a contingent process, such that if the evolutionary tape were rewound and replayed the outcome undoubtedly would be quite different,[28] but sees it as a consequence of preordained planning (requiring certain readjustments, as we shall see): "Science may not be capable of adjudicating the issue of God's possible superintendence of nature, but it certainly has discovered that nature functions in a way that at times seems most unnatural" (p. 114). Yet what is considered "unnatural" is just a discordance between past expectations or predictions based on established theories and surprisingly new discoveries.

That the investigation of nature has often provided astonishing surprises or counterintuitive results that seemed "unnatural" at the time certainly is true—one only has to recall attributing, during the Copernican controversy, an orbital revolution in the heavens to the centrally located motionless earth, or the null results of the Michelson-Morley experiments indicating that the velocity of light is invariant for all observers, or the "ultraviolet catastrophe" that resulted in Planck's introduction of an irreducible discrete quanta of energy in radiational processes. These unexpected developments certainly seemed "unnatural" at the time, but they did not lead scientists to invoke a divine cause as the explanation. *That one is able to demonstrate statistically the limitations of present theories of evo-*

lution is not grounds for turning to religion for an interpretation outside of science, but for seeking better mechanisms of explanation by science. If, when encountering some paradoxical consequence of inquiry, scientists had evoked a supernatural cause, would science have progressed as it has?

In the seventeenth century Newton's argument regarding the order in our solar system presupposing an intelligent creator resembles Schroeder's. As Newton wrote in a letter: "This most beautiful system of the sun, planets, and comets could only proceed from the council and dominion of an intelligent and powerful Being. . . . This Being governs all things. . . ." [29] But do astrophysicists today believe that the regularies in the solar system proceeded from "an intelligent and powerful Being," or do they think that it evolved according to physical laws from a nebular gaseous state? As Martin Rees states, "Now astronomers know that the coplanarity of the planets is a natural outcome of the solar system's origin as a spinning disk of gas and dust."[30] The history of science records a continuous replacement of explanations by a supervening divine power with natural causes and laws. At each crucial stage one could have devised statistical objections, based on variables and permutations, to show that further progress was unlikely. Given all the possible fractional combinations, who would have predicted that volumes of gases and groups of atoms would combine in whole number ratios, according to Dalton's "simplifying rules," thus permitting scientists to discover the atomic structure of gases such as nitrous oxide (NO), along with substances like water (H_2O) and sulfuric acid (H_2SO_4)? Even after J. J. Thomson's identification of the electron, Ernest Rutherford's discovery of the proton, Max Planck's introduction of the quantum of action, Einstein's explanation of the photoelectric effect, and Balmer's formula describing the spectral emissions of hydrogen, what were the odds that Niels Bohr would have been able to construct a preliminary model of the atom's internal structure to explain the simplest hydrogen spectra? Decades prior to the detonation of the atomic bomb, what was the probability of devising a controlled, chain, fissionable reaction? Even Heisenberg, one of the founders of quantum mechanics, did not believe in 1941 that it was possible.

Perhaps more dramatically, given all the unknown engineering, propulsion, and guidance problems what would have been the odds of predicting, in the early decades of the twentieth century, a future lunar landing? Yet all the improbabilities are swept away by unforeseen scientific "breakthroughs." So what is more likely to produce an explanation of evolution, progressive scientific inquiry based on testable hypotheses or Schroeder's appeal to a divine programmer because of the statistical improbability of attaining scientific explanations? Already there are many new discoveries in geology, paleontology, molecular biology, and genetics to challenge statistical objections to scientific explanations of the Cambrian explosion, convergent evolution, the divergent origin of humans, and the primordial conditions giving rise to organic life from preorganic chemical structures. Let's take each of Schroeder's examples in turn.

The Cambrian explosion is so puzzling because of the appearance, in such a brief time (a period of five million years), of so many diverse phyla without any fossil evidence of precursors, contrary to traditional Darwinism, which required an extended period of time to produce the gradual mutations, resulting in more complex animal forms. Although there is not yet a solution to this problem, there is evidence suggesting how it might be resolved. The sudden appearance of new phyla is driven by two essential factors: (1) a rapid rate of cumulative molecular genetic mutations, and (2) major changes in the ecology, selecting successful adaptive mutations by eliminating the less competitive. As regards the first problem, Schroeder states that such "rapid changes cannot be explained by purely random mutations at the molecular genetic level" and hence presuppose "a channeling in the flow of life that implies a teleology" (p. 87). He quotes with approval a statement by Michael Behe, a biochemist, that "biochemistry has made it increasingly difficult" to believe in Darwin's theory that evolution occurs as a result of nature selecting those random genetic mutations best fitted for survival.[31] Behe contends that if you cannot conceive how a complex biochemical process could have evolved from selected random mutations, that justifies a supernatural explanation. In contrast to Behe (who is Catholic), Murray Gell-Mann has said, "I know of no serious scientist who believes that there are special chemical forces [in molecular biology] that do not arise from underlying physical forces."[32] Edward O. Wilson also states that "in every scrap of data from every level of biology, from the chemistry of DNA to the dating of fossils, it has been the case that organic evolution by natural selection beats Creationism."[33]

The history of thought is full of examples of what at one time were considered to be inexplicable phenomena and therefore attributed to God, but which later were explained scientifically, often counterintuitively. At every stage in science explanations necessarily rest on what John Haugeland calls "unexplained explainers" whose explanation then is sought. In the past God has been the primary unexplained explainer, so that the further one recedes in history the more one finds God evoked as the final explanation, with Genesis attributing everything to Yahweh. Conversely, the more one approaches the present the less one appeals to God to explain anything, so that today one would be startled to read that a scientist in *Nature* or *Science* claimed that some inexplicable or anomalous occurrence must be due to God. It is religionists who do this! Another name for the Cambrian explosion is "biology's big bang" and there now is evidence of colossal continental shifts that could have played a major role in promoting the sudden proliferation of phyla. The discovery of this massive geological upheaval by the geologist who led the research team, Joseph Kirschvink of the California Institute of Technology, was reported in the July 25 issue of *Science*, and described in the *International Herald Tribune*:

> A colossal shift in the Earth's mass half a billion years ago caused continents to migrate rapidly from frigid polar regions to the steamy tropics, and vice versa . . . in a global upheaval that may help explain an astonishingly sudden increase in the diversity of living creatures on the planet. The dramatic discovery that the world's geography rotated 90 degrees at the same historical moment when evolution suddenly accelerated was . . . based . . . on an unprecedented analysis of the magnetic fields of rocks collected over 20 years worldwide.
>
> If confirmed, the findings could provide a long-sought explanation for an event . . . known as the "Cambrian Explosion." During this period the planet experienced a biological "big bang" that has never been repeated. New types of animals emerged at rates more than 20 times normal, leaving the first fossil records of virtually every sort of swimming, flying or crawling animal that exists today.[34]

Although these possible explanations of the Cambrian explosion have not been confirmed, they illustrate the kinds of unexpected discoveries that have occurred throughout history invalidating pessimistic foreclosures of possible scientific explanations. Schroeder himself refers to the "latent stored information" with potential genetic directives that could emerge suddenly in response to the tremendous environmental changes just described (cf. pp. 89–90). Even the primitive eukaryote cells contain enough information in their DNA to fill 1,000 *Encyclopedia Britannicas*. Who can guess what novel evolutionary structures and functions could emerge abruptly from this vast store of potential genetic information under certain conditions?

The next improbability based on statistical analyses that Schroeder cites is the convergent development of organs as complex as the eye in separate phyla. As he states, "We refer to this remarkable similarity of organs in very different animals as convergent evolution. But can we explain it? The lottery of individual random mutations at the molecular genetic level cannot be the only driving force" (p. 93). Focusing on the visual systems of five different phyla—ribbon worms, flat worms, insects, mollusks, and vertebrates—he says the "likelihood that random mutations would produce the same [genetic] combination five times is

10^{170} raised to the fifth power" (p. 92). But this statistical analysis is partially based on the mistaken conception of 'random mutations' as meaning that any cumulative mutations are equally possible, whereas in fact they are limited by the total genetic composition of the organism and by embryological constraints on which mutations can persist. As Dawkins states, "although any gene on any chromosome may mutate at any time, the consequences of mutation on *bodies* are severely limited by the process of embryology."[35]

What random mutation means is not that any possible mutation is likely to occur and produce a cumulative change, but *that there is no genetic mechanism that directs the mutations toward successful adaptations —* no teleology. The successful adaptations are solely due to the selective winnowing process of the ecology. That the mutations in separate phyla can produce a similar organ as complex as the eye suggests that even in those diverse phyla there must be some *similar latent genetic information* that is transmitted and replicated in the evolutionary process under the right conditions, but even then the structure produced is not identical but displays variations. How this occurs is exactly the kind of problem that is answered by scientists. Schroeder himself refers to a recent genetic discovery that suggests an explanation: "A gene group, Pax-6, is a key regulator in the development of eyes in all vertebrates. Its analog (a very small gene) has been found to control development of the visual systems" of the other four phyla mentioned above (p. 91). If the five phyla contain a similar gene controlling eye development, then what is the mystery in all five phyla developing analogous eyes during the Cambrian explosion?

Schroeder believes that attributing evolutionary developments solely to accidental biomolecular or genetic causes is insufficient because they require a preprogrammer to endow the latent genetic material with a propensity to develop in the right direction: "Evidence from anatomy, from molecular biology, and from the fossil record is that evolution is channeled in particular directions. In that sense, we are written into the scheme" (p. 94). But the crucial question is whether our being "written into the scheme" is to be attributed to nature or to God? If the former, then obviously nature must have had the potential to create what it has. But does this require a *deux ex machina* to explain it? What is added by claiming that God said: 'Let it be so and it was.' Do we understand the process any better? Do we know how God did it? Is the claim testable? Can we derive any predictions from it? As Dawkins succinctly states with regard to the creation of life:

> To explain the origin of the DNA/protein machine by invoking a supernatural Designer is to explain precisely nothing, for it leaves unexplained the origin of the Designer [and how he produced the effect]. You

have to say something like 'God was always there', and if you allow yourself that kind of lazy way out, you might as well just say 'DNA was always there', or 'Life was always there', and be done with it.[36]

The religionist, in my opinion and that of many prominent scientists, has always confused the issue. *Instead of realizing that processes in the natural world would not occur as they do if nature were not as it is, they claim that for nature to function as it does, it must have been created for that purpose.* This reply is similar to the argument from design based on the "anthropic principle." The latter principle states that for the universe to have developed as it has and produced a human being intelligent enough to reflect about its origins, the physical laws and constants of nature had to be so perfectly adjusted that it could not have occurred by chance, but must have been intentionally fine-tuned for that purpose. But this added assumption violates Occam's precept that explanatory principles should not be multiplied beyond necessity: instead of claiming that natural phenomena occur as they do because nature intentionally was fine-tuned to produce them, it is simpler to conclude that things exist as they do because natural conditions were such as to produce them. What is the necessity of claiming that the conditions themselves have to be accounted for? This would lead to a regress of explanations for the conditions for those conditions, ad infinitum. Explanation has to stop somewhere with some unexplained explainer, whether it be nature or God. This is well illustrated in Darwin's theory of evolution. Prior to Darwin it was believed that the unique capacities of humankind required a creator who intentionally endowed humans with these abilities. Darwin argued that this explanation could be replaced with a natural one based on chance mutations and natural selection, obviating a supernatural cause.

Accepting the religious argument leads one to look for intentional causes for everything, an application of what Daniel C. Dennett calls the "intentional stance" to all phenomena: that all phenomena have to be explained in terms of intentions or purposes, a return to primitive animism. This is evident in Schroeder, who entertains the notion that the asteroid that struck the earth sixty-five million years ago, killing off the dinosaurs and allowing smaller mammals to evolve into creatures like human beings, could have been sent by a divine providence. "This may have been an utterly random event—a pointless but significant collision. Alternatively, we can see the event as a divine retuning of the world. A force from outer space rechanneled the flow of life" (p. 99). Although introduced as a supposition like so many of Schroeder's contentions, not only is this prima facie ridiculous, but it makes God look foolish for having to resort to such drastic measures to correct his previous mistake in allowing the dinosaurs to dominate the earth. Yet it is consistent with

Schroeder's notion that having created the universe with autonomous laws, which he allowed to function on their own, God occasionally found the results unsatisfactory and therefore had to redirect the process, as in the story of Noah.

> Time and again, the Torah implies that the infinitely powerful biblical God withheld control and allowed the world to follow its own course. With this godly approach to world management, the results were not always "good" [though why they were not "always good" since they were created by an "infinitely powerful biblical God" Schroeder does not explain]. The creator then redirected the flow. . . . At each stage [in history], God withheld control to a greater or lesser extent. This allowed the world to develop according to the laws of nature created at the beginning. . . . A limited experiment was underway. If it failed, Divine retuning [a flood or meteor for example] redirected humanity. When it worked, God was pleased: "It's good." (pp. 13–14)

It would be quite surprising if many found this conception of a tinkerer God very satisfying. Would one really have much confidence in a God who, finding the consequences of 'his' creation displeasing, often had to intervene to correct the process? What would this bode for God's omniscience and omnipotence? If he were dissatisfied with his creation this implies either that he did not foresee the results or could not control them, which would limit either his foreknowledge or his power. On the other hand, if God allowed nature to take its course and then disapproved of the results, this implies poor judgment on his part. Finally, could any scientist pursue research with any confidence if it were believed that God might change the laws of nature at any time to alter its effects? This would be a return to the Dark Ages where all kinds of mysterious powers were believed to control events, thereby justifying miracles, magic, and witchcraft.

Schroeder's next attempt to harmonize science and theology leads to a most implausible emendation of Genesis. He states that according "to the biblical calendar Adam's birth occurred within the last six thousand years" (p. 126), but as Schroeder well knows this date for the creation of the first man is belied by the fossil record and geological evidence. Then, to show that the Cro-Magnons could not have been a legacy of a branching mutation from primates, Schroeder computes the statistical improbability of their evolving, due solely to random mutations and natural selection, from a shared ancestor with the chimpanzees within a period of six million years, as indicated by the fossil record. Asking what the rate of mutations would have to be "to change a common ancestor similar to a chimp into a Cro-Magnon," Schroeder calculates the difference between the genetic information carried on their respective genomes as "approximately one million differing bases" (p. 120). He then asks, given that difference,

> can we expect to have one million point mutations in DNA during the seven million years available, and have those variations retained and then have them passed on to become dominant traits in the entire local population . . . in that span of time? (p. 120)

Not surprisingly, his conclusion is that it is not possible: "the problem of producing us by the random plus selective natural processes becomes insurmountable in the time available" (p. 121). According to his computations the time required would exceed "more than one hundred million generations" (p. 121), an impossibility within the six million year time period.

But what should one accept, Schroeder's statistical calculations showing that Cro-Magnons could not have evolved from a common ancestor with the chimpanzees in six million years, or the compelling geological, paleontological, and archeological evidence that they have? Schroeder is aware of the alternative:

> Unfortunately, each time the mathematicians showed the statistical improbability of a given assumption, the response of the biologists was that the mathematics must be somehow flawed since evolution has occurred and occurred through random mutations. (p. 113)

In my opinion the biologists have the best of the argument because their evidence is more empirically secure, in contrast to statistical predictions based on questionable assumptions and our present ignorance of the biomolecular mechanisms involved that could make the pressimistic calculations otiose.

As everyone knows, statistics can be manipulated to prove almost anything one wants to prove. Essentially Schroeder's conclusion is based on *argumentum ud ignoruntium*: because we cannot explain now how a process occurred, the explanation is impossible. Applying that argument in the past would have precluded any progress in science. Schroeder's negative conclusion illustrates this very well. His calculations are based on the difference between the genetic information carried on the genome of the primate ancestors of the chimpanzees and Cro-Magnons without taking account of the full fossil evidence of the intermediary evolutionary transitions. According to the evidence, the divergence between the chimps and an early primatelike hominid was not a singular direct line of evolution to Cro-Magnons, but branched into a least two separate lineages and possibly three. The second (and perhaps third) branch led to the Neanderthals who preceded (by about 150,000 years) and then briefly coexisted with the Cro-Magnons. The Neanderthals became extinct, apparently owing to the superior tool making skills and greater adaptability of their rivals, despite the fact that the Neanderthal's craniums were nearly 10 percent larger.

In contrast to Schroeder, Jared Diamond indicates why, based on the fossil and archeological evidence, Schroeder's statistical genetic conclusions would have little relevance: "The emergence of *Homo sapiens* illustrates the paradox . . . that our rise to humanity was not directly proportional to the changes in our genes."[37] Similarly, Stuart Kauffman asserts

> that much of the order seen in development arises almost without regard for how the networks of interacting genes are strung together. Such order is robust and emergent, a kind of . . . spontaneous order that selection then goes on to mold. . . . In these cases, one hopes to explain, understand, and even predict the occurrence of these generic emergent properties; however, one gives up the dream of predicting details.[38]

If these claims are borne out, they would show why Schroeder's statistical analyses based on the detailed structure of the genes could not predict the evolutionary results.

The lineage that led to the Cro-Magnons passed through a number of species, from Australopithicus africanus, Homo habilis, erectus, and sapiens, to Cro-Magnons. The fossil record indicates that these precursors originated in Africa (not "Eden in the east") and eventually migrated throughout the world as far as Peking. None of this empirical evidence matches the ethnocentric story in Genesis that humankind descended from Adam and Eve, or Noah and his entourage, or Abraham and Sarah. Schroeder's claim that there is no disagreement between Genesis and the paleontological evidence because the Talmud and cabalist commentators (such as Nahmanides) show that there is evidence in Genesis for the existence of pre-Adam hominids, strikes me as sheer fantasy.

We are asked to believe that just as the paleontological evidence shows that a primitive form of hominid existed before Cro-Magnons, verses in Genesis attest to "the existence of pre-Adam creatures similar to humans in shape and intellect but less than humans in spirit" (p. 142). These pre-Adam, subhuman creatures were less than human because they lacked souls, even though the term 'soul' does not appear in the relevant passages. According to Schroeder, verse 2:7 in the "J" version of Genesis, which states that "God formed man of dust from the ground, and breathed into his nostrils the breath of life; and man became a living being," really means that God endowed Adam with a soul, which made him come alive, even though the passage does not say this. If such liberties of emendation are allowed, one can make the Bible say anything one wishes.

Schroeder quotes two passages regarding Adam and Eve which have a very natural and consistent meaning, but which the Talmud distorts beyond belief. After Eve had given birth to Cain and Able and the latter was slain by his brother, in the same chapter it states that "Adam *knew his wife again* and she bore a son and called his name Seth, for she said: 'God has appointed for me another child instead of Abel, for Cain slew him' " (4:25; emphasis added). Then a few lines into the immediately following chapter a different version is inserted: "When Adam had lived a hundred and thirty years, he became the father of a son in his own likeness . . . and named him Seth. The days of Adam after he became the father of Seth were eight hundred years" (5:3–4). (I quote this latter statement to show how implausible all this is.) The first assertion that "Adam knew his wife again" clearly refers to his having sexual relations with Eve after the birth of their first two sons and the death of Abel. Although the second narrative is only three verses removed from the first, the opening statement indicates an interruption in the narrative followed by a radically different version, showing that it had been inserted by another author. But despite this obvious explanation of the discrepancy between the two versions, this is how it is interpreted by the Talmud and Schroeder:

> Here, as commonly found elsewhere in the Bible, a subtle fact is being implied by describing the same event [the birth of Seth] from two slightly different perspectives [indicated in the two passages]. . . . The Talmud deduces from these two verses that followed the trauma of Cain murdering Abel, Adam and Eve separated. It was not until 130 years after Cain and Abel that "Adam knew again his wife" (Gen 4:25) {and she was able to conceive Seth at about age 150?}. The Talmud asked why the Bible states "again" in reference to Adam's relations with Eve. Eve was Adam's wife, so obviously it was with her that he had relations. The "again" is superfluous {why is the "again" superfluous when it indicates that Adam and Eve had renewed sexual relations after producing Cain and Abel?} and therefore it teaches something. The answer the Talmud supplies is that during those 130 years of separation [according to the second but not the first version], Adam had sexual relations with other beings (the nature of those beings is not clear). From these unions came children that "were not human in the true sense of the word. They had not the spirit of God." (p. 141)

Anyone who believes those two passages imply the meaning suggested must also believe in spontaneous generation, cold fusion, the tooth fairy, and Santa Claus. Why should anyone think that the "again" in the first passage is "superfluous," requiring such a fantastic interpretation, rather than indicating that after Cain and Abel were born and Abel slain, Adam and Eve "again" had sexual relations to produce Seth, as the quotation clearly and explicitly states? Is not the obvious difference between — along with the glaring discontinuity of — the two passages more reasonably explained by their having been written by two different authors, as so often occurs in Genesis? Where and how could Eve have survived separately from Adam for 130 years, as the second quotation asserts? Schroeder quotes a passage from Genesis (which was discussed previously) that refers to a people called the Nephilim, as if this supports the Talmudic interpretation (cf. p. 142). The passage reads as follows: "The Nephilim were on the earth in those days, and also afterward, when the sons of God came into the daughters of men, and they bore children to them. These were the mighty men that were of old, the men of renown" (Gen. 6:4). But since the passage refers to the time of Noah (before the flood), not to the time of Adam, it does not support the Talmudic interpretation.

Furthermore, the passage is so ambiguous and strange (as I pointed out in chapter 2), that no one knows what to make of it. Despite this, Schroeder goes so far as to suggest that these subhuman Nephilims could be considered Cro-Magnons: "The fossil record might refer to these as Cro-Magnon creatures" (p. 141). (I find it incredible that a person with a Ph.D. in physics from MIT could accept these archaic Talmudic assertions as having as much validity as paleontological evidence.) As he often does, Schroeder states this as a conjecture, but how plausible is it? In my opinion, recourse to these farfetched interpretations by the Talmud and by Schroeder show how easily one is drawn into fantasy when there are no objective constraints on one's thinking.

There also is the problem of the soul, which Schroeder believes distinguishes these creatures from Adam. Despite his excellent scientific background in physics, paleontology, and genetics, apparently Schroeder has not studied neurophysiology or the controversy over the mind/body (or soul/body) problem. If he had, he would not so blithely accept the view that what distinguishes humankind from other mammals, such as chimpanzees (ignoring their nearly identical genetic code), is that the former possess a soul. He says the Bible tells us (confirming again how literally he accepts much of the Bible) "that although mankind and animals may share a common physical origin, there is an extra spiritual input in humanity. The *meshana*, the spiritual soul of humanity, is the factor distinguishing man from beast" (p. 139). Thus "Adam, having a *meshana*, would find the Cro-Magnons [the subhuman Nephilims] inferior in spirit if not in body" (p. 142) Apart from the ludicrous conflating of the Genesis myth with modern paleontology, this ignores the fact that the vast majority of neuroscientists and philosophers no longer believe that the concept of the soul has any explanatory value, and thus is relegated to the same nonexistent status as animal spirits, vitalism, and the *élan vitale*.

There are a number of reasons why the conviction that we possess a soul was so prevalent in the past (to ensure our immortality for example), but the basic reason was that there was no direct evidence of the dependence of our conscious experiences on our brains. It was mainly during the Second World War, owing to the discovery of antibiotics such as penicillin and more effective anesthetics, that soldiers with severe wounds to their heads could survive the accompanying infection and shock, permitting the display of their terrible cognitive and behavioral disorders. It is one of the most fascinating and mysterious aspects of life that although everything we experience *depends upon* trillions of neuronal discharges going on in our brains, we have no awareness of this. What we experience is a visual field consisting of a seemingly independent natural world.[39] Though there have been remarkable advances in neuroscience in the more than half-century since the end of the war, we still are basically ignorant as to how our brains, consisting essentially of the transmission of chemical-electrical potentials, produce this three-dimensional, qualitative, 'outside' world. Yet nothing is added to this explanatory impasse by attributing our cognitive abilities to a soul—it has no more explanatory value than attributing creation to God. Thus I find the following concluding asserting by Schroeder to be totally unfounded:

> Science has confirmed the Bible's description of life as starting immediately on the cool Earth, of simple life forms developing to the complexity of the modern biosphere. Science has also confirmed the biblical assertion that less-than-human creatures with human-like bodies and brains [but without souls] existed before Adam. (p. 143)

The final denial by Schroeder concerns the possibility of even the simplest forms of life arising from an accidental synthesis of inorganic molecules: "life could not have started by chance" (p. 85). He acknowledges the remarkable experiment performed at the University of Chicago in 1953 by Stanley Miller that artificially produced amino acids by discharging an electric current (simulating lightning) into a mixture of ammonia, methane, hydrogen, and water vapor, the gases thought to have been in the earth's atmosphere when life originated 3.5 billion years ago. Because amino acids are the components of proteins which, in turn are the basic ingredients of life, this experiment was considered a breakthrough in demonstrating how life could have originated accidentally from natural conditions. Yet because vital organic functions, such as metabolism and reproduction occur in cells, whose replication is more difficult, the original elation was replaced by the sober realization that the artificial production of organic molecules is not equivalent to the artificial production of living cells. This does not prove the necessity of a God, as Schroeder admits, but it does imply that the replication of cells will not be a simple matter. As Schroeder states:

> This is . . . not an affirmation of the existence of a Creator. However, it does assert that the simplest forms of life, single-celled bacteria and algae . . . are far too complex to have originated without there being an inherent chemical property of molecular self-organization and/or reaction-enhancing catalysts at every step of their development. (p. 85)

While I have been severely critical of Schroeder's attempt to reconcile religion and science based on farfetched interpretations of Genesis, along with his claim that science has confirmed the biblical myth of creation, I do find some justification in his criticism that random mutations, understood as completely independent fortuitous genetic variations, and natural selection are sufficient to account for the progressive complexity in structures and functions displayed in the fossil record. Dissatisfied with a completely reductionist approach to explaining complex phenomena, such as the origin of life and evolution, a growing number of scientists are turning to a quite different explanatory framework embracing the emergence of new forms as described in chaos theory,[40] self-organizing dissipative systems,[41] and complexity theory.[42] Schroeder's reference to "molecular self-organization" and "reaction-enhancing catalysts" in the last line of the previous quotation indicates he is aware of these developments. But what he does not realize is that by investing nature with these inherent capacities and functions, scientists obviate the need for an initial divine programmer, the essential thesis of Schroeder. If these tendencies or potentialities are inherent in nature there is no need for a further explanation, a *deus ex machina*, outside of nature to explain their occurrence, which would raise all kinds of unnecessary questions without adding anything to our understanding.

One of the most enthusiastic proponents of this new paradigm is Stuart Kauffman. Like Schroeder and recent evolutionists, he thinks the random, contingent, "Rube Goldberg" conception of evolution held by traditional Darwinists is inadequate, but he does not subscribe to a supernatural explanation:

> . . . most of the beautiful order seen in ontogeny [embryological development] is spontaneous, a natural expression of the stunning self-organization that abounds in very complex regulatory networks. We appear

to have been profoundly wrong [in our previous explanations of complex processes]. Order, vast and generative, arises naturally.... The order of organisms is natural, not merely the unexpected triumph of natural selection.[43]

Unlike Schroeder who found it statistically improbable that life emerged naturally, that different phyla could arise suddenly in the Cambrian explosion, that human beings could have descended from a shared ancestor with the chimpanzees or evolved their unusual capacities within a six million year span, Kauffman argues that all these developments are possible if we invest nature with self-generative powers in place of purely random changes.

> I believe that life itself is an emergent phenomenon, but I mean nothing mystical by this . . . I . . . believe that sufficiently complex mixes of chemicals can spontaneously crystallize into systems with the ability to collectively catalyze the network of chemical reactions by which the molecules themselves are formed. Such collectively autocatalytic sets sustain themselves and reproduce. This is no less than what we call a living metabolism, the tangle of chemical reactions that power every one of our cells.[44]

Like the founders of chaos theory who discovered deeply embedded structural order with beautiful fractal patterns (the same intricate geometrical designs reproduced on smaller scales) that emerge from seemingly chaotic conditions, or even arise in stable systems whose periodic changes suddenly give rise to cascades of bifurcations which in turn lead to further intricate patterns, molecular biologists and geneticists began to see complex systems exhibiting unexpected dynamic properties emerging from simpler structures. Prigogine's research group also found that many systems contain subsystems that constantly "fluctuate," with a particular fluctuation destroying the preexistent order but subsequently reaching a "bifurcation point," resulting either in chaos or reorganization into a higher level of order. These latter "dissipative structures," so-called because they utilize or dissipate energy to produce the more complex levels of organization, are unforeseen and unpredictable. Thus stable systems unexpectedly can disintegrate into chaos while new levels of organization can arise "spontaneously" due to "self-organization." None of these new concepts was available earlier to explain how life might have emerged from simpler organizations of chemicals due to changes in equilibrium, or how changes in the genetic codes producing the diverse phyla during the Cambrian explosion could have been caused by tremendous geological and climatic changes, or how self-organizing molecules of nucleic acids or proteins in the genome could have produced convergent evolutionary developments of something as marvelously complicated as the eye, or how Cro-Magnons could have evolved from simpler primates. Such transitional stages producing greater complexity seem to emerge at the bifurcation points between stability and instability or order and chaos.

These theoretical possibilities have been complemented by the recent discovery that microbes can arise and exist under the most unusual physical conditions. Called "Extremophiles," these microbes exist in extraordinarily high temperatures, maximum pressures, and unusual conditions of acidity, alkalinity, or salinity challenging the view that life is extremely rare and can arise only in the most delicately balanced conditions with its development requiring extended time. Instead, it has been found that these microbes which "thrive above boiling-hot vents on the deep-sea floor . . . can swim in acid, eat sulfur, and draw energy from rock."[45] Using the latest military technology to explore deep into the ocean floor, these discoveries are transforming previous conceptions of life and its origin. As described by John Baross of the University of Washington in Seattle, who in the 1980s led the discovery of extremophiles, "This is going to tell us about the origin of organisms, the origins of life, the evolution of organisms and what sorts of metabolic processes could occur on other planets. . . . This is a total revolution in microbiology. . . ."[46] It also is a further illustration of how unforeseen discoveries suddenly can provide possible explanations of phenomena that previously seemed to require a divine cause.

All of these empirical developments tend to refute Schroeder's a priori statistical predictions that understanding the origin and evolution of life is beyond scientific explanation, although it does support his contention that this cannot be explained by the traditional interpretations of random mutations and natural selection. It also shows how futile reliance on an unchanging four-thousand-year myth is compared to the unforeseen, remarkable developments of science. Although Schroeder apposes a literal exposition of Genesis, it is clear that he believes that this archaic biblical work, as interpreted by the Talmud and ancient commentators, contains hidden scientific truths that can be decoded by correct analysis. How else could he make the astonishing claim that "the basics of western society find their origins in the Five Books of Moses," the Pentateuch (p. 9). As an undergraduate and graduate student at MIT, he took courses in mathematics, such as geometry, trigonometry, and calculus, along with science courses as physics, astronomy, cosmology, and perhaps biology, psychology, and physiology, the names of which are all of Greek derivation. Also, he must have studied electricity and magnetism, along with the atomic theory, other legacies of the ancient Greeks, as their names indicate. While none of these subjects is even mentioned in the Old and

New Testaments, they constitute the "basics" of an educated person today, at least in the sciences. As Whitehead claimed, in contrast to Schroeder, "Greece was the mother of Europe, and it is to Greece that we must look in order to find the origin of modern ideas."[47]

We also owe our institutions of democracy, constitutional government with the separation of powers, along with a vast heritage of literature, architecture, sculpture, and philosophy to the ancient Greeks, none of which is due to Genesis. I wonder if Genesis was ever mentioned in any course of Schroeder's at MIT? That Genesis could seem so important to Schroeder must be due to his personal commitment to Judaism which is so deep that it acts as a cognitive filter distorting his view of Western culture. Although the following statement is used by Schroeder to describe someone else, in my opinion it is quite self-revealing, characterizing his own thought perfectly.

> When data mount ever more convincing arguments against a favored paradigm, all sorts of mental machinations allow us to retain our preconceived notions of reality. If we have spent much of a lifetime attempting to prove the validity of a premise in question, the emotional states are high. Cognitive dissonance, humanity's inherent ability to ignore unpleasant facts, helps us in our struggle to retain the error of our ways.[48]

Previously I stated that in the West there have been two major cultural influences that formed our basic framework of beliefs: the Hebraic-Christian religion and the protoscientific tradition of the ancient Greeks. Moreover, I maintained that though one might like to reconcile these two legacies, to view them as "two perspectives on reality," as Schroeder asserted, this is precluded by their divergent origins, justifications, and claims. Based on the Old and New Testaments composing the Holy Bible, the Hebraic-Christian religion (along with the Muslim religion) derives from a prophetic tradition purporting to be the inerrant word of God as revealed in Scripture, even if Scripture itself is occasionally fallible due to human error in transmission. Not considered merely a passing phase in our cultural development, as other ancient religions such as Orphism, the Bible proclaims as an eternal truth that all of creation and human destiny are the work of a supernatural being. Although subordinating human existence to a providence whose presence and design seem remote and incomprehensible, Scripture declares that there is a transcendent meaning and ultimate purpose to life beyond our finite earthly existence. Accepting this belief system, it is claimed, can lead to a new way of life in which one's existence is profoundly transformed, the ultimate ideal of Christianity as proclaimed by Jesus and Paul.

Despite the anthropomorphic and self-abnegating features of this

worldview, it has a deeply emotional attraction constituting its basic justification since it has almost no factual support, which is why it appeals
ultimately to faith and inner religious experience. Unlike pagan religions
that have long since disappeared because of their obvious mythical content, the Hebraic-Christian religion is perpetuated by its institutionaliza-
tion, early indoctrination, and deep social and emotional needs generated
and reinforced in part by its own belief system. But owing to the unparalleled scientific discoveries and technological advances in the twentieth
century, the influence of science now greatly outweighs that of religion.
Can it seriously be doubted that the pervasive effects of science and technology on our worldview and practical techniques for dealing with
human existence largely have displaced religion in our daily lives
because the former are based on a truer, more realistic understanding of
reality? As Edward O. Wilson states:

> The true evolutionary epic, retold as poetry, is as intrinsically ennobling
> as any religious epic. Material reality discovered by science already pos-
> sesses more content and grandeur than all religious cosmologies com-
> bined. The continuity of the human line has been traced through a
> period of deep history a thousand times older than that conceived by the
> Western religions. Its study has brought new revelations of great moral
> importance.[49]

Reference still is made to a "higher power," but its status and function
have become increasingly nebulous, tenuous, and remote—except for
those desperately seeking help for a terminal illness, drug addiction,
alcoholism, or the death of a loved one. While these are poignant excep-
tions, they are due to being emotionally distraught.

THE TRIUMPH OF OUR ANCIENT GREEK HERITAGE

This triumph of the scientific outlook is a legacy and vindication of the
second major influence on Western civilization, that of those extraordinarily creative, independently minded ancient Greek philosophers,
mathematicians, and scientists. Gradually discarding the previous
mythopoetic, theogonic, and Olympian frameworks of beliefs, they were
the only people in the world to create a *sustained tradition of successive critical inquiry* into the structure of physical reality, the nature of man, and
the origin of cultural institutions, as opposed to isolated independent discoveries. Despite their other great cultural achievements, this development did not occur in Egypt, Babylonia, Persia, China, Japan, or India.
Unlike the Israelites and Egyptians whose culture was dominated by a

priestly class that maintained, based on divination and revelation, that they were the sole source of truth (as the Catholic Church claimed at the time of Galileo), the ancient Greeks attained the *extraordinary conviction that the cosmos and human existence were rationally intelligible.*

Although some Christian scholars claim that the basic assumption underlying scientific inquiry, that there is a lawful order to nature discoverable by rational investigation, was a legacy of the Christian belief that God designed and created the cosmos, this is blatantly false! The Christian belief in special creation, miracles, divination, and divine intervention *does not* instill or reinforce the conviction that the universe is organized according to immutable natural laws, but just the contrary. Even as well informed a scholar as Ian Barbour makes the following erroneous claim:

> Historians have wondered why modern science arose in the Judeo-Christian West among all world cultures. A good case can be made that the doctrine of creation helped to set the stage for scientific inquiry.[50]

Not only *can* a good case *not* be made for this, it is *completely mistaken* because there is nothing in the Judeo-Christian belief system to encourage or support scientific inquiry, as the Bible well attests since it contains absolutely nothing of any scientific value! During the Medieval Period when Christianity reached its religious zenith, there was no interest in science at all because the goal of Christians was to achieve salvation and eternal life in the body of Christ, as Paul maintained.

It is ironic that religionists should claim that the Christian belief in a divine creator encouraged and sustained scientific inquiry when the evidence is just the opposite. If anything, Christianity has impeded the development of science by maintaining that belief in Scripture and keeping the faith, regardless of the evidence, is superior to any scientific knowledge, as shown by the opposition to Galileo and Darwin. The Medieval Period is referred to as the Dark Ages precisely because of the indifference to any kind of learning except religion. The founders of modern classical science, Copernicus, Kepler, Galileo, and Newton, *did believe* that the intelligible order in nature was evidence of God's rational creation and supervision, but this belief was not derived from the Bible; it was due to reinterpreting the biblical conception of God to make it harmonious with the renewed conviction, derived from the Greeks, that it was possible to discern the laws of nature (as illustrated by the discoveries of Kepler, Galileo, and Newton, each of whom acknowledges his indebtedness to the ancient Greeks). Genesis does not portray God as imposing laws on nature, but as creating the world by verbal fiat. The assertion that "the doctrine of creation helped to set the stage for scientific inquiry" is a typical example of distorting history to justify belief in God.

It was Anaxagoras who claimed that *nous* or "mind" controls nature and the ancient atomists who asserted all events were strictly determined while chance was merely a name for ignorance. The first comprehensive astronomical system containing the hierarchical order of the seven planets revolving in uniform circular motion below the outer realm of the fixed stars was introduced by Eudoxus and Aristotle. To explain such anomalies as planetary variations in brightness and size, as well as retrograde motion (which did not fit circular orbits), Apollonius, Hipparchus, and Ptolemy emended the system with epicycles, eccentrics, and equants. Archimedes discovered the law of specific weights, as well as numerous mathematical theorems and proofs to resolve geometrical problems. The attempt to understand the causes of diseases was advanced by Hippocrates while anatomical investigations were pursued by Herophilus, Erasistratus (who anticipated Harvey's discovery of the circulation of the blood), and Galen. Where does one find any comparable investigations or discoveries by the Hebrews or the Christians?

Thus the claim that it was the Judeo-Christian belief in God that provided the rationale for scientific inquiry is completely erroneous. Nor is it true, as Paul Davies asserts, that "in Renaissance Europe, the justification for what we today call the scientific approach to inquiry was the belief in a rational God whose created order could be discerned from a careful study of nature."[51] As I have pointed out, a major cause of the Renaissance was the discovery by the Humanists of ancient Greek scientific and mathematical manuscripts, along with the transport of additional treatises to the West by the Muslims, which reawakened interest in scientific inquiry from the fourteenth through the seventeenth centuries in the newly created universities of Paris, Oxford, and Bologna. Unlike the Koran, which *does* maintain that one can discover evidence of God in the order of nature as well as in scripture, which led to significant scientific developments by the Muslims in the later Middle Ages *based on the earlier investigations of the Greeks*, there is *no* comparable evidence of a positive influence of the Old and New Testaments or even of the belief in the Judeo-Christian God on scientific inquiry. As Davies does correctly maintain, contradicting his previous assertion, "the idea that the physical world is the manifestation of mathematical order and harmony can be traced back to ancient Greece."[52]

It was the ancient Greeks beginning in the sixth century B.C.E. who gradually freed themselves from the grip of the previous mythopoetic, theogonic traditions and approached nature with an inquiring mind. Unlike the great civilizations of Egypt and China, they were not preoccupied with preparing for the afterlife and thus were motivated to investigate the existing world. Hades was not for them a continuation of this life in another world for which elaborate preparations had to be made, but a shadowy domain that had little attraction. Thus the Presocratic philosophers began to inquire into how the observable world arose from a more disorganized preexistent state and explain change and becoming in terms of common elements like water, air, fire, and earth, along with such natural principles as condensation and rarefaction, *logos*, *nous*, or necessity. Anaximander (prime 560 B.C.E.) proposed a spherical model of the universe utilizing empirical analogies such as tubes enclosing fire to represent stellar spheres and apertures to depict the fiery sparkle of the stars. He replaced intentional causes with the principle of "sufficient reason," arguing that the earth is stationary in the center of the universe because there is no reason for it to be displaced. Unlike the Hebrews, he did acknowledge evolutionary developments, declaring that all forms of life evolved from primitive sea urchins, while human beings descended from fish.

On a more rational level, after discovering the numerical ratios underlying the Greek musical scale the Pythagoreans, in one of the boldest generalizations in history, claimed that numerical ratios underlie the structure of the universe itself and that the motions of the planets display musical harmonies, an insight that resonated later in Kepler's discovery of the three planetary laws of motion. Extolling the greater importance of the sun, the Pythagorean Philolaus asserted that a fiery body was in the center of the universe around which the earth revolved, anticipating the later heliocentric theory of the universe, while Heraclides proposed that the revolution of the entire universe around the earth, as indicated by the rising and setting of the sun, could be explained more simply as an apparent motion caused by the daily rotation of the earth on its axis from west to east. Both speculations influenced Copernicus two millennia later.

Investigating the logical form of the arguments involved in explaining change and becoming, Parmenides formulated his logical principles that Being Is and Cannot Cease To Be, while Not-Being Is Not and Cannot Come To Be, principles used to exclude all division, change, motion, and becoming. Although succeeding philosophers rejected his undifferentiated, continuous, static universe, they accepted his logical tenets that change cannot involve a coming to be from nothing nor ceasing to be, principles reflected in our current law of the conservation of matter and energy. Zeno's paradoxes in support of Parmenides' position still are discussed by logicians, mathematicians, and philosophers.

Rather than selecting one of the previous elements as basic, Empedocles held that all four were fundamental, a view generally held until the reintroduction of the ancient atomic theory in the seventeenth century and the discovery during the chemical revolution of the eighteenth century that air consisted of elementary gases, such as nitrogen and hydrogen, and that water was composed of the elementary atoms hydrogen and oxygen. Empedocles anticipated Darwin in claiming that those organisms best fitted for survival persist, while others perished, and used the models of the klepsydra to explain respiration and the lantern to illustrate perception. Having observed a meteorite that fell in Aegospotane in 476 B.C.E., Anaxagoras inferred that the moon is a material body whose surface resembles the earth's in having mountains and ravines, while the Milky Way is a congery of stars so dense that their converging rays hide them, theories not confirmed until Galileo developed the telescope two thousand years later. But because the planets were believed at the time to be celestial or divine bodies, he was banished from Athens for his blasphemous views—such is the folly of humanity!

But the most astonishing intellectual breakthrough was made by the ancient atomists, Leucippus and Democritus. Every scientific discipline today, from astronomy to zoology, presupposes that macroscopic phenomena consist of and can be explained largely by microstructures, a legacy of the ancient atomists. Completely discarding anthropomorphic, animistic, and intentional explanations, they held that the atoms were eternal, indivisible, unchanging, and homogeneous, possessing the inherent qualities of solidity, shape, size, and motion. Existing in an unlimited void, their chance collision produced innumerable worlds. Anticipating the steady-state theory of the universe, these multiple worlds exist in different stages of formation and destruction, some with suns and some without, some inhabited and some not. Like modern neurophysiologists, they believed that consciousness could be reduced to physical processes, the motion of smaller, more mobile, fiery atoms. What an extraordinary accomplishment in an age dominated by superstition, magic, miracles, and divinities.

Greek speculative philosophy culminated in the writings and schools of Plato and Aristotle, the founders of the Academy and Lyceum respectively. Socrates' dialectical search for the meanings of absolute values and abstract concepts such as Beauty, Piety, Goodness, and Knowledge led to Plato's theory of the independently subsisting Forms as the objective referents of these eternal values and concepts. His emphasis on the study of mathematics as a method of freeing the intellect from dependence on the senses influenced such mathematicians as Archytas and Eudoxus, although unlike Archytas he was opposed to the application of mathematics to empirical problems believing that material objects were too imperfect and unreal to allow for exact mathematical description—even the motion of the planets.[53] Yet Eudoxus developed his theory of concentric planetary orbits, adopted by Aristotle, while a student in the Academy.

Although it would be difficult to match Plato's souring imagination and tremendous literary gifts, it was Aristotle who had the outstanding intellect, called by Plato "the mind" of the Academy. Aristotle, in fact, probably was the most comprehensive thinker of all time, his extensive writings making original contributions to what seems to be every known subject: the organization of syllogistic logic into an organon; treatises on physics, metaphysics, astronomy, biology (Darwin said he thought highly of his predecessors until he read Aristotle), psychology (the nature of the soul), memory, dreams and divination; along with systematic works on ethics, politics, rhetoric, and poetics. His theories of mechanics (explanation of various motions and investigation of statics and hydrostatics), scientific method, and organismic cosmology were the fundamental theoretical frameworks from the thirteenth through much of the seventeenth century. Although it sounds paradoxical, it is a tribute to Aristotle's extraordinary originality and achievement that it was his theory of mechanics, his conception of scientific method, his schema of explanation, and his cosmological system that had to be critically analyzed and replaced before modern classical science could be constructed on the foundations of the heliocentric theory and the reintroduced theoretical framework of atomism.

As if this remarkable burst of creative energy were not enough, it was succeeded by even greater advances in science during the Hellenistic period following the death of Alexander the Great in 322 B.C.E. and Aristotle the following year. The greatest names in antiquity in mathematics, physics, astronomy, and biology can be traced to this period: Euclid, Archimedes, Herophilus, Erasistratus, Apollonius, Hipparchus, Aristarchus, Strato, Hero, Galen, and Ptolemy. Although he chose Alexandria to be the capital of his empire, Alexander died before being able to realize his dream. It was the Ptolemies, Ptolemy I (Soter) and Ptolemy II (Philadelphus), who developed Alexandria to rival Athens, subsidizing research in the Museum and Library which actually eclipsed Athens as a center of learning during the following centuries. The recovery of the manuscripts of these great Hellenistic scholars, which had been hidden away and neglected in the dusty monasteries in the West during the Medieval Period, was a major factor in the intellectual and cultural reawakening called the Renaissance. In every case the predecessors of the founders of modern classical science can be traced either to Aristotle or to the Hellenistic scholars. As I wrote in a previous book:

> . . . the Hellenistic period . . . was not an age of great scientific-philosophical synthesis, but of brilliant mathematical, astronomical, physical,

and medical investigations and discoveries that foreshadow the classical era of modern science. The precursors of mathematical astronomy and physics, of modern trigonometry and infinitesimal calculus, and of anatomy and physiology can be traced particularly to this period. Aristarchus was "the Copernican of antiquity," Apollonius' research into conic sections provided the mathematical basis for Kepler's first two astronomical laws, Eudoxus' method of exhaustion and Archimedes' method of integration preceded the discovery of differential and integral calculus of Newton and Leibniz, Erasistratus was a forerunner of Harvey in rejecting the humoral theory and surmising the connection of arteries and veins, and Galileo was the heir apparent of Strato and Archimedes. Had not the Hellenistic period "leveled off" (Marshal Clagett's term) and finally ended as a result of the [sack of Rome and ascendance of Christianity], modern science might have begun at the beginning of the Christian era or after the achievements of Hero, Galen, and Ptolemy. But if that had occurred, there would have been no "beginning" of modern science in the Renaissance — just a continuous development of Hellenistic science.[54]

Given this extraordinary record of creative research whose legacy continues to the present, can there be any question as to whether the Hebraic-Christian religion or the protoscientific investigations of the ancient Greeks had the most lasting effect on Western civilization? Although it is true that throughout the past two millennia the Bible, along with institutionalized Judaism and Christianity, had the greatest impact on the Western world, at the beginning of the new millennium this is no longer the case owing to the remarkable advances in the various sciences, particularly during the twentieth century. While the Bible contains beautiful literature, marvelous inspirational writing, and devout exhortations to forego materialism for a more spiritual life founded on brotherly love and devotion to God, all of which contributed so much to enhance the values of love, charity, and humility, it is foolish to claim, as Schroeder does, that the Pentateuch was the basis of Western civilization. In reality, the Five Books of Moses (which were not written by Moses) have no relevance today for understanding the world and little value for addressing the complex ethical or social problems arising from the choices created by advances in science and technology: birth control and abortion, organ transplants, genetic engineering, euthanasia, cloning, detrimental environmental and climatic changes, economic disparities, and so forth. These questions are well beyond the scope of biblical ethics.

Far from providing "the basics of western society," the Old Testament has significance primarily as a Hebrew theocracy and as the source of (a qualified) monotheism in the Christian and Muslim religions. In contrast, the legacy of the ancient Greeks in philosophy, mathematics, science, technology, historical research (Heroditus and Thucydides), literature, sculpture, architecture, political theory (democracy), and constitutional government constitutes the foundation of Western civilization, and through the latter's global influence, the rest of the world. The purpose of this book has been to show that the framework of belief inherited from the Hebraic-Christian tradition, though still entrenched in Western society, is no longer viable and that one of the great challenges of the new millennium is to replace it by teaching a more adequate framework of beliefs grounded in a true conception of the universe and understanding of the evolutionary origin and biological nature of humankind. Without this grounding the endeavor to deal realistically with and to ameliorate the human condition will be chimeric.

NOTES

1. Cf. Andrew D. White, *A History of the Warfare of Science with Theology in Christendom* (New York: Appleton Publishing, 1896).
2. Cf. Paul Davies, *God and the New Physics* (New York: Simon & Schuster, 1983).
3. Cf. Karen Armstrong, *A History of God* (New York: Balllantine Books, 1993), p. 27.
4. Quoted in W. W. Hyde, *Paganism to Christianity in the Roman Empire* (Philadelphia, 1946), p. 199.
5. For a description of these contributions, see Richard H. Schlagel, *From Myth to Modern Mind: A Study of the Origins and Growth of Scientific Thought*, vol. 2, *Copernicus through Quantum Mechanics* (New York: Peter Lang, 1996).
6. R. P. C. and A. T. Hanson, *The Bible without Ilusions* (London: SCM Press, 1989), pp. 6–7.
7. Gerald L. Schroeder, *The Science of God: The Convergence of Science and Biblical Wisdom* (New York: The Free Press, 1997), p. 3. The immediately following page references in the text are to this work until otherwise indicated.
8. The report of an earlier flood covering a large land area occurs in the ancient Mesopotamian Gilgamesh legend as well as in Genesis, the former written "about 3,600 years ago and the latter "sometime between 2,900 and 2,400 years ago," according to Hershel Shanks, editor of the *Biblical Archaeology Review*. Two Columbian geologists, William Ryan and Walter Pitman, in their book, *Noah's Flood*, proposed the theory that the present Black Sea was formed 7,600 years ago when melting glaciers caused the level of the Mediterranean sea to rise overflowing the Bosporus Strait connecting the two Seas. As the rising salt sea water poured into the previous fresh water of the Black Sea, a catastrophic flood occurred. Not only covering "thousands of square miles of dry land," this deluge probably killed "thousands of people and billions of land and sea creatures," the latter when the denser salt water sank below the fresh water.

Recently the explorer Robert D. Ballard, who discovered the sunken *Titanic* in

1985, led a team of deep-sea explorers who discovered evidence of a gigantic deluge in the Black Sea from 7,500 years ago based on radioactive dating of mollusk shells recovered from the sea floor. Using sonar images, Ballard and his team located the submerged preflood shoreline exactly as predicted by Ryan and Pitman.

But while this apparently confirms the occurrence of a great deluge that occurred between 7,500 to 6,900 years ago, it does not confirm the story of Noah's Ark, as I am sure fundamentalists would like to believe. Even Ballard makes the misleading statement that " 'we wanted to prove to ourselves that it was the biblical flood.' " It seems that the oral recounting of the Black Sea catastrophe found its way into both the Babylonian Gilgamesh and the Hebraic myths, but it hardly is a confirmation of either myth if taken literally. According to the Genesis myth, *all* living creatures were destroyed except those taken into the Ark by Noah, not just those surrounding the shores of the Black Sea. The Black Sea discovery is *not* evidence of a *worldwide* flood and the biblical story that all living creatures were destroyed except those preserved in Noah's Ark is, of course, preposterous. The above account of the recent exploration of the Black Sea, including the quotations, is taken from a news item by Guy Gugliotta, "For Noah's Flood, a New Wave of Evidence," *The Washington Post*, November 18, 1999, pp. A1, A28.

9. Maurice Bucaille, *The Bible, the Qur'an and Science*, translated from the French by Alastair D. Pannell and Bucaille (Alegarth, India: Cresent Publishing Company, 1978), p. iv. The immediately following page references in the text are to this work until otherwise indicated.

10. A. Yusuf Ali, *The Holy Qur'an, Text, Translation and Commentary* (Brentwood, Md.: Published by Amana Corporation, 1983), p. 1237. This beautiful edition was given to me by a student named Altaf Sullaiman as a gift, for which I am very grateful. Bucaille refers to this edition as "the . . . remarkable English translation by Jusif Ali" (p. 161), even though it differs greatly from his translations.

11. This is true of another attempt to show that the Qur'an contained much later scientific descriptions, in this case embryological, but in a concealed language. In *Human Development as Described in the Qur'an and Sunnah*, ed. A. A. Zindani, M. A. Ahmed, M. B. Tobin, and T. V. N. Persaud (Alexandria, Va.: Islamic Academy for Scientific Research, 1994), the authors present (in translation) Islamic passages along with current embryological descriptions, claiming that the descriptive content of the two are equivalent. However, I found that the comparison was forced, with the Muslim passages being much more general and imprecise than the modern scientific ones with which they were compared. Yet the editors state, "The authors of the papers in this book are in agreement concerning the distinctiveness and compatibility of the Islamic terminology with the actual events in human [embryological] developments. This terminology fulfills all the conditions necessary for using scientific terms in this field, and the terminology actually in use today still lacks some of these conditions in some stages of development" (p. 1). But is it likely that the science of embryology, including the terminology now in use, was as developed or *more advanced* in the seventh century than today? I did not find the translations of the Muslim statements quoted suported this claim and I studied embryology as a premedical student when I was an undergraduate.

12. A. Jusuf Ali, p. 161.

13. Richard Dawkins, *The Blind Watchmaker* (New York: W. W. Norton and Company, 1987), p. 230. Emphasis added.

14. Boyce Rensberger, "In Defense of Evolution," *The Washington Post*, 8 January 1997, p. H4.

15. Stephen Jay Gould, *Wonderful Life* (New York: W. W. Norton and Company, 1990, p. 282. The immediately following page references in the text are to this work. This conception of converging evidence has been vigorously defended also by Edward O. Wilson in his book *Consilience* (New York: Vintage Books, 1999).

16. Schroerder, p. 30. The following page references in the text are to this work until otherwise indicated.

17. Rensberger, p. H.4.

18. Cf. Milič Čapek, *The Philosophical Impact of Contemporary Physics* (New York: D. Van Nostrand Company, 1961), p. 201. Also for an exposition of relativity theory see Schlagel, *Copernicus through Quantum Mechanics*, pp. 429–42.

19. Isaac Newton, *Principia*, vol. 1, Motte's translation revised by Cajori (Berkeley: University of California Press, 1962), p. 8.

20. The final quoted statement in this quotation from Schroeder is from P. J. E. Peebles, *Principles of Physical Cosmology* (Princeton: Princeton University Press, 1993), p. 96.

21. Martin Reese, "Exploring Our Universe and Others," *Scientific American*, December 1999, pp. 80–81.

22. Paul Davies, *The Mind of God* (New York: Simon & Schuster, 1993), p. 57.

23. Stephen W. Hawking, *A Brief History of Time* (New York: Bantam Books, 1988), p. 136.

24. Ibid., pp. 140–41.

25. Alan H. Guth, *The Inflationary Universe* (Reading Mass.: Addison-Wesley, 1997), p. 276.

26. Michael Drosnin, *The Bible Code* (New York: Simon & Schuster, 1998), in the Forward.

27. Richard Morin, "What are the Chances of That?!?" *The Washington Post*, 4 April 1999, B5; brackets added. For a more comlete description and excellent critical analysis see Michael Schermer, *How we Believe* (New York: W. H. Freeman, 1988), pp. 117–22.

28. Cf. Gould, pp. 238, 289, 309.

29. Quoted from Richard S. Westfall, *Never at Rest* (Cambridge: Cambridge University Press, 1980), p. 748.

30. Reese, p. 81.

31. The statement is quoted by Schroeder, p. 27 from Behe's *Darwin's Black Box* (New York: Free Press, 1996).

32. Murray Gell-Mann, *The Quark and the Jaguar* (New York: W. H. Freeman and Company, 1994), p. 112.

33. Wilson, p. 216

34. Kathy Sawyer, "A Novel Theory of Biology's 'Big Bang,' " *The International Herald Tribune*, 26–27 July 1997, p. 1.

35. Dawkins, p. 311.

36. Ibid., p. 141.

37. Jared Diamond, *The Third Chimpanzee* (New York: HarperPerennial, 1993), p. 37.

38. Stuart Kauffman, *At Home in the Universe* (New York: Oxford University Press, 1995), pp. 18–19.

39. Cf. Richard H. Schlagel, "Why not Artificial Consciousness and Thought," *Minds and Machines*, ed. James H. Fetzer, 9, no. 1 (February 1999): 3–28.

40. Cf. James Cleick, *Chaos* (New York: Penguin Books, 1987).

41. Cf. Ilya Prigogine and Isabella Stengers, *Order out of Chaos* (New York: Bantam Books, 1984).

42. Cf. Stuart Kauffman.

43. Ibid., p. 25.

44. Ibid., p. 24.

45. Kathy Sawyer, "From Deep in the Earth, Revelations of Life," *The Washington Post*, 6 April 1997, p. A11.

46. Ibid.

47. Alfred North Whitehead, *Science and the Modern World* (New York: A Mentor Book, 1925), p. 14.

48. Schroeder, p. 34.

49. Wilson, pp. 189–290.

50. Ian Barbour, *Religion in an Age of Science* (New York: HarperCollins Publishers, 1990), p. 17.

51. Davies, p. 77. In support of this claim Davies quotes John Barrow, *Theories of Everything: The Quest for Ultimate Explanation* (Oxford: Oxford University Press, 1991), pp. 6, 35, 295.

52. Ibid., p. 140.

53. Cf. Plato, *The Republic*, Bk. VI 509d–Bk. VII 530c.

54. Richard H. Schlagel, *From Myth to Modern Mind, A Study of the Origins and Growth of Scientific Thought*, vol. 1, *Theogony through Ptolemy* (New York: Peter Lang, 1996), p. 371.

CRITIQUE OF
RELIGIOUS EXPERIENCE

INTRODUCTION

T he essential thesis and conclusion of this chapter came as a complete
surprise—one of those secular epiphanies that one hopes for but
seldom attains. As I began reading a few of the voluminous publications
describing religious experiences, along with a major psychological study
of religion,[1] the more significant dreaming became for understanding religious experiences. Just as the images in dreams can be so spellbinding that
they compete with the realism of waking life, the revelatory content of
Scripture can override objective reality. As people who dream vividly and
frequently often find themselves living two lives, one in the everyday
world of experience and the other in the phantasmagoric realm of dreams,
so the religionist's reality is divided into the normal secular domain and
the transcendent realm of the supernatural. Could this be the key for
understanding the origin and appeal of religious experiences, despite the
elements of fantasy and unreality?

As others who have reflected on the development of human thought
and the origin of early myths, I had come to the conclusion that religious
belief systems originated primarily from primitive man's attempt to
make sense of human existence in a world that was completely beyond
his comprehension.[2] With almost no understanding of the origins, causes,
or effects of phenomena, it was natural that our early ancestors fabricated
stories to compensate for their ignorance. Moreover, that primitive
people perceived nature animisticly,[3] as infused with vital forces and
manifesting psychic powers, contributed to the conception of a world

273

controlled by intentional causes. All ancient societies sacrificed to the gods, believing that the outcome of every significant event in life—marriage, fertility, birth, health, harvests, and warfare—was controlled by mysterious powers personified as gods. Even today people believe in guardian angels, the Blessed Virgin, Jesus Christ, and God the Father as providential agents ministering to their personal needs.

This tracing of religious beliefs, like myths, to ignorance, animism, intentional causes, and the conviction that human destiny is in the hands of divine beings is true as far as it goes, but it does not account for the prevalence of revelation, prophesy, and divination in all early cultures. Nor does it explain the emotional force of religious symbols, the acceptance of fabulous creatures (demons, devils, cherubs, and archangels), the belief in the immortality of the soul, or the conviction that there are spiritual dimensions to reality concealed from everyday life. Yet if religious experiences are akin to dreams, hallucinations, and out-of-body (OBEs) journeys, then this would explain why the latter have played such a crucial role in religions and why human beings are so disposed to belief in the supernatural, despite the dearth of empirical evidence and rational justification. Dreams and other nocturnal adventures seem to augment the credulity of humanity because they depict a fantasy world whose origin lies deeply embedded in human nature.

How could an explanation of religious beliefs in terms of primitive forms of mentality explain such fanciful conceptions as angels floating on clouds and lifting Rubenesque bodies into heaven or the images of people being tortured by fiendish creatures in some demonic hell? What natural phenomenon would suggest the bizarre resurrection of skeletons and dead bodies from graves on judgment day at the second coming of Christ, as described in the Bible and depicted in renaissance paintings? Apart from the influence of dreams, hallucinations, and OBEs, what would have been the inspiration for the Book of Revelations, one of the most incredible pieces of literature ever written? Many artists and writers, including Dürer, Piranesi, Blake, Goya, Coleridege, Robert Louis Stevenson, De Quincey, Cocteau, Verlaine, and Rimbaud, have reported the effects that dreams and/or drugs have had on their artistic endeavors and creations.

If, as argued in previous chapters, the evidence for the belief in the existence of God has become so depleted and the rationale so attenuated as to annul its credibility, how do we explain the persistence of religions in an age dominated by scientific and technological achievements? Absent a God, what would have been the source of the epiphanies, ecstatic visions, trances, mystical reveries, divine interventions, and heavenly ascensions that form the religious dramaturgy? For though sacred writings are the foundation of revealed religions, they derive their authority from being witness to the supernatural, as proclaimed by prophets such as Abraham, Moses, Isaiah, Jesus, Paul, and Muhammad. Whereas throughout the past millennia there was little alternative to accepting the prima facie claims of religious experiences to be encounters with supernatural beings or a numinous reality, this no longer is true. Although the alternative explanation might will seem meager given the significance of the transforming experiences attested to by vast numbers of people throughout history, it is supported today by discoveries in neurophysiology, molecular biology, clinical psychology, and psychiatry. Rather than supernatural explanations of religious and paranormal (ESP) states, like dreams and hallucinations these experiences now can be attributed to the brain, as a growing body of evidence indicates.

OUR MARVELOUS BRAINS

Because there is no direct awareness that conscious experiences are dependent upon trillions of neuronal discharges in our brains, until very recently it was thought that such experiences occurred in a nonphysical spiritual entity variously called the 'psyche', 'soul', or 'mind'. With the exception of Hippocrates (who, in his book *The Sacred Disease*, attributed the terrifying convulsions and mystical-like experiences caused by epileptic seizures to abnormal excitations in the brain), and Galen (who, as physician to the Gladiatorial School in Pergamum, he witnessed horrible wounds to the brain accompanied by crippling physical and mental disabilities), both of whom recognized the brain's crucial role as the seat of consciousness, all past writers attributed consciousness to the soul or mind, occasionally locating it in the heart or chest. Even when researchers like Descartes acknowledged the close interaction of the mind and the body, they usually defined each component as a separate reality. When the body died it commonly was believed that the freed soul or spirit journeyed to another world.

Because ordinary conscious processes do not disclose their underlying neurophysiological conditions, until very recently the brain was not considered the neuronal substrate of the mind. It was mainly during World War II, owing to the discovery of medications such as penicillin and more effective anesthetics, that soldiers with terrible head wounds could survive the accompanying infection and shock displaying the awful effects of their injuries. In the following decades there have been many studies describing the complex disruptions or distortions in cognitive functions, behavior, and personality traits caused by chemical imbalance, brain injuries, lesions, or aneurysms.[4]

These studies, along with a greater knowledge of brain structures and their functions, the biomolecular composition of the brain, the electrochemical nature of neuronal discharges, and pharmaceutical treatments in psychiatry have led most scientists to dismiss the soul or mind as having any explanatory function. If neuroscientists refer to the mind at all, they usually regard it as "the summation of brain processes." Although conscious states *as experienced* (sensations, feelings, sensory qualities like colors, sounds, and tastes, mnemonic images, and thoughts) have properties different from neuronal discharges, they nonetheless "occur in and are caused by" (John Searle's description) the neurophysiological structures of the brain.[5] So while mental states are qualitatively different from brain states, neurophysiologists claim that their existence and explanation depend wholly on brain processes — there is no separate discipline studying an independently existing spiritual or mental substance. Psychoanalysts and psychiatrists describe and analyze the conscious manifestations of these brain states, particularly when displayed in abnormal behavior, but their etiology is investigated by neurophysiologists and biochemists.

Early attempts to delineate the causes of phenomena were mistaken because they were based on superficial resemblances, projected intentionalities, and the fallacious logical inference of *post hoc, ergo propter hoc*: that if an unusual event followed a peculiar occurrence it could be attributed to that occurrence. Thus an eclipse, appearance of a comet, a bizarre dream, or cry of a distant animal before a fatal accident or disaster would be considered its cause. But rumbling thunder is not an expression of angry gods, terrifying lightning is not a thunderbolt of Zeus, psychotic behavior is not demonic possession, nightmares are not (as the term literally signifies) visits by evil spirits, and birth defects or natural disasters are not punishment by the gods. As difficult as it may be for some people to accept, modern research indicates that dreams, nightmares, visions, trances, inner voices, possession, speaking in tongues, mystical states, and out-of-body experiences can be correlated with and explained as the effects of unusual brain processes. But is it possible that an evolved organ weighing less than three pounds and shaped like an enlarged walnut could be the source of religious, paranormal, and esoteric experiences formerly attributed to supernatural beings?

This will not seem so incredible if one realizes that the vast panorama of human perception, as well as all the evolved capacities of human beings, have their origin in the brain. If our early ancestors had known of the powers of the brain they would have built shrines to commemorate its existence, altars for sacrificial offerings, and gods named in its honor.

DREAMS, PROPHESIES, AND DIVINATION

As Descartes argued, if perceptual representations of the world occurred only when external physical causes were present, how do we explain dreams which can be every bit as realistic even though the usual physical causes are absent? Because of the apparent autonomy of waking and sleeping states, throughout the past the enigmatic information conveyed in dreams often was considered more significant than normal wakefulness. The medium by which gods, angels, departed souls, or demons transmitted cryptic messages for good or evil, their divination could make the difference between death and disaster or life and laughter.

How different the history of Israel would have been if Joseph had not interpreted correctly the Pharaoh's dream of seven "sleek and fat" cows being devoured by seven "gaunt and thin" cattle succeeded by another dream of seven seeds of grain "plump and full" subsequently destroyed by seven "thin and blighted" grains (Gen 41:1–8). Would Jesus have become the inspiration for a new religion if Pontius Pilate had followed his wife's advice to release Jesus, rather than Barabbas, when she sent word to him that he should "have nothing to do with that righteous man, for I have suffered much over him today in a dream" (Matt. 27:19). What would have been the future of Christianity if Constantine, in the early hours before the battle of Milvian Bridge, had not had a dream commanding him to have his soldiers draw on their shields "the symbol of Christ" and advanced into battle behind a standard bearing "the initials of Christ interwoven with a cross"? This so inspired the Christians among his troops that this could have been the decisive factor in his defeat of the forces of Maxentius, who fought under "the Mithraic-Aurelian banner of the Unconquerable Sun."[6] Or closer to our own era, how different would the history of the United States from 1963 have been, especially regarding the Vietnam War, if President Kennedy or his security guards had heeded the warnings of the psychic Jeane Dixon who had dreamt of his assassination in Dallas the following day?

Considering that more than one-third of our lives is spent sleeping and that dreams account for between one-fifth and one-third of sleep time, a significant portion of our existence is given over to dreaming. Moreover, from 2000 B.C.E. to 1500 C.E. even a larger portion of time was spent sleeping because dreams were deliberately induced by hallucinogenic drugs, magic spells, ritual trances, and "incubations" (spending the night in a sacred place where one submitted to various preparatory procedures and ceremonies) to provide needed guidance at times of personal or national crises. Throughout the world it generally was held that dreams could prophesy the future (precognition), reveal the occurrence of distant events (clairvoyance), foretell the onset of a disease and propose cures (prodromic), predict the beneficial times for important ceremonies and ventures (divination), and offer solutions to pressing problems (oneiro-mancy). In addition, it was believed that during sleep the soul could leave the body and visit the netherworld, a trepass forbidden to the living. Thus reality encompassed much more than met the wakeful eye.

There are striking differences in the dream continuum from normal to nightmares, including "Old Hag" (a dream where a grotesque figure enters the room by the dreamer's bed often pressing on one's chest),[7] lucid, out-of-body astral projections, alien abductions, and near-death encounters (those having these latter experiences often consider them more than dreams, but at least they begin as dreams and end in bed). While they can include other sense modalities such as sounds and smells, usually they are visual, people referring to "seeing" their dreams and "being in" their dreams (although being spoken to by the gods is a common occurrence as evident in the Old Testament). Thus dreaming is a kind of perception, especially "lucid dreams" when the dreamer is wide awake with open eyes and clearly aware of the immediate surroundings, yet realizes that what is experienced is not perceptual 'reality,' but a dream. Dreams occur when the usual external physical stimuli are not producing sensory responses in the brain nor evoking the ordinary behavioral responses, allowing the relaxed brain the freedom to fabricate images or verbal commands to satisfy some psychic need (the neuro-physiological processes underlying dreaming will be described in more detail later).

These nocturnal experiences can be unbelievably creative with the dreamer flying above buildings and mountains, breathing underwater in beautiful coral reefs, drifting effortlessly though solid walls, or reuniting with deceased loved ones in public places they frequented when the deceased was alive and seen by the person they are with but not by others. Yet they also can be terrifying with the dreamer being stabbed, raped, strangled, thrown from high places, or attacked by grotesque crea-tures. While many people (like myself) only experience innocuous hazy dreams that are difficult to recall, others have extremely traumatic dreams in technicolor which are so lifelike that they dominate the imme-diate waking period and color the day.

Because dreams are not constructed according to the usual realistic principles of waking experience, often being distorted, grotesque, or féerique, provoking feelings of euphoria, anxiety, or terror, there arose a class of soothsayers or diviners devoted to their interpretation. Having a symbolic rather than a literal meaning, it was the task of the interpreter to explain what they signified. Just as in waking life where the symbolism of ordinary language is used to represent and express our everyday experiences, dreams have a symbolic meaning whose obscurity requires skilled interpreters, whether ancient priests or modern psychoanalysts. What distinguishes modern analysts from ancient soothsayers is their contrasting views of the source of the dream symbols, methods of interpretation, and meaning. In ancient times dreams were believed to be cryptic messages from supernatural beings whose intentions could be benevolent, capricious, or malicious. These occult agents were thought to possess a foreknowledge of and influence over events which they could disclose in dreams.

Following the eighteenth-century enlightenment, this supernatural interpretation tended to be dismissed as superstition by the nonreligious. By the end of the nineteenth century the time was ripe for Freud's revolutionary approach to dreams presented in *The Interpretation of Dreams* published in 1899 (but with a publication date of 1900). Dreams still had a symbolic meaning whose obscure significance had to be interpreted by a skilled analyst, but Freud attributed the cause of dreams, along with their disguised meanings, to unconscious wish fulfilling desires: primarily repressed infantile sexual or instinctive drives. He distinguished the experienced "manifest content" of dreams from their "latent" or hidden origin in the unconscious. By dividing dreams into segments and helping the dreamer to form free associations with the various parts of the dream, through a lengthy subtle process the successful analyst gradually enabled the dreamer to interpret dreams as disguised repressed desires too repulsive for conscious admission.

By symbolically concealing the abhorrent latent desires in the manifest dream, the unconscious protected the individual from being awakened by such disturbing influences. Freud referred to dreams as "the Royal Road to the unconscious" and as "the protector of sleep," thereby explaining their function. These repressed infantile desires could be manifested also in physical and psychological disorders, such as hysteria, paralysis, hatred of a parent, and frigidity. The purpose of psychoanalysis was to enable the patient gradually to recognize the latent cause of her dreams and distressing symptoms, thereby becoming free of its disturbing influence. Thus while dream interpreters in the ancient world had the responsibility of deciphering the *prophetic* meaning of dreams produced by some supernatural agency, the function of the analyst, according to Freud, was to help the dreamer become aware that the actual symbolic meaning of the dream was a disguised manifestation of an unacceptable unconscious repression. For Freud the unconscious replaces supernatural beings and self-understanding replaces revelations.

The evidence for the dominant role of dream interpretation throughout history is well documented by Norman MacKenzie in his excellent book on "Dreams and Dreaming."

> As soon as human beings developed a written language, they began to set down their dreams and record ways in which they might be interpreted. Few early records survive, but even in the fragments that have been preserved from ancient Egypt—written in hieroglyphics that were themselves a series of picture symbols—we find evidence of the importance that the Egyptians attached to dreams and to oneirology, or dream interpretations.[8]

Nearly 4000 years ago "the Egyptians believed that the gods revealed themselves in dreams" and that dreams "were simply the perception of things that existed but could not be seen or heard in waking life" (p. 26). Yet by "various means, ranging from divine inspiration to ritual incantations, and even the use of potions and ointments to summon the 'invisible spirits,' Egyptians tried to make contact with this other world" (pp. 26, 28). By these means "they derived warnings, advice, success in love or other ventures, recovery from illness, or merely pleasurable experiences" (p. 28). The dreams of the great Egyptian magician, Setme Khamuas, contained "many of the elements of the 'world-savior' myths—prophesying the coming of a miraculous leader—that were widespread in antiquity throughout the Near and Far East" (p. 30). One can see in the British Museum the famous Chester Beatty papyrus, written around 1350 B.C.E., that recounts some "200 *omina*" or dreams with various interpretations of the dream symbols (cf. p. 28).

Most ancient civilizations had their "dream books," which were guides to how recurrent dream images with their symbolic meanings should be interpreted. According to MacKenzie dreams could be classified into three types: (1) those in which the gods commanded some pious act, such as the construction of a statue or a temple (as when Yahweh commanded the Israelites to build a temple in the desert); (2) those in which the gods conveyed advice or warnings; and (3) those that were deliberately evoked by rituals, potions, and incantations, as during incubations, to reveal solutions to problems. "A whole caste of priests, called 'Masters of the Secret Things' or 'Scribes of the Double House of Life,' devoted themselves to such services, and practiced their mysteries in special temples" (p. 30). Often individuals, believed to have extraordinary endowments such as healing powers, after their death were elevated to the status of gods and temples erected in their honor where the ill could seek cures. This was true of Imhotep who lived about 2980–2950 B.C.E. and whose most important temple was in Memphis, along with the Greek physician Asclepias who lived about 1100 B.C.E. and whose incubation center was near the Oracle's Temple at Epidaurus (cf. pp. 30, 43). These sacred places were precursors of present-day healing shrines, such as the Grotto of Lourdes where piles of crutches are displayed as witness to the successful cures.

Even earlier than the Egyptian *Book of the Dead* were dream books from Assyria, Babylonia, Sumeria, and Mesopotamia.

> The Assyrians certainly depended on dream books for help. This much we know from clay tablets found in Nineveh, in the library of the Assyrian king Ashurbanipal, who reigned between 669 and 626 B.C. This library, the oldest directly known to us, was a repository of learning reaching back to the dawn of civilization—possibly to 5000 B.C. The Nineveh tablets, in fact, provide the link in a chain of dream theory that stretches from the most remote past to our own time. It is believed that Ashurbanipal's dream book was used by the Roman Soothsayer Artemidorus (about A.D. 140), whose work has in turn inspired almost every subsequent compiler of dream books. (pp. 34–35)

Furthermore, as MacKenzie points out:

> There seems to be little doubt that in Assyria, as in Egypt, dreams were used in therapeutic processes. . . . Anticipating contemporary psychoanalysis, the Assyrians believed that once the enigma presented by the dreams had been worked out the disturbing symptoms of the affliction would pass. But whereas modern psychoanalysis uses the dream to illuminate the hidden conflicts and repressed anxieties of the patient, the Assyrians believed either that a demon must be exorcised, or that the appropriate deity would reveal the means by which the sufferer could be treated. (p. 34)

It was from these more advanced civilizations that the Israelites, especially during their years of captivity in Babylonia, derived their own culture of dream interpretation. As MacKenzie states, "the largest collection of Jewish sacred writings—the Babylonian Talmud—was set down between the sixth and second centuries B.C. It is full of references to dreams, rules for the interpretation of dreams, and the means of avoiding evil dreams" (p. 36). There are numerous examples of dream interpretation in the Old Testament, although occasionally the Lord speaks directly to the individual, as he does to Moses.

> "If there is a prophet among you, I the Lord make myself known to him in a vision, I speak with him in a dream. Not so with my servant Moses . . . with him I speak mouth to mouth, clearly, and not in dark speech. . . ." (Num. 12:6–8)

In Job young Elihu describes how Yahweh appears "in a dream . . . when deep sleep falls upon men, while they slumber on their beds . . . he opens the ears of men, and terrifies them with warnings . . ." (Job 33:15–16).

As the example of Joseph and Pharaoh illustrates, the Jews were often called upon to interpret the dreams of gentiles. In the second year of his reign, having had a very troubling dream, the Chaldean King Nabuchadnezzar summoned to his court "the magicians, the enchanters, the sorcerers" to interpret his dream, telling them that they would "be torn limb from limb and your houses . . . laid in ruins" if they failed (Dan. 2:1–5). When these "wise men" admitted they were unable to interpret the dream, Nebuchadnezar ordered them to be slain, with Daniel and his exiled companions from Judah chosen to be their executioners. However, Daniel asked the king to permit him to interpret the dream. The meaning "was revealed to Daniel in a vision of the night," and Daniel gave thanks to God who " 'reveals deep and mysterious things . . . for thou hast made known to us the king's matter' " (Dan. 2:19–23).

In contrast to pagan religions the followers of Jesus were opposed to magic, divination, and astrology, so there are fewer references to dream interpretation in the New Testament, but there are some, usually conveyed by Gabriel or "an angel of the Lord." In Matthew there is the well-known example of Joseph, the husband of Mary, having "an angel of the Lord appear to him in a dream" informing him that he should take Mary as his wife and call the son she was bearing "Jesus" (Matt. 1:20–21). Then, after the wise men had visited Mary and the infant Jesus, they were "warned in a dream not to return to Herod" with word of the birth as Herod had instructed (Matt. 2:12), for when he earlier had heard the wise men refer to the Christ child as "he who has been born king of the Jews," he decided to have him killed (Matt. 2;2). But again an angel appeared to Joseph in a dream, saying, " 'Rise, take the child and his mother and flee to Egypt . . . for Herod is about to search for the child, to destroy him' " (Matt. 2:13).

There are several references to the "an angel of the Lord" appearing in dreams to the disciples. According to Acts, when Herod arrested Peter and had him imprisoned, one night when he was bound in chains sleeping between two soldiers with sentries guarding the prison door, "an angel of the Lord appeared, and a light shone in the cell; and he struck Peter on the side and woke him saying 'Get up quickly.' And the chains fell off his hands" (Acts 12:7). Paul, too, had several dreams in which the angel of the Lord appeared, one during his final tumultuous sea journey to Italy. During a tempest when the ship was "violently storm-tossed" so that "all hope of being saved was at last abandoned," Paul appeared before the crew saying, "take heart, for there will be no loss of life among you" because "this very night there stood by me an angel of the God to whom I belong and whom I worship, and he said: 'Do not be afraid Paul; you must stand before Caesar . . .' " (Acts 27:22–24).

When we turn to the interpretation of dreams by the ancient Greeks, we find additional confirmation of the central thesis of this book that of the two major cultures that formed Western civilization, the revelatory tradition of the Hebraic-Christian religion and the empirical-rationalistic outlook of the Hellenes, it is the latter that has proven correct. While the average Greek accepted the conception of dreams prevalent at the time, philosophers like Plato and Aristotle proposed a more rational explanation. Like other Near Eastern cultures, the Greeks had a long tradition of dream interpretation extending to Homeric times when it was believed that Zeus and other gods either appeared directly in dreams, or like the Christian god, sent heralds as emissaries.

Thus, as MacKenzie points out, there were two different approaches to dreams in ancient Greece. The first is the more traditional conception of dreams as divine revelations while the second

> is the emergence of a more rational and, indeed, inquiring attitude to dreams as natural phenomena: Plato, Aristotle, and some other philosophers seem to have approached more nearly to the modern conception of dreams than most writers in the intervening centuries. One might say, in fact, that the division between oneiromancy as a mystical or magic system and the serious treatment of dreams really begins in classical Greece. . . . (pp. 41, 42)

Among the Greeks who began to take a more scientific and less credulous view of dreams are the following. In one of his fragments the Presocratic philosopher Heraclitus says: "To those who are awake, there is one ordered universe common (*to all*), whereas in sleep each man turns away (*from this world*) to one of his own."[9] Based on this fragment MacKenzie asserts that

> Heraclitus, who lived from 540–475 B.C.E., was the first man known to have made the simple but vital statement that each man retreats in sleep into a world of his own. In one sentence, he thus detached the phenomenon of dreaming from the supernatural and made it a common human fact—but a fact, he seemed to think, that had no special meaning. . . . (p. 47)

Although Hippocrates, the father of medical science, acknowledged the existence of divine dreams he was particularly interested in "dreams whose symbolic form reveals what we now would call a morbid physiological condition," the kinds of dreams (prodromic) that foretell illnesses. (p. 47)

In the *Republic*, Plato justifies the good life as an end in itself by contrasting the tumultuous soul of the "despotic character" with the harmonious soul of the "philosopher king." In so doing, he graphically describes the kinds of dreams produced by the uncontrolled appetites of the despot, anticipating Freud's theory of the origin of dreams.

> Those which bestir themselves in dreams, when the gentler part of the soul slumbers and the control of reason is withdrawn; then the wild beast in us, full-fed with meat or drink, becomes rampant and shakes off sleep to go in quest of what will gratify its own instincts. As you know, it will cast away all shame and prudence at such moments. . . . In fantasy it will not shrink from intercourse with a mother . . . man, god, or brute, or from forbidden food or any deed of blood. In one word, it will go to any length of shamelessness and folly.[10]

Yet Plato does not restrict such dreams to despots, adding that "in every one of us, even those who seem more respectable, there exist desires, terrible in their untamed lawlessness, which reveal themselves in dreams."[11] In attributing vile dreams to uncontrolled instinctual drives Plato was foreshadowing modern Freudian theory.

Aristotle wrote two brief treatises on dreams, one explaining their cause and the other a critique of divination or prophesy, both displaying his remarkable intelligence and acute analytical powers. In the tract *On Dreams* it is obvious he made a careful empirical study of dreams, noting that dreams usually occur soon after one falls asleep and shortly before awakening, that they can be commonplace or "confused and weird" depending upon the state of the body, that some people dream while others claim they do not, and even identified what are now called "lucid dreams," when the dreamer is awake with open eyes and aware of the environment, yet realizes that what is being experienced is not perceptual reality but a dream world: "some very young persons . . . though looking with wide open eyes, see multitudes of phantom figures moving before them, so they often cover up their heads in terror."[12]

In his explanation of dreams Aristotle distinguishes between the two faculties of the soul involved, sense perception and intelligence. While perceptual representations originate from sense perceptions, their categorization and identification depend upon an intelligent judgment. Deception, illusion, or error can occur if either one of these faculties is defective: for example, if intelligence is adversely affected by drinking too much wine or by emotion and if sense perception is distorted by fever or injury. It is the same faculty that produces waking illusions and dreams: "the faculty by which, in waking hours, we are subject to illusion when affected by disease is identical with that which produces illusory effects in sleep"

(p. 619). This is remarkable because it places dreams within a naturalistic explanatory framework devoid of supernatural causes.

Because in dreams the normal stimulation of the senses is absent, the sensory image does not convey an *actual* representation of anything real, yet nonetheless *residual sensory movements present* what at the time *appear* to be something actual, however distorted:

> . . . it is manifest that the stimulatory movements based upon sensory impressions, whether the latter are derived from external objects or from causes within the body, present themselves not only when persons are awake, but also then, when this affection which is called sleep has come upon them with even greater impressiveness. (p. 622)

No other writer in antiquity proposed such a sensible explanation of dreams, claiming that they are produced by abnormal residual states of the body. As MacKenzie says, "Such rational consideration led Aristotle away from much of the superstitious muddle that surrounded dreams three centuries before the Christian era" (p. 49).

Aristotle's treatise *Prophesying by Dreams* shows the same reasonable approach, along with an unusual open-mindedness, indicated in the first paragraph (the quotation is in McKeon).

> As to the divination which takes place in sleep, and is said to be based on dreams, we cannot lightly either dismiss it with contempt or give it implicit confidence. The fact that all persons, or many, suppose dreams to possess a special significance, tends to inspire us with belief in it, as founded on the testimony of experience; and indeed that divination in dreams should, as regards some subjects, be genuine, is not incredible, for it has a show of reason; from which one might form a like opinion also respecting all other dreams. (p. 626)

Still, he is not convinced by this.

> Yet the fact of our seeing no probable cause to account for such divination tends to inspire us with distrust. For, in addition to its . . . unreasonableness, it is absurd to combine the idea that the sender of such dreams should be God with the fact that those to whom he sends them are not the best and wisest, but merely commonplace persons. If, however, we abstract from the causality of God, none of the other causes assigned appears probable. For that certain persons should have foresight in dreams . . . seems to be something . . . the explanation of which surpasses the wit of man. (p. 626)

It would be difficult to find a more astute assessment.

As Aristotle primarily is concerned with evaluating the divine or prophetic nature of dreams, he focuses on whether dreams are "sent" by God for a purpose:

> . . . forasmuch as certain of the lower animals also dream, it may be concluded that dreams are not sent by God, nor are they designed for this purpose [to reveal the future]. They have a divine aspect, however, for Nature [their cause] is divinely planned, though not itself divine. A special proof [of their not being sent by God] is this: the power of foreseeing the future and of having vivid dreams is found in persons of inferior type, which implies that God does not send their dreams; but merely that all those whose physical temperament is, as it were, garrulous and excitable, see sights of all descriptions. . . . (p. 628; brackets in original)

Just as he does not believe that dreams are sent by God, he does not have much confidence in prophesy. The fact that "many dreams have no fulfillment is not strange" because it is bodily "movements . . . that cause 'presentations', as a result of which sleepers foresee the future . . ." (pp. 628–29). But since these bodily "movements" are not preordained they do not have any necessary connections with future events, hence their causal "presentations" have no prophetic value. It is a matter of chance if one proves correct; moreover, he reiterates that if God had chosen to communicate in dreams he would have done so in the clarity of daylight and to the most intelligent, not in the obscurity of night to the ignorant and deranged.

Because the Romans generally were tolerant of other religious cults as long as they also paid tribute to the Roman gods, including deified emperors, they assimilated the dream practices prevalent throughout the empire. Dream interpretation, in fact, was taken so seriously by Emperor Augustus "that he made a law that anyone who dreamed about the commonwealth must proclaim it in the market place."[13] It is reported by Plutarch that Caesar's wife Calpurnia dreamt of his assassination by stabbing and that some emperors dreamt of their own assassinations. Supporting Plato's interpretation of despotic dreams, Nero had terrifying dreams "of being covered by swarms of ants, of being dragged by his wife into a dark place . . . and of various anatomical distortions" (p. 50). That these dreams seemed to be a symptom of his madness led his trusted advisor Petronius to conclude that it " 'is neither the gods nor divine commandments that send the dreams down from the heavens, but each of us makes them for himself' " (pp. 50–51).

Cicero, the great Roman orator, prose writer, philosopher, lawyer, and statesman, whose life was fatally affected by a dream, wrote a critical treatise *On Divination*. As MacKenzie relates, Cicero dreamt that Octavius would become the supreme ruler in Rome, leading Cicero and his brother to align themselves with Octavius against Anthony. Although Octavius and Anthony had been rivals, when Octavius became Augustus he allowed Anthony to put Cicero's and his brother's name among the proscriptions, decreeing their death in 43 B.C.E. Despite this fateful acquiescence in one dream, *On Divination* Cicero displays the same skepticism toward dreams as Aristotle, asking how one can distinguish between true and false dreams, why gods should reveal themselves in the obscurity of the night and in the visions of "drunkards and madmen," and why these nocturnal communications were necessary when the gods had provided men with intelligence for planning their futures. Hence, he shrewdly concludes that dreams have no value as a guide in life.

> "If, then, dreams do not come from God," he wrote, "and if there are no objects in nature with which they have a necessary sympathy and connection, and if it is impossible by experiments and observations to arrive at an interpretation of them, the consequence is that dreams are not entitled to any credit or respect whatever." (p. 53)

The person considered the greatest interpreter of dreams in antiquity was the Roman Artemidorus who lived in the second century C.E. As mentioned previously, his book *Oneirocritica* had been the primary source book on dreams in the ancient world and had the most influence of any dream book until Freud's *The Interpretation of Dreams*. Unlike Aristotle and Cicero, he considered the prophetic dream a valuable guide in life, claiming that " 'dreams and visions are infused into man for their instruction' " (p. 54). He anticipated Freud in claiming that what is essential in dream interpretation is the associations evoked by the dream, although he differed from Freud in believing that it was the associations derived by the interpreter that were significant, not those formed by the dreamer, as Freud insisted. As MacKenzie states, Artemidorus devoted his entire life to the study of dreams.

> He was interested in the question of recurrent dreams, in the intensity of emotion that different dreams evoked, in the manner in which prodromic dreams seemed to anticipate illness, and in the way in which dreams were related to such similar phenomena as visions, oracles, fantasies, and apparitions. But, above all, he was concerned with the distinction between two classes of dreams: the *somnium*, which was a reference to the future; and the *insomnium*, the product of ordinary life.... "The lover occupies himself with his sweetheart, the fearful man sees what he fears, the hungry man eats, the thirsty one drinks." (p. 55)

He proposed six critical issues for the interpretation of dreams: "whether the events in the dream are natural, lawful, and customary for the dreamer, the conditions under which it was dreamed, and the occupation and name of the dreamer" (p. 55). By means of such lines of inquiry the interpreter could uncover associations that would explain the dream.

After the fall of the Roman Empire and the triumph of Christianity over the pagan religions, throughout the Medieval Period dreams had the same significance they had in the Old and New Testaments. That the Hebraic-Christian religion is considered revelatory attests to the significant role of prophetic visions in the Bible, while Buddhism[14] and the Muslim religion were based directly on the dream-trances of Buddha and Muhammad. The text of the Koran, unlike the Bible, has undisputed authenticity because it was personally dictated by Muhammad to scribes (since Muhammad like Jesus was illiterate). The question of how Muhammad came to have the revelations composing the Koran is an intriguing one: how could an illiterate person dictate over a period of twenty years one of the most influential books ever written? As Jews and Christians claim of the Old and New Testaments, Bucaille writes that for him "there can be no human explanation to the Qur'an."[15]

The many references in the Koran to the Old and New Testaments confirm that Muhammad was thoroughly familiar with the Bible, even though he acquired this knowledge orally. He considered Jesus a prophet similar to Moses and Isaiah; furthermore, although he was a merchant by profession, when he approached his forties he became more and more troubled by religious matters, often withdrawing during the holy month of Ramadan "to a cave at the foot of Mt. Hira three miles from Mecca and spent many days and nights in fasting, meditation, and prayer. One night in the year 610, as he was alone in the cave, 'the pivotal experience of all Mohammedan history came to him.' "[16] As described by his major biographer, Muhammad ibn Ishaq and quoted by Durant:

> "Whilst I was asleep, with a coverlet of silk brocade whereon was some writing, the angel Gabriel appeared to me and said, 'Read!' I said, 'I do not read.' He pressed me with the coverlets so tightly that methought 'twas death. Then he let me go, and said 'Read!' . . . So I read aloud, and he departed from me at last. *And I awoke from my sleep*, and it was as though these words were written on my heart. I went forth until . . . I heard a voice from heaven saying, 'O Mohammed! thou art the messenger of Allah, and I am Gabriel.' I raised my head toward heaven to see, and lo, *Gabriel in the form of a man, with feet set evenly on the rim of the sky*, saying, 'O Mohammed! thou art the messenger of Allah, and I am Gabriel.' "[17]

More visions evoked the Koran. "Often, when they came, he fell to the ground in a convulsion or swoon; perspiration covered his brow. . . ."[18] As

Durant states, it is possible "his convulsions were epileptic seizures; they were sometimes accompanied by a sound reported by him as like the ringing of a bell—a frequent occurrence in epileptic fits."[19] When pressed to describe how he received the revelation,

> he answered that the entire text of the Koran existed in heaven, and that one fragment at a time was communicated to him, usually by Gabriel. Asked how he could remember these divine discourses, he explained that the archangel made him repeat every word. Others who were near the Prophet at the time neither saw nor heard the angel.[20]

No one else "saw nor heard the angel" because the visions undoubtedly were vocal and visual hallucinations of the kind experienced by epileptics and schizophrenics.

ALTERNATIVE EXPLANATIONS OF THESE VISIONS

The pressing question is which is the most reasonable interpretation of Muhammad's visions: that Gabriel "in the form of a man, with feet set evenly on the rim of the sky" was sent by Allah to reveal the Koran which "existed in heaven," or that Muhammad was suffering from recurring dreams or hallucinations, possibly caused by epilepsy or by the days and nights spent in a cave "fasting, meditating, and praying"? Were there no other analogous experiences of successively recurring dreams during which lengthy discourses were dictated, we would be forced to accept the explanation provided in Muhammad's dreams, even though that would beg the question since it was itself part of the dream.

But the fact is there are other reports of lengthy recurring narratives in dreams, although Muhammad's is one of the most extended and remarkable. We can at least concede that he had the greatest powers of coherent dreaming and recall ever recorded—indicative of an extraordinary brain. Yet there are analogous examples. According to MacKenzie, Jerome Cardan, a sixteenth-century "Italian philosopher, mathematician, astrologer, and man of letters," wrote his most famous work, *De Subtilitate Rerum*, "because of a recurring dream" (p. 73).

> In the dream Cardan was shown in detail the plan and subject matter of a large book: the dream was so insistent that he decided it must be written. While he was doing so the dream continued to recur, being especially frequent when he was indolent, but entirely ceasing after publication of the first edition. (p. 73)

This *insistence* and *recurrence* is what Muhammad also experienced, only his occurred over a period of twenty years. William Blake also experienced many vivid dreams, some of which he reproduced in his engravings: "On one occasion he saw God's face looking at him through the window, on another a tree full of angels" (p. 88). One cannot help wondering what the face of God looked like.

The best-known and most vividly dramatic personal description of one's dreams in English is Thomas De Quincey's *Confessions of an English Opium Eater*. Taking opium as a sedative at night it produced a spectacular panorama of dreams that evoked, in his words, "deep-seated anxiety and funeral melancholy," though occasionally an "unearthly splendour" (p. 129). These "hypnagogic illusions," as MacKenzie calls them, were described by De Quincey as a kind

> "of painting . . . upon the darkness [of] all sorts of phantoms. . . . In . . . 1817 this faculty became increasingly distressing to me; at night, when I lay awake in bed, vast processions moved along continually in mournful pomp . . . concurrently with this, a corresponding change took place in *my dreams*; a theatre seemed suddenly opened and lighted within my brain, which presented nightly spectacles of more than earthly splendour." (p. 129)

As MacKenzie states, the "horrific, yet dazzling, complexity of De Quincey's dreams may no doubt be attributed largely to opium. No one else has left such an elaborate record of his dreams over a period of years as De Quincey, nor described them so vividly" (p. 131).

Unlike De Quincey who recounted his dreams but did not make use of them as a source of literary composition, his contemporary, the poet Coleridege, who also was taking opium describes its stimulating effects on his writing. As recounted by MacKenzie, in the summer of 1797 just before falling asleep he read the words:

> " 'Here the Khan Kubla commanded a palace to be built. . . .' Three hours later he woke from his opium-induced doze, with the complete poem in his head. All the images rose up before him, 'as things, with a parallel production of the correspondent expressions, without any sensations or consciousness of effort.' " (p. 131)

He then began writing the poem from memory, but when he was interrupted by a caller and returned to recording the poem he " 'retained some vague and dim recollection of the general purport of the vision, yet . . . all the rest had passed away like the images on the surface of a stream' " (p. 131), as usually happens with dreams. While this represents only a partial recording of a dream, as compared to Muhammad's recurrent dictations of the suras, it does illustrate the brain's capacity to produce dream images and narrations that can be used to compose literary works.

As a final example there is the testimony of Robert Louis Stevenson whose dreams were not a result of taking opium, but due to the fevers produced by the tubercular condition that eventually killed him. In addition to causing some delirium, they may have kept his sleep stage at the light level which we now know to be the most productive of dreams. But what is especially significant about his dreams, beyond their extensiveness, is that he dreamed in sequence, his dream the following night resuming where he had left off the previous night—just as was true of Muhammad.

> In his book *Across the Plains*, Stevenson described the evolution of his dreams. He tells how, in early life, they often came in the form of nightmares; these . . . were succeeded by scenery and travels. The third phase started when he began to dream complete stories and, while still a student, *to dream in sequence. Each night he could take up the fantasy life envisaged in his dreams at the point at which he had quitted it; each morning he returned to reality.* (p. 133; emphasis added)

Yet even this is not as remarkable as the fact that when he began to support himself by his writings there appeared in his dreams "Little People" (schizophrenics also claim that "little creatures" dictate things to them) who aided in the creation of stories that were marketable, even sharing Stevenson's financial worries. Although this is not identical to having the angel Gabriel dictate sutras of the Koran to Muhammad, it is similar enough to support the claim that the brain is capable of producing a scenario where fantasy creatures are conspiring in the writing of serial episodes of a continuous story. Moreover, these hallucinatory creatures were capable of creative thinking to fulfill the wishes of Stevenson.

> What he described as the "Little People" not only set before him "truncheons of tales upon their lighted theatre," but also seemed to know when to perform for the dreamer. "They share in his financial worries and have an eye to the bankbook; they share plainly in his training; they have . . . learned like him to build the scheme of a considerable story in progressive order . . . they can tell him a story piece by piece, like a serial, and keep him all the while in ignorance of where they aim." (p. 133)

Thus as MacKenzie states, Stevenson

> had the knack of putting the demand for saleable stories to his sleeping self. He *actually regarded his conscious self simply as a kind of agent, writing down and doing the general mechanical work of authorship*—as well as

enjoying its material rewards—*while the "Little People" did the creative part.* (p. 133; emphasis added)

It seems to me that this account of Stevenson's brain during sleep constructing fantasy creatures to take over his creative role as a writer, as well as his financial problems, to the extent that he felt that he was *their* agent or instrument, not that they were *his*, is precisely analogous to Muhammad's dream experiences of having his religious anxieties resolved by the (hallucinated) archangel Gabriel communicating to him and having him repeat, fragment by fragment, the Koran. Like Stevenson, he believed that these verses were dictated to him and that he was just a "messenger" for their expression, although in his case the source was due to his religious concerns.

This explanation of the origin of sacred documents in terms of brain process, rather than supernatural powers, does not lessen the extraordinary nature of the occurrence. Yet these dream experiences are hardly more strange or puzzling than other psychological phenomena, such as multiple personalities, somnambulism, or the bizarre Capgras delusion, a mental derangement caused by brain damage. Those suffering from this affliction believe that someone close to them, such as a husband or wife, has been supplanted by someone else, an imposter who has similar characteristics to the person they displaced and who subsequently disappeared. In the past this abnormal state undoubtedly would have been considered demonic possession.

Nor is the capacity of the brain to store information and then reveal it in an unexpected, autonomous manner all that unusual. There is the oft repeated case of the woman who in later life suddenly began speaking fluent German, a language she did not realize she knew. This, too, would have been considered in ancient times an example of some kind of possession or speaking in tongues, but in her case it was discovered that when she was very young she had heard German spoken around her without consciously learning the language, yet her brain had assimilated this linguistic competence without her knowing it. Everyone probably has had some experience of hearing "inner voices," either as admonitions of parents or as echoes of the beloved voice of a deceased relative. The Old Testament essentially is the record of Yahweh's commands to his prophets. Thus what in antiquity were regarded as divine revelations or commands now can be explained as dreams or hallucinations, similar to those that have inspired writers and artists.

Thus I agree entirely with the following excellent statement by MacKenzie:

> Self-knowledge, or creative inspiration, may come in the form of dreams.... How it comes, and what part dreams play in its coming, seems to vary from one person to another. Some merely dream, some hear voices or see visions [for example Moses, Paul, Joan of Arc, De Quincey, and Billy Graham], some read off their work, as it were, from their minds, as if it were inscribed complete in some hinterland of consciousness [Muhammad, Coleridge, Stevenson]; some sink almost into a trance when about to write or compose [Buddha and Muhammad]. All, however, seem to be tapping some source of creative energy not directly accessible to waking consciousness in order to release images and thoughts that whirl in the darker reaches of the mind. (p. 129)

Attributing these autonomous cognitive functions exhibited in dreams and hallucinations to the brain will be less difficult to accept if one remembers that *conscious* creativity also depends upon our brains. None of us, when creating something, knows how the brain enables us to produce the results; we call it "inspiration" to disguise our ignorance. Even as I write this, what I write seems to come to me from "I know not where." Obviously it depends upon some previous research and reflection, but what actually is written appears somewhat as a 'revelation'. Another name for very creative people is "gifted" because their inherent talent came as an endowment which they feel was just bestowed upon them.

If one remains unconvinced by the examples just presented, that religious revelations are remarkably similar to the hallucinatory inspiration of writers and artists and therefore probably have the same cause, then perhaps the extensive clinical evidence of schizophrenia will succeed. Schizophrenia is a mental disorder affecting about two percent of the population who manifest various kinds of behavioral abnormalities depending upon the severity: hearing commanding voices, seeing fantastic hallucinations, perceiving distortions of space and time, being frightened by a loss of ego or self, experiencing a general sense of disorientation, and responding to questions in an irrational manner. Because of their peculiarities the response to schizophrenics in the past was varied: sometimes their strange behavior led to their being selected as shaman or priests, although at other times they were considered insane and a threat to society.

NEUROLOGICAL DISCOVERIES OF LOCALIZED BRAIN PROCESSES

The fact that both the hallucinations of schizophrenics and the dream world of sleepers often have a similar religious motive implies, I believe, that they have the same neurological cause. Recent research apparently has located this cause in the left temporal lobe, although this is not to say that a belief in deities is innate. The temporal lobe obviously is innate, but the particular thematic content of the dream or hallucination depends upon the individual's biochemical physiology, background experience, and personal predilection. This explanation of hearing hallucinated voices, at least, has been advanced by several neurological discoveries since the nineteenth century that have identified the primary centers of speech. In 1861 Paul Broca, a French pathologist and surgeon announced the discovery, based on an autopsy of a patient's brain who had suffered severe impairment of speech called aphasia, the area responsible for the disability. Now known as Broca's area and aphasia, it is located on the left frontal lobe and is responsible for the motor production of speech, the physical ability to talk. Just ten years later a German neurologist, Carl Wernicke, identified a type of speech impairment or aphasia quite different from Broca's. Whereas the person with Broca's aphasia loses the physical ability to talk, except for a few words, Wernicke's patients could talk profusely but their speech was nonsensical and unintelligible. One of his patients, a storekeeper, when asked "Who is running the store now" would reply incoherently as follows: " 'I don't know. Yes, the bick, uh, yes, I would say that the mick daysis nosis or chipickters. Course, I have also missed on the carfter teck.' "[21]

As Broca, Wernicke also identified the area causing the aphasia, locating the lesions in the posterior part of the dominant temporal lobe, including some of the parietal area. But in contrast to Broca's area which is permanently located in the left hemisphere, in children up to ages six or seven there is enough plasticity in the brain that if a major lesion occurs in the Wernicke area of the left hemisphere, the speech mechanism is taken over by the right hemisphere. Although there is some variance, normally in right handed people both speech centers are located in the left hemisphere, while for left handed people Wernicke's area usually is located in the right hemisphere. Whichever hemisphere contains the speech center, left or right, is called the "dominant hemisphere" while the other is named the "minor hemisphere."

As important as the localization of these psychoneurological functions were, understanding their significance depended on further discoveries in the twentieth century. In addition to containing the speech centers, the normally dominant left hemisphere controls the right side of the body (thus people with a stroke in the left hemisphere are paralyzed on the right side) and receives perceptual information from the right visual field, whereas the right hemisphere controls the left side of the body and receives visual data from the left visual field. Despite this asymmetrical lateralization of brain functions in the two hemispheres, we normally are completely unaware of it. Although some of our brain functions are localized in one or the other hemisphere, our experience comes unified or holistic. That our visual field, speech, and bodily movements are not bifurcated or segregated we owe to a four-inch-long bundle of nerve fibers with a diameter about the size of a pencil, called the corpus callosum, which connects the two hemispheres.[22] The information and directives from both hemispheres transmitted through this central neural cable normally are so well synchronized that earlier brain scientists believed the hemispheres must be symmetrical, mirror images of each other.

Then, in an effort to save patients who were dying from epileptic seizures because the hyperactive neuronal discharges were being transmitted to both hemispheres, in the 1940s a neurosurgeon, W. P. Van Wagenen, took the desperate measure of cutting the corpus callosum.[23] Not knowing what the side effects might be, he was relieved to find that not only were the seizures eliminated, there also appeared to be no mental or motor impairment from the corpus callosum being severed, apparently supporting the symmetry hypothesis. A decade or so later Roger W. Sperry, Ronald E. Myers, and Michael S. Gassaniga performed a number of exacting experiments on epileptic patients who had undergone the split brain operation, as it has come to be called, to determine whether severing the corpus callosum actually had no effect, as it appeared.[24] They found, of course, that after the operation the two hemispheres of the brain functioned independently as separate brains, but the most significant results occurred when not only the corpus callosum, but also the optic chiasm (the crossover of the optic nerves connecting both hemispheres) was severed, so that instead of information from both halves of the visual field being transmitted to both hemispheres, as normally occurs, information from the right visual field was transmitted solely to the left hemisphere, and information from the left visual field transmitted only to the right hemisphere, the one normally lacking the speech center.

Although the operation did not affect the person's intelligence or personality, it did produce some unusual side effects confirming that the speech center and analytical reasoning for most people (who are right handed) are located in the dominant *left* hemisphere, while spatial orientation, musical talent, and visual pattern recognition are located mainly in the minor *right* hemisphere. It also showed that when the usual synchronization of the two hemispheres was disrupted, *each performed independently without knowing what the other was experiencing or doing*! For example, using slides with pictures of various objects, when the images were projected only to the *left* visual field and thus transmitted solely to the nonverbal *right* hemisphere, when asked what the subject saw, she responded that she did not see anything at all, that her visual field was blank. Yet when she was directed to select by her left hand what she had seen, she could do so, contradicting what she had said. The right hemisphere not being able to communicate to the left hemisphere what it had seen, the verbal left hemisphere was prevented from knowing and describing what the right hemisphere experienced. The only way the right hemisphere could communicate this was by using the left hand to pick out or write down what it saw.

When a word such as 'heart' was projected in the center of the subject's visual field, so that the letters 'art' fell in the right side and communicated to the left hemisphere, while the letters 'he' fell in the left side and communicated to the right hemisphere, when asked what word was seen, the subject answered art, oblivious to the other word 'he'. Yet one experiment was designed especially to show that the subject was aware of both words, as Julian Janes reports.

> If two different figures are flashed simultaneously to the right and left visual fields, as, for example, a "dollar sign" on the left and a "question mark" on the right, and the subject is asked to draw what he saw, using the left hand out of sight under the screen, he draws the dollar sign. But asked what he has just drawn out of sight, he insists it was the question mark. In other words, the one hemisphere does not know what the other hemisphere has been doing.[25]

These experimental results are especially interesting because of the rare glimpse they offer of our dependence on the autonomous functioning of our brains in performing simple mental acts. For example, when asked to verbally identify red or green flashes on his left visual field and transmitted solely to the right hemisphere, at first the subject could do so only randomly because the verbal responses of the severed left hemisphere were not cued to the visual information projected to the right hemisphere. Soon, however, the erroneous answers were corrected because the right hemisphere, having heard the wrong answer given by the left hemisphere, signalled the mistake in such as way that the left hemisphere (or person) could correct it.[26] Note how natural it is to begin talking as if the separate hemispheres were having the experiences and responding or not responding for the subject, *so that the subject seems to be merely passive, as in revelatory, dream, and hallucinatory experiences.*

Even more astonishing is the fact that the right hemisphere can recognize objects in the left visual field and direct the left hand to correctly manipulate the objects *without the person being at all conscious* of the activity. If the right hemisphere (which can comprehend speech but not produce it) is asked to pick out with the left hand (which it controls) the object it has seen, it will do so without the person having any *awareness of what is occur-*

ring.[27] This seemingly lack of consciousness in the right hemisphere led some investigators, such as the Nobel Laureate John Eccles, to conclude that only the dominant hemisphere with the speech center is conscious, implying that speech is a necessary condition for consciousness.[28]

But when experiments were performed to test this hypothesis it was refuted. For example, if among the objects flashed to the left visual field and transmitted to the right hemisphere an image of a nude woman is included, although the subject had no consciousness of the image and denied seeing it, she indirectly showed her awareness by blushing and giggling. When asked why she reacted that way, she said she did not know.[29] Moreover, other experiments indicated that the right hemisphere could make verbal inferences, draw logical conclusions, and thus reason independently of the person being aware of it.[30] This supports the belief throughout the ages that by means of dreams or hallucinations the brain provided clues or reasoned answers to problems without conscious awareness, as revealed in prophetic and prodromic dreams. Thus the fact that split brain subjects are not aware of what occurs in the right hemisphere does not mean that hemisphere is not conscious, but that because of the severance with the left hemisphere it cannot convey its experiences to the person so as to be conscious of it!

JULIAN JANES'S CONCEPTION OF THE BICAMERAL MIND

These results led Janes to an intriguing explanation of the inner voices or verbal commands that in the past were attributed to the gods or other supernatural beings. First he asserts that the "Gods are what we now call hallucinations"[31] which originate in the "temporal-parietal region" of the right hemisphere. Recall that in children this area of the *right* hemisphere can take over the speech functions of the Wernicke area normally located in the left hemisphere. The split brain operation has disclosed the independent functions of the two hemispheres and the curious results from their disconnection and lack of synchronization and communication. When severed, it is as if the person were located in the dominant hemisphere with the speech center cut off from whatever the minor hemisphere was experiencing.

Janes' thesis is that in the fourth and third millennia B.C.E., when ancient civilizations were being formed and some of the great religions arose, the Wernicke area in the right hemisphere functioned autonomously, conveying commands through the commissure fibers to the left hemisphere which experienced them as objective voices of the gods—not as coming from the right hemisphere. As Janes states, "the speech of the gods was directly organized in what corresponds to Wernicke's area on the right hemisphere and 'spoken' or 'heard' over the anterior commissures to or by the auditory areas of the left temporal lobe" (p. 105). It was as if human brains at that early time were split, in the sense that they functioned independently of one another, and yet connected in such a way that the right hemisphere could transmit verbal commands to the left hemisphere, appearing to come autonomously. But owing to various social changes and pressures, the introduction of writing, the interchange and conflict with other societies, and frequent chaotic social conditions arising when nations were invaded and conquered, according to Janes, the independent functioning of the Wernicke area in the right hemisphere was repressed, although it still has a vestigial function in children and perhaps a prominent recurrent one in schizophrenics, to the extent that it invades and controls their consciousness.

The mental state in which the two hemispheres functioned as independent beings, the left the person and the right the gods, with the right hemisphere unilaterally sending commands to the left, is called by Janes the "bicameral mind" and the religious epochs in which this occurred the "bicameral epoch."

> If this brain model of the bicameral mind is correct, it would predict decided differences in cognitive function between the two hemispheres. Specifically, we would expect that these functions necessary for the man-side would be in the left or dominant hemisphere, and those functions necessary to the gods would be more emphasized in the right hemisphere. Moreover, there is no reason not to think that the residuals of these different functions at least are present in the brain organization of contemporary man. (p. 117)

One advantage of this bicameral mind is that it would allow the gods to direct human action while leaving the left hemisphere free for human speech. There must have been some evolutionary advantage to allowing one hemisphere to direct human behavior disguised as the voice of the gods, perhaps an advance over merely instinctual behavior in the transition to full consciousness. In addition, it could have provided some emotional comfort in thinking that we are not alone in the universe but are supported by divine beings. Furthermore, Janes believes that the bicameral mind evolved as a means of social control with the development of language.

> The bicameral mind is a form of social control . . . which allowed mankind to move from small hunter-gatherer groups to large agricultural communities. The bicameral mind with its controlling gods was

evolved as a final stage of the evolution of language. And in this development lies the origin of civilization. (p. 126)

This is an intriguing hypothesis to explain the origin of the belief in
divinities due to the experience of hearing the voices of the gods, and the
crucial role this had in the history of religions, along with the supporting
neuroanatomical evidence previously described. But religions are too
diverse, rich, and complex to be explained by a single hypothesis. While
hearing the threatening voice of the gods in dreams and hallucinations
undoubtedly was one of the major sources of revelatory religions, as evident in the Bible, there were other sources as well: the mysteries of life
inciting narrative explanations; the animistic belief that natural events
have intentional causes; the transference of parental authority to a higher
power; the yearning for some greater sanction and retribution for our
moral actions; the emotional need for religious symbols, rituals, and ceremonies to cement social cohesion; and the haunting awareness of the
contingencies of life, especially the specter of death. No one can claim to
know which was the first or what was primary. They all played some role
at some time and their relative significance probably shifted with the
wiles of time.

EVALUATION OF RELIGIOUS EXPERIENCES

In this last section I shall consider other kinds of religious experiences:
the commonly reported presence of God, conversions and mystical experiences, out-of-body projections, and near death encounters. A large accumulation of research material, summarized by Michael A. Persinger and
others, indicates that these experiences, too, can be explained in terms of
brain processes. Before writing this book I believed, like many of my colleagues, that people today who believe in supernatural beings do so out
of ignorance; otherwise, they would understand that what we have
learned in the past century, especially, precludes such beliefs. As I argued
previously, the plausibility of religious beliefs varies inversely with our
scientific knowledge of the universe. In the early stages of human history,
when humankind knew almost nothing about the physical world,
explaining the origin of the universe, the creation of man, the intricate
design of organisms, and the seasonal cycles of nature as the intentional
cause of a supernatural being was understandable.

But as scientific investigations progressively led to alternative verifiable explanations of these phenomena, they either diminished or
destroyed the rationale for the religious interpretation. Thus on the ratio-
nalistic assumption that religious beliefs originate primarily in quasi-

rational explanations of natural phenomena, they ought to have disappeared with the development of science, except among the most uneducated segment of society. But while this *is* true to some extent, it does not explain the resurgence of conservative religious movements in the Muslim, Christian, and Hebrew religions. So the humanist claim that the cure for religion lies in attaining a greater scientific knowledge of the universe and raising the general level of education, as necessary as these are, is not sufficient.

What I came to realize in writing this chapter is that subjective God experiences are far more important as sources and justifications of religious belief than theological explanations of natural phenomena, despite what religionists claim about the origin of their beliefs. Moreover, the very nature of these experiences, such as the reassuring presence of Christ, the Blessed Mary, or God, are so personally compelling and self-authenticating as to seem immune to any doubt or critical analysis. When confronting others who do not have these experiences, it is tempting for those who do to feel select, smug, and superior, like the "chosen people" of old. As we shall find, those who have out-of-body experiences, like astral projections or alien abductions and near-death encounters, also believe they have been granted a privileged access to other dimensions of reality. But does this mean that we have to accept uncritically religious experiences as interpreted by the people having them, any more than we accept as reality what is presented in dreams or hallucinations? Although it is undeniable that individuals have dreams, hallucinations, trances, out-of-body, near-death, and God experiences, we can question whether these states represent something objectively real or are merely subjective illusions produced by the brain. Normally when we describe someone as having had a dream or hallucination, we do so to contrast that experience with a veridical one. The question is whether this distinction also is valid of out-of-body, near-death, and religious experiences. I shall try to show that empirical evidence indicates that it is, though this is by no means conclusive. I realize that those who believe that religious experiences are beyond the pale of empirical inquiry and scientific explanation will not be convinced, but at least I hope to have drawn the issue at the crucial point.

Although I have never seen a report of the percentage of the world's population who have had what they would identify as religious experiences, the accounts of such experiences are legion. Ranging from the terrifying to the sublime, I now believe they have been the major source of religious beliefs, reinforced by dreams and hallucinations. In contrast to mystical experiences (which we shall consider later), where one feels one's ego or self submerged in unity with the Infinite One or Cosmic

Consciousness, "like raindrops falling into the sea," in Western religions the individual often feels embraced by the *presence* of an Otherness. As described by Rudolf Otto in his great classic, *The Idea of the Holy*, this presence is felt as a "mysterium tremendum."

> The feeling of it may at times come sweeping like a gentle tide, pervading the mind with a tranquil mood of deepest worship. It may pass over into a more set and lasting attitude of the soul, continuing, as it were, thrillingly vibrant and resonant, until at last it dies away and the soul resumes its "profane," non-religious mood of everyday experience. It may burst in sudden eruption up from the depths of the soul with spasms and convulsions [epileptic seizures], or lead to the strangest excitements, to intoxicated frenzy [Holy Rollers and the Dervish], to transport, and to ecstasy [Plotinus and St. Teresa]. It has its wild and demonic forms and can sink to an almost grisly horror and shuddering. It has its crude, barbaric antecedents and early manifestations, and again it may be developed into something beautiful and pure and glorious. It may become the hushed, trembling, and speechless humility of the creature [St. Francis] in the presence of—whom or what? In the presence of that which is a *mystery* inexpressible and above all creatures.[32]

Except for the use of the term 'soul', rather than 'brain', and assertion of an inexpressible mystery, this is an excellent description of the range of religious experiences. Why do I object to its beings attributed to the soul and called an inexpressible mystery? The reason is that we now can locate the cause of these experiences in the brain (due to electromagnetic waves, excessive neuronal discharges, or biochemical imbalances) and have some slight understanding, at least, of what produces them. Furthermore, because epileptics, schizophrenics, and psychotics have similar experiences owing to their abnormal brain conditions, we know that at least some of these experiences are produced by the brain and therefore are not occult. Attributing them to the soul does make them mysterious because we know nothing about the soul and how it could cause these experiences. Where does the soul exist? What is it composed of? How does it interact with the body to have the physiological effects it does? Attributing these experiences to the soul, like invoking God as an explanation of anything, tells us absolutely nothing about how or why the process occurs. It is only people who do not know what an explanation should consist of who are satisfied by these kinds of claims.

The issue is not whether people actually have the religious experiences they report having, but whether the best explanation is that they are, in fact, produced by supernatural beings or whether they are projections of the brain, similar to dreams and hallucinations. Moreover, the sincerity and authenticity of the reports are not in question, as a few typical testimonies will illustrate. The first is by a fifty-year-old woman who felt lonely and distraught after her last child left home for the university.

> "I was sitting by myself beside the fireplace; I couldn't sleep very well during the previous nights, something just didn't seem right. I thought about my life and what it was like when I was a child. Then there was an odd sensation and I felt as if my heart had been embraced. The warmest experience I had ever felt touched me and I knew that God was there."[33]

Similarly a young man says:

> "At the time I was under great emotional duress, I didn't know what to do with my life. I spent my days drunk and my nights with loose women. Then suddenly, I felt the presence of God and just knew it was He. He called my name and I had the most joyous experience of my life, a Commune with the Creator." (p. 24)

Analogous accounts are reported by Timothy Beardsworth in reply to a newspaper request for descriptions of religious experiences:

> ". . . in a very gentle and gradual way it began to dawn on me that I was not alone in the room. Someone else was there, located . . . about two yards to my right front. Yet there was no sort of sensory hallucination. I neither saw him nor heard him in any sense of the word 'see' and 'hear', but there he was; I had no doubt about it. He seemed to be very good and very wise, full of sympathetic understanding, and most kindly disposed towards me." [34]

As conveyed in another reply:

> "There was no sensible vision, but the room was filled by a Presence which in a strange way was both about me and within me. I was overwhelmingly possessed by Someone who was not myself, and yet I felt I was more myself than I had ever been."[35]

There are several important features to note in these reports: (1) the first two occurred under extreme emotional stress, but the latter two under calmer conditions; (2) the experiences occurred to the four persons without any deliberate seeking on their part, an apparent response to a deep need; (3) they had an overpowering sense of the presence of someone, God in the first two cases and just an unidentified benevolent presence in the latter two, without any auditory or visual images; and (4) the experiences were very reassuring and comforting. In other cases, however, the person actually 'hears' and 'sees' God. The following report was by a young person with a high fever who was seriously ill with scarlet fever.

> "As I drifted in and out of consciousness, I felt I was going to die. Then suddenly I heard a voice say, 'Don't worry, I am with you.' I looked up and saw a soft white ray coming through the window. The voice said, 'I am Christ, through me there is salvation.' I knew I had seen God. I was no longer afraid." (p. 32)

The perception of a ray of white light associated with Christ or some Divine Being is characteristic of near-death experiences as well, as we shall find.

A somewhat similar experience was reported by a woman whose husband Fred had just died. She felt as though her world collapsed and that nothing had any meaning or value, until she, too, was reassured by a vision, although of a different kind.

> "The fourth night after he died, I lay in bed, trying to piece my life together. I lay there for hours. Suddenly, I felt Fred's presence. . . . I looked over and saw him standing beside me. He was dressed in his old work clothes and had a big smile on his face. He said 'Don't worry Maud, I'm in heaven now. God has let me come to you. All our friends are here too. It's all true, what we believed about God. . . .' The next day I felt good, the sun was shining again, there was meaning to my life." (pp. 33–34).

Reports of similar experiences were sent to the Religious Experience Research Unit:

> "At one time I reached utter despair and wept and prayed [to] God for mercy instinctively and without faith in [a] reply. That night I stood with other patients in the grounds waiting to be let in to our ward. . . . Suddenly someone stood beside me in a dusty brown robe and a voice said 'Mad or sane, you are one of my sheep'. I never spoke to anyone of this but ever since . . . it has been the pivot of my life." [36]

Like the first two religious experiences reported previously, these occurred under considerable emotional stress, the last person apparently a mental patient in a hospital. They differ from the first four, however, in that the experiences included more than an acute sense of the presence of someone, but also an actual perception of a voice and a person, the first Christ, the second the woman's deceased husband Fred, and the third someone in a "dusty brown robe." The fact that such experiences often occur when the person is in a disturbed physical state (fever, delirium, dying, and so on) or under great emotional stress strongly suggests that they have a neurological basis.

Moreover, that these experiences are related to the person's particular culture, family background, personal memories, and individual history further implies that they are the brain's resolution of deeply disturbing problems, as we have seen earlier, rather than communications from supernatural beings. The report of a dream by a graduate student in psychology is quite revealing in that respect. It begins like other religious visions before turning into a bizarre denouement, combining his religious upbringing with memories of alien abductions and a television series.

> "One night I had a wonderful dream. I was standing near Christ on the Mount of Olives. Many other people were standing around as well. Suddenly, a cloud appeared over Christ's head and the people ran back in terror. Just before he began to rise into the sky, I ran up to him and got caught in some kind of force beam. I remember looking down upon the faces of the people below me as I moved further and further away. Suddenly, I looked into the clouds and saw a spaceship, with the sides slowly opening, like the side doors of a helicopter. As I moved up towards it, being carried by the same force as Christ, I saw they were aliens. The next thing I remember is being on the ship and seeing Christ standing there. He smiled, and slowly took off his mask like on Mission Impossible. He was an alien too! He then turned to the others and said, 'That should condition them.' " (p. 29; emphasis added)

The ending has a further interesting twist.

> "Then suddenly, they saw me standing there. I was told to go back onto the earth but that I would be guarded by a special piece of knowledge [as is true usually of alien abduction reports]. At that moment, I woke up, wide awake and quickly grabbed some paper . . . and wrote it [the special piece of knowledge] down. It said, 'Propriety is the propensity for procreation.' " (p. 29)

Why, if these kinds of experiences were manifestations of supernatural beings, do they appear in the context of the personal experience and problems of the individual? The conflating of Christ with an alien abductor surely is an indication that this was merely a dream, as the student recognized. But given its striking similarity to religious experiences or visions, on what basis can the two be distinguished? Does it not imply they have the same cause? Would Jews, Muslims, Hindus, or Buddhists hear the voice of or have visions of Christ or of aliens? Why doesn't the God of the Jews or Allah speak and appear to Christians? Are there different Gods speaking to different people or does God change his persona with his cultural audience? Rather than the manifestation of transcendent deities, these religious experiences seem to be very ego- and ethnocentric, as one would expect if they were projections of the brain. What if scientific theories varied with particular cultures and individuals, how much confidence would we have in their universal and objective truth?

Turning to specific scientific explanations of these experiences, one investigator in particular has had spectacular results. In his book, *Neurological Basis of God Beliefs*, Michael A. Persinger claims, based on clinical research, that "God Experiences are the products of the human brain . . . tempered by the person's learned history . . ." (p. x).

> God Experiences are predicted to be correlated with transient electrical instabilities within the temporal lobe [also the speech center] of the human brain. These temporal lobe transients (TLTs) are normal changes that are precipitated by maturation, personal dilemma, grief, fatigue, and a variety of physiological conditions. Productions of TLTs create an intense sense of meaningfulness, profundity, and conviction. (p. x)

When activated they "contain common themes of 'knowing,' forced thinking, inner voices, familiarity [déjà vu], and sensations of uplifting movements [heavenly ascensions]. In more extreme conditions, God Experiences are associated with personality disorders and epileptic-type hallucinations." (p. x)

These experiences are the very kind which were attributed to supernatural beings in the past because of their mysterious origin and nature. "Shorn of their poetic language, the descriptions of most religious leaders indicate temporal lobe abnormalities. If they were alive today, they would have much less appeal. There appears to be something magical about psychiatric symptoms when they are centuries old" (p. 18). These temporal lobe transients (abnormal electrical activity) can occur with or without seizures and accompany the religious experiences just reported, as well as the dream experiences of artists like Blake and writers like Coleridge and Stevenson described previously. At the time life appears bleakest and empty, if a temporal lobe transient occurs, "we suddenly experience a sense of understanding and a feeling of knowing" (p. 16). As for the artists and writers, people with "psychic seizures" in the temporal lobe without convulsions "experience vivid landscapes or perceive forms of living things. Some of these entities are not human, but described as little men [Stevenson's dreams of landscapes and "Little People"], glowing forms, or bright shining sources." (p. 17) These bright beams of light occurred in two of the dream experiences reported above, and are typical of alien abduction dreams and near-death encounters, as we shall find later.

Unlike the more severe cases of temporal lobe seizures, "*the God Experience is a normal and more organized pattern of temporal lobe activity* . . . precipitated by subtle psychological factors such as personal stress, loss of a loved one, and the dilemma of anticipated death. There are no convulsions and few bizarre behaviors" (p. 19) They commonly are described as " 'being touched by God,' " or " 'being at one with the universe' " (p. 19). "Forced thinking is experienced as being 'implanted with the words of God,' " as in the case of Abraham, Moses, Jesus, Paul, and Muhammad (p. 19).

Temporal lobe epileptics do display more unusual symptoms: "the behavior of the temporal lobe epileptic has been characterized by the persistent theme of religiosity. Their lives are full of repeated peaks of mystical experiences and multiple conversions" (p. 19). Psychotics with a temporal lobe disorder have even more bizarre symptoms described by Slater and Beard and quoted by Persinger:

> "Mystical delusional experiences are remarkably common. One patient said that God, or an electrical power was making him do things; that he was the Son of God. Another said he felt God working a miracle on him. Another felt that God and the Devil were fighting within him and that God was winning. . . . Hallucinations were often extremely complex and were usually full of meaning, often of a mystical type. Nearly always there were auditory hallucinations at the same time. One patient saw God, heard voices and music and received a message that he was going to heaven. Another had a vision of Christ on the cross in the sky, and heard the voice of God saying, 'You will be healed, your tears have been seen.' "[37]

There have been numerous other studies documenting the correlation of religious conversions and mystical experiences with temporal lobe epilepsy. In a classic article by Kenneth Dewhust and A. W. Beard, they summarize previous literature from the early nineteenth century on the " 'religiosity' of the epileptic" that includes mystical and conversion experiences usually involving hallucinations.[38] They also analyze six case histories of patients with temporal lobe epilepsy, reporting their mystical and conversion experiences. Finally, they review the conversion experiences of such mystics and saints as St. Paul, St. Teresa of Avila, Joseph Smith (the founder of the Morman religion), Francis Libermann (a Jewish convert to Christianity), Hieronymus Jaegen (a German mystic) St. Thérèse of Lisieux, and Catherine dei Ricci (a Florentine saint), all of whom exhibited some typical symptoms of temporal lobe epilepsy: severe headaches, violent trembling at times, terrifying visual and auditory hallucinations, visions of a pillar of light, temporary loss of consciousness or sight, mystical unions, and cosmic visions.

Among the descriptions of their religious experiences reported by the five patients with temporal lobe epilepsy were the following: (1) being "suddenly overcome with a feeling of bliss" as if "literally in Heaven"; (2) "suddenly feeling God's reality," "seeing a flash of light," "having a series of visions in which he felt that his past life was being judged," and "hearing heavenly voices abusing him"; (3); "becoming intensely interested in following the teachings of Jesus Christ," having "a very vivid dream of the Crucifixion" and a daytime "hallucination in which he saw angels with their harps, praying and worshipping," then after discontinuing anticonvulsants he had fits every few hours" during which "he suddenly realized he was the Son of God," that "he possessed special powers of healing" and "believed he could understand other people's thoughts"; (4) a young woman suffering from petit mal attacks and on rare occasions a grand mal seizure reporting having hallucinations in which she "saw an arm with lights coming out of the fingers, eight-sided rockets" and heard "the Almighty's voice . . . on several occasions"; and (5) a patient who, after a seizure, woke up saying "I had now found my situation in life and . . . had been specially selected by God . . . to carry out my belief that the greatest power is the love of God" and "to find some way to prove that the Bible was true." While it always can be argued that "God works in mysterious ways" and therefore chose epileptic seizures to bring about conversion and mystical experiences, the claim hardly seems persuasive. As Aristotle and Cicero argued, one would have expected God to choose better subjects and circumstances for his revelations. It is more likely that it is the brain that works in "mysterious ways" to bring about these 'religious' experiences, especially with all the clinical evidence.

In contrast to these *scientific* explanations of the origin of dreams, hallucinations, and religious experiences in terms of abnormal discharges in the temporal lobe exhibited by severely distressed persons, schizophrenics, epileptics, psychotics, as well as well-adjusted religious people, William Alston defends a *religious* interpretation. Arguing that just as everyone believes we are *justified* in accepting ordinary perceptions of physical objects as veridical, unless there is counter evidence (hallucinations, mirages, visual distortions, and so on) for doubting this, religionists, according to Alston, are justified for *the same reason* in accepting their 'perceptions' of hearing, seeing, and sensing the presence of God as veridical, unless there are sufficient grounds for doubting this.

Drawing an analogy between people having sensory and those having religious perceptions claiming with certainty that what they were perceiving was real, Alston argues that this is *prima facie justification* for accepting religious beliefs as valid because the evidential basis is comparable. Concisely stated: "If S's belief that X is O based on an experience in which, so it seems to S, X is appearing to S as O, then that belief is prima facie justified."[39] Initially this seems dubious because it would imply that whenever something X appears to someone S as a particular entity O, then that person is prima facie justified in believing in X. One could substitute for O angels, devils, "Little People," "the Old Hag," pink elephants, a deceased spouse, hallucinated snakes, or God. As dreams, hallucinations, and illusions illustrate, the mere appearing of something to someone is not prima facie justification for believing it is a manifestation of something real. The reason we accept ordinary perceptions as disclosing 'real physical objects' (within the context of ordinary experience) is that this has been *verified throughout the ages by all people*. Has there ever been a culture that has not accepted the reality of physical objects based on perceptions? In contrast, even though most people throughout the past believed in some kind of deities, they have not claimed to perceive them nor have they agreed on their objective characteristics.

To avoid this objection Alston appeals to a "socially established doxastic practice," by which he means a socially accepted means of forming beliefs.

> My main thesis . . . is that CMP ["Christian mystical practice" or perceptions of God] is rationally engaged in since it is a socially established doxastic practice that is not *demonstrably unreliable* or *otherwise disqualified* for rational acceptance. If CMP is, indeed, a socially established doxastic practice, it follows that . . . it is prima facie rational to regard it as reliable, sufficiently reliable to be a source of prima facie justification for the beliefs it engenders. (p. 194; emphasis added)

However, unlike ordinary perceptions that normally are universally accepted as encounters with real entities (desks, automobiles, rocks, squirrels, trees, and so on) for which there is no alternative explanation for such experiences, there is no universal agreement that people "perceive God" (in fact, most people who believe in God or some higher spiritual power never have claimed to have perceived God), while the experience of God (like the contents of dreams and hallucinations) *can* be explained in terms of temporal lobe discharges. In ordinary perceptions our sense organs and brains are necessary for perceiving physical objects but not sufficient, because the causal effects of an external world also are required. This is not true of dreams or hallucinations nor of the perception of God, as least by epileptics and schizophrenics. The striking difference is that while everyone agrees that perceiving ordinary physical objects (in normal circumstances) requires their existence, there is much less consensus, even within the religious community, that claiming to perceive God is justification of God's existence. So the prima facie evidential basis of the two cannot be the same.

Furthermore, Alston's argues that *perceiving God* is the best justification for believing in God, not that *positing the existence of God* is the best reason for explaining the experience of God, the usual argument. But most people learn about God before they claim to have experienced God and therefore evoke God *ex post facto* as the cause of the experience, the reverse of Alson's argument.

> The thesis defended here is not that the existence of God provides the best explanation for facts about religious experience or that it is possible to *argue* in any way from the latter to the former. It is rather that people sometimes do perceive God and thereby acquire justified beliefs about God. (p. 3)

Alston apparently presupposes that the direct *awareness* of God is analogous to the direct *perception* of ordinary objects, even though the vast majority of people have never claimed to have perceived God, while epileptics, schizophrenics, and psychotics have. Alston admits to being a "direct realist" as regards religious experiences, just as he is a "direct realist" regarding sense perception.

> In the same way, if one is a direct realist about sense perception, as I am, one will be inclined to hold not that internal facts about sense experience provide one with premises for an effective argument to the existence of external objects, but rather that in enjoying sense experience one thereby perceives external physical objects and comes to have various justified beliefs about them, without the necessity of exhibiting those beliefs . . . as the conclusion of any sort of argument. (p. 3)

Although he qualifies this claim, he nonetheless is saying that the "belief in the *existence* of God is susceptible of a perceptual justification," just as belief in the existence of the book you are reading is susceptible of a perceptual justification (cf. p. 3).

While a full reply to this argument is beyond the scope of this book, I think it has two crucial flaws: (1) Alston's acceptance of a direct realist interpretation of ordinary perception, and (2) his analogy between perceiving God and perceiving physical objects. Another term for "direct realism" is "naive realism" and such a view is truly naive. Although it appears as if we directly perceive the physical world, we know this process is mediated by physical stimuli of the sense organs, intricate neuronal discharges, and complex cerebral processing. That the world appears as it does in perception is not because that is the way the *independently existing* physical world is, but because the various physical effects (light and sound waves, radiation, chemical stimuli, tactile pressures, and so on), in affecting our different sense organs, are transduced into neuronal discharges conveyed to the brain which are experienced by us as colored, noisy, fragrant, tasty, hard, warm, and so forth. It is the physiological transmissions within our sense organs and the neurological processes in our brains that transform the *physical* stimuli into *sensory* perceptions. The world we experience is the outcome of very complex processes, not the mirror image of an independent reality.

Because of their diverse physiological natures, the world appears differently to other organisms: dogs see the world in grays and hear high frequency sound waves, some snakes and insects respond to ultraviolet light, while further down the phylogenetic scale organisms probably do not experience the world in the forms it has for primates. Who knows how physical objects would appear to extraterrestrial creatures with a different biochemical and neurological constitution. As Kant maintained, the world we experience is "objectively real" but "transcendentally ideal": that is, given the kind of creatures we are, we *appear* to directly experience the world as it is, but remove us from the world and these appearances would disappear. But while Kant believed that "things in themselves" independent of our experience were completely unknowable, by probing nature experimentally scientists have discovered something of their "inner natures" and "secret powers" in terms of particles, waves, charges, forces, fields, and so on. The latter are considered 'the real physical world', not the one we directly experience, however external and real the latter appears to our direct sensory perceptions. When we look at the sun we seem to see it as it exists now, but in fact we are seeing its radiational effects after a lapse of eight minutes.

Thus Alston's acceptance of a "direct realist" view of ordinary perception that is opposed by considerable scientific evidence undermines his argument. Nor does the fact that we only experience the world as it *appears* to us, because of the kind of creatures we are, lend support to his claim that we can accept the existence of God on the grounds that he *appears* to people in their perceptions. Like dreams and hallucinations, god appearances can be accounted for in terms of purely physiological causes (as in schizophrenics, epileptics, and psychotics), whereas we cannot explain how the world normally appears to us without evoking an external physical reality. Based on their subjective experiences, people have claimed to have perceived all kinds of creatures (demons, dragons, unicorns, leprechauns, centaurs, witches, and angels) that do not exist, but it is difficult to deny the existence of the ordinary world as we experience it and maintain one's sanity.

Secondly, Alston's equating "perception of God" with "perception of physical objects" is flawed in another way. One obvious disanalogy is that while we can describe the ordinary physical objects we perceive in great detail, who can describe their perception of God in a similar manner? We can draw pictures or photograph physical objects, but can anyone draw a picture of or photograph God? Religionists who claim to have perceived God are convinced that something objective produces the experience, but contrary to what Alston claims, they have little idea of what that objective existence is. Theists describe 'it' anthropomorphically as a personal God (all loving, all knowing, all powerful, infinite perfection, and so on), while in negative theology 'it' is characterized as transcending any recognizable traits and thus is ineffable. With god experiences one does not describe *God* but one's alleged *experience* of God, whereas in ordinary perception one does not describe the experience of perceiving the physical world, but of what is perceived: an apple, a flower, a bird, or a person. This is just the reverse of what Alson claims. It seems to me that there is a world of difference between the two forms of perception, precluding drawing any conclusion from their similarities.

The basis of this difference is the process by which the two 'perceptions' occur. We can give a detailed explanation of any sensory perception like vision in terms of the nature of the stimuli (light waves or photons), the sense organ (eyes containing a lens, iris, and retina with rods and cones), and the chemical-electrical transmissions of the nerve stimuli through the optic chiasm to the visual centers of the cortex. In claiming to "perceive God," can Alston describe the various processes involved: what God is like to cause the effect, where and how the effect is produced in the human organism, how it is transmitted, and so on? Like most arguments of religionists, Alston's position depends upon uncritical acceptance of an imprecise analogy. If it is true that religious experiences are produced by temporal lobe sensitivities, then the experience of perceiving God is like dreaming, hallucinating, and having visions, not like normal perception and this is what the evidence indicates.

What I think Alston is justified in claiming is that some religionists do have experiences that they take to be perceptions of God which are considered by some within the religious community to be rational justifications of the belief in God. Scientists also have experiences which they take to be evidence of microstructures and processes which are considered within the scientific community to be rational justifications of the belief in such entities as electrons, DNA, dopamine, and hydrogen). Some philosophers of science claim that this justification basically depends on the *consensus* of the scientific community, as Alston is arguing for religious beliefs, but this ignores the fact that scientific theories are submitted to rigorous *objective* tests, so the results are not just dependent on what some scientists experience or on what the scientific community believes, but on what nature discloses and confirms. What scientific theories are taught depends upon the consensus of the scientific community, but the consensus itself depends upon rigorous experimental confirmation with nature often disproving theories.

Religionists argue that it is because God reveals Himself to the individual that one has the religious experience one does, but the evidential basis of the experience still is wholly subjective, similar to dreams and hallucinations, in contrast to scientific evidence which is objective or intersubjectively confirmable. We cannot confirm someone's experience of God in the way we can repeat Newton's prismatic discovery of colored light rays, identify a particle interaction in a cloud chamber, or verify the helical structure of DNA. Scientists have developed experimental techniques for testing whether the consensus of the scientific community is correct. Religionists usually answer that it is the nature of religious experience that precludes objective testing similar to science, but then they have to accept the fact that because these experiences can be explained on other grounds, they are not self-validating. It is reasonable to believe in God if one wants to have the positive consequences of the religious experiences (as William James argued in the "Will to Believe"), *but having the experience is not a justification for believing that there is a God.* Religious experiences have been generated by worshiping many divinities that we no longer believe exist (Zeus, Isis, Orpheus, Apollo, and so forth). Thus having these experiences is no justification that their presumed causes exist.

The next type of religious experience, conversion, can be dealt with briefly because it is similar to mystical experiences, especially when the effects are transforming and permanent. There is no denying that alcoholics, drug addicts, criminals, and despondent people have been "lifted out" of their desperate conditions by believing in a "higher power" or a "spiritual energy" that will assist them. A typical example is reported by Alston:

> "When I was middle-aged and the second World War upon us, there came a night when I was in deepest distress of mind. I was alone in my bedroom, pacing the floor. . . . Suddenly, I heard a voice firmly say 'Be still and know that I am God!' It changed my life. I got into bed, calm and confident."[40]

But beliefs can have powerful effects ("you will burn in hell for eternity if you have pre-marital sexual relationships or commit adultery") without being true and there are various explanations for this.

Just as hearing the commands of God for most people can be an extension of the youthful experience of hearing the inner directives of their parents, so the reliance on a "superior being" can be a replacement for the early dependence on our fathers, as the expression "God the

Father" implies. From an early age theists are told that "God is forever with you" and that they can always "turn to God in times of need." Moreover, as God is referred to as "the Almighty," there is nothing He cannot do if He chooses. This belief is devoutly expressed by one individual, as reported by Persinger:

> ". . . do I believe in laying on the hands and the Spirit entering a group of people in prayer, of course I believe. How else could I help build a church in which we worship? Or go to the service every week? Or tell my children that God will protect them forever. Of course God exists, for if He did not, which to me is inconceivable, how could man survive? How could I survive now and forever after? What *meaning* would there be at all?" (pp. 42–43).

But this person believes this partially because he has been taught to do so. There are a billion people in China who, brought up under a communist regime, do not think that it "is inconceivable" that God does not exit or that life could have no meaning without God. Suppose we started afresh, not teaching children biblical stories but describing the vastness of the universe, the wonders of life, and the trememdous novelties and beauties of nature, recounting the great achievements of Galileo, Newton, Darwin, Rutherford, and Einstein. And rather than telling them that the meaning of life depends on an afterlife, they were taught that the meaning of life is what you make of it, that it depends upon your character. Would they still find belief in Santa Claus necessary?

When one feels that one is in a desperate situation, religious beliefs can have a tremendously uplifting effect, especially when reinforced by "the congregation," "the brotherhood," or "the fellowship." Because language itself often has such a powerful effect on our emotions, just uttering the words "God the Savior," "Christ the Redeemer," or "Allah is Great," especially when said within the sanctity of a temple, church, or mosque, can cause a neurophysiological response producing a calming, joyous state. But these responses depend upon the background of the person. The statue of a fat seated Buddha does not inspire reverence in a Christian, but neither does an emaciated figure nailed to a cross instill awe in a Buddhist.

ASTRAL PROJECTIONS

Although the next kind of religious experience to be considered, out-of-body experiences (OBEs), normally are not classified as religious, there is considerable evidence to suggest that they could have been a major contributor to belief in supernatural and heavenly ascensions. As for the supernatural, the description of the "denizens of invisible worlds" described by some astral projectors resemble the fiendish creatures or radiant deities described in the Bible and portrayed in many religious paintings. As described by Carol Eby,

> the different kinds of entities occupy the different levels and subdivisions of the invisible worlds. Some are depicted as hideous monsters in horrible hells, delighting in the torment of humans. Others are seen as benevolent deities in glorious heavens. . . . Esoteric literature presents an elaborate hierarchy of beings at various levels of spiritual development to inhabit the invisible worlds. . . .[41]

The "benevolent deities" are further depicted as "majestic beings of radiant matter clad in shimmering robes," so typical of the Bible, while the "elaborate hierarchy of beings" recalls the nine orders of the celestial heavens in Catholic theology. Could they, too, have originated from astral flights believed to be ascensions into heaven?

One of the most direct references to a heavenly ascension as a possible out-of-body experience is that of the apostle Paul. Although to avoid self-glorification he attributed the experience vaguely to a "man in Christ," it is obvious that he is referring to himself and "to visions and revelations of the Lord" (2 Cor 12:1).

> I know a man in Christ who fourteen years ago was caught up to the third heaven—whether in the body or out of the body I do not know, God knows. And I know that this man was caught up into Paradise—whether in the body or out of the body I do not know, God knows—and he heard things that cannot be told, which man may not utter. (2 Cor. 12:2-4)

The Roman mystic Plotinus (205–270 C.E.) describes a similar out-of-body experience, one of at least four that he reported to his disciple Porphyry when he ascended to a higher emanation.

> Many times it has happened: lifted out of the body into myself; becoming external to all other things and self-encentered; beholding a marvelous beauty; then, more than ever, assured of community with the loftiest order; enacting the noblest life, acquiring identity with the divine. . . .[42]

While these OBEs seem incredible to those of us who do not experience them, apparently they have been as common in the past as they are today.

Scientific research has found evidence indicating the universality of OBEs. Researchers estimate that about one in five to ten normal adults will experience the sensation of leaving their bodies at least once during a lifetime. Based upon analysis of over 70 different cultures throughout the world, studies approximate that 95 percent of them consider OBEs a valid supernormal experience. (p. 124)

Whether these OBEs took the earlier forms of visits to the underworld, heavenly ascensions, or presently as astral projections and alien abductions depends upon the historical context and culture, a further indication of their subjectivity!

Despite the fact that these astral projections are related to hypnagogic and hypnopompic dreams (the former occurring as one is falling asleep and the latter when one is awakening), the projectors are convinced that they actually leave their physical bodies (usually in bed) and, acquiring an astral form, travel to distant places. Eby describes a voyage when "I 'awoke' in my astral body away from home, traveling over the countryside somewhere" (p.15). Unfortunately she does not identify where she was when she awoke, what condition she was in, or how she returned in her awakened state to where she left her physical body, which might have confirmed the experience as actual. According to traditional astral projection theory, which has a gloss of fantasy, "a silver-colored cord" connects the astral body to the physical body, so that if, "during an astral journey, the connection is ever severed, supposedly the physical body dies" (p. 94). As Eby observes, for obvious reasons there is no evidence indicating whether this ever occurred.

As is true of dreams and hallucinations at the time one is having them, as well as religious revelations and mystical experiences, a feeling of complete certainty accompanies the OBEs (according to Persinger this feeling is a function of temporal lobe transiency). Eby says, "I have had OBEs that were so realistic that I thought I was actually functioning physically, in the physical world, until such paranormal phenomena as floating or passing through a wall convinced me otherwise" (p. 103). During one OBE "the astral world appear[ed] as substantial as the physical world — every bit as real as the paper holding these words" (p. 120). Despite the conviction of certainty held by the astral voyager, this is not a confirmation of the reality of what has taken place because such convictions accompany nearly all of these experiences, whether real or not. Claiming that ordinary people have seen her in her astral form, Eby asserts that she deliberately self-induced an OBE in order to visit her friend Jean, who was working at night in a laboratory in a cement plant, having alerted her beforehand to expect her.

On July 21, 1990, at 11:56 P.M., Jean was in the lab, running a chemical analysis, when she felt my presence. She said either I stood where she was standing or she stood where I was standing, she did not know which, but she stepped aside. We talked and Jean asked if I was on my way to Judi's, to which I replied "yes." Jean wished me a "sunshining trip." (pp. 105–106)

But vague assertions of "detections of astral form" and "feelings of presence" are not very substantial evidence to support such a radical claim. Whether they had talked, as Eby asserts, could be confirmed by a tape recorder, but no attempt was made to do so. Eby claims that the "literature on astral projection contains examples of . . . another person in physical waking consciousness seeing the person appear in astral form" (p. 104), but again no effort is made to confirm this by photograph or video camera. If a normal person can see them, they should be detectable in some other way. She reports even more implausible experiences, such as projection *before it had opened* to a casino filled with people, and later visiting it *after it had opened* and recognizing it just as she had seen it in her projection (cf. p. 12).

She also claims that she has visited social gatherings in her astral form and that people recognized her.

> The first time I consciously approached beings on the astral plane, I was in an unfamiliar, though ordinary appearing house whose . . . occupants were strangers to my conscious memory. I thought it was quite likely that I was invisible, but I was wrong. To my surprise and embarrassment, the people in the house not only saw me, but they recognized me and spoke to me! To this day I have not determined who they are. . . . (p. 134)

If this had been an astral visit, rather than a dream, one would expect that some names and addresses would have been taken as identification to verify the experience. That there is no attempt to provide some kind of convincing evidence for these experiences is exasperating. It is as if the mere fact of having them were prima facie justification of believing them! Other reports are even more incredible.

> One time I was floating along, minding my own business, when I was grabbed and nearly captured by two humanoid astral entities. While I struggled to escape, I looked into one of the strangest faces I had ever seen—a furry animal face with a long snout and beady eyes! (p. 124)

It seems to me this is more the stuff of nightmares than of reality! She also relates the experience, when in bed one night, of seeming to be present when an airplane skidded along the runway and exploded into flames and then seeing the very same crash on television the next morning (cf. p. 89). Two of these experiences definitely are examples of precognition.

The most substantiated case is that reported by her friend Sue, who at the time lived in Colorado Springs, and her close friend Bob who lived in West Burlington, Iowa. He had telephoned Sue in a troubled state but before explaining anything had "abruptly hung up." Anxious because she had not heard further from Bob, the next morning Sue went for a walk in a nearby park and as she sat on a swing she suddenly "was in the place where she had never been before, the pharmacy where Bob worked" (p. 100). While she was there in astral form, Bob looked directly at her, saying he would call her between 5:00 and 5:30. Another worker who was standing nearby overheard him and asked in a puzzled voice, "why he would call her?" Not realizing that he had said anything, Bob replied, "What?" Then when he called Sue at the appointed time she told him about her experience of 'seeing' him in the pharmacy, describing what he was wearing, which he confirmed (cf. p. 100).

What sense can one make of this? It does not appear that these reports were deliberately fabricated, yet if they were true our conception of the universe would have to be radically revised to include foretelling future events (precognition), along with projecting to distant places in astral form and communicating with real people. I admit to being mystified, though unconvinced. Eby gives as a final example: "The most impressive being I have ever seen during any of my astral projections . . . appeared one night after I floated out of my upstairs bedroom window in astral form. I clearly saw, standing on my porch roof, a figure that looked like depictions of Jesus Christ (p. 134). Although Eby usually does not interpret her astral projections in a religious context, this experience suggests that they are not unlike religious visions or dreams.

While many of Eby's statements make it appear that she had no doubts about the reality of her astral experiences, at one point in her book she asks the same sensible questions that anyone would ask.

> Where are the invisible worlds? In another universe? In the imagination? Here? Do the invisible worlds only exist in our minds during alternative states of consciousness? Are they clever illusions created by our brain chemistry for reasons of which we are still unaware? Or are they part of our external environment, a part of objective reality, which can be perceived by more than one person? (p. 111)

These are excellent questions which she should make a greater effort to answer. She also presents an especially reasonable assessment considering her earlier positive claims: "We still lack proof that the invisible worlds are internal or external, or that they exist at all" (p. 111). Considering the kind of incredible universe implied by these astral projections, for which she offers no independent evidence, I think it likely that they are "clever illusions created by our brain chemistry for reasons of which we are still unaware."

Furthermore, current research into the morphology of the brain along with the biomolecular and physiological causes of dreaming offer a scientific explanation of these bizarre experiences. As summarized by Edward O. Wilson in his book *Consilience*, there now is considerable empirical evidence that the cinematic play of dream sequences projected by the brain when free of external sensory stimuli can be traced to nerve impulses originating in the brain stem that are modulated by specific neurotransmitters.

> During sleep, when almost all sensory input ceases, the conscious brain is activated . . . by impulses originating in the brain stem. It scrambles to perform its usual function, which is to created images that move through coherent narratives. But lacking moment-by-moment input of sensory information, including stimuli generated by body motion, it remains unconnected to external reality. Therefore, it does the best it can: It creates fantasy.[43]

The wakeful state of the brain influenced by external sensory stimuli which directs voluntary muscular responses is due to "amines such as norepinephrine and serotonin" (p. 82), neurotransmitters which permit this input of sensory stimuli along with outgoing bodily reactions. Sleep comes owing to the opposing effects of the neurotransmitter acetylcholine blocking the admission of external sensory stimuli by the amines, thereby eliminating the usual sensory inputs and behavioral responses, but leaving unaffected the autonomic nervous system controlling such vital functions as heart beat, breathing, digestion, and the rapid eye movements (REMs) characteristic of dreams. The experience of muscular paralysis reported in "Old Hag" and abductee dreams is caused by the acetylcholine blocking the normal muscular activation of the amines.

While *inhibiting* the firing of certain neurons in the brain stem, acetylcholine *activates* other neurons producing PGO electrical discharges. These are the actual initiators of dream images when transmitted

> from the pons (the P of PGO), a bulbous mass of nerve centers located at the top of the brain stem, upward to the lower center of the brain mass, where it enters the geniculate nuclei (G) of the thalamus, which are major switching centers in the visual neuronal pathways. The PCO waves then pass on to the occipital cortex (O), at the rear of the brain, where integration of visual information takes place. (p. 83)

Explaining how the sleeping brain, impervious to the regulating constraints of the external senses coordinated to muscular movements, draws on the visual images stored in its memory banks (the hippocampus and hypothalamus) to create the fantastic scenarios experienced in dreams, these discoveries also can account for the curious dreams of flying through space or of out-of-body experiences, like the astral voyages just described or alien abductions (to be described shortly).

> Because the pons is also a principal control station for motor activity when the brain is awake, the signals it passes through the PGO system falsely report to the cortex that the body is in motion. But of course the body is immobile — in fact it is paralyzed. What the visual brain does then is to hallucinate. It pulls images and stories out of the memory banks and integrates them in response to the waves arriving from the pons. Unconstrained by information from the outside world, deprived of context and continuity in real space and time, the brain hastily constructs images that are often phantasmagoric and engaged in events that are impossible. (p. 83)

It is this deceptive signaling by the pons to the visual cortex that the body is in motion, when integrated with visual images, that produces the dream experiences of flying, or of leaving one's body behind to explore distant places, or of being carried by aliens to spaceships, or of walking through a long tunnel to encounter deceased relatives (to be discussed in the last section). This account, typical of scientific explanations, provides a plausible demystifying understanding of phenomena which will not appeal to those who would prefer to find in them a deeper significance.

> We fly through the air, swim in the deep sea, walk on a distant planet, converse with a long-dead parent. People, wild animals, and nameless apparitions come and go. Some constitute the materialization of our emotions triggered by the PGO surges, so that from dream to dream our mood is variously calm, fearstruck, angry, erotic, maudlin, humorous, lyrical, but most of the time just anxious. There seems to be no limit to the combinatorial power of the dreaming brain. And whatever we see we believe, at least while sleeping; it rarely occurs to us to doubt even the most bizarre events into which we have been involuntarily thrust. (pp. 83–84)

That the brain is a sophisticated chemical-electronic processor of data supplied by our external senses and proprioceptors producing all of our conscious experiences, including dreams, paranormal, and religious experiences, is now maintained by nearly all neuroscientists and philosophers. While sensory stimuli from the external world are necessary for experience, it is the central nervous system and brain that transduces and transforms these stimuli into our conscious representation of the external world. It also is the microprocessing of the brain that makes possible such indispensable cognitive functions, noted since Aristotle, as discriminating, remembering, generalizing, classifying, abstracting, conceptualizing, symbolizing, inferring, analyzing, and synthesizing. Despite considerable progress, neuroscientists are just beginning to get some inclination of the infrastructures of the brain that underlie macroconscious processes. But I am not advocating the reductionist position that macroconsciousness will be reduced to or replaced by microstructures: to explain is not to explain away, unless the explained entities never existed in the first place, such as demons, souls, phlogiston, or the ether. Explaining consciousness in terms of brain processes no more eliminates consciousness than explaining water in terms of H_2O eliminates the phenomenal properties of water or explaining heat as the motion of particles eliminates the sensation of heat.

ALIEN ABDUCTIONS

What makes the appraisal of the reality of these astral voyages even more difficult—or easier if one is already convinced they are merely weird dreams—is that they are strikingly similar to those experiences reported by alleged aliens abductees. John E. Mack, who has risked his professional reputation as a respected Harvard psychiatrist for taking these accounts seriously, has presented detailed case histories in his book, *Abduction: Human Encounter with Aliens*, to support his contention that these reports "raise profound questions about how we experience the world around us and the very nature of that world."[44] In response to critical reviews of his book, charging that he was encouraging weird cults, superstitious beliefs, and irrationalism, he replied that after several years of investigation he was convinced of the "experiential truth of the abduction phenomena," despite its challenge to the current worldview of science.

> The information that I obtained during the several years of this investigation has been communicated in case after case with such power and consistency that a body of data formed which seemed to point clearly to the experiential truth of the abduction phenomenon, whatever its ultimate source might prove to be. (xii)

But this statement is equivocal in that it affirms the truth of the abduction *experience*, but is noncommittal about its *cause* or reality. Yet like religious visions and astral projections, the question is not whether those having the *experience* are sincerely convinced, but whether the experience should be taken as prima facie justification of the *reality of the occurrences*. Are such experiences produced by the brain or are they actually real? It appears that Mack has arrived at the latter conclusion when he states:

> The fact that what the experiencers are describing simply cannot be possible according to our traditional scientific view would, it seems to me, more sensibly, yes *rationally*, call for a change in that perspective, an expansion of our notions of reality. . . . (p. xii)

While I agree that these experiences, *if actually real rather than projections of the brain*, should not be dismissed merely because they do not fit into the framework of science, the essential question is whether the whole edifice of science, built on very solid experimental foundations, should be revised because of the *subjective* experiences of a *minority* of people who can provide scant additional evidence for their claims. Although it would be unfair to dismiss their realistic interpretations on the a priori grounds that they are implausible in terms of what we otherwise know about the universe, one should also be cautious in conceding these experiences to be real based solely on the sincerity and convictions of those having them. As we have found, this acute sense of certainty is characteristic of the whole spectrum of these kinds of experiences, some of which we would dismiss as phantoms. Yet Mack, like Alston and Eby, accepts these experiences as real based on the reports themselves: "My criterion . . . for including or taking seriously an observation by an abductee is whether what has been reported was *felt to be real* by the experiencer and was *communicated sincerely* and with powerful affect appropriate to what is being reported" (p. 16; emphasis added). On this basis he says, "this work has led me to challenge the prevailing worldview or consensus reality which I had grown up believing . . ." (p. 3). But obviously more is required for accepting a view that challenges our prevailing conception of reality than that it "was felt to be real" and "communicated sincerely and with powerful affect," otherwise we would have to accept the worldview of schizophrenics, epileptics, and psychotics. In fact, of course, Mack does search for objective criteria in terms of publicly observable evidence and has ruled out psychopathological explanations: "Psychological testing of abductees has not revealed evidence of mental or emotional disturbance that could account for their reported experiences" (p. 4). While this generally may be correct, it was not true in the case history of Scott, one of his patients.

But it is troubling that most of these experiences are revealed under hypnosis, in some cases decades after the alleged experiences when the individual had grown to maturity. One of Mack's colleagues cautioned "that although hypnosis could be of benefit in 'producing new material,' it does not 'guarantee accurate recall' and 'can be extensions of a personal fantasy experience' " (p. 59). Indeed, we have previously seen how extraordinarily creative the brain can be in fabricating fantastic dreams and hallucinations; there seems to be no limit to the brain's creative powers. Furthermore, Mack's descriptions of childhood abductions include some experiences that the reader will recall were similar to the *dreams* of Coleridge and Stevenson, along with the experiences reported by epileptics and astral projectors.

> Indications of childhood abductions include the memory of a "presence" [Old Hag and religious dreams], or "little men" [Stevenson's "Little People"], or other small beings in the bedroom [epileptics and astral projectors]; recollections of unexplained intense light in the bedroom or other rooms [epileptics and astral projectors]; a humming or vibratory sensation at the onset of the experience [OBEs and neardeaths]; instances of being floated down the hall or out of the house [astral projections]; close-up sighting of UFOs; vivid dreams of being taken into a strange room or enclosure where intrusive procedures were done; and time lapses [astral voyages and alien abductions] of an hour or more . . . in which the parents may have been unable to find the child. (p. 14)

If these are merely additional variations of dream experiences (Mack admits "the experiencer may at first call what is happening a dream" [p. 18] until further questioning convinces him otherwise, which could be the result of the investigator's power of suggestion), rather than actual abductions, then the particular UFO-alien motif could be explained by the person's having watched *Star Trek* on television or seen films of *Star Wars* and aliens. Recall the dream of the psychology graduate student who conflated Christ with aliens.

It being impossible to describe in all their subtle variations and lifelike detail the individual case histories of the abductees, when allegedly taken to spaceships where they experience traumatic encounters with aliens who perform intrusive physiological examinations, I shall present Mack's summary description of these occurrences.

> When abductions begin in the bedroom [or other places], the experiencer may not initially see the spacecraft, which is the source of the light and is outside the house. The UFOs vary in size from a few feet across to several hundred yards wide. They are described as silvery or metallic and cigar-, saucer-, or dome-shaped. Strong . . . light emanates from the bottom of the craft . . . and also from porthole-like openings that ring its outer edge. After they are taken from the house, abductees commonly

see a small spacecraft which may be standing on long legs. They are initially taken into this craft, which then rises to a second larger or "mother" ship. At other times they experience being taken up through the night sky directly to the large ship and will see the house or ground below recede dramatically. Often the abductee will struggle at this and later points to stop the experience, but this does little good except to give the individual a vital sense that he or she is not simply a passive victim. (p. 19)

Often the bedroom, house, or yard where the abductee is sleeping is illuminated by bright lights prior to the abduction and little aliens are seen entering the room after which "the abductee is commonly 'floated' . . . down the hall, through the wall or windows of the house, or through the roof of the car" (pp. 18–19). Like astral projectors who report similar experiences, they "are usually astounded to discover that they are passing through solid objects, experiencing only a slight vibratory sensation" (p. 19). Is there any corroboration of this? As Mack admits, and he is conscientious in presenting contrary evidence, "independent witnessing of an abduction does occur, but is, in my experience, relatively rare and limited in nature" (p. 20). One colleague, named Hopkins, recounted a case "where a woman made an unsolicited report to him that from the Brooklyn Bridge she saw his client, Linda Cortile, being taken by alien beings from her twelfth story East River apartment into a waiting spacecraft that plunged into the river below" (p. 20). While this report is being investigated, there is no indication of a confirmation which one would expect if the "spacecraft plunged into the river below." In the case of one of Mack's patients named Scott, when he told his father of seeing a flying saucer outside their home, his "father got his gun and went outside and there was nothing but nature" (p. 83).

The evidence for the UFOs and the abductions consist of

the visual sightings or radar spotting of UFOs, light and sound phenomena associated with them, the burned patches of earth that they sometimes leave, aborted pregnancies, and lesions on the surface of or implants left in abductees bodies following these experiences. (p. 16)

Yet as Mack admits, none of this evidence constitutes proof: "As in so many aspects of the phenomenon, the evidence may be compelling, yet at the same time maddeningly subtle and difficult to corroborate with as much supporting data as firm proof would require" (p. 20). Without "firm proof," how can the evidence be "compelling"?

Astrophysicist Jill C. Tarter and astronomer Christopher F. Chyba, who are researchers at SETI Institute (Search for Extraterrestrial Intelligence) in California, wrote the following in the End-of-the-Millennium

Special Issue of *Scientific American*: "Despite tabloid reports of aliens and artifacts everywhere, scientific exploration so far has revealed no good evidence for any such things."[45] This again reflects the difference between critical scientific investigations and human gullibility or the propensity to want to believe in the extraordinary, occult, or supernatural. Even the kinds of evidence mentioned by Mack are suspect. Abductees often report "cuts, scars, scoop marks, and small fresh ulcers that appear on their bodies after their experiences . . . related to the physical procedures performed on the ships," but "these lesions are usually too trivial by themselves to be medically significant" (pp. 26–27).

Yet considering the kinds of examinations that abductees report, including having long needles inserted into their heads, tubes pressed into their abdomens, eggs removed from their ovaries, fetuses taken from the uterus, there should be more confirming physical evidence of these procedures (the explanation that the aliens remove all traces before the abductee is returned home seems contrived or self-serving). Female abductees report that they have been impregnated and have had the fetus removed, "but there is not a case where a physician has documented that a fetus has disappeared in relation to an abortion" (p. 27).

Some abductees claim to have seen on later visits human forms that resemble them, along with fetuses in containers and even hybrid babies raised in incubators. "Experiencers may also see older hybrid children, adolescents, and adults, which they are told by the aliens or know intuitively are their own" (p 24). Yet Mack admits that we have "no evidence of alien-induced genetic alteration in the strictly biological sense, although this may have occurred" (p. 24). This is not surprising because inter-species breeding does not seem to be possible on our planet, and the aliens as described certainly are of another species. What is surprising is that this is not mentioned by Mack.

While many of the physical examinations are extremely embarrassing, sexually offensive, painful, and traumatic, especially because the victims feel they have lost all control over the situation, generating resentment, hatred, and rage; however, some do come away with an "altered sense of their place in the cosmic design, one that is more modest, respectful, and harmonious in relation to the earth and its living systems" (p. 35). The aliens often talk of the careless manner in which humankind is destroying the ecology of the planet, raising the specter of a kind of biblical apocalyptic destruction of all life. Sometimes they seem to be warning humans for their own good, at other times they imply that they want to save the planet for themselves. As a result of these warnings some of the abductees believe they have been given a sacred mission upon returning to help save the planet.

The aliens are seen in a number of varieties, some dark and others blond, some tall and others short or even tiny, some are grotesque others are attractive (especially a few of the 'females' who were quite seductive), some appear to be neuter while others seem to have sexual organs. Some are threatening and cruel, others are sympathetic and reassuring. There is a kind of hierarchical organization beginning with a leader, those who follow his instructions, and inferior creatures who just obey orders (cf. p. 22). It is the arms, legs, heads, and eyes that are the most dramatically prominent. Abductees describe the eyes of the aliens as disturbingly large and black, capable of penetrating and controlling the thoughts of their captives, determining what they will remember and when. This capacity of mind control is the most striking and alarming feature of the aliens. Communication takes place telepathically, not verbally, with each communicator seeming to know immediately what the other is thinking. They allegedly have the ability to anesthetize or immobilize the sleeping husbands or wives because they never are awakened by the abductee's movements, even when they are screaming (cf. p. 20).

Surprisingly, although the abductees have a vivid recall of being taken from their homes to the spaceship, they have little memory of returning. After an especially terrifying experience one said she "blanked out" and the "next thing I was back in bed, waking up" (p. 107). Although the consensus of the abductees in these reports lend credibility to them, they still resemble nightmares. For those unfamiliar with the great nocturnal fabrications of the brain, it must seem that only reality could produce such similar spectacular experiences. But while this could be so, there are reasons for thinking they are just further theatrical extravaganzas of the brain.

Even though I have tried to be impartial and sympathetic, there are characteristics of the case histories of these patients that should make one suspicious in accepting their reports as valid. All of the people described have very vivid dreams (Scott had hallucinations with epileptic seizures and was diagnosed as having a split-personality) and a number of them had a strong interest in UFOs that could have induced these dreamlike experiences. Moreover, it is curious that in so many cases other siblings, usually the mother, and the children of the abductees also had these experiences, but not the fathers, as if the capability were genetically inherited. Most of the experiences have to be recalled under hypnosis with very dramatic physical effects: sweating, thrashing, screaming, and brief states of paralysis (the latter previously explained by Edward O. Wilson as due to the effects in the brain stem of the neurotransmitter acetylcholine), although at the termination of the sessions the abductees claim to feel unburdened and therefore more relaxed and at peace. Some undergo pronounced psychological transformations emerging with a sense of intellectual development and cosmic enlightenment, along with a kind of missionary dedication to preserve the earth and its living creatures.

These alien abductee experiences are similar to religious conversions and to the belief of astral projectors that they are privileged in being able to explore other dimensions of reality or invisible worlds. Abductees, too, sometimes describe their experiences as "not occurring in our space/time universe" and of being exposed to "vast other realities beyond the screen of this one, beyond the 'veil" with a "deeply felt sense of opening up to or returning to the source of being and creation or cosmic consciousness . . ." (p. 17). This is rather heady stuff, especially when compared with the scientific view of the universe in which humankind is a late development from very primitive beginnings with no evidence of cosmic significance.

NEAR-DEATH ENCOUNTERS

There is a third type of out-of-body experience, called "near-death encounters," that have some features resembling astral projections and alien abductions, along with distinctive characteristics of their own. I shall rely on the descriptions provided by Raymond A. Moody because his unusual background includes a Ph.D. in philosophy as well as an M.D., uniquely qualifying him to evaluate the validity of these unusual experiences. From 150 case histories he has selected those that fall into the two following categories:

1. The experience of persons who were resuscitated after having been thought, adjudged, or pronounced clinically dead by their doctors.
2. The experiences of persons who, in the course of accidents or severe injury, or illness, came very close to physical death.[46]

From these cases he has arrived at the following composite profile based on the common features of near-death reports.

A man is dying, and as he reaches the point of greatest physical distress, he hears himself pronounced dead by his doctor. He begins to hear an uncomfortable noise, a loud ringing or buzzing, and at the same time feels himself moving very rapidly through a long dark tunnel. After this, he suddenly finds himself outside of his own physical body, but still in the immediate physical environment, and he sees his own body from a distance, as though he is a spectator. He watches the resuscitation attempt from this unusual vantage point and is in a state of emotional upheaval.

After a while, he collects himself and becomes more accustomed to his odd condition. He notices that he still has a "body," but one of a very different nature and with very different powers from the physical body he has left behind. Soon other things begin to happen. Others come to meet and to help him. He glimpses the spirits of relatives and friends who have already died, and a loving, warm spirit of a kind he has never encountered before — a being of light — appears before him. This being asks him a question, nonverbally, to make him evaluate his life and helps him along by showing him a panoramic, instanta- neous playback of the major events of his life. At some point he finds himself approaching some sort of barrier or border, apparently representing the limit between earthly life and the next life. Yet, he finds that he must go back to the earth, that the time for his death has not yet come. At this point he resists, for by now he is taken up with his experiences in the afterlife and does not want to return. He is overwhelmed by intense feelings of joy, love, and peace. Despite his attitude, though, he somehow reunites with his physical body and lives. (pp. 21–23; italics in origial)

There are obvious similarities between this description and the pre- vious accounts of OBEs. As was true of astral projectors and alien abductees, the word most commonly used by the near-death patients to describe their experience of leaving their "spiritual bodies," as Moody calls them, is "floating." Like astral projections, this spiritual body is weightless, invisible to live humans, can hover over the 'dead' body or view it from a detached position near the ceiling, and is able to "float" through solid objects such as doors and walls. As alien abductees in their etherial form, they can hear people around them speaking (doctors and nurses, as well as family and friends), but they are not able to talk to them even when they desperately want to, yet they can communicate their thoughts directly to whomever they encounter in the other world beyond the living. They can describe their experiences to some extent, although much of it is ineffable or not expressible in common language.

Regarding the differences in the near-death OBEs, they occur just before or at the time the patient is thought to be either clinically dead or near death and the time of resuscitation. In addition, unlike the previous OBEs where one leaves one's physical body for another state, but still feel they are in the same bodily shape and form, near-death subjects report that their separated state is an amorphus one, variously described as "a mist, a cloud, smoke-like, wispy, an energy pattern" (p. 47). As other OBEs who have a sense of being in another space-time dimension, "almost everyone remarks upon the *timelessness* of this out-of-body state." They describe being taken very swiftly through some kind of dark space, "a cave, a well, a trough, an enclosure, a tunnel, a funnel, a vacuum, a void, a sewer, a valley, and a cylinder" (pp. 30–31).

But the most distinctive feature of the near-death encounters is seeing other spiritual beings, often people they knew from the past who had died and who greeted them in a very friendly way. As one woman said:

> "They were all people I had known in my past life, but who had passed on before. I recognized my grandmother and a girl I had known when I was in school, and many other relatives and friends. It seems that I mainly saw their faces and felt their presence. They all seemed pleased. It was a very happy occasion, and I felt that they had come to protect or to guide me." (pp. 55–56)

There is a unanimous report of seeing an indescribable brilliance, a dazzling white light which, despite its intensity, did not harm the eyes. It was not a physical light, like that of the spaceships in alien abductions, but a *personalized* light described as an "angel," "Christ," or just "a being of light" depending upon the person's religious beliefs. Although it did not have a human form it would directly transmit questions and exchange thoughts. Primarily concerned with what the individuals had accomplished in their lives and if they were prepared to die, in these reports, obviously, the light-being conveyed the decision that the person was not ready to die and thus would have to return to his or her body. In the words of one woman:

> "I knew I was dying and there was nothing I could do about it, because no one could hear me. . . . I was out of my body . . . because I could see my own body there on the operating room table . . . but then this really bright light came. . . . It was tremendously bright; I just can't describe it . . . yet it didn't prevent me from seeing everything around me — the operating room, the doctors and nurses, everything . . . and it wasn't blinding.
>
> At first, when the light came, I wasn't sure what was happening, but then . . . it kind of asked me if I was ready to die. It was like talking to a person, but a person wasn't there. The light . . . was talking to me, but in a *voice*.
>
> Now, I think that the voice that was talking to me actually realized that I wasn't ready to die. You know, it was just kind of testing me more than anything else. Yet, from the moment the light spoke to me, I felt really good — secure and loved. The love which came from it is just unimaginable, indescribable." (pp. 63–64)

A further remarkable aspect occurs during the thought exchange with the light-being (although it can occur independently), a review of the person's life similar to reports of people nearly drowning seeing their lives flash before them. The light-being apparently possesses knowledge of the person's entire life, while the individual experiences the review as an incredibly real and vivid flashback of images from childhood to the present. Some people have the impression of being able to recall everything, others only the highlights of their lives. As one person described this:

> "After all the banging and going through this long, dark place, all of my childhood thoughts, my whole entire life was there at the end of this tunnel, just flashing in front of me. . . . It was just all there at once . . . not one thing at a time . . . but it was everything. . . ." (p. 69)

Yet the review was not intended as a "judgment day" accusation followed by biblical fire and brimstone; it was more like a learning session where the person could recall and recover from her mistakes. The emphasis was on love, caring for others, self-improvement, and enlightenment. One person said the light "kept stressing the importance of love . . . [and] things that had to do with learning . . . that there will always be a quest for knowledge . . . so I got the feeling that it goes on after death" (pp. 67–68). At times the person feels very isolated and alone, but as Moody says, "that spiritual rebirth can be brought about by isolation is an integral part of the belief systems of many cultures . . . including *The Bible*" (p. 174). The near-death experience removes the fear of death replacing it with a positive expectation of a better afterlife. As with other OBEs, once the experience is over most people "report that they simply . . . 'went to sleep' or lapsed into unconsciousness, later to awaken in their physical bodies" (p. 82).

Again we are faced with the question of what to make of this? Does the marked agreement of these near-death descriptions, despite some differences, confirm their otherworldly communications or, on the contrary, do they simply imply a common neurological response to the most traumatic of experiences, that of nearly dying? Unlike the previous accounts of OBEs, Moody presents and evaluates attempted scientific explanations—pharmacological, physiological, neurological, and psychological (isolation experiments)—the latter involving dreams, hallucinations, and delusions, none of which he finds convincing. What I find most striking about these near-death encounters is that they seem to provide the most corroborative evidence of their actual occurrence. Analogous to Sue's astral projection described previously to the pharmacy where her friend Bob was working in another state permitting her to describe accurately his clothing, in the near-death encounters the person allegedly leaves his 'dead' physical body in another form enabling him to 'see' what was being done to resuscitate him, describing the procedure so accurately (despite having no medical background) that the physician was astonished. As Moody states:

In several cases, persons have related to me how they amazed their doctors or others with reports of events they had witnessed while out of the body. While she was dying, for example, one girl went out of her body and into another room in the hospital where she found her older sister crying and saying, "Oh, Kathy, please don't die, please don't die." The older sister was quite baffled when, later, Kathy told her exactly where she had been and what she had been saying, during this time. (p. 99)

Moody presents other firsthand reports of similar cases.

"After it was over, the doctor told me that I had a really bad time, and I said, 'Yeah, I know.' He said, 'Well, how do you know?' and I said, 'I can tell you everything that happened.' He didn't believe me, so I told him the whole story, from the time I stopped breathing until the time I was kind of coming around. He was really shocked to know that I knew everything that had happened. He didn't know quite what to say, but he came in several times to ask me different things about it." (pp. 99–100)

Unlike the previous example where the dying person had to go to another room to *see and hear* her sister, the present example could be explained (implausibly, I admit) on the grounds that somehow the patient was still conscious during the whole procedure. This is true also of the following case, even though it is more involved.

"When I woke up after the accident, my father was there, and I didn't even want to know what sort of shape I was in, or how I was, or how the doctors thought I would be. All I wanted to talk about was the experience I had been through. I told my father who [the person was who] had dragged my body out of the building, and even what color clothes that person had on, and how they got me out, and even about all the conversation that had been going on in the area. And my father said, 'Well, yes, these things were true.' Yet, my body was physically out this whole time, and there was no way I could have seen or heard these things without being outside of my body." (p. 100)

It is true that one would assume that the shock of the accident would prevent the young man's body from conveying information about the surroundings which the brain could process, but he cannot be certain that, despite his injuries, in some way his brain was not registering what was happening.

There is a final account, more than justifying the amazed and perplexed response of Moody. As it is quite long, I will try to make it as succinct as possible without distorting what occurred. This patient was facing dangerous surgery complicated by the fact that he had "a severe case of bronchial asthma and emphysema," which made administering the necessary anaesthetic extremely dangerous. The patient was so upset by the prospects that his hand shook when he shaved. Then when he was in the hospital four days before the scheduled operation, he said that

> "a light appeared in the corner of the room, just below the ceiling. It was just a ball of light, almost like a globe . . . no more than twelve to fifteen inches in diameter, and as this light appeared, a feeling came over me . . . of complete peace and utter relaxation. I could see a hand reach down for me from the light, and the light said, 'Come with me. I want to show you something.' So . . . I reached up with my hand and grabbed onto the hand I saw. As I did, I had the feeling of being drawn up and of leaving my body, and I looked back and saw it lying there on the bed while I was going up towards the ceiling of the room.
>
> Now . . . as soon as I left my body, I took on the same form as the light. I got the feeling . . . that this form was definitely a spirit. It wasn't a body, just a wisp of smoke or a vapor . . . [but it] had colors . . . orange, yellow, and a color . . . I took to . . . be . . . indigo, a bluish color." (p. 102)

Although the spiritual form did not have a body, it extended a hand but later returned to a spherical light when the gesture was over. When the patient reached up to grasp the hand, he did so from his out-of-body form, seeing his physical hand and arm limp in bed by his unconscious body. Drawn to the light he was led to the recovery room several floors below.

> "So, I was drawn up to the same position the light was in, and we started moving through the ceiling and the wall of the hospital room, into the corridor, and through the corridor, down through the floors . . . to a lower floor in the hospital. We had no difficulty in passing through doors or walls. They would just fade away from us as we approached them. . . . And in a moment I realized that we had reached the recovery room . . . in the corner . . . near the ceiling, up above everything else. I saw the doctors and nurses walking around in their green suits and saw the beds that were placed around in there." (p. 103)

The patient explains that the purpose of the visit was to show him where he would be brought after the operation, especially the bed in which he would be placed: "the bed on the right just as you come in from the corridor . . ." (p. 104). The light wanted to reassure him that though he would have died, there was nothing to fear and that while the light would not be there when he arrived in the recovery room, it "would be overshadowing everything that happened and would be there for me at the end" (p. 104). After telling him this, the light returned him to his former hospital bed where he saw his physical body and "instantaneously" returned to it. Then on the morning prior to the scheduled operation, the realization that he was going to die struck him and he became worried about leaving his wife alone to raise an adopted nephew who was causing problems. He began writing a letter to his wife and nephew explaining his concerns, but after completing two pages he broke down sobbing. At that point he felt the presence of something without seeing any light who 'asked' why he was sobbing, saying, " 'I thought you would be pleased to be with me' " (p. 106). When the patient answered that he would have been except that he was anxious about his wife and nephew, the presence replied, " 'Since you are asking for someone else, and thinking of others . . . I will grant what you want. You will live until you see your nephew become a man' " (p. 106). With that the patient stopped sobbing, destroyed the letter to his wife, and underwent the operation the following morning.

Elaborate preparations had been made with very sophisticated equipment to assist his recovery after the operation. The procedure was successful and as he regained consciousness in the recovery room (which he had visited with the light) he said to his physician, " 'I know exactly where I am,' " to which the latter replied: " 'What bed are you in?' " The patient answered: " 'I'm in that first bed on the right just as you come in from the hall.' " Apparently not knowing what to make of the answer, the physician " 'just kind of laughed, and . . . thought that I was just talking from the anaesthetic' " (p. 106). When the doctor who had performed the operation asked the anesthesiologist, who had set up the elaborate equipment expecting a precarious recovery, what he could do to help, the latter replied, " 'There's not a thing . . . [to] do. I've never been so amazed in my life. Here I am with all this equipment set up and he doesn't need a thing' " (p. 106). To this the surgeon responded, " 'Miracles still happen, you know' " (p. 106).

While there are many bewildering aspects to this case, initially it does appear to provide some corroboration of these kinds of experiences. How could this patient and the others, along with Sue described previously, identify or describe things they could not have experienced because their physical bodies were not in the vicinity at the time? Presumably clinically dead, it hardly seems possible the brain could produce images of things to which the sense organs had no access. Yet the difficulty is that the patients are recounting their experiences after the fact in such a way as to make them seem as coherent as possible, without realizing that the brain can play all kinds of tricks or deceptions on the subject, especially when under a powerful anesthetic which can produce very realistic hallucinations. (When I related this case to a student of mine who several years previously had a brain tumor removed under the strongest anaesthetic possible, she told me to what extent her brain confabulated her experiences and how bizarrely realistic the apparitions appeared at the time, to the extent that afterward it was impossible in some instances to decide which were hallucinatory and which were actual.)

How, then, when reporting his experiences to Moody, could the patient distinguish between what occurred while he was awake and what were the confabulated effects of being anaesthetized? Even dreams can be as unusual as this clinical account without having anesthetics as the cause. So which is the most plausible: that the brain could contrive this strange scenario or that it actually occurred? None of us knows for certain, but I would consider the former much more likely. Still, I find myself empathizing with Moody when he says, "I am left, not with conclusions or evidence or proofs, but with something much less definite—feelings, questions, analogies, puzzling facts to be explained" (p. 183). As tempting as it would be to try to ignore or explain away these reports Moody, like Mack, declares that these "near-death experiences were very real events to these people, and through my association with them the experiences have become real events to me" (p. 183). Yes, but are they actually real?

Persinger has tried to put this question to the test by demonstrating that mystical experiences (MEs), UFO abductions, and near-death experiences (NDEs) are caused by temporal lobe sensitivities. Constructing an electromagnetic device enclosed in a helmet which, when worn by a subject, can be made to generate "a wavering magnetic signal that . . . matched brain wave activity in the temporal lobes," he showed that paranormal experiences could be replicated.[47] As described by Denis Stacy based on his interview with Persinger: "The helmet was then hooked up to a computer, which directed the firing of the magnets in a carefully timed way. 'This controlled pattern,' Persinger explains, 'generated a magnetic vortex that reached the site of the temporal lobes' " (p. 114). Stacy then goes on to describe the specific results:

> The first thing Persinger set out to do with his helmet was to study the claims of UFO abductees. To participate in the study, subjects who had never reported a close encounter wore the helmet while its magnetic vortex massaged their brains. As the helmet whirred, Persinger told them to imagine they were emerging from a woods and could see a light in the sky. (He had actually set up a pulsing overhead light in the lab.) Then he asked them to free-associate, giving vent to the images pouring into their brains.
>
> Unbelievably, these ordinary subjects began spinning stories chock-full of the details repeatedly reported by professed abductees. From gray-skinned, slit-mouthed aliens to blue beams of light to horrific reports of medical probes, the scenarios were the same. (p. 114)

To ensure that these experiences were produced by his magnetic helmet and not by suggestion, a control group was placed in the same situation but without the magnetic helmet. Only the group wearing the latter reported the UFO abductions. He also performed a similar experiment to induce mystical experiences (MEs).

> Persinger used the same approach to study other forms of the ME, from the sense of a foreign presence to déjà vu. Time and again he found that subjects donning the helmet were much more likely to have a mystical experience. And from one person to the next, the details in a given category of experience were, almost without exception, the same. (p. 114)

So with his magnetized helmet Persinger was able to induce a kind of mild epileptic discharge in the temporal lobe artificially producing the experiences usually attributed to some kind of esoteric cause. If valid, the device confirms his theory that temporal lobe sensitivity

> accounts for an otherwise bewildering variety of paranormal experiences, including classic OBEs, NDEs, UFO abductions — even a visitation from God. In fact, the theory has allowed Persinger to define the ME in a new way. It is, he says, "any event that involves a widening of emotional meaning, such that things not typically considered significant would now be considered meaningful. After an ME, a person may even view himself in relationship to a larger entity — wholeness if he's a mathematician [or mystic], or God if he is a Christian [Jew or Muslim]." (p. 60)

Furthermore, Persinger believes that he has demonstrated that this magnetic vortex stimulating the temporal lobe also shows that the latter is the source of the vivid *conviction of certainty* that is the *primary* basis for believing these experiences are real: "the experience will be perceived as extremely real because those functions of the temporal lobe that are recruited are the same ones that assign meaning and significance in the first place" (p. 60). If what Persinger claims is true, then this would provide almost conclusive evidence that these experiences, rather than being actual or real, are projections of the brain.

CONCLUSION

As we begin a new millennium, we face a choice as to which of the two preeminent cultural influences will prevail (there being absolutely no basis for a reconciliation, in my opinion): the regressive religious beliefs so dominant from the dawn of civilization or the progressive scientific worldview that increasingly directs our thinking and behavior. For while the religious explanations of natural phenomena by intentional causes now are generally discarded, if the kinds of subjective experiences just discussed, from sensing a divine presence to out-of-body projections and near-death encounters, were to prove to be not fabrications of the brain but disclosures of hidden dimensions of reality occupied by all kinds of arcane creatures, then the theoretical framework of science would have to be reconstructed to accommodate these experienced phenomena.

On the other hand, if applying the current techniques of scientific inquiry not only show that it is the only sound method for understanding physical reality, but also can explain the cause of the paranormal, transcendental, or numinous experiences that largely have produced and sustained religious beliefs throughout the past, then its success is assured. Although at this point in history we cannot be certain of the outcome, by the end of the new millennium humankind will know whether the gods have been vanquished by science or whether, as Hamlet said, "There are more things in heaven and earth, Horatio, than are dreamt of in your philosophy." Given the historical record of the disproof of the occult, the magical, the miraculous, and the esoteric, the most recent victim being "crop circles," my expectation is that the gods will be vanquished, not that their existence will be vindicated.

The celebration of the new millennium could be considered confirmation of the essential thesis of this book, that the worldview of science, a legacy of the ancient Greeks, has prevailed over the Hebraic-Christian belief system because of its truth. Consider their different forecasts of the future. Drawing on apocalyptic predictions in both the Old and New Testaments of a final cosmic cataclysm preceding the arrival or return of a saving messiah, the global wars, mass exterminations, and terrible holocaust that have decimated the twentieth century, along with alarming climatic and ecological abuses that appear to be causing an increase in natural disasters such as hurricanes, floods, mud slides, and earthquakes, were seen by many religionists as signs of the impending Armageddon. As centennially prophesied during the past two millennia, the forces of good and evil personified by God and Satan would engage in a final battle with Goodness triumphantly crushing the forces of Wickedness, following which (according to Christianity) all those who lived in faith and righteousness would be resurrected in the new Kingdom of God. But none of this turned out to be true; the old millennium passed smoothly and peacefully into the new.

In stark contrast to the religious fatalistic denouement, special millennium editions of magazines such as *Forbes* and *Scientific American*, addressing the future prospects of scientific and technological research, were either daunted or confounded by the wealth and depth of future possibilities. As indicated on the cover of the End-of-the-Millennium Issue of *Scientific American*, the kinds of questions pursued by scientists represent realistic appraisals of the future: "Can Physics Be Unified?" "What Secrets Do Genes Hold?" "How Was the Universe Born?" "How Does the Mind Work?" "Can Robots Be Intelligent?" "Is There Life in Outer Space?" "How Much Do We Change the Climate?" Unlike the false prophesies of religionists, these portentous questions affecting the future of humanity lie entirely beyond the purview of religion. Even the choice of Einstein as "Person of the Century" by *Time* magazine confirms the striking shift in the relative importance of science and religion during the past century, despite the number of people who still cling to religion. But human beings have become too dependent upon the creative initiatives of science and their view of the universe too imbued with its concepts, theories, methodology, and expectations—despite lapses into more primitive frameworks of belief—to withstand the imperatives of science. So though in the past humanity claimed religious faith for its salvation, it now increasingly evokes scientific inquiry in its quest for a better life and hopes for the future.

NOTES

1. Cf. David M. Wulff, *Psychology of Religion* (New York: Wiley Publishers, 1991).

2. Cf. Richard H. Schlagel, *From Myth to Modern Mind: A Study of the Origins and Growth of Scientific Thought*, vol. 1, *Theogony through Ptolemy* (New York: Peter Lang Publishers, 1996), chaps. 1, 2, 3.

3. Cf. Heinz Werner, *Comparative Psychology of Mental Development* (New York: Science Editions, Inc. [1948]1961), p. 69.

4. Three well-known classic studies are the following: Oliver Sachs, *The Man Who Mistook his Wife for a Hat* (New York: Harper & Row Publishers, 1970); A. R. Luria, *The Man with a Shattered World*, trans. Lynn Solataroff (New York: Basic Books, Inc., 1972); and Howard Gardiner, *The Shattered Mind* (New York: Vintage Books, 1974).

5. I have tried to describe the prevalent position of neuroscientists in a way that avoids extreme reductionism while also denying traditional mind-body dualism. See my article, "Why not Artificial Consciousness and Thought," *Minds and Machines* 9, no. 1 (February 1999): 3–28.

6. Will Durant, *The Story of Civilization*, Part III, *Caesar and Christ* (New York: Simon and Schuster, 1944), p. 654.

7. Cf. David Hufford, *The Terror that Comes in the Night* (Philadelphia: University of Pennsylvania Press, 1982), p. 202ff.

8. Norman MacKenzie, *Dreams and Dreaming* (New York: The Vanguard

Press, Inc., 1965), p. 26. This is a superb study of the role and significance of dreams and their interpretation throughout history. My indebtedness to this book will be apparent and it is a pleasure to acknowledge it. The immediately following references in the text are to this work until otherwise indicated.

9. Kathleen Freeman, *Ancilla to the Pre-Socratic Philosophers* (Oxford: Basil Blackwell, 1962), p. 30, frag. 89.

10. Plato, *The Republic*, trans. Francis Cornford (Oxford: Oxford University Press, [1941]1972) [Bks. VIII-IX, 569-71], pp. 296-97.

11. Ibid. [Bk. IX, 571], p. 297.

12. Richard McKeon, *The Basic Works of Aristotle* (New York: Random House, [1941]1968), pp. 624-25. The immediately following page references in the text are to this work until otherwise indicated.

13. MacKenzie, p. 50. The immediately following references in the text are again to this work until otherwise indicated.

14. In the last quarter of the fifth century B.C.E. Gautama Buddha, following five previous dreams predicting his enlightenment, had a vision while seated under a bo or bodhi tree that was the source of his religious conversion. The principles of Buddhism were derived from this experience of enlightenment.

15. Maurice Bucaille, *The Bible, the Qur'an and Science*, trans. from the French by Alastair D. Pannell and M. Bucaille (Aligarth, India: Crescent Publishing Co., 1978), p. 125.

16. Will Durant, *The Story of Civilization*, Part IV, *The Age of Faith* (New York: Simon and Schuster, 1950), p. 163.

17. Ibid., pp. 163-64. Emphasis added. Durant's quotation is from R. A. Nicholson, *Translation of Eastern Poetry and Prose* (Cambridge: Cambridge University Press, 1922), pp. 30-40.

18. Ibid., p. 164.

19. Ibid.

20. Ibid.

21. Richard Restak, *The Brain* (New York: Bantam Books, 1984), p. 238.

22. Cf. ibid., p. 245.

23. Julian Janes, *The Origin of Consciousness in the Breakdown of the Bicameral Mind* (Boston: Houghton Mifflin Company, [1976]1990), p. 114.

24. Cf. Richard H. Schlagel, *Contextual Realism: A Meta-physical Framework for Modern Science* (New York: Paragon House Publishers, 1986), pp. 10-12.

25. Janes, p. 115.

26. Cf. Michael S. Gazzaniga, "The Split Brain in Man," in *Perception, Mechanisms and Models*, eds. R. Held and W. Richards. (San Francisco: W. H. Freeman and Co., 1950), p. 32.

27. Cf. Richard H. Schlagel, *Contextual Realism: A Meta-physical Framework for Modern Science*, p. 11.

28. Cf. John Eccles, *Facing Reality* (New York: Springer-Verlag, 1970), pp. 78-79.

29. Cf. Gazzaniga, p. 34.

30. Cf. Michael S. Gassaniga and Roger W. Sperry, "Language after Section of the Cerebral Commissures," *Brain* 90 (1967): 131-48.

31. Janes, p. 74. The immediately following page references in the text will be to this work until otherwise indicated.

32. Rudolf Otto, *The Idea of the Holy*, trans. W. Harvey, 2d. ed. (Oxford: Oxford University Press, 1950), pp. 12–13; brackets added.

33. Michael A. Persinger, *Neurophysiological Basis of God Beliefs* (New York: Praeger, 1987), p. 35. The immediately following page references in the text are to this work unless otherwise indicated.

34. Timothy Beardsworth, *A Sense of Presence* (Oxford: Religious Experience Research Unit, 1977), p. 122. Quoted from William P. Alston, *Perceiving God: The Epistemology of Relgious Experience* (Ithaca: Cornell University Press, 1991), p. 17.

35. Ibid.

36. Beardsworth, p. 91. Quoted from Alson, pp. 18–19.

37. E. Slater and A.W. Beard, "The Schizophrenic-like Psychoses of Epilepsy. I. Psychiatric Aspects," *British Journal of Psychiatry* 109 (1963): 95–150. Quoted by Persinger, pp. 20–21.

38. Kenneth Dewhurst and A. W. Beard, "Sudden Religious Conversions in Temporal Lobe Epilepsy," *British Journal of Psychiatry* 117 (1970): 497–507.

39. Alston, p. 100. The immediately following page references in the text are to this work unless otherwise indicated.

40. Cf. Beardsworth, p. 92. Quoted by Alson, p. 19.

41. Carol Eby, *Astral Odyssey* (York Beach, Maine: Samuel Neiser, Inc., 1996), p. 114. The immediately following page references in the text are to this work untill otherwise indicated.

42. Plotinus, *The Enneads*, trans. Stephen McKenna, 2d. ed., rev. by B. S. Page (London: Faber and Faber Limited, 1956), Bk. IV, 8: 1, p. 357.

43. Edward O. Wilson, *Consilience* (New York: Vintage Books, 1999). This excellent study of the convergent interrelatedness (consilience) of scientific theories is another testimony by a leading scientist of the truth of the scientific worldview. The immediately following page references in the text are to this work until otherwise indicated.

44. John E. Mack, *Abduction: Human Encounters with Aliens*, rev. ed. (New York: Ballentine Books, 1995), p. xii. The immediately following page references in the text are to this work until otherwise inicated.

45. Jill C. Tarter and Christopher F. Chyba, "Is There Life Elsewhere in the Universe?" *Scientific American*, December 1999, p. 123.

46. Raymond A. Moody, *Life after Death* (New York: Bantam Books, 1976), p. 16. The immediately following page references in the text are to this work unless otherwise indicated.

47. Denis Stacy, "Transcending Science," *Omni*, December 1988, vol. 11, 3. The imediately following page references in the text are to this work until otherwise indicated.

BIBLIOGRAPHY

Ali, Yusuf A. *The Holy Qur'an, Text, Translation and Commentary*. Brentwood, Md.: Amana Corporation, 1983.

Alston, William P. *Perceiving God: The Epistemology of Religious Experience*. Ithaca: Cornell University Press, 1991.

Anderson, Bernhard W. *Understanding the Old Testament*, 4th ed. Englewood Cliffs, N.J.: Prentice-Hall, 1986.

Aquinas, Thomas. *Summa Theologica*. In *Basic Writings of St. Thomas Aquinas*, ed. by Anton C. Pegis. New York: Random House, 1945.

Aristotle. *Metaphysics*, Bk. 12, ch. 7, 1072b 23–29. Trans. W. E. Ross.

Armstrong, Karen. *A History of God*. New York: Ballantine Books, 1993.

——. *In the Beginning*. New York: Ballantine Books, 1996.

Arts, Frederick B. *The Mind of the Middle Ages: A.D. 200–1500*. New York: Alfred A. Knopf, 1962.

Barbour, Ian. *Religion in an Age of Science*. New York: HarperCollins Publishers, 1990.

Beardworth, Timothy. *A Sense of Presence*. Oxford: Religious Experience Research Unit, 1977.

Bebe, Michael. *Darwin's Black Box*. New York: Free Press, 1996.

Bible. The Revised Standard Version. New York: Thomas Nelson and Sons, 1953.

Bruce, F. F. *Paul: Apostle of the Heart Set Free*. Grand Rapids: Eerdmans, 1977.

Bucaille, Maurice. *The Bible, the Qur'an and Science*, trans. from the French by Alastair D. Pannell and M. Bucaille. Alegarth, India: Cresent Publishing Company, 1978.

Čapek, Milič. *The Philosophical Impact of Contemporary Physics*. New York: Van Nostrand, 1961.

Crossan, John Dominic. *Jesus: A Revolutionary Biography*. New York: HarperCollins, 1994.

Dawkins, Richard. *The Blind Watchmaker*. New York: W. W. Norton & Company, 1986.

Dewhurst, Kenneth, and A. W. Beard. "Sudden Religous Conversions in Temporal Lobe Epilepsy." *British Journal of Psychiatry* 117 (1970): 497–507.

Diamond, Jared. *The Third Chimpanzee*. New York: HarperPerennial, 1992.

Drosin, Michael. *The Bible Code*. New York: Simon & Schuster, 1998.

Durant, Will. *The Story of Civilization*, Part 3, *Caesar And Christ*. New York: Simon and Schuster, 1944.

——. *The Story of Civilization*, Part 4, *The Age of Faith*. New York: Simon and Schuster, 1950.

Eby, Carol. *Astral Odyssey*. York Beach, Maine: Samuel Neiser, Inc., 1996.

Eccles, John. *Facing Reality*. New York: Springer-Verlag, 1970.

Eusebius. *Ecclesiastical History*. Trans. G. A. Williamson. Harmondsworth, Middlesex: Penguin Books, 1965.

Fox, Robin Lane. *Pagans and Christians*. New York: Penguin, 1986.

Freeman, Kathleen. *Ancilla to the Pre-Socratic Philosophers*. Oxford: Basil Blackwell, 1962.

Friedman, Richard E. *Who Wrote the Bible?* New York: Harper & Row Publishers, 1987.

Funk, Robert W., and Roy W. Hoover with the Jesus Seminar. *The Five Gospels: The Search for the Authentic Words of Jesus*. New York: Macmillan Publishing Co., 1993.

Galilei, Galileo. *Sidereus Nuncius*. Trans. A. Van Helden. Chicago: The University of Chicago Press, 1989.

——. "The Assayer." Trans. by Stillman Drake and C. D. O'Malley. In *The Controversy on the Comets of 1618*, ed. Stillman Drake and C. D. O' Malley. Philadelphia: University of Pennsylvania Press, 1960.

Gardner, Howard. *The Shattered Mind*. New York: Vintage Books, 1974.

Gazzaniga, Michael S. "The Split Brain in Man." In *Perception, Mechanisms and Models*, ed. R. Held and W. Richards. San Francisco: W. H. Freeman & Company, 1950.

Gazzaniga, Michael S., and Roger W. Sperry. "Language After Section of the Cerebral Commissures." *Brain* (1967): 90.

Gleick, James. *Chaos*. New York: Pengiun Books, 1987.

Gould, Stephen Jay. *Wonderful Life*. New York: W. W. Norton & Co., 1990.

Goulder, Michael D. *The Evangelist's Calendar: A Lectionary Explanation of the Development of Scripture*. London: SPCK, 1978.

Greene, Brian. *The Elegant Universe*. New York: W. W. Norton & Company, 1999.

Hanson, R. P. C., and A. T. Hanson. *The Bible Without Illusions*. London: SCM Press, 1989.

Hobson, J. Allen. *The Chemistry of Conscious States: How the Brain Changes its Mind*. Boston: Little, Brown, 1994.

——. *Sleep*. New York: *Scientific American Library*, 1995.

Hufford, David. *The Terror that Comes in the Night*. Philadelphia: University of Pennsylvania Press, 1982.

Hume, David. *Enquiries Concerning Human Understanding*. Reprinted from the posthumous ed. 1777 by L. A. Selby-Bigge. Oxford: At the Clarendon Press, 1902.

Hyde, W. W. *Paganism to Christinity in the Roman Empire*, Philadelphia: University of Pennsylvania Press, 1946.

Jacobson, Thorkild. "The Cosmos as a State." In H. Frankfort and H. A. Frankfort, *Before Philosophy*. Baltimore: Penguin Books, 1949.

Janes, Julian. *The Origin of Consciousness in the Breakdown of the Bicameral Mind*. Boston: Houghton Mifflin Company, [1976]1990.

Jewett, Robert. *A Chronology of Paul's Life*. Philadelphia: Fortress Press, 1979.

Kauffman, Stuart. *At Home in the Universe*. Oxford: Oxford University Press, 1995.

Kee, Howard Clark. *Understanding the New Testament*, 5th ed. Englewood Cliffs, N.J.: Prentice-Hall, 1993.

Kierkegaard, Søren. *Concluding Unscientific Postscripts*. Ed. and trans. Howard V. Hong and Edna H. Hong. Princeton: Princeton University Press, 1992.

Kuhn, Thomas S. *The Copernican Revolution* (Cambridge: Harvard University Press, 1957.

Luria, Alexander. *The Man with a Shattered World*. Trans. Lynn Solotaroff. New York: Basic Books, 1972.

Mack, Burton L.. *Who Wrote the New Testament?* New York: HarperSanFrancisco, 1995.

Mack, John E. *Abduction: Human Encounters with Aliens*, rev. ed. New York: Ballantine Books, 1995.

MacKenzie, Norman. *Dreams and Dreaming*. New York: The Vanguard Press, Inc., 1965.

MacMullen, Ramsey. *Christianizing the Roman Empire: A.D. 100–400*. New Haven: Yale University Press, 1986.

McKeon, Richard. *The Basic Works of Aristotle*. New York: Random House, [1941]1968.

McNeill, William H. *Plagues and Peoples*. New York: Doubleday, 1976.

Meeks, Wayne. A. *The First Urban Christians*. New Haven: Yale University Press, 1983.

Mill, John Stuart. *Utilitarianism*, ed. J. M. Smith and E. Sosa. Belmont, Calif.: Wadsworth Publishers, 1969.

Miller, Ed. L., ed. *Believing in God*. Upper Saddle River, N.J.: Prentice-Hall, 1996.

Moody, Rayond A. *Life After Death*. New York: Bantam Books, 1976.

Murray, Gell-Mann. *The Quark and the Jaguar*. New York: W. H. Freeman & Company, 1994.

Newton, Isaac. *Opticks*. Based on the fourth edition, London, 1730. New York: Dover Publishing, 1952.

Nicholson, R. A. *Tanslation of Eastern Poetry and Prose*. Cambridge: Cambridge University Press, 1922.

Otto, Rudolf. *The Idea of the Holy*. Trans. John W. Harvey. 2d ed. (Oxford: Oxford University Press, [1922]1950.

Pagels, Elaine. *The Gnostic Gospels*. New York: Vintage Books, [1979]1989.

Paley, William. *Natural Theology*. Edited by Frederick Ferré. New York: The Liberal Arts Press, 1963.

Payne, Robert. *The Dream and the Tomb: A History of the Crusades*. New York: Stein and Day Publishers, 1984.

Persinger, Michael A. *Neurophysiological Basis of God Beliefs.* New York: Praeger, 1987.

Plato. *The Republic.* Translated by Frances Cornford. Oxford: Oxford University Press, [1941]1972.

Prigogine, Ilya, and Isabelle Stenger. *Order out of Chaos.* New York: Bantam Books, 1984.

Restak, Richard. *The Brain.* New York: Bantom Books, 1984.

Sachs, Oliver. *The Man who Mistook his Wife for a Hat.* New York: Harper & Row Publishers, 1970.

Sagan, Carl. *The Demon-Haunted World.* New York: Random House, 1995.

Sarton, George. *A History of Science.* Vol. 2. Cambridge: Harvard University Press, 1959.

Schlagel, Richard H. *Contextual Realism: A Meta-physical Framework for Modern Science.* New York: Paragon House Publishers, 1986.

——. *From Myth to Modern Mind: A Study of the Origins and Growth of Scientific Thought.* Vol. 1, *Theogony through Ptolemy.* New York: Peter Lang, 1995.

——. *From Myth to Modern Mind: A Study of the Origins and Growth of Scientific Thought.* Vol. 2, *Copernicus through Quantum Mechanics.* New York: Peter Lang, 1996.

——. "Why Not Artificial Consciousness and Thought." In *Minds and Machines,* Edited by James H. Fetzer, 9, no. 1 (February 1999).

Schroeder, Gerald L. *The Science of God: The Convergence of Scientific and Biblical Wisdom.* New York: The Free Press, 1997.

Shapin, Steven. *The Scientific Revolution.* Chicago: University of Chicago Press, 1996.

Slater, E., and A. W. Beard. "The Schizophrenic-like Psychoses of Epilepsy. I. Psychiatric Aspects." *British Journal of Psychiatry* 109 (1963): 95–150.

Spong, John Shelby. *Liberating the Gospels.* New York: HarperCollins Publishers, 1996.

Stacy, Denis. "Transcending Science." *Omni,* 2, no. 3 (December 1988).

Stark, Rodney. *The Rise of Christianity.* San Francisco: HarperCollins, 1997.

Taylor, H. O. *The Medieval Mind.* Vol. 1, 4th ed. Cambridge: Harvard University Press, 1962.

Weinberg, Steven. *Dreams of a Final Theory.* New York: Vintage Books, 1992.

Werner, Heinz. *Comparative Psychology of Mental Development.* New York: Science Editions, Inc., [1948]1961.

Westfall, Richard S. *Never at Rest.* Cambridge: Cambridge University Press, 1980.

Wilson, Edward O. *Consilience.* New York: Vantage Books, 1999.

White, Andrew D. *A History of the Warfare of Science and Theology in Christendom.* Vol. 1. New York: Appelton, 1896.

Whitehead, Alfred North. *Science and the Modern World.* New York: A Mentor Book, 1925.

Wulff, David M. *Psychology of Religion.* New York: Wiley Publishers, 1991.

Zindani, A. A., M. A. Ahmed, M. B. Tobin, and T. V. N. Persaud, eds. *Human Development as Described in the Qur'an and Sunnah.* Alexandria, Va.: Islamic Academy for Scientific Research, 1994.

INDEX